Take City Hall!

"Put a sign on your door that says 'Mayor' and you are revered like the Pope. People open doors for you and take your coat. People give you T shirts and ties and books in foreign languages.

If I'd known that being a Mayor is this much fun, I'd have become one much sooner. So my advice to young people, when I visit schools, is to become a Mayor as soon as you can."

Take City Hall!

*Mayor Tom Whalen
and the Transformation of
New York's Capital to an
"All-America" City*

Daniel E. Button

**Whitston Publishing Company, Inc.
Albany, New York
2003**

Library of Congress Control Number 2002112295

ISBN 0-87875-542-X

Printed in the United States of America

Front cover is a partial depiction of a color lithograph generously donated by the artist, Hy Rosen. It shows Albany's City Hall early on a summer morning soon after Mayor Whalen began his final term. The Mayor's office is behind the three narrow windows in the lower right corner. In the foreground are Academy Park (left) and the statue of General Philip Schuyler.

For the memory of Thomas M. Whalen III:

> Be not afraid of greatness.
> Some are born great.
> Some achieve greatness.
> And some have greatness thrust upon them.
>
> —William Shakespeare
> in *Twelfth Night*
> (Act II, scene v)

Table of Contents

PART III
THE LONG YEAR

PART IV
ON THE GROUND RUNNING, *RUNNING*

The "Why" and the "How" of
Take City Hall!

For Albany, Tom Whalen was the man for his time. As Mario Cuomo once declared, he fit his city perfectly.

These pages seek to recapture the essence of the Whalen Decade (Albany's Mayor, 1983-1993) and, as objectively as possible, to survey its origins and weigh its accomplishments and note its stumbles, to provide a perspective on its significance—not merely for Albany but for all those concerned about autocracy where it exists. For Mr. Whalen inherited an autocratic municipality and his administration exemplified a classic example of reform. One scholar states that "he created a modern municipal government."

Take City Hall! reflects his monumental achievements for the city and its citizens, but in no sense is it to be read as a memorial token. The author's task of recording and evaluating was complete before the tragic evening of March 4, 2002. Driving home alone, Mr. Whalen dozed at the wheel—that dreadfully silent hazard familiar to so many of us—and his car drifted off the road. Though this cruelly untimely accident cut short a vibrant, productive life, his service as Albany's chief executive was immovable history, which already had been gathered and harvested for these pages.

It is worth noting that the Mayor and this author had been of very different political backgrounds and beliefs, he a lifelong Democrat who had never renounced his early and long attachment to the O'Connell Organization, and I, elected as a Republican to serve our area in the United States Congress. When I was three times a candidate, I would have had reason to assume that he had worked against my interests. It was his instantly brilliant performance in office which persuaded me, early in his administration, that his instincts and choices for Albany were offering an admirable example of efficient and effective government. This resulted in Albany's regaining a lost civic pride, an acceptance of citizen participation and responsibility through a renewed confidence in the integrity of the City's Mayor and his policies. As he was leaving office, we agreed that I would undertake to relate and interpret the dramatic dimensions of that career.

To accomplish that, I considered it essential to describe the background of Albany's governance—how it reached the condition he had found when he came to office—and his personal background that had prepared him for the problems he would confront. The first two sections of this book, "Follow the Money" and "Precepts and Preparation," review these two prior circumstances. A third section, "The Long Year," analyzes Mr. Whalen's responses in a unique period when his predecessor, Erastus Corning, was largely unable to direct his city government. The fourth section, "On the Ground, Running, *Running*," reports on and interprets many aspects of the Whalen administration. Obviously, the extent of this close attention must be selective, and though widely representative of issues and answers, challenges and opportunity, personalities and perplexity, not every day's occupation could be chronicled.

* * *

What makes a book?

"As writers, all we have is language and nothing else. We've got these 26 letters of the alphabet and some punctuation marks—that's it." This point by Tim O'Brien, a journalist and author, is joined by Frank O'Connor's famous four words, "Get black on white," or as poet Brendan Galvin wrote, "It all comes down to that open notebook on the desk," and Bonnie Morris's ode to "the organic feel of nib on paper, ink on callused middle finger, spiral notebook flopped open on warm knees—that intimacy of creation." Simon Schuma, the historian, warns that the writer must be "an intermediary between the audience and the past." And H. G. Bissinger's "Writing books is hard—and if you're trying to get it right, you really do suffer with the facts you have." Peter Ackroyd, whose works include a life of Thomas More, argues that accounts such as this book should "issue from imagination and intuition as much as from scholarship and research." Whereas Susannah Lessard considers that "fact is the underpinning of morality." All these aspects of the author's responsibility to the reader (and to the subject) have impinged on the several stages of *Take City Hall!*, conception to completion. And, finally, I can relate to words of the essayist Michael Frank, who tells us this of William Butler Yeats: "He wrote and rewrote, erased and spliced and sharpened. . . . He worked hard and he reworked hard."

* * *

The chronological continuity of the events described here was achieved through the best form of history that mankind has ever devised—the columns of the daily newspaper. For Albany, that continuity has meant relying on the *Knickerbocker News* (until 1988) and much more extensively on the *Times Union*, an institution for which I retain a warm regard (in spite of the inevitable tendency of institutions to occasionally disappoint and sometimes vex). Having served as its editor for six years in the rather distant past (1960-1966), I cherish the ideal of its role in the community. Although I not infrequently dissented from the nature of its coverage and comment on Mayor Whalen and his policies and performance, I am greatly in debt to these newspapers' record as revealed by many, many hours of the whirring Microfilm reader. Frequently, throughout these chapters, the papers' account is the basis for quoted statements, an advantage for which I am grateful.

* * *

The book's successive drafts have been too many years in process, from pen to typewriter to computer (in other hands) even prior to the publisher's magic in reproducing it all. It's sadly regrettable that Mayor Whalen did not live to see the finished product emerge, but he did know that the contents had been completed, and I'm confident that this fact was very satisfying to him. We spent hundreds of hours together for our conversations. Those sessions were in a variety of settings, probably none so frequent as a breakfast table in a picture window, with one of his hands typically lowered to rub the head of Daisy, our terrier who sat at his side worshipfully. Tom Whalen was—as was remarked in his eulogy—dog's best friend, and Daisy was firmly convinced of that endearing quality.

So this book and I owe much to him for his patient cooperation which was essential to making possible this bit of history. At no time did he try to influence its theme, content, or language. He contributed factual information, offered many of his personal opinions (as the reader will find, for they are so identified), and provided insights drawn from his unique experience. But the interpretations, evaluations, and conclusions presented in the text are mine alone, formed with the benefit of my own experience and also the valuable crosscurrents of other individuals' views and commentary.

Thanks to the generosity of my former colleague Hy Rosen—artist, sculptor, and editorial cartoonist of the Albany *Times Union* (1945-1989)—his striking watercolor of City Hall graces the cover of this book. In addition, he graciously made available some of his on-the-mark illustrations from among those that illuminated the editorial pages for many years. Hy's distinctive commentaries effectively augment my account of the Whalen years. I am very grateful for this significant artistic underscoring of my prose version.

And I am indebted to numerous others for their interest, encouragement, or assistance at various times over the years. Among these, I must enthusiastically include Michael O. Laddin, president of the Whitston Publishing Company, a valuable Albany-area asset. He early saw the merits of the manuscript at an important stage in its development. To his colleague Jill M. Wolcott, I am also highly appreciative for her expert help in perfecting a manuscript into this final form.

Donna M. Devlin's expert assistance was crucial in several stages of the manuscript's completion in the form in which you see it. Without that loyal help, its preparation for the publisher would have been notably less feasible. Publication of the book would have been later and its accuracy less assured. She has my wholehearted gratitude.

Joseph Goodman, II, during his all-too-brief life and brilliant career in the law (Harvard J.D.), was a dedicated student and keen analyst of public affairs, including the Albany political scene. He became an early inspiration for me in arriving at the concept of this book. I found particularly valuable as background Joe's detailed—and pointed—information and commentary on the city's experience in the O'Connell era, as he wrote of it in a thesis for a seminar at his alma mater, Williams College, with James MacGregor Burns, the noted historian and political scientist. I am grateful to Joe's parents, Diane and Dick Goodman, for having made the thesis available.

I have special thanks for members of my family, most especially and most gratefully so for my wife. Rena's patience and support were enduring as the manuscript made its way through endless drafts. Her wise (and fearless) comments and insightful suggestions after each of her re-readings were priceless. But most precious of all was her steadfast belief in the eminent worth of the project and in my capacity to bring it to completion. Inspiring as well as practical, her confident support was essential throughout.

I acknowledge with all due appreciation these friends and associates who, among others, were significant in seeing the manuscript through, from inception to "The End": Richard J. Barrett, Virginia B. Bowers, Joseph M. Curtin, the late John E. Holt-Harris, Alan V. Iselin, Harriet S. Langley, Joseph E. Persico, Kenneth J. Ringler, Marcia S. Scharfman, the late Karl H. Schrade, and Peter J. White.

Also, Ed Dague, Norman Brickman, Harold Rubin, John J. Kelliher, James Patrick, Peter R. Kermani, Richard P. Nathan, Carl E. Touhey, Robert E. Lynk, the Most Reverend Howard J. Hubbard, William E. Rowley, William H. Swire, United States Representative Michael R. McNulty, James M. Gallagher, the Reverend Robert C. Lamar, Stephen T. Longo, the late Albert J. Abrams, Lewis C. Rubenstein, and Assemblyman John J. McEneny.

But in addition to—or perhaps I should say, before and beyond—all those who in some certain way helped directly, this book was importantly though more indirectly aided by the generous contribution of numerous persons who in past years gave freely of their time, confidence, encouragement, patience, skill, and insight toward preparing this writer for some phase of his careers in journalism and public affairs.

I give grateful credit to two individuals who helped ignite the spark when, at 12 years, I decided that I wanted to become something I knew nothing about—a reporter. A junior high school teacher, Emily Oliver Wright, took the unusual initiative of making an appointment for me to meet with the city's newspaper publisher, D. Hiden Ramsey. For the better part of an hour he talked with me about his trade—and from then on the juvenile ambition became an unquenchable one. That hour, the gift of two kind people, remains with me after nearly three-quarters of a century.

Subsequently, assistance has been offered by many— teachers, employers, editors, colleagues, friends. At the risk of unintentionally omitting some highly deserving of inclusion in these acknowledgements, I will thankfully cite these:

Mary C. Dennison, Alice Mayhew, Douglas S. Freeman, Walter B. Pitkin, A. Sydney Blatt, Henry T. Claus, Carl T. Wise, Joseph H. Nicholson, Gardiner Mulvaney, Francis J. Murphy, James E. Allen, Jr., Frank Porter Graham, Ralph McGill, Gerald R. Ford, John V. Lindsay, Oliver Pilat, Paul H. Davis, Richard A. Ahlstrom, James C. Ross, William S. Carlson, Richard E. Deems, Robert Price, Charles B. Harding, Bennett Cerf, and Gene Robb.

D.E.B.

Part I:
Follow the Money

Introduction

Before all the election victories, before a Mayor Corning or a Mayor Whalen, there were the county committee and its committeemen. Political committees exist everywhere, but in Albany the committeemen's functions were perhaps unique.

They were assigned to help win those annual victories, to "get out the vote." But their actual duties, as prescribed, were vastly broader than the civics textbooks had envisioned. The committeeman was required to be intimately familiar with his own slice of the city. And to be as effective as he'd want the election-night totals to prove, he had to nosily learn a lot about his district's occupants, door-to-door—and what would influence their voting practices. The system thus rested on citizens' uneasy anticipation that, depending on their being known for voting "right," they could win the favor of the powers behind and above the committeeman—or, to the contrary, fear the consequence.

Soon after the end of the 40-year mayoralty of Erastus Corning, which ushered out this era, its requiem was composed by an editor of the *Knickerbocker News*, William M. Dowd. Noting that Albany "is only beginning to awaken from a decades-long slumber into which it was lulled" by Machine manipulation, Dowd wrote that the city had "commonly accepted that the Machine will provide, the Machine will guide, the Machine will decide." Because "Citizens were obliged to see their committeeman rather than being able to meet with the proper elected or appointed authority," he called this "bureaucratic red tape in its ultimate form" which "stifled residents' true participation in the running of their community" and "scares off outsiders who could bring improvements." (Improvements already were arriving for Albany, but through a native son, who was an outsider only in the Machine's viewpoint.)

The system's inception dates from World War I, when a 30-year-old lawyer, Edward J. O'Connell, charted an assault on the then entrenched Republican machine. What he had wrought was an enormously successful organization that would survive him by decades. The network's immediate purpose, of course, was to grasp and then to solidify success at the polls, and so to hold public office at many levels—controlling decision-making, establishing public policy, determining who got what, gaining power, power, power.

To what end? The answer may be in the homely old maxim, "Money makes the mare go."

The ten chapters that follow consider some ingredients of life in Albany in those days of the committeeman.

The Past Is . . .

"Albany offers a rich political scene, both for the participant and the observer."[1]

"Destiny is not a matter of chance," the storied theologian and democrat William Jennings Bryan volunteered in one of his countless silver-tongued orations. "Destiny is a matter of choice," explained Mr. Bryan, who himself experienced a few frustrating brushes with destiny. "It is not a thing to be waited for. Destiny is a goal to be achieved."

His comment, unquestionably, is equally sound and profound today, fit for the ears of ambitious Americans.

The text for today, though, is Destiny's descent, after many post-Bryan years, into one of the nation's most colorful political theme parks. It's a modestly sized town that developed from a riparian hillside fort to be the vaunted capital of Empire. Heroes have emerged from Albany en route to an even greater Destiny. All this is told with trumpets in the history books, though on another scale of significance Albany proportionately stands only an ignoble thirty-first in size among capital cities. "Lots of famous people get involved in Albany politics," notes James MacGregor Burns. The distinguished novelist and memoirist William Kennedy glories in his city's "historical presence in every facet of the nation's life." As another perceptive modern-day commentator has written of his hometown, "Albany is a theater of political intrigue. . . . Albany always has been in the big league of politics albeit as a small-market team. A move from the Executive Mansion to the White House always seems in reach."[2]

Throughout much of the century following Bryan, a less heroic political structure was built there and efficiently nurtured and maintained. Its numerous flaws not only were evident but well advertised. This structure, identifiable as the O'Connell-Corning Organization, was often, more unkindly, known as the O'Connell-Corning *Machine*. Organization or Machine, whether we regard its control or its results, it paralleled those of contemporary bosses named Curley, Hague, Crump, Daley, and Pendergast. Classic form, slighter scale. Albany's people, as one of the Cornings speculated, perpetually are more interested in the great game of politics than are citizens of any other place except the District of Columbia.

Through its endless stratagems, the Albany Organization retained tight control of its city, installing Democrats as Mayor in 21 consecutive elections up to the end of the twentieth century (and other officeholders virtually as regularly). The Organization was put together by two sets of brothers who were from the nineteenth century, but it thrived into a second generation, past wars, depression, 13 presidents from Wilson to Reagan, 11 governors from Smith to Cuomo. In that same period, Albany elected but three mayors.

The one constant throughout was the last survivor from the founding group, Daniel Peter O'Connell, who almost by default became popularly credited with the prolonged record of successes—and abuses. For more than 30 years, after his early associates were all dead, he was undeniably the Boss.

* * *

Many "political animals" with an ear for the profession's lore find intriguing fascination in Dan O'Connell and his fabled reputation as a man often ranked with those who put their stamp on America's big cities. But he outlived all of them, a champion of unrivaled election victories (by his candidates;

after his early close victory, never himself) and incomparably
stifled opposition.

Ancient Dan O'Connell had once been Young Dan, one
of those so proudly named for the revolutionary firebrand
"Liberator of Ireland," the Daniel O'Connell who "mobilized
the masses as no European political leader had ever done
before."

Born in the first months of Grover Cleveland's presi-
dency (and shortly after Ulysses Grant's cortege, honoring
Albany with a stopover, had paused outside the same City Hall
where employees one unlikely day would bow and curtsy to
Boss O'Connell), Dan had yet another early footnote to history:
His birth had exactly coincided with Parnell's deal with the
Tories in Parliament in the noble cause of Home Rule for
Ireland. This stroke of timing seemed surely a portent when
the news from abroad arrived in the South End: A destined
career in public affairs, perhaps.

But quaint association with large events aside, he himself proved to be intent on maintaining a dull status quo. Not
without cause did his motto as boss become "The Usual." A
sprat grown into corpulency, a drifter become torpid in his
maturity, he was well into his 30s before finding any discernible "career." A grade-school dropout, he savored accounts
of battles and tacticians' battlefield stunts, but he preferred to
hear these read to him by confederates who, with his aggressive consent, had attained a status he couldn't hope for.
Denied normal symbols of respect, he retreated to a virtual
mountain top, lama-like, and survived into his tenth decade. A
correspondent for a national magazine, visiting Albany, found
him an "irascible recluse, painfully shy, totally out of touch
with life as it is lived today."

He demonstrated power by requiring those seeking his
blessing to come to his bunker—and averting such perils as
traceable telephonic communication and the vulnerability of a
paper trail. His desires and commandments were made
known in one-on-one conversations or in tiny select groups
(always the same trusted few) and only within his own low-

ceilinged walls. If he ventured out, his publicly recorded observations were meaningless parodies of genuine speech. He was never seen at City Hall, rightfully his own capitol, and his furtive visits to his party's command post were rare though it too was secured.[3]

Nearly ten years after his death, a marker was placed on South Pearl Street outside what was described as his birthplace at the corner of Second Avenue.[4] Reporting on the modest little dedication ceremony, the Albany *Times Union* repeated this popular embellishment of the legend: "It was O'Connell . . . who wrested control from Republican boss William F. "Billy" Barnes, Jr., after more than 20 years of an Albany GOP machine."

In the legend's weaving, Dan O'Connell's reputed role was immensely augmented by acts of God: the early deaths of his comrades in manipulation, men much more qualified and personally successful—but who had the bad luck to die young.

And therein lies what the populist commentator Paul Harvey would call "the rest of the story."

* * *

Younger than Dan by two years, Edward J. O'Connell had the misfortune of dying three or four decades too early for legend to build around his name and deeds as it later built the reputation of his scapegrace brother.[5]

Dan died at 91, having lived 38 years beyond Ed, and approximately that much longer than their two brothers, Patrick (Packy) and John (Solly), whose walk-on roles in the early O'Connell story have long been shadowed by Dan's and all but buried in local lore. As an example: A Schenectady *Gazette* columnist wrote in 1993 that "The Albany Democratic Machine was born in 1919 when . . . Dan O'Connell decided to challenge the organization that then ran the city. . . ." In the column's several hundred words, Ed O'Connell's name never appeared. The prosperous Corning brothers, Edwin and Parker, won mention for having supplied Dan with money.

Until his very sudden death at 51, Ed was the prime mover in the O'Connell wing of the Democratic organization of Albany County. In his lifetime, he was popularly recognized as an heroic figure grown into outsize proportion from humble origins. An astute and successful lawyer who had played football and excelled in academics at Union College and then earned his law degree at the affiliated Albany Law School, Ed joined a slightly younger Law alumnus, Samuel E. Aronowitz, in establishing a successful partnership. He kept the home fires burning while Dan sailed away in the World War I Navy and Sam was wounded and decorated in France. Like Dan, Ed married in his forties (both after their mother's death). He had found Kitty, a striking young woman, behind the counter at Stittig's candy store when he stopped in for ice cream. (His partner also was an admirer of Kitty's.) They lived comfortably in a landscaped brick mansion atop one of the thank-you-ma'ams rising on South Manning Boulevard—while Dan established himself in his well-advertised plebeian headquarters just beyond Second Avenue's steep climb above their South Pearl neighborhood.[6]

By appointment rather than through a general election, Ed took over the influential position of County Attorney early in the Corning-O'Connell hegemony, thus attaining control over a lot of the public's small-bore governmental decisions. As the only lawyer in the ruling group, he stood shoulder-to-shoulder (and eye-to-eye) with the O'Connells' eminently formidable allies, the Corning brothers. For years, he was the party's hard-fisted county chairman. Those strategic positions, based in the original South End stronghold and modestly supplemented by Dan's single term (1920-1923) as one of the city's assessors, constituted the O'Connells' power base for the first 20 years of their collaboration with the Cornings.

Perhaps significantly, the breakthrough years for Albany Democrats coincided with the turbulent years in Ireland leading up to what many regarded as Ireland's own declaration of independence in 1921—comparable to the 18th century revolutions in America and France. The fever in

Ireland became a fervor worldwide in Irish cities such as Albany, and to this can be attributed a political solidarity contributing to the O'Connells' stirring successes in mobilizing their compatriots.

The O'Connells bossed the shabby streets of Albany and the city's blue-collar satellites within the county's boundaries. Their domain included hundreds of disciplined party workers; long series of second-, third-, and fourth-tier public elective and appointive positions whose officeholders were screened and selected; plus thousands of routine, undemanding, frequently menial—invariably low-paying—jobs on public payrolls. These they closely monitored, a rigor sustained by flying-buttress support from an electorate increasingly apprehensive of the consequences of dissent. It was not a handsome picture, but a striking one.

* * *

The eminent historian Allan Nevins took note of the enmity between the O'Connells and their fellow Democrat, Governor Herbert Lehman (1933-1942). Both Dan and Ed, he wrote, "but especially Dan, were rough, self-centered, and rigidly conservative."[7]

After noting that Upstate New York in that period had "only one powerful Democratic leadership" organization, Nevins credited the O'Connell brothers with an "astute strategy" between 1925 and 1940. In that time, he said, they converted Albany into "one of the staunchest Democratic fiefdoms in the state," thus likening it to Tammany Hall and the parallel organizations in Brooklyn and the Bronx. (Nevins was ignoring the Cornings in this account.)

Ed and Dan "took no interest in social measures," the historian wrote, "were hostile to the Big New Deal in Washington and the Little New Deal in the state, and remained isolationists in foreign affairs." They had opposed Lehman's nomination for governor in 1932, and as governor he tried to "avoid any open quarrel with them . . . but he found the gulf between his ideas and theirs unbridgeable." On his very first day in office, in fact, he became entangled in a dispute with them over a judicial appointment.

When the man who ultimately succeeded Lehman in the governor's chair, Thomas E. Dewey, ran against him in 1938, he "assailed the O'Connells and the 'vicious mess of corruption in the very shadow of the capitol.'" This of course anticipated some of Dewey's actions when he became governor in 1943.

*   *   *

But, demonstrably, it was the complementary but contrasting partners, the "aristocratic" Corning brothers and eventually Edwin's sons who laid claim to high political and public office and aspired to other preferential privilege. They also were capitalists and CEOs whose holdings eventually embraced a very lucrative insurance agency from which the revenues included commissions on policies written for local governmental entities.

Among the four principals, Edwin Corning was far and away the greater political entrepreneur, organizer, captain, and candidate—while he lived. He outshone and outranked everyone else connected with the Albany County Democratic organization from 1919 for the next decade and a half.

The pairs of brothers had joined in a common enterprise though from clearly disparate motivation and ambition. Among the elements linking them apparently was the attraction of a shared social diversion. Albany's historians occasionally make much of the involvement by the barkeeping O'Connells and the clubby "patrician" Cornings in the underworld of cockfighting competition.

Much Depends on Dinner, a culinary anthropological commentary published in 1986 by the Canadian teacher and author Margaret Visser, offers an incisive interpretation of this attraction. "Men from widely different social backgrounds," she wrote, "have always met and mixed at cockfighting bouts. . . . The discovery of a common base-line fellowship among lords, workers, peasants, and bourgeois makes it part of the essence of the exercise.

". . . The master of a cock, in many societies, has been found to identify himself, and especially his sexual prowess, closely with his bird. . . . Cockfighting is like wrestling, a celebration of rampant virility. . . ."

Undoubtedly, there are those who would declare that politics, with its incessant contests for preferment, ranks beside cockfighting competition. In any case, the O'Connells and the Cornings found pleasure in both sports.

* * *

When in 1921—two years after the joint enterprise got underway—the cabal needed a plausible candidate who could win Albany's City Hall, it was Edwin whose banking contacts enabled him to bring forward an obscure hymn-singing Baptist bachelor—William S. Hackett—who charmed the new female voting block and was able to sidestep the ferocious anger of the "Wets" whose cause had just been outlawed by the Eighteenth Amendment. The triumph, achieved in a severe recession with high unemployment contributing to resentment toward the GOP, was the first of the 21 victories for the party's mayoral candidates over an eight-decade span.

The next year the other Corning brother—Parker, nine years older than Edwin—was elected to the U.S. House of Representatives by elbowing out another Democrat—the popular Congressman Peter G. Ten Eyck. Albany County's turnout that fall provided a handy plus for Alfred E. Smith in winning back the governorship he had lost in 1920 after a single two-year term. Edwin's strategic success and influence became so obvious that Smith installed him as the party's state chairman and then, in 1926, brought him onto the state ticket at age 43 to run successfully for lieutenant governor. In a remarkable show of consolidated strength, his overwhelming vote led the entire countywide ticket (including his brother's reelection to

Congress) in record-breaking majorities. These local victories were credited to the organizational skills of the party's county chairman, Ed O'Connell. Dan O'Connell, then known primarily as "the leader of the South End," rolled up a big win in the Second Ward.

With Smith aiming for the White House in 1928, Corning was widely conceded to be the probable candidate for governor that year. But well before campaigning began, Edwin's "health collapsed" (a euphemism for a variety of plagues) and he resigned as the party's chairman and withdrew from politics.

In this contretemps, Edwin Corning unwittingly emerged as the foil for the renascent political career of an old Groton schoolmate, Franklin D. Roosevelt, who successfully claimed the governorship nomination in his first step back from invalidism.

After years of agonizing illnesses, Edwin died—only 50 years old—alone at his Maine retreat. (It may be worth noting, with a certain degree of admittedly irrelevant continuity, that Tom Whalen, the future mayor, was born in the last year of Edwin Corning's life—precisely seven months prior to the latter's death on August 7, 1934.)

The *New York Times* obituary said of his career in politics: "He is generally credited with turning Albany County from Republican to the Democratic column." No other Corning or any O'Connell was allotted a share of the credit as it was understood at the time. Eventually, it turned out to be Dan, the survivor, who inherited this footnote to history, which he readily accepted.

Contrasted with Dan O'Connell's sixth-grade education and his involvement with baseball gambling pools (which led to his incarceration at one stage), Edwin Corning was a product of the Albany Academy, Endicott Peabody's Groton classes, and Yale. For many years he was president of the Ludlum Steel Company, forerunner of the more familiar Allegheny Ludlum; and he was simultaneously an officer of another business heavy with Corning family influence, Albany

Felt, antecedent of the present Albany International Corporation.

He was exposed to one potentially explosive political vulnerability, though none of his opponents ever capitalized on it. He led Ludlum Steel into a patent deal with the Krupp Steel Works of Essen, Germany, and became the chairman of the board of Krupp Mirosta Company, organized to handle Krupp's alloy steel patents in this country. Krupp was then associated, as was to be historically recognized, with Germany's war machine and its industrial might. The very name was a liability from which virtually any American political figure would shrink.

As a gentleman farmer on the "Upper Farm" adjoining his older brother's "Lower Farm" near the Hudson River's shoreline in a rather rural suburb, Edwin Corning raised what were termed "thoroughbred cattle." He'd been born into a family with a strong political aura—his arrival in the fall of 1883 was just a year after his father was defeated by Grover Cleveland for the Democratic nomination for Governor of New York.[8]

Beyond his political and manufacturing careers, Edwin took on other responsibilities including a sizable personal establishment and five children. He had the foresight to engage in a sideline, a profitable insurance agency. Ultimately, this offered his son Erastus 2nd the only employment in private enterprise he ever had. In an especially timely as well as thoughtful gesture, Edwin organized the agency in 1932, the year that Erastus was turned loose by Yale into a land populated by those new growth-communities—Hoovervilles. And as a crowning example of Corning-O'Connell coordination, before his death Edwin was able to persuade his opposite number, Ed, that Erastus should enter politics as soon as possible. So months after Edwin's departure from the scene, Erastus, at the age of 25, was selected to run for the State Assembly, the Legislature's "lower house," even though this move meant displacing a Democrat who had held that office for several years.[9] This was the beginning of a very long public career—46 years—for the young man, but it was coincidentally the real beginning of the O'Connell eminence in Albany County. The next year, Parker Corning retired from his job in the Congress. And this, incidentally, also made it possible for Ed and Dan to execute a clever ploy on the checkerboard they toyed with, advancing Erastus one square, up to the State Senate.

All this took place while Ed O'Connell was still the party's county chairman.[10] The strategy did not change after his death in 1939, however, for a year later Albany's Mayor was persuaded to resign and seek a minor judgeship which conveniently happened to be immediately available for him. Senator Erastus was put on ice for a year until the next city election. At 32, after six years of undistinguished legislative chair-warming, he was elected Mayor of Albany for the first of 11 times.[11] Having rehearsed well, he played the role of Boy Mayor through several acts, then that of the graying matinee charmer, in continuous performance under the experienced direction of the veteran trouper, Daniel P. O'Connell, whose own role could fairly be described in the playbill as "Survivor" and who is the only one of the founding four known to virtually any living person today.[12]

* * *

Politics was a natural and normal second trade for many barkeeps, and easily a random goal for an indolent, purposeless man such as Dan O'Connell seemed in his 20s and early 30s.

Often known as "the poor man's friend," the barkeep traditionally offered services and comforts probably unavailable otherwise. His saloon—and the proprietor himself— stood at the center of almost all action in a city's confusing world. The saloon, so attractive to so many—especially for the regular patronage—frequently resembled a club. And served modestly as employment bureau, union headquarters, immigrant way station, bank and credit agency, and reliable neighborhood charity.

Running for office—and, eventually, contriving to run everything—was a logical step upward in the community for a man who personified these significant fringe benefits for people who lived on the fringe.

The scores of saloons on South Pearl and its neighboring streets were an ideal backdrop for the making of a politician (especially when running against a "Dry," as Dan O'Connell was privileged to do). Such a handy—not to say, essential—population pocket was to become the nucleus for all that came later.

However, O'Connell's only race for public office, in 1919, came near to blighting his political career before it started. He was elected only by a recount and a hairbreadth margin, made possible by the two controversial issues of the early post-war era. The momentum for the election's swing vote was in the emotion-packed pro-and-con sentiments on Prohibition and women's suffrage.

Both were controversially stirring fodder for hot-button arguments far surpassing more loftily remote questions on League of Nations membership or the "Red scare" response to international communism. The Eighteenth Amendment had been ratified by the obligatory 36 states in January, only two months after the Armistice. Already, Albany's 300 saloons were being shuttered against the day when national Prohibition became effective, January 16, 1920.

O'Connell was one of four candidates for two positions as tax assessors in the city. Another candidate, John Franey, had accepted support from the aggressive Prohibitionists. As the *Times Union* reported, "In all the downtown wards there was every evidence of Republicans slashing Franey. South Enders of every party object to Franey's Prohibition endorsement and declare they will have nothing to do with anybody who accepted 'Dry' support."

In the November voting, according to the *Times Union*, "The women of the South End frequently wheeled their babies up to the polling booth where there was always plenty of men about to mind them while the mothers voted." And, no doubt, to remind the mothers on how they were expected to vote.

Congress had sent the Nineteenth Amendment (voting "shall not be denied because of sex") out for state ratification only in June, but New York's early endorsement was in time to make women's right to vote effective with the local off-year elections of 1919. Generations of obstinacy on this issue finally had been overcome and a key rampart of male supremacy was toppled. Since only men could vote on the suffrage question, the women's victory obviously represented the ultimate caving of resistance.

The *Times Union*, which made little effort to conceal its partisan preferences under editor Martin Glynn (who had been Democratic Governor of New York for 14 months as well as a Congressman, State Comptroller, and Lieutenant Governor), reported that "O'Connell made a wonderful run throughout the city and especially in the South End, where he is a very popular young man."

O'Connell finished well behind the top candidate, a Republican in the pocket of the vaunted Barnes machine, but 163 votes ahead of Franey, the next-best Republican candidate. Early returns had shown him trailing but in the recount he was able to pull ahead just far enough. His margin was 50.12% against Franey's 49.88%. When the victory finally was tabulated, the winner was not to be found. He had gone off hunting for squirrels to shoot. (Albany later abandoned this method of selecting its assessors.)

Propelled by the shifting mores of post-war America, Dan O'Connell's squeaker offered a small beachhead for his brother Ed and the Corning brothers to plot the next move. It hardly seemed a momentous triumph and, in itself, it wasn't. In fact, their candidate for Mayor and almost all the rest of the ticket were defeated.

The task of building on this wedge of credibility, creating an efficient organization, and winning the city lay in an uncertain future. In no real sense were Daniel O'Connell's 163 marginal votes found in the recount, the decisive blow that turned Albany away from Barnes and nobly into Corning-O'Connell's hands.

* * *

Edward O'Connell and Edwin Corning were the Organization's kingpins for the first 20 years, and Dan became county chairman only in 1945. He immediately named Leo Quinn, a man in his own image, to run the shop with a suitably heavy hand day to day.

Heavy-handed was, without question, the O'Connell style both before 1945 and thereafter. The over-familiar popular name of "Uncle Dan"—outside his earshot—was ironic and, at best, perhaps unconsciously subservient. From within the Organization comes this description: "Our people who get to see Dan are terrified of him. They tell him only what he wants to hear" (a recipe for disaster). Another witness tells of seeing such major figures as a pair of judges, John Pennock and John Clyne, hardliners well and happily known to the Boss, displaying surprising obeisance to him beyond respect, and even Erastus Corning deferring unconscionably. The extent of his followers' apprehension was comically visible when the Boss showed up at a public gathering. He rarely took off his familiar broadbrimmed brown hat in those surroundings, so his county committee's meetings were said to "look like an Orthodox synagogue." (Fortunately for the Loyalists' palates, few of them would be on hand for a favorite meal of the Boss's, a menu described as "a nice mess of sweetbreads and eels.")

O'Connell's shy insecurity inevitably led to his acquiring, at an early age, an attribute he never lost—a notably low profile, creating only awareness of a shadowy presence somewhere else. He shunned the company of his subordinates and inferiors at bars—as a patron, that is; after all, he had spent many years as the bartender. He was not, in fact, seen to drink in public. As he went his own egocentric way, he offered no gregarious side despite his origins and his prime occupation. He was kissing no babies, shaking no stranger's hands, and still ignoring the wakes and funerals that chronically are a second home for so many politicians. To a reporter who approached him with a question about a current political development, he snapped a curt reply: "I don't talk about politics here" (at a meeting of the party's county committee which would nominate the election slate he had dictated.)

During this time, another reporter, the *Times Union*'s Chuck Malley, received word that the Boss would welcome the visit he had proposed.

"What I remember most was the coughing that Dan was into, the smoke curling around the room, the raspy voice hard to understand, Dan sprinkling my name, Chuck, throughout his answers to my questions, as if I were an old friend of his instead of someone he'd never seen nor perhaps likely never really knew of except through my byline.

"And I remember the very strong eyes, though they were difficult to see behind those bifocals. They were street-smart eyes, sharp enough to cut you in half with a glance. They were eyes that said, 'Ok, you're a college-educated guy and I only went to grade school, but I'm smarter than you are.'

"I told him that I was from Cohoes. I believe he had a warm place in his heart for Cohoes people because the Democrats there were under his thumb as long as the Albany city Democrats had been. I told him that as a kid I used to see Mike Smith, the leader in Cohoes, go by in his big Packard. I'm sure he thought Mike was too flamboyant, with his cowboy hat, cigar, and chauffeur. O'Connell was turned off—embarrassed, maybe—by the high profile, arrogant ways of some politicians he had to deal with. If you were smart, and wanted Dan on your side, you would avoid that."

Chuck's meeting with Dan resulted in a birthday reminiscence, better than the frustrating experience of most other reporters who might wangle an audience only to find they had obtained nothing publishable. (Sometimes, reporters who were in the Organization's pocket—a well-established custom shocking to journalism professors—were complimented by being brought to the Whitehall Road house or the camp in the hilly Helderbergs for a shot or two, a cigar, some bluff, big-boy talk including a private word on the newest party line—but never any actual news.)

All this was puppeteering, signifying nothing. The visitors whom the imperious ancient permitted without invitation across his protective moat and who were most welcome within the lair were his judges—a select panel altering in stripe with the passage of years, but who invariably were his own "made" men. They could more reliably bring true assessments of ambition and performance, substance versus appearance, rivalries and feuds, promising sprouts or neglected promises. They could affirm more impartially his own estimates and conclusions of who was not only capable but loyal, or where treachery might be festering. They could repeat jokes at the expense of the latest posturing at the newspaper office.

These judges could bring their own sly sources of useful knowledge or gossip. In Albany County Court, Surrogate's Court, State Supreme Court, State Court of Appeals, and Federal District Court, they were privy to an endless variety of tales, many of them quite informative and frequently also accurate. And they would humor him with one more rehash of well-worn Civil War yarns because Dan had made himself into a reputed authority on that era. (One judge even wrote a book as an offshoot of these seminars.) And they would take turns reading to him—often, on the war—choosing up nights they'd make their time his. A judge of high repute and station would cook for him on his particular evening. All this within the four walls, with only the mice to eavesdrop.[13]

* * *

In 1986, when the O'Connell plaque was placed on South Pearl Street, the then Mayor proposed that "In a political sense, nobody has made a greater impact than Dan O'Connell on Albany in the twentieth century." This thought was marginally correct if the judges' eyes were closed to Nelson Rockefeller and the extreme physical changes he caused to be wrought, with all their implications for a very long future. But among those who greatly affected Albany, it's not possible to overlook that same Mayor who, in his relatively few years in

office, did so much to undo what O'Connellism had contrived
to put together.

NOTES

[1] From *Albany Ahead*, a report by the Mayor's Strategic
Planning Committee, 1985.

[2] Paul Bray, writing in the *Times Union*, May 1999.

[3] Author's Note: Not completely secure, however. I personally recall the thrill of joyously waving from one of its windows to
an ecstatically raucous knot of my supporters ten floors below in
State Street. The occasion was an impulsive "no hard feelings" visit
on Election Night, 1966, but it became just an impudent intrusion
into the Democratic County Committee's offices—which turned out
to be vacant, left open by Democrats who had run out in apparent
stunned confusion after an unheard-of debacle.

[4] The marker, resembling the state's historical blue and gold
plaques, was placed by the Albany Tricentennial Commission
under Lewis A. Swyer's leadership in 1986. Its largest legend reads
"Uncle Dan," followed by reference to his birthdate, November 13,
1885, and to the birthplace No. 1 Second Avenue, but inaccurately
describes him as "Albany Democratic Leader, 1923-1977."

It seems a shame, in fact, to have to observe that almost
everything about the plaque and its location was in error. As has
been pointed out by Virginia B. Bowers, the city's historian, Daniel
Peter O'Connell was not born anywhere near the building designated as his birthplace. The family residence and saloon in 1885 were
a mile up Second Avenue's dangling dogleg of a hill, near its intersection with what rightly enough came to be known as O'Connell
Street. Dan was born over the saloon that his father operated there.
The grandfather of Dan's generation had resumed his occupation
from the old country and gone into farming on land in that area.
(He and his son John, Jr.—Dan's father—were Republicans.)
Somewhat later, the O'Connells migrated eastward to South Pearl

Street, living at First Avenue, while the business was relocated to a corner at Fourth Avenue. It was there that Dan helped out behind the bar, his chief occupation until he joined the Navy in World War I. There never was an O'Connell connection with the building at the corner of Second Avenue where the plaque stands. So much for legend!

5 Another example of the proposition that basic facts can't be allowed to interfere with a good story: The political biography of Thomas P. (Tip) O'Neill, a former Speaker of the House of Representatives, places "the O'Connell brothers" in Washington conferring with the then Speaker, Sam Rayburn, during the 1950s. But by then, three of the four brothers were dead and only Dan was alive. That errand, perhaps apocryphal, was said to have been arranged by United States Representative Leo W. O'Brien of Albany. It enabled "the O'Connells" to appeal successfully for Rayburn's help in obtaining a tax settlement with the IRS. In return, the gratified "O'Connells" promised Representative O'Brien's vote to the Speaker on a controversial issue where he needed support. All this was O'Neill's version. His book, *Man of the House*, was published several years after the deaths of Leo O'Brien (who also admired a story well told), O'Connell, and Rayburn.

As for the merits of the very questionable "deal" which O'Neill so blithely described (presumably related to him by either Rayburn or O'Brien), in which a Congressman's vote was being bartered for the Speaker's assistance in a private matter with the U.S. government: at best it hardly would reflect credit on any of the principals, including the storyteller—if it all actually took place. Speaker Rayburn would not be happy with such an account tingeing his high reputation.

6 Author's Note: Ed and Dan were "vastly different in character," I was told by Sam Aronowitz, Ed's partner, who at the time was representing me in defense against a 1963 inquisition bearing Dan's stamp.

7 *Herbert H. Lehman and His Era* by Allan Nevins. Published 1963 by Scribner's.

8 Had there been a Governor Corning rather than a Governor Cleveland, we certainly never would have had a President Cleveland. In a rivalry bearing an interesting parallel to this "what-if," local legend insists that if Edwin Corning's health had held up in 1928, there never would have been a Governor Franklin

D. Roosevelt—and therefore no President Roosevelt, or New Deal. Or the occasion for a First Lady named Eleanor Roosevelt. Or a President Harry Truman, etc., etc., etc. Some parallels and variations on such quixotic prospects can be found in the 1999 volume *What If?*, published by G. P. Putnam's Sons; edited by Robert Cowley.

[9] The Corning-Ludlum-Krupp liaison did not limit the political career of Erastus, who was first elected to public office in a year when the Reverend Charles E. Coughlin and other demagogues were denouncing "the merchants of death" in international arms dealings. In that period of international tension and apprehension, for many Americans "Krupp" was an epithet linked to the growing power of Adolf Hitler. By 1946, when Erastus was the Democratic candidate for New York State's No. 2 office, Krupp was one of only three German industries being prosecuted by the World War II victors for war crimes. He lost that election, but not because this was a factor. Governor Thomas E. Dewey and his running mates swamped the Democratic ticket.

[10] In New York State's 62 counties, either major party's county chairman can be, and often is, a significantly influential individual. His position (or hers, for somewhere there must be instances of a county chairwoman) grants wide authority, as broad as any autocrat may elect to make it. Obviously, there are some passive or simply inadequate chairmen, and some who will act as a front for another's commands; and undoubtedly research would disclose examples of mere appetite for money or the public payroll. But potential power is inherent in the chairmanship, which is far more than calling the meeting to order and approving the minutes. An aggressive county chairman can impact the prospects of his party's candidates, restrict the options of local officeholders, adjust the governmental agenda, boost or modify the hopes of state and national aspirants, inspire or cloud the mores within his territory, and by any of numerous means affect the daily existence of all the inmates of his little sphere. The advantages are sufficiently flexible that a chairman may use his post for deal-making that will bring him a judgeship, while on the other hand judges have been known to forsake the bench for simply a hope of winning the chairman's office. The Democratic tradition in Albany County once strongly leaned toward vast influence, even if only to legitimatize the chairman's behavior and dictates. Ed O'Connell enlarged on the effi-

ciency of top-down discipline and enforcement. His brother greatly magnified it; the title served to authenticate his instincts and
whim. Corning played in the same league but, as will be noted
later, he was considered to lack certain essential credentials. Save
for Harold Joyce's foreshortened bid to regain an O'Connell-style
leadership, the sway of the five post-Corning Democratic chairmen
has been steadily declining. Among Republicans, the only strong
and effective Albany County chairman within the past half-century
was Joseph C. Frangella (1966-1974).

[11] Since his return from Yale and subsequent marriage in
June 1932, he had been formally listed as a resident of suburban
Glenmont. But just before needing to be an Albanian for appearance's sake (or for legal reasons) before being announced as
Albany's Mayor-to-be, he developed an official "Southern
Boulevard" address. The compilers of the city directory couldn't
figure out where this new residence might be on a rather short,
middle-class street, so the directory's section on streets and their
residents listed Erastus Corning 2nd at 000 Southern Boulevard. As
the mayoralty became a reality, he adopted 3-C in the apartment
tower at 397 State Street as his official address, but the young
Corning family (there were two children) lived at their familiar
"Kenwood" estate south of the city. After World War II he officially
became a resident of his mother's home on South Lake Avenue.

[12] When the O'Connells and Cornings began forming their
formidable Organization immediately after the World War I
armistice, one of their co-strategists was a Whalen. (He was not
related to the Tom Whalens.)

Respectfully and deferentially referred to as "Sir Robert" by
Dan O'Connell, Robert E. Whalen (1874-1951) was a "lifelong
Democrat," famed, however, for "never having made any bones
about how he felt toward the New Deal and its chief creator—he
was strictly against it."

An Albany lawyer (Whalen, McNamee, Creble & Nichols)
for more than a half-century, he was invariably chosen to argue for
the state and county Democratic committees in any major court
challenge. He would "drop all else" for those cases. "Unrelenting to
his enemies," he was steadfast in his "deep convictions and rugged
character." Politically, he was wholly in tune with the conservatism
of the O'Connells and Cornings. For nearly a half-century, the
Robert E. Whalen Homes on Colonie Street in Arbor Hill had repre-

sented part of the city's effort to provide low-cost housing. He probably would have deplored the social changes they embodied, but they were constructed after his death. When he died unexpectedly at the Red Lion Inn in Stockbridge, Massachusetts, the *Times Union* and *Knickerbocker News* published identically phrased page-one obituaries. Reading their lines (and between them), it's very possible to hear a commanding voice in the shadows: "That's the way I want it to be—and that's the way you're going to print it!"

[13] Tom Whalen, a judge in the City Court for six years, did not believe that he visited O'Connell's residence during that period (1970-1975). He recalled only a few conversations on other occasions throughout his career before O'Connell's 1977 death.

Voice of the Boss

In an era when many a man at the top would have hired a "mouthpiece" rather than a "spokesperson," Leo C. Quinn was "chief spokesman" for Dan O'Connell and the Albany County Democratic Committee.[1]

Born in a small Pennsylvania town in the year Teddy Roosevelt became President, Quinn was reputed—as a "frequent visitor" at the White House—to have "personally known" Presidents Franklin D. Roosevelt, Harry S. Truman, and John F. Kennedy. His line of presidential intimacies ended there, for just two months after Kennedy was assassinated, Leo Quinn died suddenly.

Just what had attracted him to Albany as a 30-year-old lawyer without clients is obscured by accumulated years but equally by the certain way the O'Connells conducted their affairs. Little enters the public record when a new operator turns up in a town and first puts a foot on the bar rail. Young Leo's brogans showed up at just about the time Dan O'Connell was experiencing real problems with the law because of his baseball pool connections.

All the O'Connell and Corning brothers were alive and active then, but only Dan was still standing by the time Leo was knighted as the county committee's point man—titled the executive secretary. He took over from Jack Murphy just after the Organization had beaten back Governor Thomas E. Dewey's vain efforts to break the party's control of Albany County. "Second in command" was the cliché aptly applied to his status, as was the term "Dan's first lieutenant." Over the next two decades, in the Boss's name he exercised to the fullest the derived power he had won. Whatever truth supports the description of his lofty Washington contacts strongly indicates the range of his deputized missions abroad and his impressive imprint on what people thought, said, and did at home.

Leo Quinn was a tough man for a tough job. And many persons who came into contact with him found him to be accordingly gruff and far from easy to deal with. But, countered one account searching for obituary compliments, he was considered to be a generous person. To lend credibility to this, he was reported to have once donated $500 to his alma mater, Catholic University.

Beyond his party responsibilities, he had earned a sensitive spot on the county payroll—superintendent of the tax delinquency office—at $100 a week, which for Leo Quinn was cigar money. In his bachelor suite at the Democrats' favored hotel, the DeWitt Clinton, he and Dan O'Connell held their regular one-on-one sessions where strategies and tactical decisions were made and other very private matters were talked out without the perils of bugs or paper trails.

It was there one wintry Monday morning when—suffering with a cold—he died in his chair, alone. He was 63. (The timing coincided with the accession of an O'Connell intimate, Jack Pennock, to the State Supreme Court, and of yet another, Francis Bergan, to New York's highest bench as an associate judge of the Court of Appeals following his uncontested statewide election.)

His 78-year-old friend and patron, also down with a chill, was unable to join a throng of other old friends charitably estimated to exceed 1,000 at the funeral service in St. Mary's, the historic and handy downtown parish. It developed that Leo had been carefree about what morticians call "arrangements," so Dan O'Connell made room for him in his own plot at St. Agnes Cemetery.

That closed a final curtain on Leo Quinn's public role. But simultaneously a small team of true insiders searched diligently—and fruitlessly—for the committee's bankroll he controlled.   Legend intimates that, however promptly they showed up, they had begun their urgent search too late. The game in Leo's rooms this time was "Finders keepers."

NOTE

[1] The TV guru Bernard Kalb has effectively termed the political "spokesman" as "the second oldest profession." In Albany, Leo Quinn elevated that profession to include the art of intimidation. An insight into the O'Connell attitude on public issues appears in a comment about a parallel organization. In his fascinating introduction to the book *Plunkitt of Tammany Hall*, Peter Quinn—no connection—wrote: "The dislike of the Tammany leadership for public statements or speeches is legendary."

The Hour Strikes

*"Moments come and go: Here is the time, seize
it, do your best."* —David McCullough[1]

The Organization finally was humbled by one of its
own, a native son, 49 years of age when he took over, a family
man of Irish descent, strong in the dominant faith of his towns-
folk, with a very decent practice in the law, and a previously
unblinking association with the O'Connell-Corning party, having previously refrained from offering question or objection,
complaint or reformer's zeal.

His intent was neither to wreck the Organization nor to
change the party (though he affected both in major degree) but
rather to save his city and its government from fiscal disaster;
next, to install sound policies of administration, then to establish for it a reputation of honorable intent and performance.
And ultimately to salvage its civic soul. As Mayor of Albany,
he was described by a subordinate as a leader who "wanted a
victory every day."

Without announcing his personal tenets or an official
creed, he swiftly set in motion a series of acts, initiating and
carrying out a program of policies which implicitly renounced
the concept of governing by fear and favor. And he governed
long enough not merely to gain respect and admiration for his
administration and its high achievements, but more importantly he restored the elements of civic self-respect to the citizenry, almost without its needing to note that fundamental
changes had taken place.

This accomplishment was by dint of personal strength. He had seen the need for a clean break with the recent past— even though he had come to his responsibility under the auspices of the heavy hand of that past. He had discerned the specific ways and means to remedy the city's ills. And he had summoned the steadfast courage to match deed to vision. Physically (and fiscally) he succeeded, in considerable degree, in repairing a broken and broke city; it was broke in more ways than one—and he fixed it. In the insightful analysis of Vincent O'Leary, then the president of the State University of New York at Albany, "Despite his long connection with the city's political machine—and to the consternation of its minions—he turned out to be a reformer who created a modern municipal government."

The greater triumph, though, was in lifting—partly by force of example—its spirit. The people of Albany were indeed regaining a lost pride in their city. In a different, and deeper, sense, however, they came to realize pride in themselves as individuals, as responsible and respectable citizens able to vote freely, to express themselves openly, to dissent without fear of consequence.

Concerning Albany's "soul": Many years' acceptance of fiscal shenanigans compounded by cynical manipulation had created an apathy that perpetuated both unilateral control and cynicism itself. Too many in Albany did not consider it advisable to inquire, protest, or object. Their logo was the turtle, which knows it's safer when the neck is not out.

* * *

The protagonist in this adventure? He was a hardy, husky throwback to the tough times that his ancestors survived, whether those in Dublin and Galway generations ago or, perhaps, to another forebear, Captain John Parker of the Lexington Minutemen, who at his country's decisive moment commanded, "Stand your ground! Don't fire unless fired upon. But if they mean to have war, let it begin here!"—this before falling in a hail of musket fire from the Redcoats.

As a young man he shipped out as a cook on a slow boat to Europe's North Atlantic ports and on a string of other summers he was a day laborer with a union card, a pick-and-shovel man in crews laying utility lines. Many days, he viewed the world from the bottom of a trench.

In his day, he was a quarterback and, in baseball, a third baseman, guarding the "hot corner" (so called for good enough reason) playing in fast company, on an otherwise all-black, semi-pro team. Later he competed in squash in a tough league; teamed up with eight or nine compatriots to golf regularly at Tralee or a half-dozen other courses in Ireland, and—at home—began many a summer's morning with a round before breakfast, in large part for the walking it mandated. He and his wife, Denie, would hike enthusiastically in the countryside or tramp the west coast of Ireland; climb a couple of dozen Adirondack peaks; and enter cross-country skiing competitions. And past his fiftieth birthday, he wholeheartedly took up competitive sculling, a demanding sport likened to "aquatic tightrope walking requiring both enormous precision and guts."

He not only enjoyed such physical activity but found it "a necessary component to mental health, not merely for pleasure but energizing for everything else I do."

So saying, then, it hardly can come as a surprise that on a day pivotal to the rest of his life, one that altered everything that had come before, he went canoeing down an Adirondack river.

Our protagonist, Thomas Michael Whalen, third in the family to bear those names, had for the past 17 months held public office as the president of the Albany Common Council, a position that placed him as the lawful inheritor of the mayoralty in the event of a vacancy. O'Leary considered that the party's leadership should have "known better" than to trust this "iron-tough, affable, ruddy-faced Irishman" who would spend summer Sundays at Tanglewood for an afternoon of Mahler or Bernstein. This critique really centered on, not "the party's leadership," but the decisive judgment of the man

Whalen was now about to succeed in office. With increasing degrees of responsibility to be shouldered, he had been unofficially assuming many duties of Erastus Corning 2nd, for 41 years Mayor of this ancient politically focused city, who lay critically ill in Boston, four hours' drive to the east.

* * *

In mid-spring, a *Times Union* columnist, R. L. McManus, Jr., had looked ahead to the changeover and commiserated with Whalen:

> "You knew that Erastus Corning was going to be a tough act to follow, but you never imagined it could be like this.
> "You're Tom Whalen, mere mortal, operating in the shadow of a not-quite-departed legend." He described troubles Albany was facing with the State, with KeyBank, with the bond market, with the police force, with the FBI and with other matters that included citizens' demands on his time and attention—"and you have to know that it's only just beginning."
> "But," the columnist concluded, "you're Tom Whalen and your shoulders are broad."

* * *

Spring was more than a little late in 1983 and May was especially rainy. By the start of the Memorial Day weekend, the east branch of the Sacandaga River, flowing through the lower reaches of Upstate New York's immense, mountainous, and wild Hamilton County (population 2.5 per square mile), was rushing with freshets fed by its endless tributaries. This was the stream that Tom Whalen set out to canoe on that Saturday morning with his friend, strapping John Krueger.

Fresh from an inspirational talk ("A man's true wealth hereafter is the good he does in this world to his fellowman") to Veterans Hospital volunteers looking ahead to the holiday, he was eager to head north from Albany on Friday so they could launch their canoe early next morning.

Good friends for several years, they made an impressive pair: sturdy Tom Whalen whose stocky 5-11 was overshadowed by Krueger, who'd played gung ho varsity basketball at Valparaiso University back home in Indiana. Arriving in Albany to represent an insurance company, John found Tom a worthy opponent at squash, and so a firm, if competitive, friendship began. John drove the 72 miles northwestward to the Whalen chalet at the hamlet of Wells, but it was Tom who concocted one of his own favorite seafood pastas—shrimp in garlic butter—for the supper they shared, sitting on the pew-like benches pulled up to the big pine table in the lodge's aptly named "great room."

Saturday morning they fried a few eggs, packed a sandwich lunch in backpacks and, in sneakers, T shirts and jeans, by 8:30 had put the canoe in the river below the dam at Wells, trending south 18 miles as the Sacandaga skirts the county's main arterial, Route 30. The water was high and fast and they scraped a few rocks en route. About halfway down their course they pulled off to a sandbar and dozed there for a while, hectored by black flies.

Their destination was the boat launch at Northville on the tip of Great Sacandaga Lake, where they would pull the canoe ashore. The lake's still waters were a challenge for the last few miles, and both canoers were exhausted by 3 o'clock, when they reached their destination. By arrangement, they were to rendezvous there with the eldest Whalen son, 20-year-old Thomas Patrick, a rugby player known as Tommy, at a riverside spot near the boat launch. After stepping ashore, the men lounged in the mid-afternoon sun among rocks and grassy outcroppings.

At the end of about an hour's wait, the family's 1977 Olds wagon pulled in. Tommy and his cousin, Mike Gaynor, climbed out and walked slowly toward them. Tommy's expression was so serious that his father peered beyond him at the wagon to see if perhaps they'd had a fender-bender on their drive up. When the younger men came within shouting distance, he learned the reason.

"Dad!" Tommy called with barely concealed excitement. "Bad news! The Mayor has died!"

The end had indeed come a few hours earlier for Erastus Corning. He had not seen the Mayor's office for more than 11 months. Tom Whalen thereupon became Albany's seventy-third Mayor.

Though not exactly on a truly comparable scale, the word that came this bright Saturday afternoon to the Adirondack foothills for Albany's second-in-command was more than superficially parallel to the news rushed out on a rainy Friday night to another deputy, Theodore Roosevelt, on a remote mountaintop—the Adirondacks' highest—three generations earlier. In each case, the summons was not "for whom it may concern" or for "a few good men," but instead constituted a call to destiny for a single individual of unproven capacity to address the challenge. The demands thrust now upon each were, in their unique degree, as striking as were the scenarios, and the responses to those demands contained a jack-in-the-box surprise that might confound many but would delight the multitude.

On their voyage southward, the canoers had noted that State Troopers seemed unusually active on the highway as it repeatedly wound near and across the river. They were impressed by the patrols' diligence, without finding cause to suspect that the Troopers had a mission beyond monitoring holiday weekend traffic. The Troopers had been scouting for them on the strength of an emergency call from Tom Burke, Albany's police chief: "Find Tom Whalen and tell him he must call Albany!"

* * *

Heading back to Wells, speeding away from the city, Tommy drove while his father tried to think through this turn of events. Although Corning's death after his hospitalization of nearly a year was hardly unexpected, the sudden fact and impact of it forced an urgency of appropriate response.

"I was trying to figure out," Whalen explained, "'How do I do this and still do justice to the memory of Erastus Corning?' I knew very well that there were things I had to do for the city—soon.

"It had been obvious to me through the whole scenario that when the moment arrived, people would be focusing more on his extraordinarily long service than on acquiring a new Mayor.

"How was I to handle that in a politic way? I had to be discreet in public actions and words. But exactly how to achieve that? What should be said after I was sworn in?"

Callers were repeatedly interrupting the solemn atmosphere. Nancy Connell of the Albany *Times Union* tracked him down at what her story termed his Adirondack cabin.[2] She had to be satisfied with nothing meatier than "It is premature to discuss any plans for changes." Denie and other family members were heard from, somber and questioning. Whalen handled them all standing by a wall phone near the back door.

The final caller was Jimmy Drislane, great friend and mentor from the law firm. His connections in the Democratic party had turned to him to locate the Corning successor, and he immediately assumed responsibility for initiating arrangements for the swearing-in. Because of ingrained habit, in crisis the most basic mechanisms of Albany's government were operating—but unofficially, through the party that dominated it.

This was the essence of his message now, referring to the judge who would administer the oath of office:

> "Jack Pennock will be available tomorrow.
> You need to call him and work out the when
> and where."

And then he added: "Don't delay! The city
needs to have its Mayor!"

* * *

By 7 o'clock, Whalen was on the road for Albany, with
John again driving. En route, he started jotting an outline of
what he might say to his constituents after taking office. His
pencil stub's marks were far more blunt than was the fine line
he would need to toe so scrupulously.

By the time they reached the city and approached the
Whalen home at the end of placid South Pine Avenue, the twilight was anything but quiet. A few dozen reporters and pho-
tographers from newspapers, radio, and television were
crowding the street and overflowing not only the Whalens'
lawn but neighboring yards. A series of spotlights flooded the
entire front of the house. The evening dusk of late spring had
darkened all else.

From several rods' distance, the further chaos which
would result if their quarry suddenly turned up in their midst
was only too apparent.

Still collecting his thoughts about what to tackle first in
the immense task that lay immediately ahead—how to assume
a responsibility that had lain virtually dormant for so long, and
when to appropriately grasp the reins without appearing pre-
sumptuously eager—with all this in mind, the new Mayor was
loath to be forced to respond to shouted questions with
answers that could better await a more temperate occasion.
Intuitively, he would try to avoid being drawn into careless
reference to the city's problems, with which he was far from
comfortable. No good would be served by stressing the negative at such a time. Accept the responsibility, do your job, and
see what happens.

Discreetly, Krueger threaded his way through the mob
scene with an unrecognizable profile and torso slouched into
the cushions beside him. Then, having parked in the driveway
around the corner on Cortland Street, on foot they approached

the empty house through a rear gate in the back yard, their path screened by a stand of pines the Whalens had planted as a means of gaining some privacy from the two streets bordering their home. From inside, without lights, they surveyed the journalistic frenzy in the street for several minutes before slipping out the way they had entered. No reporter or cameras saw the new Mayor that evening.

They said goodnight on a firm handshake as Krueger dropped his friend off at the home of his brother, Dr. Michael Whalen, a few blocks away on Manning Boulevard, for an impromptu family reunion. As the news began to spread through the city, Denie Whalen had retreated there with the children during the afternoon.

* * *

Albany's flags were at half-staff on Sunday morning as the Whalen family went to Mass at St. Vincent De Paul Church, their home parish. His mood was deliberately downbeat, restrained, as it continued to be for the next days.

When a friend on the street called out, "Good morning, Mr. Mayor," an observant reporter noted that the unfamiliar salutation failed to bring a prompt response. To a question from a ten-year old, "Are you going to be Mayor?" the answer came with a quiet diffidence, "I guess so."

The restraint lingered. He was visibly on hand, but chose to remain in the background. Inevitably, however, there had to have been a sense of relief: He had borne the responsibility of the Mayor's duties—sharing them, too, with the city's lawyer, Vinnie McArdle, though increasingly called upon to accept the lead—while still lacking the proper authority to enforce decisions. After many days in the office, without portfolio, not even with an "acting" title, he had found ways to show initiative, to institute change. As Mayor, he could know that he had finally acquired the authority that really would be needed to tackle the job effectively. He had passed through a most unusual situation, an enforced kind of on-the-job training. But now it was for real.

Though eminently respectful of Erastus Corning, he no longer would need to dissemble, claiming that the Mayor knew all about what was going on, was aware and approved of pro-active events, even had initiated them. For more than 90 days, none of that face-saving for the dying man had been remotely true. In a dire situation largely created by Corning's refusal to let go, the city had barely survived because the ability to decisively act was effectively blocked. Now would be the time for show-and-tell. Was Tom Whalen up to it?

Sunday's *Times Union* devoted several pages to stories, photos, an editorial, a melancholy Hy Rosen cartoon, and tributes. Corning's prolonged critical illness had made it possible for virtually all the necessary obituary material to be ready for publication.[3] There was even room for a story about the city's new Mayor, though with scant illumination as to how he might shoulder the tasks he would have to master.

His review of the news account was brief because he needed to sit and encapsulate his thoughts on what must be said: Not extensive, simple, in keeping with the very special time, focusing on Corning's memory. He was interrupted in his musings and jottings only by three callers, Lew Swyer and Jim Drislane, both close friends and advisers, and Judge Pennock.

Public utterance aside, his private feelings were mixed. One major emotion was of relief from the pressures which had built up over the months. Now that he realized he could legitimately engage, all out, in doing what was so badly needed in running the city, he was eager to get going: "I'll have a chance to do this only once—and I want to do it the right way," a thought that was to recur frequently. He recognized that he must anticipate conflict, that he would confront inbred political anger and in-house resistance within City Hall. (Later, he would ruminate many times that he hadn't fully realized how difficult politically his chosen course would become.)

True, he was by then well aware of problems—taking in the full range of issues in trying to govern—and he was stirred by a mild degree of anxiety: "Am I up to the challenge?"

Mingled with this was a recognition of his obligation not to deviate from an appropriate reserve during the public mourning—even though work was urgently awaiting his hand.

* * *

The new Mayor and Pennock, who would swear him into office, had readily agreed on the Albany County Courthouse, 100 yards up Eagle Street from City Hall, as the proper setting for the small ceremony. City Hall itself, still emotionally the property of Erastus Corning, clearly would be inappropriate. A courtroom on the third floor of the courthouse was set aside and a Sunday mid-afternoon hour was arranged as most suitable.

The long morning finally over, he drove Denie the three miles to the government center on Eagle Street and took an empty space for the Olds in front of the Court of Appeals. As they walked, more slowly than usual, to the adjacent courthouse, he found that, rather than the dramatic events of that day, his innermost thoughts were sentimentally turning to a principal influence which had steered him to this opportunity—his late father, whose fiscal wisdom and political instincts had been instrumental in instilling the ideal of public service. His counsel, his confidence, and his comradeship were grievously missed at this crucial stage.

Some six dozen spectators were somberly on hand, ranging from family to commissioners, plus a throng of reporters and cameramen. Among those pressing close to hear the oath, the Mayor-to-be caught the eye of his uncle Jim, his cousin (also named Denie), Aldermen Pete Horan and Joe Lynn, and Chief Burke.

On the rim of the gathering, Vincent McArdle, Albany's corporation counsel, hovered, out of range of the cameras, avoiding chance interviews while pondering the loss of his chief. For six months or more, he and Tom Whalen had formed a team—sharing leadership's responsibilities, making joint decisions, and screening information about the city government's functioning in Corning's absence. But in early spring, the task of substituting for a Mayor who couldn't make informed judgments, and couldn't be heard or seen, devolved upon the one person clearly destined to take over eventually. Then, as Whalen stepped toward center stage, McArdle instinctively moved closer to the prompter's box.

"During that difficult period, Vinnie and I never had any major disagreement or misunderstanding," Whalen said. "This positive relationship eased the transition for me. Vinnie was and is savvy in politics, in professionalism, and in personal connection. If it looked as if he should take a step back, he would do so without my needing to say a word."

Given this acute sensitivity, the city's lawyer was in the shadows in the courtroom. John E. Holt-Harris, ranking adviser to Whalen and to Corning, placed McArdle "at the top" of all those whom he assayed as most friendly to Whalen's efforts at the outset of his administration. "He was totally loyal to Tom and to his own principles, and he was in perhaps the best place to make the new Mayor's responsibilities work out."

Bill Keefe, Corning's right-hand man for nearly ten years, was unobtrusively busy, carrying on, ensuring that the requisite tools for the occasion were readily available. He handed the judge the appropriate book that contained the proper oaths for a variety of offices.

Judge Pennock, in his robes, held open the book and read the relevant 43 words, which promised support of the respective constitutions, federal and state, and the faithful discharge of unstated duties "to the best of my ability."

Pens were ready for the judge's and the new Mayor's signatures, attesting to their acts. The ever-efficient Keefe had seen to this detail, too.

Whalen's remarks after the swearing-in were subdued and terse, emphasizing Corning's memory rather than any declaration on his own behalf; not a word of whatever expectations or even hopes for the city he might have. "I plan to do all I can to keep the city government functioning as well as possible," were his only words looking to the future. It was apparent to the gathering that he considered this an hour to be sensitive to the citizenry's need to pay tribute.

"It is appropriate at this time that we focus our thoughts on Erastus Corning and all he did for the city of Albany," was the heart of his message to the city that had become his.

Altogether, a lonely, difficult period confronted the successor who, with even one poorly chosen word, could become resented as an interloper.

Years afterward, Whalen recalled that "I didn't pay much attention to a great deal of what was going on, it was all so new to me. I had to try to comprehend and digest my new responsibilities. I just needed to block out some aspects. The best course was to stay low-key and let people get through the time for mourning, the wake, the funeral. For four decades, after all, Mayor Corning had a bigger-than-life effect on the whole city."

* * *

On Monday morning, a member of the cleaning crew brought word to Bill Keefe in the Mayor's office that there'd been an uncredentialed visitor there at an odd hour before dawn Sunday. The visitor, a woman, was reported to have disappeared into the private office and to have carried something off when she left. Informed of this disturbing episode, Mayor Whalen made a prompt decision: Tighten security and pass the word to any of the people who might feel they could take advantage of the changing of the guard. Keefe said he was satisfied that the visitor's description fitted Polly Noonan, whose special friendship with Corning had titillated Albany for nearly 50 years.

On Tuesday, as Albanians by the thousands entered the Episcopal cathedral in tribute, the six men whom Corning had designated to advise him in his absence[4] held to their scheduled meeting time—and it was their last of some 40 sessions. Whalen, the sixth man appointed to the select group, was now the first, in charge and to be held accountable. To dispel any lingering doubt about the lawful succession which had dealt him accountability, he immediately announced the dissolution of this "Regency" group. Though not its chairman, he decisively seized the occasion to disband it unilaterally.

As the meeting ended, Holt-Harris put an arm around the new Mayor. By common consent, he had chaired all the group's sessions.

"Tom, you are now your own man," he said.

Who will be making decisions? a reporter asked.

"The city has a Mayor!" Whalen pointed out emphatically. Though seemingly innocuous, for Albany it was, in its way, a bold statement of leadership.

When the question was repeated, he pointed vigorously to his chest with his right thumb.

"Me!"

He was giving his city a graphic symbol of his acceptance of responsibility and accountability. And he was conspicuously freeing himself to formulate his own judgments and decisions, regardless of the advice he might receive from others, including Corning's counselor, Holt-Harris.

Few could foresee the emerging impact of his readiness.

* * *

On Thursday, the day after the funeral, the reporting on the Episcopal service at the Cathedral of All Saints included reference to "a sea of politicians . . . in their best suits," and suggested that Mr. Corning "no doubt would have been pleased by such homage." It was said that "no national figure" was present, despite the attendance of the state's two United States Senators. The presence of Daniel Patrick Moynihan, a Corning antagonist whom the old mayor reviled, was remarked behind many hands. Corning had refused to support him for the Senate in a heated 1976 primary, and he was ignored by the Albany County party in his 1982 reelection campaign.

(Nevertheless, Moynihan had gone out of his way to pay a call on Corning in the Boston hospital.) Mayor Edward I. Koch of New York was not to be seen although "there was a seat set aside for him." It was not too difficult to understand why Koch might find a way to be busy elsewhere that day. After all, Corning was still being advertised as the man whose support had been critical to his defeat by Cuomo only eight months earlier. Koch had loudly proclaimed himself—at least half-seriously—as New York City's "mayor for life." As it turned out within a few years, he didn't realize such an ambition. But in his own town Corning had, and before the curtain came down on the final act, he'd taken one of the leading roles in blighting Koch's larger dreams.

The Cathedral dean's sermon (published verbatim by the morning paper on page one) referred to the passing of "a man of great importance and influence, a man loved by many, many persons . . . who, to greater or lesser degree, has influenced the lives of all of us."[5] Overtones of that very influence may have occasioned this unusual break with the Episcopal order of service.

That day, both Albany newspapers distributed a 20-page tabloid "Keepsake" supplement as a memorial.[6]

And this was the day the successor arrived at Room 102 in City Hall to begin a new era for Albany and for himself. For the old quarterback, it was first down, goal to go.

* * *

As Albany's tribute came to an end, the tasks that the new Mayor was inheriting were uppermost in the minds of many who had led the mourning.

On the morning after the funeral, the *Times Union*'s leading editorial welcomed Whalen as Mayor in the context of "the serious problems the city faces."

"The picture of city finances" described in the most

recent report by the state Department of Audit & Control
"chills the blood," the editorial graphically commented.   It
termed Albany, "debt-ridden and battered in the bond market,"
as being "in worse financial shape than any other city in
upstate New York."[7]

These horrified comments also reflected a statement
issued earlier by Standard and Poor's noting that the reasons
for having changed Albany's rating three levels downward
"included the consistent record of overspending, deficit financing from debt proceeds, reduced liquidity, and increased cash-
flow borrowing."

This aspect of the Corning legacy for months had
boiled spasmodically to the surface of the public's awareness.
Although entirely muted among the cascade of tributes, this
"blood-chilling" crisis had to be faced, promptly and effectively, with a clear-eyed appreciation of the existence of manifold
problems.   But—more importantly—the looming difficulties
were compounded by a hangover productive of many a long
headache.   Curing it would be virtually the sole responsibility
of just one person, but he would need to find skilled, dedicated helpers.

In these earliest hours, Tom Whalen was at least subliminally impressed and influenced by a sentence in a published commentary[8] that he'd clipped and saved during the
spring.   It read:

"History is not kind to idlers."

* * *

"When I came to office I believed that most Albany citizens wanted reform," Whalen commented later.   "I could
anticipate that my biggest hurdle in changing things was most
likely to come from within the party.   In this forewarned expectation I was right, as many future events would prove!"

Seventeen months earlier, Whalen had walked into City
Hall on New Year's Eve of 1981 with a map in his head.   Over

the previous years, ideas had percolated there in contemplation of what could make Albany a better city.

The sketchy map unfortunately didn't offer a clue as to how to get There from Here, for its lines were only figurative. Had it been actual, his map would have resembled a jigsaw of uncharted geography in a land we might as well call Figment.

But on that day, Tom Whalen, citizen, became Thomas Whalen, civil officer, second-ranking elective official in his hometown. Though its implications remained unknowable, the key to Albany's long-range future had just been placed in his hand. Better described, perhaps, as the code for bringing logic to all the map's scrambled chaotic pieces.

The pieces would become his to assemble because of his lifetime—nearly a half-century by then—spent within the city, a lawyer whose daylight hours downtown had gained for him unusual opportunities to understand its commerce. He held title to a home-owner's perception as well as a P-and-L perspective on the city's fiscal and tax structure. And somewhere among the pieces was his modest history in the dominant political organization, earning there a corporal's stripes plus a battle star and the requisite Good Conduct Medal.

In rescuing Albany from itself—from the clutch of its ironbound traditions, the bonds of its shriveled expectations, plus the more perilous pitfalls dug by his presumed allies—Tom Whalen called upon very unusual credentials: his quarter-century exposure to the special world of money-men; his seven months' drenching in the cold shower of official Albany's exotic bookkeeping; and—most of all—a bravado worthy of Don Quixote in Wonderland.

The multitude of perplexing lessons he had just learned while Corning still lived, though unwelcome, had been genuinely fortuitous. For, along with headaches and heartburn, they had brought insights, comprehension—and a growing reputation. He could hardly plead innocence when the hour struck. He'd been as forewarned as an inhabitant of a barrier island in September.

And forearmed; he innately recognized the incubus

he'd inherited along with a title and a desk. To his credit, he accepted without quibble the responsibility: he could not merely drape the title around him or pose behind the desk. The acceptance meant standing his ground; righting disorder; confronting challenge both figurative and active; making nice, as the old ethnic term has it, but saying "No." And demonstrating the determination he must truly possess or go under along with the city put in his charge.

The city hoped, but remained uncertain.

The practicality of her people's ancient political loyalties, their long-submerged imagination and rusted creativity, the assumption that because Erastus Corning had survived through the lifetime of their own memories his way of doing (not doing) things was standard—the fact that all such beliefs had now faded, left Albany's populace appalled and awed. A new leader, if he was indeed to lead, must move quickly though respectfully; act decisively, though with untested authority; show calm confidence though beset by contradictions and questions. The hand he had drawn must be played coolly, a Bogart facing Lorre and Greenstreet across the table. A case of do or die.

But, in truth, he'd had another option: He could have quit; he could have tossed down the hand of deuces and treys and abandoned the game as hopeless. Even as responsibility arrived, he could read that nothing much was expected of him, all was transient and temporary. He had private issues of his own, not the least of which was his professional career and the living it afforded the six at home, another responsibility he accepted with equal gravity.

But these were only theoretical options. To Tom Whalen, he had zero choice. Mentally, for years past, he had creatively structured the way things ought to be in his city. Together with opportunity, duty had descended on him. There never was a real question that he would stay. Try. Do his best. Damn the torpedoes. Not for nothing had it been said of him that, like Emily Dickinson's father, he "steps like Cromwell."

"Being his own man—that would become the most

remarkable part," was the summary opinion of the man who stood above and beyond all the turbulence of the Whalen years. Holt-Harris, a very highly regarded lawyer, was an O'Connell intimate who knew the Organization from its insides, where his stature was appreciated and respected. He had been the closest male friend of Whalen's predecessor. And yet he was both objective and protective in his view of Whalen individually and as a public official.

"The odds were against him from the outset," said Holt-Harris, who also could colorfully cast a candid eye on his own qualities, from the tenacity ascribed to his Welsh ancestry, to parallels between his character and that of John Bunyan's Pilgrim.

"The Old Guard didn't like him—couldn't comprehend his honesty and bluntness. They saw him as a usurper. He had a good many enemies in the ranks. They thought Corning should not have designated him for the position where he became the obvious successor. There were those I call the 'strict constructionists' who claimed that Erastus hadn't really appointed him and that he hadn't intended for Tom to be Mayor.

"Whalen had one commissioner who hated him and thought City Hall was his own province.

"But Whalen had some strong points behind him," Holt-Harris added. "He did have the legal right to the office— once he got there. He was helped, in fact, by being close to a big portion of the population—Irish Roman Catholic—who could assume he knew what the term 'Protestant Ascendancy' signified to them. He had the support of Mario Cuomo, who wanted him to succeed because Corning had picked him. He had the good wishes or the active involvement of a range of well-intentioned people who were in a position to be of help. His entire adult life had been in preparation for public office and for competent discharge of its duties."

* * *

Fundamentally, of course, Albany's inescapable problem, and his, was the city's dire fiscal posture. Sense had to be brought to the chronic imbalance in Albany's deployment of its only-too-finite resources. Beyond the intricate juggling act and skilled diplomacy which this feat would entail—tasks daunting enough in themselves—credibility must be infused into all the endeavors that underlay any hope of financial stability. Exposing, then caulking up, the systemic leaks also meant explaining, if not justifying, the *why* and the *where* of the city's available resources, unaccountably depleted. This adventure in itself was perilous, sowing distrust and breeding poisonous enmity.

And even these vital aspects of recovery were dwarfed by an ultimate necessity: A single individual of intrinsic honor, one with the integrity to "do the right thing because it is the right thing to do," and—equally, perhaps—with the courage to stand before doubt and damnation, plus the stubbornness to see it through. Character would be the answer.

* * *

Albany quickly ran through a serial quartet of City Hall structures in its first 200 years, but the fifth has endured handsomely and began its second century precisely when Tom Whalen took office.

Perilously but courageously, an Albany Mayor does his thinking, receives his phone calls, greets his visitors directly beneath some 70 yards of New Hampshire granite and a massive collection of cast iron among which one piece alone weighs a ton.

This is the City Hall's 10-story tower and its carillon, rising high above the main bulk of the structure. If one were contemplating a medieval drama it would be possible to imagine a mayoral captive within this tower, huddling close to its base and wary of the narrow windows allotted him, seeming little more than dungeon-like slits. Even so, he can labor there, fret there, dream there, receive complaints and supplications there, even issue commands there day after day, unmindful of the pile rising above his head—unmindful, that is, save for its clock's faithful quarter-hour reverberations that measure every four-year span in 15-minute intervals, 140,256 of them. So it has been for five score years, and more, for 20 of Albany's Mayors.

Slightly below the crest of State Street's majestic hill, it might have dominated the city save for the overpowering State structures all about. An early, almost poetic interpretation of its Romanesque granite solidness by Mariana Griswold Van Rensselaer,[9] called its 202-foot tower an "expression of civic authority."

The cornerstone was wedged into place in 1881, a few months after fire destroyed its 50-year-old Philip Hooker-designed antecedent. The replacement was hustled to completion in only a year and a half, compared with the Capitol's quarter-century of construction. Its unusual, striking lines were drawn up by the eminent architect Henry H. Richardson, one of the nineteenth century's greatest.[10] He had come to town on the Capitol project, so his incidental engagement to design City Hall was almost happenstance. Nonetheless, he proudly termed it one of the best of all his renowned designs. At a cost of $325,000, Richardson's City Hall might well be evaluated as Albany's biggest bargain ever.

Richardson gave the Mayor one window that provides a southerly vista out Eagle Street toward the Executive Mansion of New York's Governors, but the office's principal view is through shaded parks toward the Capitol. That massive bulk looks eastward down at the Hudson, whereas Albany's own statement of governance faces westward, conveying in spirit a sweep of progress and opportunity. In its own front yard, it confronts the brazen coattails of an outsized Philip Schuyler, who poses resolutely atop a pedestal which hides a forgotten time capsule of the 1920s.

* * *

From his windows, draped as they were in an imported velvet he'd had cut to emphasize their narrow height, Erastus Corning mused—toward the end of his life—that "I have looked at the Capitol from across the street hundreds of times every week."

This was a reflective Corning, revealing a quality that he rarely could afford to put on view. What else did he do in that room other than receive penitents and beggars, grant reprieves, and compile the Orders of the Day? It turns out that all was not the stress of command:

> "As a Capitol-watcher, I have had a good time," he conceded. "Capitol-watching has been a lot of fun, and always interesting, most of the time exciting." As he regarded the building's mass, he found sermons in stones, too: "I have learned some of the things that change—and some of those that do not."

His remarks came in a paper—very clearly one of his own composing—for a symposium on the Capitol's history and significance. The paper was informal, insightful as to both his real self and the larger picture, anecdotal and humorous without seeking to be comic, disclosing a man big enough to give credit to an ancient foe (he called Thomas E. Dewey the state's "best administrator") and deep enough to understand and enjoy history. He showed himself as a sensitive human being capable of sentiment and of knowing—and recapturing—delight and sorrow, an individual with a richness known to only too few Albanians, even at this late hour.

"I can look back," he wrote, "to the time when Governor (Nathan) Miller lost his bid for reelection (1922), and he and his wife and seven beautiful daughters left Albany and my 12-year-old heart was terribly saddened, if not broken."

* * *

Corning, whose complex and contradictory life dated
from the Edwardian era in a year when a greengrocer was
Albany's Mayor, mirrored a jest of a New Haven newspaper
columnist who gazed across the campus and sneered about
"the sense of privilege imbibed from four years at Yale
University." Except for that period and a few preppie years
earlier, he had spent seven decades around Albany, a substantial majority of them in City Hall. He'd been Mayor 80% of his
adult life, and in public office—placed there by Albanians—
92% of his years since turning 21. Albany was truly his life, as
Holt-Harris observed.

A revealing sidelight on how his reputation as a master
politician flourished as his city shrank and shriveled was heard
by a national television audience as he prepared to take office
for the last time.

"There are many things that are important to the people," he said in a CBS network program. "They may not be
important to me, but I early came to the conclusion that what's
important to the people is important to me."

On that same program, broadcast in the weekend of his
eleventh inaugural, Corning won mostly laudatory attention
("reasonable and fair," he judged). The occasion was an interview included in Charles Kuralt's renowned "Sunday
Morning" series. He was called a "Hudson River patroon," and
identified as "the last of the big-city bosses," which was stretching the literal truth. Finally, he was hailed as "the real power
in Albany." This, of course, was a much more factual reference,
but to it was added an odd comparison. His power was
termed by the show's script writer to be greater than that of
Nelson Rockefeller, the former governor who left Albany eight
years earlier—and who had been dead for three years.

* * *

City Hall's central court, reaching three stories upward,
is surrounded by a warren of modest offices. The Mayor's
suite is nestled in the southwestern corner of the main floor.

His space incorporates his private chamber, a small foyer, his assistant's reception room, a larger work area for the secretarial staff, and a sizeable conference room.

Albany's Mayors, as they have sat facing toward an extraordinarily large—and unused—fireplace and mantel, may have been inspired over the years by an heroic likeness of Pieter Schuyler, their very first predecessor in the long line of the city's chief magistrates. Even its outsize frame claims another noted architect, Marcus T. Reynolds, as its designer.[11]

As the Mayor eased behind his desk in the early hours of each business day, his eyes were likely to make contact with a steadfast challenge prominent on the mantel:

ASSIDUITY, it reads, proclaiming this unforgiving watchword that is an integral part of Albany's ancient coat of arms.

Diligence, it demands. *Unremitting attention*, it requires. *Persistent application* to the daily chores, no matter how mean they appear to the incumbent at that moment.

And at the end of his arduous and diligent efforts for the day, the mayoral eye may well again pass across the official motto which will have become his own. But now *assiduity* is not so much a challenge as an inquiry:

Were you equal today to the obligation which we have laid upon you?

Undoubtedly, some Mayors have proved themselves able to supply more satisfactory answers than have some others.

NOTES

[1] Mr. McCullough was describing an attitude of Theodore Roosevelt, in *Brave Companions: Portraits in History* (Simon &

Schuster: A Touchstone Book; copyright 1992 by David McCullough).

2 The "cabin" is a 1975 chalet-style retreat, a sturdy and comfortable three-level structure that easily sleeps eight under its pitched roof. It is dominated by a large room where a sitting area fronts a big stone fireplace. Three wide glass doors look westward, beyond foliage hiding Route 30 and the Sacandaga, toward the 3,250-foot height of Hamilton Mountain. A 10-foot-wide deck wrapping around most of the house is perfect for watching a mountain sunset, a twilight feast for the eagle eye of the man who would be Mayor, for such moments a stout Cortez upon his own Darien peak.

3 In truth, Corning had died "on the Knick's time"—that is, early in the afternoon on Saturday, providing an opportunity for a very timely Extra edition on the day of his death. The *Knickerbocker News* too had been thoroughly prepared. But preparations on the presses for the Sunday *Times Union* foreclosed the possibility of the Extra. And since the paper wasn't published on Sundays and holidays (Monday was the official Memorial Day), the Knick was relegated to bringing three-day-old "news" to its remaining readers on Tuesday afternoon, following on a hundred columns of detailed coverage in the *Times Union*.

4 Detail on this "Regency" is to be found in the chapter "The Badly Tangled Web." (In Section III: The Long Year.)

5 Great minds, etc.: In more informal remarks upon the death of Daniel P. O'Connell six years earlier, the Roman Catholic Bishop, Howard J. Hubbard, said that his "life has influenced the lives of countless people."

6 Ironically, this edition described by the publishers as a keepsake was printed on standard newsprint, a paper that ages and deteriorates rapidly, particularly on exposure to light.

7 Just four days earlier, on what might be termed "the morning after," the newspaper had editorialized that "under Mayor Corning's guidance, the city worked." This presumably was intended to mean that it had an efficient and effective municipal government. The editorial cited that Albany had "not a great deal of crime" or "problems with traffic congestion," and that its schools, police, fire protection, and other services were "adequate." "The mayor's stately manner greatly enhanced the reputation of Albany," for which his "elegance, urbanity, and sophistication" established him

as "a classy ambassador." But the later follow-up editorial had finally recognized some of the shadows on this picture, finding problems more serious than traffic congestion.

[8] From a Report (April 1983) of the National Commission on Excellence in Education.

[9] From *Henry Hobson Richardson and His Works*, by Mrs. Schuyler Van Rensselaer. Published by Houghton Mifflin and Company in 1888. Copyright by Dover Publications 1969, in an unabridged republication.

[10] Much of the information on the City Hall is from *Albany Architecture*, edited by Diana S. Waite, and published in 1993 by the Mt. Ida Press and the Preservation League of New York State. Copyright by Matthew Bender IV and the Mt. Ida Press Partnership.

[11] He drew the plans in 1902 for that striking structure designated as 35 State Street, originally the home of the Albany Trust Company and the firm of Cooper Erving Savage, so intimately linked with one occupant of City Hall. The building is noted for its distinctive rounded-corner configuration and Renaissance Revival exterior detailing. Subsequent ownerships included the First Trust Company, Bankers Trust, First American Bank, and, since 1993, Key Bank of New York, which uses the property for its private bank.

Toward Reform:
Stumbling Steps

"Fear was a big factor in Albany politics then," Whalen attested in recalling the O'Connell period. "If you didn't do things the way the Organization wanted them done, or if you didn't adhere to the party line, you could be banished politically, never to surface again."

In the first 20 years of the Boss's leadership of Albany County Democrats, the party lost one election, to Jack Tabner, a young Republican lawyer who won one of the county's three State Assembly seats in the first Eisenhower landslide. Democrats held all other principal offices in the city and at the county level, including members of the state and national legislatures. A reform ticket headed by a young Protestant clergyman, a newcomer who was horrified by what he'd seen during his brief residence, was turned back casually by Corning. A Democratic lawyer waged lonely primary campaigns for the State Legislature against the Boss's slate, only to be humiliated each time—and with inaudible applause for his brave efforts. Occasionally, a Republican candidate would mount a well-conceived campaign but without substantial support or promising effect. Otherwise, the true will of the hapless Albany County Republicans was open to question. O'Connell and Corning (his protege? partner? front man?) were constantly invincible. Little wonder that the Organization appeared sure it could govern in a manner that pleased the Boss and returned appropriate reward to various levels of certified Loyalists.

"According to stories," Whalen said of the O'Connell period, "some party characters were on the fringe of illegal conduct—and others were downright shady."

Some of the leading figures—he mentioned Julian Erway, Donald Lynch, and the Ryan brothers specifically—"all had their deals and were the beneficiaries of the spoils system."[1]

The Boss and his men—particularly the Law and Order system from patrolmen to prosecutors to judges—scorned doubters and objectors and all who failed to enroll as Democrats.

The above-the-law attitude was exemplified in 1963 in a high-handed series of demands by O'Connell's prosecutors (legitimated by a captive grand jury). The newspapers' publisher and editors were haled before the jurors and required by a District Attorney to explain, under oath, news reports and commentary they had published.

Ultimately, the fruit of this abuse of power was a rebellion which, while political in expression, was also broadly civic in essence.[2] The rebellion marred most of Dan O'Connell's final decade. It was a combination of circumstances, perhaps attributable in part to the Boss's age—he was just past 75 when Nelson Rockefeller bollixed Albany's demographics for good by ripping the left ventricle of O'Connellism right out of the city's center for his fabled "South Mall." He turned 81 in the November of the first real stirring of a Republican insurgency and was just short of 90 when it petered out. Another critical factor was the surprising vigor of the Republicans under a new leader, Joseph C. Frangella, a brashly determined and combatively effective county chairman. And, finally, there was at last a responsive electorate—O'Connell's opponents elected 16 candidates in Frangella's eight-year chairmanship. In addition, Democrats were hard-pressed in other campaigns where their margins of victory were significantly reduced. The competition became so close that one important officeholder, an O'Connell intimate, was reelected only through a recount (and even then serious doubt remained about the legitimacy of that outcome). In no instance was a Republican elected to any office in Albany city government, although some still maintain that evidence existed showing the official result of Corning's ninth election (1973) had been corrupted by the theft of enough ballots that would have given the election to his opponent, Carl E. Touhey. (Were Corning's narrow victory by some 3,000 votes turned around, resulting in a Touhey victory, the advent of Thomas M. Whalen, III to the Mayor's office just ten years later never would have occurred. But Corning, declared the winner, continued to serve throughout those ten years, with two more reelections along the way.)

* * *

Thus, Dan O'Connell's closing years severely compromised his legendary reputation as the infallible Boss of a stronghold whose votes were to be delivered to any candidate—local, state, national—whom he chose to endorse.

Dissent and discord, previously unknown, burst into the open. His Organization dreaded the idea of an elected school board and its power to levy a real-property tax distinct from that dictated in City Hall. But at one of the peaks of the insurgency, the old three-man board (a pair of Organization lawyers[3] and a gynecologist) was turned out and a new board chosen by popular vote. It was a serious dent in the O'Connell armor—and its fearsome repute.

Simultaneously, the Organization fought a movement to grant union representation to its uniformed employees. The Police and Fire departments traditionally were among the intimidating bastions of control. To have their pay and work rules subject to review and argument—even agitation, as easily could be foreseen—seemed unthinkable. But the rank-and-file won in a showdown, repudiating the paternal grip directed, as they knew, by Dan O'Connell. In effect, he was seen as turning his back on his own people, a concept that understandably rankled.

The State Commission of Investigation returned to

Albany with a new vigor and a renewed campaign of inquiry all the more stinging because of the commission's lack of success—beyond publicity—over the many years of its onslaught against the O'Connell fortress. Erastus Corning was now obliged to bring his faulty memory, swearing to speak the truth but exhibiting an Astaire's fancy footwork as he danced about his insinuating questioners, taunting them with chilly insolence. Worse, as an unforeseen but probably inevitable dividend of the probing, the SIC's lawyers did draw blood from the cheek of a prime Organization debater and hassler—and a judge, at that—Jack Pennock, who over the years had become a friendly counselor for Whalen. For what amounted to little more than poor judgment in ruling against the SIC in a rather trivial and technical matter that was, nevertheless, a case of "judicial misconduct," he was rebuked by a panel of appellate judges, all of whom just happened to have been Republican in orientation. His defender before this august group, arguing an essentially hopeless case of technicalities, was Whalen, who was still a judge in City Court. Picked for this difficult and thankless duty by Pennock himself, he offered a defense in a courtroom manner notably contrary to Pennock's prickly combative style.[4] (Whalen later considered that the case was, altogether, a boost for his reputation within the profession.)

And to top off the depressingly prolonged downhill slide, Daniel P. O'Connell himself was being cruelly denigrated, even by the people who had for years benefited by his patronage. With each defeat at the polls, new restlessness appeared among these confounded friends—"Is Dan slipping?" When old strategies finally were recognized as damagingly outdated and counterproductive—"Is this our infallible wise man? Have the unkind years withered his judgment?" When his handymen from so long ago, the Ryan brothers, seemed unduly flamboyant—"Is it Dan who's really making the decisions?" When Corning blatantly persisted in a personal relationship O'Connell was said to abhor—"Isn't the Boss strong enough to stop that?"

To such contretemps, there could be added unprece-

dented instances of followers having resisted—if not flouted—
offers and decisions from on high, such as Donald Lynch's
quitting the county committee's key position; young Tom
Brown's finally disdaining his prized reward, a seat in the
Legislature; Eugene Devine's costly willingness to go to bat for
the firemen against the Corning and O'Connell position; the
inability of one bishop of his church to control some progressive, provocative priests who were annoyingly out on Albany's
streets—and the irksomely nonconformist views of yet another imported bishop. And, perhaps, even including the willingness of Tom Whalen—who had shown such promise—to say
"No!" twice when new candidacies were enticingly dangled
before him.

In his last election—four months before he died—when
he was too ill, tired, and aged to care much, Dan O'Connell saw
his party elect a farmer, a Georgia Baptist, as President; a scholar who actually wrote books, as a New York Senator; and a
mayor of Schenectady, as his Congressman. Despite the legend, political time had marched out from under this man
whose watchword remained "The Usual."

NOTES

[1] Webster's describes spoils system as a "practice of regarding public offices and their emoluments as plunder to be distributed
to members of the victorious party." Julian Erway was a lawyer
whom O'Connell twice sent to the State Senate for 14 years within a
26-year period (1942-1968), serving as District Attorney in an interim period. His political career ended in 1968 when defeated by
Walter B. Langley. He and Lynch formed Erly Realty, and profited
substantially from land development deals on which they had
obtained an inside track. Lynch and the Ryans enter this account
elsewhere.

[2] Author's Note: I can testify as to the validity of a direct connection between the O'Connell attack on a free press and the opposition's uprising. My successful campaign in 1966 against an Organization candidate (for the Congressional seat centered in Albany city and county) was inspired and given forceful commitment by the prosecutorial abuses and by the oppressive climate they characterized. I had experienced both firsthand. "Just one of those things," was O'Connell's public comment on this first big election he had ever lost. I felt greatly rewarded to have accomplished this while the Boss was still at the height of his power.

[3] A school board seat was one of Holt-Harris's assignments. One of his colleagues there was another O'Connell favorite, Neile F. Towner, who was a law partner of Julian Erway, the Senator and D.A.

[4] Pennock won his place as Albany County Attorney (an appointive position) precisely because of the sharp mind behind that sharp, no-nonsense combativeness. He was rewarded by selection as the Organization's candidate for the Supreme Court in the seven-county Third District and was elected to a 14-year term in the month that John F. Kennedy was assassinated. At the end of that term, he was believed to be in bad repute among voters because of his official rebuke three years earlier, but he won reelection largely through strenuous and judicious campaigning by his son, by Whalen, and not many others. He died some eight years into his second term.

A Financial Fairyland

On the day Corning was elected for the last time, his city government was mired in accumulated deficits of more than $9 million. It was November 1981 and he had held the office—through two generations—for exactly 40 years. Within a few months the debt had to be "forgiven" by the State Legislature because the city had no way to pay it off.

According to projections made later by Whalen's budget director, the fiscal year that had ended just five days before the election was the fourteenth in a row in which the Corning administration had operated in the red. (This was a particularized revision of fiscal history, presumably made possible by the budget director's expertise and special opportunity to review the way the books had been kept. Previous reports had found three years of deficits.) Operations in the prior year, 1980-81, alone cost $4.2 million beyond the city's lawful revenues. For better or worse, however, the Mayor had provided additional revenue—but it was revenue somewhat less than lawful.

For many years, his fiscal policy had entailed merely unwritten priorities for acquiring and disbursing municipal resources. Justified only by his own judgments and commitments based on data existing solely in his head, these were subject to no one's knowledge or scrutiny. The city's financial officers, the Comptroller and Treasurer, though elected separately from the Mayor, were wholly under his thumb. The fiscal oversight of the Common Council was a joke. Even Daniel

O'Connell, innocent as he surely was in any area of sophisticated finance, had been exempted from actually passing on
Corning's fiscal imagery. Like a balloon in a spring breeze, the
city's finances had bounced along for decades, though each
year carrying more ballast.

The ballast had grown unsupportable in very recent
years because of a trio of interlocking, festering causes:

> (1) Most recently, and most crucially,
> Corning's prolonged absence and his even-
> tual inability to participate even passively
> in decision-making had finally brought the
> city's underlying ills to a near-tragic climax.
>
> (2) But at the core were two long genera-
> tions of tight control by a pair of aging men
> who imposed a system which invited abuse
> while denying an inert public its right to
> true participation in decision-making. The
> people of Albany were not accustomed to
> problem-solving in public. They were
> accustomed to being told what was best for
> them. And theirs was not to reason why.
> Four decades earlier, an astute journalist, I.
> F. Stone, had visited Albany long enough to
> enable him to write that the city "exhibits
> the slatternly side of the democratic
> process," and that "Albany is contented in
> its corruption" with "respectable elements"
> which "share widely in the benefits of
> machine government." He identified "dis-
> honest practices" that "no one could wish to
> condone—except the property-owners and
> lawyers who benefit by them, and their ben-
> eficiaries are many."[1] His 1940s comments
> could as easily have been written early in
> the 1980s.
>
> (3) Compounding this inherent weakness
> was the subverting of Corning's attention
> for five years before his final illness. He had

taken on the county chairmanship of the
Democratic Party after his mentor's death.
The historic range of this strictly political
role implicitly mandated that he greatly
enlarge his stern oversight of Albany
County's government which was in the
hands of a man he distrusted. As a party
insider said in 1979, "Corning has absolute
control over everybody, as far as the county
is concerned, the same as in the city. No
decision is made on the county level of any
consequence or substance that he doesn't
make." He was seen as "coldly and effectively" dominating the county "in a way
that Dan O'Connell never did." These new
duties distorted his span of attention and
relegated the city's affairs to second or third
place in his priorities. Meanwhile, problems multiplied, compounded by the nature
and quality of his managerial judgments.

They were complicated by the absence, with rare exception, of a truly competent layer of administration. This was
directly attributable to the Corning style of insisting on managing everything himself. His department heads were figure-
heads—largely unqualified party Regulars. And when his
overview and direction of these incompetents became over-
loaded because his attention was focused elsewhere by the
competing demands, his non-functional staff simply let too
many essentials fall through the cracks. By his own creation,
this formula for calamity was far worse than the costly ineffi-
ciencies of day-to-day, year-to-year malfunctions.

Administratively, the picture that the Corning mayoralty presented could be said to hark back a century and across
the Atlantic to the heyday of Prime Minister William E.
Gladstone, who so completely involved himself in detail that if
he was absent from Whitehall his Cabinet considered that "it
was as though he had 'left us mice without the cat.'"

The closed-door policy of Corning's government

brought on its own unique problems, all of them much more related to long-term outcomes than with contemporary problem-solving. Hand-in-hand with the deals worked out behind the doors was the implicit expectation that partisan politics properly belonged as an integral characteristic of government, very deeply involved there, an unchallenged right. The Organization received first consideration, whatever the issue might be. Primacy was awarded to the eternal requirements of maintaining control and, naturally, of staying in power. Input from individuals or private organizations was specifically unwanted; the deals were to be accomplished quietly—more speedily and, in their way, more efficiently.

In 1973, the year in which Corning barely survived a reelection challenge by Carl Touhey, a biting report from the State Commission of Investigation warned his administration that "There is plainly a line which must be drawn between governmental operations and partisan political considerations." This stricture was ignored, and the interweaving of opposing purposes continued unabated.

In truth, "policy" in such circumstances was subordinated to effective means for retaining a political party's control of the machinery of government. Its needs and purposes were dominant. The game was as crude as any Ponzi scheme. The outcome necessarily would be chaos.

Was mismanagement an issue? Asked this question, Whalen replied narrowly: "Yes, I think there are a lot of cases where people"—not identified—"didn't pay as much attention to the financial operations of the city as they should have."

Corning chronically relied on three inappropriate devices: He optimistically overestimated how much money the city could expect to take in. He underestimated how much he intended to spend. And he included, among anticipated revenues, purported "surpluses" that did not exist. His merry estimates regularly overstated the anticipated revenues by millions of dollars, leading to sizable deficits.

Each year the dominoes continued to fall. His borrowing inevitably was necessary to make up the difference between estimate and reality. The result was higher taxes to pay off his borrowing follies. Tax increases spurred residents' flight from the city. A cycle of diminished property-tax base followed. Censure by Audit & Control. Punishment from the bond-rating agencies.

Corning's year-after-year practices went unnoted by almost all of his constituents, who reelected him in 1981 with 72% of the vote. In effect, he was "forgiven" before his city's debt was.

But the nature of his record was not unnoticed everywhere. The State Comptroller, Edward V. Regan, whose office monitors municipalities' fiscal health,[2] complained in November 1982 during the fifth month of Corning's absentee mayoralty that "The city's principal financial problem continues to be large annual operating deficits." His report covered Albany's operations over a four-year period that represented almost all of Corning's go-it-alone mayoralty after O'Connell's death. (Unhappily, release of the report coincided with announcement of the budget for 1983 prepared not by Corning but by Whalen and three colleagues.) The comment on Corning's fiscal practices was biting:

"The city's unrealistic budgeting practices . . . have plagued the city for numerous years and . . . have contributed to the city's financial condition."

Albany was in "financial crisis," the Comptroller said, and called for a series of salvaging reforms in the city's fiscal policies. He indicated a need for stringent controls to be imposed by the State.

The crisis and the failings that had created it were attributable to this one man, who magisterially retained preparation of those budgets in his own hands, ultimately producing forecasts that frequently were unsupported by fact, and employing loose practices that the Comptroller termed "improper" as well as his favorite term, "unrealistic." Corning's budget for 1982 later proved to have the same dismal shortcomings as those the Comptroller's report complained about: a $2.56 million deficit attributable to his having overestimated by $2 million the revenues from sales and property taxes and from parking fines, and to his optimistic but wrong guess that the city would sell $1.5 million of its properties.

That budget, the last to be prepared by Corning alone, was a thing of shreds and patches, only too typical of all those that it followed. Lacking any information that could help make sense of its figures, it offered no written narrative, not even a table of contents, to assist the bewildered reader. The city's new property-tax rate went unmentioned. No reference to a capital fund was to be found. A frustrated reporter who had undertaken an analysis found his efforts an "exasperating experience" and labeled the budget "a mystery tale with few clues." Or, as Churchill remarked (speaking of the Soviet Union), "It is a riddle wrapped in a mystery inside an enigma."

The Mayor was regularly taking money that had been borrowed ("ostensibly," as the Comptroller noted) for construction and other capital purposes, and "improperly" diverting it to make up for the shortfall in income for current operating expense.[3] He used a similar diversion for money that was "required to be held in reserve for debt redemption." Thus "cash shortfalls that otherwise would have occurred with operating deficits of this size" were covered by Corning's irregular practices.

"The city has been able to remain solvent, despite deficits of this magnitude," the Comptroller cautioned, "only by using funds (legally) restricted to other purposes."

Albany was taking on long-term debt to fund—illegally—current requirements. This amounted to covering up the fact of an empty treasury. The Mayor could do this only because of his parallel habit of "extensive borrowing in excess of needs," thereby creating a renewable pool of funds to draw upon so long as each new indulgence provided walk-around money for him.

In other words, he could describe potential capital projects that never were carried out. If, however, some eventually had to be done, they would materialize only years later, when more borrowing would be required for their completion. The

year-by-year accumulated debts became monumental in relation to the cash flow. "Forgiveness" by the Legislature was a
direct reflection of this malady.

This "haphazard capital program," together with "inadequate accounting controls," "contributed heavily" to the
"financial crisis" of 1981-1982.

The need for capital planning, the Comptroller's report
stated bluntly, was shown by:

> • The existence of "borrowings made in
> excess of amounts needed, (providing) cash
> to fund the operating deficit";
> • Capital projects started before any for-
> mal approval was obtained;
> • Projects authorized and borrowings
> made, but work never undertaken;
> • Many recurring expenditures impru-
> dently financed by borrowing rather than
> through annual appropriations of current
> revenue.

Corning's happy-go-lucky approach to fiscal detail may
in fact indicate a slyly designed state of confusion, a companion piece to the irregularities of his costly purchasing and contracting practices. Invariably, the result was written in glaring
red ink and chagrining contrasts.

Among seven Upstate cities listed by the State
Comptroller, Albany was the only one carrying a debt load that
exceeded its constitutional limit. Albany's debt reported in a
new Comptroller's statement (issued two weeks before
Corning's death) was $82.28 million, or 116.5% of the $70.60
million limit. For other New York cities, the average of the
debt was only 35.3% of their respective limits, less than one-
third of Albany's disastrous figure. Had Corning been physically answerable, he'd have experienced considerable difficulty in offering a "not guilty" response, for every cent in the miserable record was attributable to his own stewardship.

Similarly, only Albany's debt burden exceeded the

annual revenue. It was nearly half-again as large as the revenue, surpassing it by 43.8%. In sharp juxtaposition, the debt load in the six other cities (Binghamton, Buffalo, Rochester, Syracuse, Schenectady, Troy) was less than their revenues, averaging no more than 60% of their funding sources. Comparably, Albany's record in this respect revealed practices that produced a fiscal situation twice as negative as these other cities'.

Another of Regan's complaints was of a "structural deficit" in the city's financial position. Occurring when a governmental body's current revenues are insufficient to pay both current expenses and the interest on its accumulated debt, the structural deficit in Albany's case was a burden that existed for most of the Corning decades as the price of his own practices. The Comptroller's unhappiness produced no desired result, nor was there a realistic possibility of effecting one.[4]

In addition to comparing the principles of budgeting with some of Albany's practices, the Comptroller's report included major segments of commentary, replete with negatives. Operating deficits received due attention, but so did bidding requirements, purchase of insurance, payrolls, personnel records, taxation, assessments, indebtedness records, and revenue sharing. Operations were scrutinized in the City Comptroller's, Treasurer's, and City Clerk's offices, the city's courts, and the water department. The landfill and the city's management of a theater and a hotel were critiqued.

Certain comments were very detailed. The segment on bidding requirements listed 24 vendors in 15 categories who had, over three years, received $6,063,000 for goods and services that were supplied without the necessary competitive bidding. A plumber received $650,000 including a markup of 100% or more for materials. An electrician was paid $450,000, a printer $504,000. Seven trash haulers got $904,000. Four wrecking businesses obtained $715,000 for demolition of city properties or privately owned condemned properties. In two years, a supplier of trees received $659,000. Without question, some goods and services were provided; the hanging question was in the markup.   The runoff from it financed the Organization, whose funds, the highly knowledgeable Holt-Harris believed, were augmented by operations at the O'Connell brewery and, ultimately, from its sale to a national beer distributor toward the end of the O'Connell years. The brewery's product under the brand name of Hedrick had enjoyed universal—"or else"—availability and priority in Albany bars. (The fact that Holt-Harris could not be completely certain that the beer was funding the party suggests the secrecy guarding the Democrats' sources of money.)

Of the 24 businesses identified by the State Comptroller as recipients of large amounts of public money for non-bid work or materials, two-thirds became defunct within a short time after Whalen's reforms began. The record implies that some, at least, could have been conduits for funds intended for little tin boxes unrelated to the purported services or supplies.

"Even though all this was essential for the party's finances," Whalen explained, "it really was also designed to take care of a select few most handsomely. A dozen vendors became very wealthy.

"As George W. Plunkitt described his guiding principle in the 1800s heyday of Tammany Hall, they operated in keeping with its blunt declaration: 'I seen my opportunities and I took 'em!'"

An overall similarity to Tammany characterized the O'Connell-Corning regime, in Whalen's retrospective, binocular view.

In Albany, if you wanted to seize your own "opportunity" (to eventually share the rewards) you were expected to work in one of the ward committees, preferably as a trusted leader. You needed to exhibit obvious diligence, results—and loyalty. Over the years, the opportunist who paid his dues by producing the desired vote for Organization candidates felt he was entitled to some of the harvest.

* * *

After enumerating and decrying bid and purchasing abuses, Comptroller Regan tried two tactics:

First, his 1982 report included a plaintive appeal to "the Common Council and other responsible city officials" to start to pay attention to the state's critical and admonitory message. (Mayor Corning was never mentioned in its 20 pages.) This pointed suggestion was coupled with a reminder that "Responsibility for financial condition rests with both the executive and legislative branches of the city's management and both must exercise the fiscal restraint necessary so that the city can operate within its resources."

Unfortunately, the appeal and the admonition were as unrealistic as the Mayor's budgeting. Without doubt, the Common Council's history as a blind follower (a news analyst's column referred to the members as "aldermice"), was eminently clear to the political realists in the Comptroller's office.

Regan's second tactic potentially boasted more muscle. Except for the changes in the Mayor's office, it almost certainly would have been imposed on Albany. It proposed—threatened—financial controls to be exercised by the State "as a means of restoring the city's financial well-being." Albany was teetering on the brink of surrendering to strict, obligatory oversight by the Comptroller plus a mandated three-year plan for honest budgeting. The city would be placed under the state's thumb, essentially as New York City had been in the 1970s, with a figurehead mayor, as was true of Abraham Beame.

In preparing Governor Carey for the prospect of the state's takeover of the capital city, Regan informed him that Audit & Control had "repeatedly brought our concerns to the attention of the city officials," staunch members of the Governor's party. "Our continued evaluation . . . leads us to believe," he said, "that there is no hope for self-improvement" by Albany's government. New York's fiscal watchdogs had abandoned faith in Erastus Corning's intentions.

"What would Albany be today," an editor of the *Knickerbocker News*, Duane LaFleche, had asked in 1968, "if Mr.

Corning had put his keen intelligence, his obvious charm, his inherited prestige, his administrative and political talents to the utter service of the city and less to the service of a political machine?"

NOTES

[1] In *The Nation*, May 1944.

[2] During the 14 years when Regan served as Comptroller, including all but the final eight months of Whalen's term, the designation of the department was informally changed to Office of the State Comptroller but this was never pushed through as a legislative and constitutional change. Throughout this book the official title of the department is employed.

[3] This practice apparently was employed at least as far back as Corning's first term in the 1940s. I. F. Stone (quoted earlier) wrote in 1944 that "Albany's city government seems to have been holding down its tax rate by paying current expenditures out of capital borrowings." He also mentioned another impression: "Assessments seem to be adjusted to aid the deserving and teach the independents a lesson."

[4] Inherited by Whalen, the structural deficit extended not only through his administration but well beyond it. By the end of the century it remained intact in the audits of Albany's accounts.

That Old Gang of Mine

In Albany, the traditional "insiders" of politics prefer to call themselves Loyalists. For decades—generations—small knots of men (and a very rare female) successively created a corps whose single-minded fealty to Leader and Organization—and to one another—would never be doubted. "Political people live according to standards of loyalty," it's been accurately stated by Edmund Morris, the biographer of TR and Reagan. As more philosophically expressed by the astute writer Jack Beatty, "In the romance of American politics, politicians may habitually betray the electorate, but they always keep their word to each other."[1] One important aspect of the brotherhood was summed up in Corning's apt phrase, "I like doing business with my friends." If their trustworthiness toward one another was unquestioned, they also possessed the attribute of being unquestioning.

The loyalty exacted was "a discipline" in the judgment of John Holt-Harris, who stood cannily apart from the rigor of it all but who nonetheless also sat exceedingly close to the power propelling the machine—Corning and O'Connell. The closeness of the associations endowed him with insights and credentials for keen analysis and strong opinion.

Four constituent elements were compounded in "the discipline," Holt-Harris surmised, these being

Fear   Respect   Love   Ambition

"These made it all work," he theorized, even while inserting at least one element surprising to many an observer of the same process. "These were what made everyone loyal to what the men at the top wanted."

The Loyalists never considered Tom Whalen one of their crowd—and he accepted the demarcation. This was no less true during his two positions over 12 years in City Hall than it had been in previous years.

And it was true even though he had already played valuable roles in support of quintessential insiders, Corning himself and the skilled infighter Judge Jack Pennock.

* * *

Within the months immediately after O'Connell's death in the waning hours of February 1977, pent-up ambitions, antipathies, and antagonisms were unleashed, conflicts that otherwise would have remained suppressed.

Like impoverished cousins and long-lost nephews barely able to wait for the reading of a childless miser's will, the would-be inheritors of O'Connell's hoard of power closed in for the spoils.[2]

Dan O'Connell, who had briefly held but one minor elective office, inherited his political office as Albany County Democratic chairman from his brother Ed, as we read in the opening chapter. And after more than 30 years of his chairmanship there was now a natural heir, by virtue of the rules of the county committee. Erastus Corning held the first vice-chairmanship. Logically and legally he had a right to take the chairman's reins at least until the party could regroup. Probably the law of natural selection operated in this respect, as well, for almost no one other than a Corning or an O'Connell had held the county chairmanship for the past 56 years.

Corning, however, found himself facing a double-barreled challenge. In assuming the chairmanship, and thus promptly grasping its accompanying power and prerogatives, he viewed an enlarged landscape. That, in turn, meant diverting his attention away from his mayoral duties, though he continued to function from City Hall.

Leo W. O'Brien (the former O'Connell Congressman, 1952-1966)[3] was dubious that Corning could handle all that he had inherited. "Corning is tough, and he can say 'No,' which is what's required of a leader," O'Brien once said in a private conversation. "But he can't say 'No' the way Dan could. When Corning says 'No,' it rankles.

"Why? Because he comes out of the Fort Orange Club. Without an Irishman as a partner, he couldn't make it and I don't know of an Irishman who could be his partner."

Corning did pick "an Irishman" as a limited partner in 1981. How well that partnership might have functioned over time is problematic because as it took shape Corning was already beginning to fail and the partner had to gear up to become his successor. In the five years following O'Connell's death, however, Corning had flunked O'Brien's test. He'd shown that indeed the whole was too much for him to control—he let his city, his basic responsibility, slide to the brink of disaster. Additionally, he still had a "Polly problem," one which had irritated O'Connell. Dorothea (Polly) Noonan had maintained a decades-long relationship with Corning which at its baffling best was ambiguous. She was invariably described in print as the Mayor's "confidante." And she exercised—and flaunted—a powerful influence within the party's county committee both by virtue of her association with Corning and her control of a significantly large women's club on the fringes of the Organization. She took an instant dislike to Tom Whalen as soon as he emerged as the probable successor to Corning, and for years her enmity was one of the strongest of the negative factors he struggled with in the party.

Promptly in 1977, in an unprecedented primary for the party's nomination for Mayor, Corning's opponent was the county's State Senator, Howard C. Nolan, who argued that "The city desperately needs open, honest, progressive government," an amazing allegation by one Democrat holding elective office, speaking of the long-term administration of another Democrat, in fact the party's star. Similarly, a sharp attack on "the ugly and indecent attitude" of that administration toward "working people," including public employees, was launched by a labor union (Civil Service Employees) in a city where unions had been formed in four major departments of Albany's municipal government only in recent years.

To turn back Nolan, Corning called together a half-dozen men who would help devise and direct his response. One of the select group was Tom Whalen.

But was Whalen on the right side?

Having successfully defeated Carl Touhey and Arnold Proskin, the two strongest Republican vote-getters after Walter Langley had retired undefeated from the Senate, Nolan felt like a world-beater—specifically, one who bore a bitter grudge for slights and slurs. He had defied the Organization in seizing the senatorial nomination in the first place. His challenge to Corning was a credible one, regardless of the elements of high-flying ambition or personal rivalry. His war cry of "open, honest, progressive government" for the city deserved a decent hearing—and the primary's results showed that a solid three-out-of-eight Democrats gave it to him. The implications were broad for not only the city's governance but the county's, and also the party's structure and mode of operation.

Clearly Corning likewise deserved a hearing in this unprecedented contest and, holding almost all the face cards, he obtained a comfortable degree of support—though, with all the organizational advantages and a 36-year record of presumed accomplishment, the support hardly was reassuring.

When "choosing up sides" was taking place that summer, Whalen's choice undoubtedly was influenced by the compliment of having been invited and by the prospect of joining well-regarded associates in counseling the region's No. 1 politician. Basically, however, the choice was a fit with his previous overt political decisions: his "to get along, go along" willingness to perform a committeeman's dreary scut work a decade earlier, and his 1969 judgeship candidacy on the Corning ticket when the party needed a clean new face.

* * *

As a relative outsider allowed to witness life among the Loyalists, Whalen now was admitted to their sanctum along with such proven members as the inevitable Holt-Harris; Ray Kinley, the emissary from State Bank of Albany who could perform many tasks unofficially for his good friend Erastus; Tom Brown, of Whalen's generation, who had shown his abilities as a strategist and campaigner with freewheeling elections to the County Legislature in 1967 and State Assembly in 1970; and Doug Rutnik, the Noonan-in-law lawyer who was deeply involved in Corning's affairs both political and commercial and who, along with Holt-Harris, stood at the top of the list of the Mayor's very closest male associates. Rutnik, on the other hand, maintained close ties with William Powers, a Rensselaer County politician (who later was to become a powerful chairman of the Republican State Committee) and other leading Republicans.

Holding only slight political credentials in his résumé, why was Whalen drafted by the Mayor to advise on a survival struggle? Quite likely, he was proposed by Kinley, who regarded Tom Whalen warmly, having known his father well, and then recommended by Rutnik, who also had cordial contacts and impressions. Both of these Corning advisers were extraordinarily influential at City Hall.

The appeal of having a fresh voice in the councils, one conspicuously lacking a party-line reputation, could have been a plus in Corning's thoughts. And he, assuming correctly that Whalen would not be bringing a hidden agenda to the table, understandably would be attracted by Whalen's range of involvement in the do-good, not-for-profit agencies where his performance commanded attention even from a Mayor. Corning, making some of his courtesy drop-ins at such agencie's annual dinner meetings, had plenty of opportunity to observe young Tom Whalen in charge, earning both familiarity and respect from the top-drawer citizenry attending.

The Mayor's advisory group met every week that summer over breakfast in a private upstairs room at that favorite Corning haunt, the Fort Orange Club. Occasionally during those sessions before the September primary, the newcomer ventured to speak out against the prevailing wisdom on various bits of campaign tactics. In one instance, he bucked the prevailing sentiment and derided as foolhardy the idea of establishing an "enemies list," a sensitive topic those days when the sod was still damp from the unearthing of Richard Nixon's own unholy roster. His argument carried the day, and occasionally he spoke out decisively on other items, too, causing Erastus Corning to sit back and take due note.

The advisers adopted a ho-hum campaign slogan, "Mayor Corning knows how to get things done," and this low-pressure standpattism was sufficient to defeat Nolan, who received nearly 10,000 votes (out of about 25,000 cast) or 38% of the vote.[4]

Nolan's sizable vote reflected a surprising turnaround within the fundamental Organization constituency. His appeal was to the disgruntled, and his strength—contrary to expectations—was in the "machine wards." He had turned into the candidate of minorities and organized labor, including the police union and the unionized Public Works crews. Their agenda, basically "more money," was frightening to the white-collar "country wards" in the western portion of the city. Accordingly, this area became Corning's stronghold, where he was viewed as a guardian of the status quo, the man who would hold the line on costs and taxes. The sharp and totally surprising geographical switch in the anti-Corning vote was a huge change from the lineup four years earlier when the Mayor narrowly escaped defeat by Carl Touhey, a contest whose closeness was attributable to the challenger's strength uptown—but this time, Corning territory.

* * *

In Corning's interview with the *Times Union*[5] before his 1981 reelection, his questioners focused on such timely topics as the forthcoming 1982 tax rate, his budget preparations, his unprecedented tenure in office, his attitude toward his opponent, his expectations for Whalen—and also on a much more timeless topic: his party's network of committeemen.

At the time, the strategically placed members of the county committee had blanketed the city for exactly 60 years. Its effectiveness was demonstrated regularly in the results of every election within the city and virtually every primary too.[6]

"It's a good system," Corning responded, declaring his belief that the committeemen had not lost any of their effectiveness over the years. (They would, in fact, bring in a 72% favorable vote for him three weeks later.)

But the interviewers' question was armed with a jab considerably more pointed. *Are you personally comfortable with the system?* In effect, he was asked to evaluate the extent of, and the appropriateness of, an invasion of privacy by putting the party's committeemen into familiar contact with the daily lives of residents.

And, the questioning implied, could he comprehend that a citizen's awareness of this intimacy might create an atmosphere of fear?

His "Yes and No" answer actually was far from ambiguous. Yes, he was comfortable with the committee system. No, he did not envisage it encouraging apprehension among his constituents. This was a bland denial of a truth inherent in a practice that he had encouraged and promoted, had benefited from personally time after time, and as an intelligent observer and keen analyst, surely recognized as self-evident. His own lieutenant of many years, Dick Conners, was known for a colorful aphorism, calling the committee system "the yeast that makes the party's bread."

One dissident committeeman has described the system as "100% a control mechanism."

"It was their way (the Organization's) of maintaining control—dominance—over the citizen and the city. There was an absolute prohibition on responsible citizen action. You had a question on the water bill? You were to go to your commit-

teeman with it. You went only through him in a chain of command like the Army's—and it was just about as democratic!"[7]

(Yes, this freethinker continued to do the committeeman's assignment. He had a job with the county.)

Whalen, in his turn, affirmed that, as of the period to
which Corning's appraisal was directed, "the ward system was
functional." To the Loyalists, "the party is everything—not the
efficacy of the government," said Whalen. "This was inculcat-
ed as not merely tradition but virtual law. Party and government were so intertwined there remained little difference
between them, or none." As presumed proof, he cited the continued existence, year after year, of the "Welcome, Stranger"
property assessment practices for taxation (and intimidation)
purposes. Newcomers, acquiring a home, promptly found
their committeeman bearing tidings of sharply increased real
estate taxes, which were either payable or destined to be sub-
jected to a graphic demonstration of the Organization's whimsy and powers.

In practice during the decades of the party's control of
the city, the effect was indeed a sticky residue of latent intimidation, though the process could resemble the reverse. One of
those "longtime observers" that a diligent reporter always can
unearth, let fly with this pungent description of Albany
Democratic politics: "A shrewd combination of something *for*
everyone and something *over* everyone." A newcomer to
Albany in years past offers a personal testimony of an instance
which certainly was replicated in tens of thousands of similar
situations over several decades in the middle half of the twentieth century.

When he bought his home in Albany, many years ago,
two committeemen—both were lawyers—dropped by one
evening. They mentioned that it was likely that the assessment
probably would go up inasmuch as this was the custom following such a purchase. There was a grave shaking of heads.
But, they added, the newcomers had no reason for concern
because an objection could be filed by the homeowner. In
fact—and here a folded paper was produced from a jacket

pocket—"We just happen to have the necessary form right here and—if you will just sign—we'll see that it's taken care of." A favor done? In reality, the taxpayer had let himself become another intimidated citizen / voter—one whose citizenship had just been ever-so-slightly compromised. This occurred a few weeks before one of the elections in which Corning was to be reelected, and he recognized what was expected of him.

The roller-coaster policy on real property taxes—raising the tax only to reduce the assessment following a costly appeal—created a deliberate hazard, which was true in spades for business proprietors.

"Each year we had to retain a lawyer to ensure that our real estate taxes were adjusted back to the previous year's level," recalls William Swire, of a family-owned furniture store downtown. "What was true for our business was true for virtually every real estate owner.

"It was one of a number of ways that Albanians were reminded to be constantly aware of the power of the political machine to financially influence their lives. It reminds me of stories of Old World cities that were tightly governed in centuries past by provincial royalty granted absolute control by a distant monarch."[8]

The plain fact and effect of such encounters between Organization and taxpayer was an exercise in demonstrated *power* for power's sake. Just a bit of a threat, cloaked in a favor. "We can do this for you." Or not.

Power!

* * *

The two committeemen of the newcomer's tale assuredly were well above the norm for their assigned responsibilities and duties. They had their parallels—roughly speaking—in each of the 132 districts throughout the city, under a leader for every ward. All were schooled in delivering the Organization message of power. With varying degrees of efficiency or officiousness, they were functionaries all in the Albany County Democratic Committee.

A principal strength in the Organization's controls was cleverly concealed within the seemingly mundane fact that large numbers of the committeemen (and their families) were lodged in the city's payroll. There, they were captives of their basic tools for survival. They were expected—required—to not merely come out and vote for the Organization's candidates but to get out and work for their election. This very special patronage was, in Whalen's word, "big."

Another form of patronage was less formalized but equally effective, and always potentially more remunerative. Service as a committeeman was important for any lawyer who hoped to take part in the spoils spilling over from the courts where O'Connell's judges could employ their discretion. Well-paid refereeships, guardianships, and trusteeships, handed out at those judges' decision, were the coin of reward.

In most cases, personal or professional friendships were a principal element in the awards. Over a period of several years, Whalen's practice was augmented by refereeships (in such matters as foreclosures) distributed in Supreme Court by Pennock. Whalen's expertise in bankruptcy was regularly recognized through trusteeships ordered by the third of the Ryan brothers, Jack, or later by Justin Mahoney. At County Committee headquarters, guardianships were monitored for potential appointments that would be made in Surrogate's Court.

There was no City Committee, for that would violate an O'Connell operating principle, adopted in 1936, toward the end of Edward J. O'Connell's chairmanship, in order to further centralize and focus control over the party's operations and influence within the county's borders. In many of the years of O'Connell control, the city's population and voters outnumbered all those in the rest of the county. An Albany city committee would divide the authoritarian powers attainable through one invincible mechanism, the county committee they operated. Democrats in the towns and smaller cities of the county maintained their own local committees with widely varying results in both organization and effectiveness.[9]

In the city, one of the committee system's main effects was to stultify citizen participation in the kinds of activities—both political and merely civic—that are commonplace in most cities.

The mechanism constituted far more of an enforcement agency than did the Boss tradition itself—even though the Boss authenticated it and was at its top. Albany had, in effect, an intelligence network most graphically personified by the self-serving legend that *"They know how you vote!"* but one also effective on a day-to-day, bread-and-butter basis. Albanians didn't want to be known as being out of line. They didn't know what penalty might follow indications of independent thinking, and they were reluctant to find out. *Power!*

(Is it appropriate here to revive the pungent observation of that oft-quoted British historian, Baron John Acton, as to the absolute corrupting influence of absolute power?)

* * *

Tom Whalen, just turned 30 and newly a partner at Cooper Erving, was earmarked in 1964 by Alderman Abe Dorsman as a good bet to take on a committeeman's chores under his tutelage in the Thirteenth Ward. Shortly, he was recruited to join his fellow attorney on duty in this large area within the heart of an aging residential area of Pine Hills.

Dorsman had been teamed with another lawyer, Jack Rehfuss, as the committeemen. But he was going it alone most of the time since his partner resigned upon becoming a City Court judge. An unusual degree of ferment within the County Committee's ranks currently was stirring enough uncertainty to make it advisable to staff the party's positions as completely and efficiently as possible. A vague aroma of discontent was in the air and primary elections—new to the party, where actual contests were at best a novelty—were being visited like locusts and boils upon the Democrats by young George Harder.

A party stalwart's son who had served in the FBI and emerged as a liberal-leaning lawyer, Harder was brashly—and bravely—compulsive in repeatedly launching kamikaze assaults. He stubbornly concentrated on running against the most entrenched officeholder on the ticket, Frank Cox, a journeyman Assembly member. Loyalists everywhere were alarmed and alerted by the spectre of challenge and competition within the ranks. These primaries did not encompass Whalen's ward, but he possessed the attributes to be useful, particularly since the Whalen family was so well known in the area.

In Pine Hills, the houses—a mix of "modest" and "mansion"—were adorned with some grass and shade, in contrast to the landscape in much of the rest of the city. Even the numerous dwellings that held two families conveyed respectability and a degree of prosperity. Horse-drawn wagons still brought bread and milk right to the front door. Schools were within walking—"home for lunch"—distance and their pupils seemed universally to fit Garrison Keillor's maxim for Lake Woebegon's children: they were all above average. The householders were disproportionately state employees, merchants, or other white-collar (and pink-collar) workers. Nary an O'Connell or a Corning dwelt there, though in pre-war days the most successful of all the O'Connells, Ed, had lived and died in a brick mansion on South Manning Boulevard.

For 30 years, the Whalens had been Pine Hills residents—in a short series of homes that regularly upgraded their comfort and space—ever since Mary ("Pat") and Tom, Jr., had moved from Troy so he could more easily take a Depression job with the state. Young Tommy grew up in three different dwellings in the tight-budgeted 1930s and 1940s, went to both grade and high schools only blocks from home and—after four years' absence in college—studied law on a nearby campus. Upon marrying soon afterward, he and his bride, Denis O'Connor, established their home on South Pine Avenue in the house where Denie had grown up. It was an obscure block, virtually a dead-end, resembling a street out of a Donna Reed movie. Close neighbors, with a certain kind of small-town diversity, included the next-door DeLancey Palmers, the prominent real estate people; on the other side, Rudolph Pauly, a Sterling Winthrop pharmaceutical director; the large and ebullient household of the Victor Obertings; widowed Maude Redmond; Ralph Bloomsburg, the insurance executive on one corner, and Wilbur Crannell, the lumber dealer, whose house at the far end of the quiet block was bought by the Whalens later. And on the opposite corner lived Gilbert Tucker, strong advocate for Henry George's "single tax" theory who as a young man had survived the *Titanic's* sinking.[10]

Like Tom and Denie, his brother and sisters all had settled in the same sprawling middle-class section. The name "Whalen" rang a familiar bell when committeeman Tom carried the party's handbills and brochures to doors up and down Pine Hills' leafy streets. As one of the 132 committeemen and committeewomen charged with tapping the public pulse and spreading the gospel message, he would appear to be a natural.

Just one problem: He hated the role. Knocking on doors with a smile and a handful of leaflets was tolerable, but his earlier experience Election Day poll-watching was a painful bore out in the boondocks in remote precincts of outlying towns, where the youngest lawyers always were consigned. His assignment at a firehouse was far out in Colonie, near the Schenectady County border. And the pre-election briefings where the committee members were jammed into a South Pearl Street barroom were tasteless exhibitions of bossism.

The setting, at the corner of Fourth Avenue, was the site of the old O'Connell saloon, and was known to many of the faithful as "Little City Hall." (At one time, a conductor on a South Pearl Street trolley line regularly called out "City Hall" at his Fourth Avenue stop.) Dan O'Connell himself showed up in his native hearth to welcome the committeemen and the scattering of a few committeewomen in the large back room behind the bar. Then a city judge would call out instructions, ward by ward, for getting out the vote—in clear violation of judicial canons of conduct. Whalen felt remote from the proceedings, as an unattached and uncommitted observer might.

He endured a very few years in committeeman's sheep-like clothing, then was rescued from the role's obligations by becoming a judge. When that term ended, he never went back to the committee, nor was he invited.

* * *

Though the old committee system survived, its inherent power suffered a series of downgradings. In Corning's five years beyond Dan O'Connell's bossy lifetime, some restlessness was inescapable. Because O'Connell had been seen as infallible as the Pope, occasional questions and squabbling erupted which never would have occurred in his time. Dissent from the party line had been unthinkable, and no longer was a differing opinion deserving of excommunication—except in those instances when Erastus Corning's newly won primacy was challenged.

O'Connell continued to hold "the reins pretty tight" in his declining years, according to Holt-Harris, who was on hand. (This view contradicted a fairly general supposition that Corning had asserted himself with increasingly enlarged effect over a period of a half-dozen years.) "Erastus was there (at O'Connell's home) every Monday at noon," his close friend said, "regardless of their other sessions together, to report on what he was doing, to receive updated instructions, and to talk over just about anything such as where to plant a tree pleasing to someone."

On the other hand, Corning was given more or less a free hand on an item that would seem to have major importance—decisions on commercial development within the city. Ironically, the decision-making in this area never really amounted to much. And with additional irony, it was O'Connell-Corning policies, giving the city a certain obnoxious repute, which were discouraging investment, speculation, and opportunity. Albany's economic staple remained the state government, with some supplement from colleges and hospitals. The city, once a transportation and commercial hub, steadily lost ground in these once-essential industries, together with many related enterprises.

Only when Corning became the party's county chairman did the ward leaders go to him. While O'Connell lived and held the chairman's title, the entire Organization looked to him for instruction and permission, for critique and approval, and for their own status on the leash of transient authority.

Following Whalen's election as Common Council president in 1981, baseless speculation intimated that he would for the first time acquire genuine status in the party as well as in government. He'd be installed as first vice-chairman of the county committee.

When given a chance to remark on this theory, Corning observed that he'd been allowed to ascend to that particular office only after his first 30 years as Mayor. (The idlers circulating the gossip got the point.)

NOTES

[1] *The Rascal King: The Life and Times of James Michael Curley.* Addison-Wesley Publishing Company. Copyright 1992 by Jack Beatty.

[2] The explosion of competition extended beyond political preferment. In that same season, an O'Connell grandnephew sued to contest the Boss's will. His suit declared that his granduncle had been mentally incompetent and was improperly influenced by another relative in disposing of his estate, valued at up to $100,000. In a beautiful touch of irony, it was his one-time protégé (later cast out), Judge Lawrence E. Kahn, whose ruling opened up Dan O'Connell's medical records to hostile inspection.

[3] Not to be confused with J. Leo O'Brien, Mayor of Watervliet, who was the County Chairman 1983-1990.

[4] Two minor contests that year produced interesting results.

Nancy Burton, a rebellious outsider, was elected to the Common Council in the Sixth Ward for the first of three terms. (She later was elected and reelected as the city's Comptroller.) In the Eleventh Ward, another outsider, David Sawyer, defeated the party's designee, Gerald D. Jennings. After the primary, "I was in Corning's office one day," Whalen said later, "when Jennings called asking for permission to run as an independent. The Mayor's answer was, 'You can't.' Corning was the Godfather, I think." Sawyer left town soon thereafter and Corning appointed Jennings to fill the vacancy.

5 Until the Spring of 1982, the *Times Union*'s name included a hyphen. The fussiness of its removal rivaled the *New York Times*'s abandonment of a period in its nameplate (formerly, *The New York Times*) as a typographic conceit.

6 In the 1977 primary, a poll by the *Times Union* 10 days before the election showed Nolan with a 19-point lead. Corning's 62% of the primary vote represented a 24-point victory. One interpretation can be argued that the committeemen had done their job!

7 Such an ironclad arrangement seems in conflict with the Corning legend that his door was open to all comers with complaint or query. It raises a question parallel to the one that asks, What were the four gatekeepers doing outside his office door?

8 Speaking of the Whalen years, however, he adds: "Now it was no longer necessary to retain the lawyer to appeal our assessment. Gone were the quid pro quo arrangements that had prevailed for almost every transaction involving the city."

9 When Mayor Whalen tried to encourage formation of a city committee several years after Daniel O'Connell's death, the idea went nowhere—fast. He could find no support for it in the County Committee's membership, reflecting the strong opposition of the county chairman.

10 A colorful recounting was told in the October 1998 newsletter of the Friends of Albany Rural Cemetery (where Gilbert and other Tuckers are buried). Gilbert, third generation in a family that published newspapers for farmers, was 31 years old, unmarried, when returning from a family trip to Europe he met Margaret Hays, a young woman traveling with her Pomeranian and with two other women. He decided that propriety demanded that they— especially Margaret—be properly escorted. Happenstance placed them all in a lifeboat as the Titanic prepared to respond to the iceberg collision. All, including the dog, made it safely to New York

harbor, where they parted. Though lacking the lurid detail of the 1997 movie, the newsletter's article sets the record straight on a number of legends and myths. And it lacked a romantic ending, for Gilbert and Margaret never did get around to marrying one another.

Apres Moi . . .

Four years before Erastus Corning decided on the man to be in place when—and if—he vacated Albany's mayoral office, a *Times Union* editorial offered him a prescription for selecting that person. It happened to fit Tom Whalen very well indeed.

Having reached the startling hypothesis that even though Corning was an indestructible icon his power base showed definite signs of erosion, Donald W. Haskins, the newspaper's editor of the editorial page, also arrived at several related judgments about the city's future beyond the Corning era.

- Because the Republican party was still unable to mount a realistic challenge in the city, the Democrats would retain power indefinitely.
- All indications suggested that it would be Corning who would make the choice of a successor.
- It was important, therefore, that he should not try to foist some nondescript hack on the community when inevitably he had to bow out at last.

With all these assumptions placed before them, the *Times Union*'s editorial board agreed that Haskins would write an editorial incorporating them. His draft was shortly approved and promptly published—on the day of Corning's 1977 reelection. It was probably the first—and for a long time the only—serious comment on an Albany minus Erastus.

The editorial embodied an eerily foresighted quality. It saw far-reaching significance in the Mayor's new term. Corning, it said, had "one more opportunity—perhaps his biggest challenge—still ahead."

"That challenge is to come up with a plausible, acceptable, and successful successor."

Such a successor, the editorial conceded, would have to arise "from the ranks of those whose party he has served so long and faithfully."

Whalen's credentials in his profession, in the community, in his personal life (and, to a lesser degree, in the party) certainly made him a *plausible* nominee for the Common Council's presidency and the prospective successor as Mayor. He could reasonably be assumed to be *acceptable* to the city's voting residents. The chances of pleasing the Organization itself could be less obvious, though he did qualify as an Albany County Democrat. As for being *successful*, there could be no guarantees, but Whalen's experience as a lawyer within the business and financial arenas could suggest an ability to manage a realm that Corning certainly would have acknowledged as Albany's major problem.

Corning's animus toward Albany's newspapers renders it doubtful that the editorial would have promptly put him on the trail of a "plausible and acceptable" person to take over eventually. Nevertheless, some degree of response seems apparent. A few weeks later, after being sworn in for his tenth term on January 1, 1978, he stated publicly that he considered it to be his last. (This, of course, is in conflict with a credible belief that he never really expected to retire—as he did not.)

And ultimately he did push aside the lackluster ward politicians who'd been next to him and did choose a man with the prescribed credentials. Although the name "Erastus Corning" was still on the ballot when the next election came around, it remains noteworthy that Haskins's three judg-

ments for the longer-term future all developed precisely as predicted.

* * *

The dim picture of his own future and the city's after
four decades on the job certainly had to be evident to Corning
as 1978 began. For the first time he'd been forced to turn back
serious opposition in the party. The shock to his system
incurred on the operating table, plus the difficulties he experienced in getting back on his feet, were reminders of approaching old age. Observers remarked that he was noticeably thin-
ner.

Just before his reelection, he had turned 68. His mother, the only member of the Corning family to live beyond, or
even into, their 60s, had recently died. And even though his
way was finally open to ruling as Albany County's undisputed
boss, this had become possible within the past year only
because of another death. Time was at last claiming its toll,
impossible to ignore.

The justification about concern for the outcome of
another term—beyond the issue of succession—is pointed up
by the fact that, of three goals Corning enumerated for the
tenth term, none was achieved or even effectively put into
motion. The 1978-1981 goals were described as: Creating a
new housing program that would supply capital funding for
Albany's poorer residents in the form of city-backed second
mortgages; working with the state to convert Union Station
into a records center; completing two parks in the Pine Bush.
Even assuming full and sincere intent to take on these programs, in the end the will to actually propel them into action
was lacking in the Mayor and his responsible commissioners.

As his ninth term creaked to a dreary close throughout
December, City Hall staffers had needed to bring the ever-lap-
ping tide of official papers to him, first in the hospital and then
out to his rather remote home beyond the city line.

The municipal government could be maintained in reasonably orderly shape through relays of messengers lugging bundles of documents to him. This turned out to be a precedent for a much more complicated relay five years later. When invalided by emphysema and asthma in 1982, Corning was again able, though with diminishing credibility as months passed, to maintain the illusion of actually being in charge of Albany's government.

* * *

"I spend a lot of time reading because I find it rewarding to the spirit," Corning once told Haskins, the editorial writer. Indicative of his range on a daily basis was this incident: One morning, upon reading a good-humored, change-of-pace remark in the editorial column about the city's absence of sparrows, Corning promptly called Haskins. The easily recognizable reason—as he teasingly pointed out—was the disappearance of horses from city streets, while in the countryside the sparrow thrived as ubiquitously as ever.

Haskins understood and appreciated the Mayor's fascination with political power, seeing it comparable to that of other silver-spoon-fed personalities having what he regarded as coarse, Kennedy-like backgrounds. His view of Corning was as the typical flawed aristocrat, in the old sense of the term "a gentleman," even though possessing a darker side. He did admire Corning's breadth of interests, especially his familiarity with art and literature—and even architecture.

His acquaintanceship with the Mayor fostered insights in crafting worthwhile commentary on the Corning administration such as the 1977 editorial on responsibility for identifying a mayoral successor.

"What Would You Think . . . ?"

Dusk was settling in though March was in the process of departing lamb-like; an added hour of daylight wouldn't arrive until the weekend.

Adhering to his long habit of discreetly placing his own personal calls, Erastus Corning dialed an unlisted number, glancing at his watch—it was 4:15—before the response came at the other end of the line, then spoke only a brief sentence: "Why don't you stop on your way up?"

* * *

His visitor shows up within an hour. Almost leisurely but inevitably, they speak first of concern about the tenuous condition of Ronald Reagan following the assassination attempt that day, and then of the coincidence that in the face of such big news Walter Cronkite had just handed over his CBS anchor's chair to Dan Rather, who had been on the scene when John Kennedy was shot. Corning mentions with some resentment the blame he places on Cronkite for "having defeated Carter" in the previous year by his nightly refusal month after month to let the hostages in Iran be forgotten.

The ensuing dialogue proceeds something like this:

"I've really got to do something about Jimmy Giblin—now."[1]

Aware of Corning's concern about the public's impression of Giblin—second-ranking officer of the city—as "just a typical Organization man," the caller replies, "I've thought you might be reaching this point. So what do you have in mind?"

"I do have a solution in mind. I must replace him on the ticket, and make a decision on it right away. . . . *What would you think of Tom Whalen?*"

"Frankly, he hadn't occurred to me. Offhand, though, I can answer this way: The only Mayors of Albany I've ever known were WASPs, all the way back to Hackett, sixty years' worth. What you're suggesting would be quite a departure from the political philosophy that this organization has always known."

The conversation is punctuated by Corning's spells of coughing and the pauses to catch his breath. Finally, "Yes, that's true—but I'm not sure it isn't time for a change. Tell me what you think of Tom."

Still surprised, the visitor does not hesitate.

"He's honest to a fault. His integrity is beyond question. That's the opinion of lawyers and judges. And, I think, many people in the community. I don't have much of a basis for evaluating his judgment. But altogether, I think Tom would be very good indeed for what you need him for."

He adds an aside, not wholly irrelevantly. "You know of my own experience with Dan, when he was looking me over as someone he could put forward to do certain things the right way. He asked me about my religion, and when I said, 'Anglo-Catholic' he just asked, 'Is that the same as Erastus?' I told him 'Yes,' and that was all he needed to hear."

* * *

Corning's visitor that penultimate day of March 1981, John E. Holt-Harris, left City Hall with some mixed and unspoken thoughts stirring in his lawyerly mind. He was convinced Erastus Corning knew he was quite ill and even had been unsure in past months about whether he even wanted to run for reelection once more. And Holt-Harris wondered if he had been right to neglect enlarging on more of his personal impres-

sions of a man whom he thought of as a complex yet straightforward character. He put aside the question as irrelevant in
the circumstances, but he did not forget it.

In any event, he strongly believed, that evening, his
friend Erastus was without doubt in the process of picking his
successor as Albany's Mayor. "A political decision," he told
himself, "but at least he's going about it in the right way, looking for the very qualities he should be!"

* * *

Holt-Harris's relating of this encounter is an anecdote
sufficiently disarming that we can easily miss the deep meaning buried within it.

Corning's question, "What would you think of Tom
Whalen?" was in the context of a suitable replacement for his
Common Council president. Implicit within it, of course, was
the unspoken recognition—an awareness by both men—that
charter and precedent established the holder of that relatively
insignificant office as the lawful successor to any Mayor who
vacated his position during an elected term.

The question was wholly innocent on its face. But Holt-
Harris's response, and then Corning's, immediately moved on
to another realm. Their conversation embodied a virtual
code—perhaps like Bill Bradley's and Jerry Lucas's private
communication on the court during New York Knicks games.
Neither needed to acknowledge their true concern there in the
gloaming around the Mayor's desk. They were not speaking
merely of a man who could somehow upgrade the traditional
duties of presiding over the legislative body and representing
the city at minor functions.

Without having specifically acknowledged as much,
their references were to Whalen as a potential Mayor of
Albany, the successor to Corning himself. This is why unspoken words send the signal:

The signed-and-sealed giveaway was Holt-Harris's
quick mention of religious affiliation as an element in the selec-

tion. Jimmy Giblin, Dick (Red) Haggerty, and Dick Conners were far from his mind when he spoke of Whalen, a Roman Catholic, as breaking a precedent. Those predecessors in the Council's presidency also were Roman Catholics. Holt-Harris was envisioning Whalen as Mayor, not in a lesser office—and Corning accepted his interpretation exactly that way.

Without question, then, that early spring evening, Corning was choosing Albany's next Mayor. His eyes were open, unblinking at reality. Intentionally and purposefully, he was placing Tom Whalen in line to follow him—able to take over if necessary; otherwise, in a position to lay claim to consideration eventually. The dangling issue—a good conversational gambit in Albany for years—as to whether Corning had known what he was doing, was truly a non-issue.

Assuredly, he had to be gratified to hear Holt-Harris's words of commendation. He was already close to making his choice. Those words were positive, reassuring, appropriate to Whalen's acceptance by the public (perhaps even by the party) and also promising for his performance in public office. The favorable opinion from his closest friend was warmly welcomed.

And he had another respected endorsement as well, this one from Polly Noonan's son-in-law, Doug Rutnik, with whom he had shared so many confidences. In the same decisive season, Doug—when queried—had responded tersely, "Tom is the man."

But at this point in his life—71 years along, ailing and hurting on more days than he liked to admit, his town's most eminent and honored figure, without serious challenge in this election year, never having wanted for any material thing his whole life long—his small and symbolic one-man search committee—himself—was hardly looking for character references. He certainly didn't want a bright young comer, a yes-man on his way up. He needed and wanted an experienced, savvy person capable of standing his ground when the going got rough, as might be anticipated when the age of Albany bossism finally came to a close.

In Whalen, he had found a solid citizen (one such as Whalen himself would seek fruitlessly a dozen years later), ready to accept political life—in addition to being acceptable. This citizen had a bit of experience within the party, had run successfully once for office, was familiar with Albany's limits and her limited expectations. He had demonstrated acute loyalty to Corning by choosing to support him instead of one of his own contemporaries (Nolan) or the old Whalen family friend (Ryan) when they contested his office and power.[2] That counted, too. He had invested time and energies in doing good things in recognizable civic endeavors while doing well in his profession. That he actually had a profession was novel in itself, for the men who had preceded him in the Council's presidency—and even Corning himself—lacked this particular distinction; they were all salesmen of one kind or another.

And Corning could thankfully check off a highly important aspect of that professional experience: Whalen had combined the practice of law with unusual familiarity in fiscal practices and mastery of their mysteries. Banks and their exotica were prominent in his background. He'd been a protégé within more than one generation of Albany's men who moved money around.

* * *

So how was it that Tom Whalen's name, like Abou Ben Adhem's, finally came to lead all the rest for Erastus Corning? Halfway through Corning's five-year solo flight as Albany's Boss, a *Times Union* reporter preparing a speculative article on Albany's politics apparently had been able to find only one Democrat willing and ready to be publicly quoted with comment connecting the Mayor to his governing style.

"Corning is someone," Whalen said in a moderately outspoken analysis, "who doesn't particularly like to delegate functions. He likes to do things himself"—a masterpiece of understatement. Far from bold on the face of it, it was the only direct quote the reporter could wean from all the old city's sea of politicians, large and small.

So there it hung, fearless black ink on credulous white newsprint for the scrutiny of the morning's readers and for the everlasting record. No one else in cautious Albany was prepared to venture as much.

"No place else," Whalen added with a bit of further brashness, "will you find a place as dominated as Albany is by the Mayor." And in the closing months of the 1970s, his was a thoroughly sane judgment.[3]

And so it followed, "There isn't much of any significance the Mayor isn't involved in," a beautifully provable daily truth about decision-making in Albany. In other words, Corning's thumb was in every pie.

In the repressed atmosphere of those days, these were boldly expressed comments from within the party fold—and Tom Whalen, as of that time, had done little to impressively distinguish himself from the sheep. As with Bill Clinton two decades later, incidentally, the critical verb he employed—"is"—tended to define what was diplomatic to say about Corning, who was very much among the quick.

What did Corning think of such outspokenness?

"I never got any comment on it from him, then or later," Whalen told associates. "If he actually read it, he could have taken it as a compliment, perhaps. He liked to be the powerful man I said he was."

* * *

Such an artless display of a secure sense of self or, perhaps, of a rare candor and courage almost surely shaped into a factor stored away in Corning's intricate calculations. An omnivorous reader and a newspaper scanner, he was ever vigilant to find in any sparrow's fall its subtle significance for himself. Certainly he had "actually read" the well-displayed article. It held the making of an eye-opener ("Well, there's a fellow who's not afraid, even, of me!"). But, with much greater prob-

ability, Whalen's keenly bald observations merely wedged
another small brick of credibility into a solid structure erected
at length within Corning's mind. It had been building for a
dozen years or longer, at least since they first ran on the same
ticket in an unusually sensitive year.

Only some 15 months later, he was ready to finger this
brash younger man for the city's No. 2 hierarchical position
and to smash whole shelves of sacred vessels in doing so. Like
the cunning fox that he was, he quickly jumped over decades
of lazy-dog assumptions (and the japanned layers of ancient
expectation) to endow this outspoken man with a few of his
own singular powers.

After years of reflection, Whalen himself offered a partial answer—only a teasing fragment—to this question that has
bugged many Albanians. The riddle is worth scrutinizing
because "Why him?" was an integral part of the hostility that
was felt and expressed by so many in his own party, whence
his help should have come. The probably true reason amply
justifies Corning's selection.

"My name was recommended to him, though I really
don't know by whom,"[4] Whalen said. But unconsciously he
was blocking, in a not very imaginative way, a realistic view of
the possibilities. The list had to be very short if, in fact,
Corning had opened up for suggestions. Reasonable doubt
can exist as to whether he required a search committee's help
in identifying a suitable candidate. For numerous reasons—
ranging from the Whalen and O'Connor families' long-standing friendly view of Albany Democrats, and Tom's one successful election campaign on the Corning ticket, to his helping
hand in the Mayor's most recent reelection and his solid reputation in a profession that solidly combined law and finance—
Corning was amply armed to be his own recruiter. For all his
legendary open door to all mendicants, he kept his own counsel. He was at the very top; no other officeholder or elder
statesman merited his consultation. His party position was
that of a Caesar crowned by the same tradition which had
descended to him. He was not the first among equals; in
Albany he was first indeed.

As for others of decent rank, he had either made them, had defeated them, or perhaps deigned to tolerate them: He scorned a seeming counterpart, the County Executive; he had crushed his State Senator who had once stood up to him; and the Representative in Congress he had lured into the Albany district was by now a disappointed and remote figure living in Maryland virtually free of local care.

Additionally, Corning's governing style mandated that very, very few individuals even had the status to be close enough to Corning to have an inkling of his desire to replace Giblin.[5] Few indeed would have had the temerity to volunteer a suggestion much less offer a "recommendation" (to employ Whalen's term). And the number who would creatively brush aside the obvious, routine Organization choices and understand Corning's situation clearly enough to see the possibilities in Whalen—well, put them all together and they spell out a couple of names, perhaps a threesome, no more: Ray Kinley (the elder) and Doug Rutnik. Jack Holt-Harris would have been an immediate suspect, but he testified that it was Corning who brought Whalen's name forward only after the Mayor's own consideration of it was well advanced.

The most likely scenario appears to be that Corning, extremely knowledgeable about virtually everything in his city, sifted out the chaff and came up with Whalen's name. And then understandably wanted to check out his impressions with those two or three trusted intimates. Among these, Holt-Harris—the best witness we've had—may have offered a definitive affirmation of Corning's instinct.

* * *

With a high degree of coincidence, Whalen—after several years of avoiding opportunities to seek other public positions—had primed himself that same winter to actively consider a candidacy.

"By instinct, I had always dismissed out-of-hand the idea of the Council presidency. But for some reason"—he was unsure of the cause of his reassessment—"I began to think, 'This is the time for me to do it.'"

It seems improbable that he would have considered seeking an obscure office that had been a dead end for others without having realistically recognized that its holder might eventually gain a clearer shot at the Mayor's chair. Such a calculation by no means need involve a macabre assumption as to Corning's longevity—but the man was, after all, in his seventies.

Whalen did not explicitly confirm such speculation, but in another context he volunteered that he arrived at the Council presidency with a head brimming with ideas for measures that could make the city more livable—and governable.

Because the habitual practice in Albany politics was to ask permission ("Yes, Jimmy, you may be excused," but substitute "run" for "be excused" in this instance), Whalen obtained an appointment with Corning and confessed his ambition. Corning "as always was non-committal."[6] The Mayor's supplicant guessed that he would then have "spoken with Doug Rutnik and Holt-Harris, looking for feedback." And we know about that: The remaining question is the sequence of these few critical conversations.

Was Whalen's timing (he couldn't place the date of his meeting with Corning) so unpredictably but happily precise that his appearance in Corning's doorway provided a quick answer to the Mayor's screening and recruiting? In the absence of contrary evidence, it appears possible that Whalen himself acted as the catalyst, the impetus for the question, *"What would you think of Tom Whalen?"*

Earlier, Whalen had ventured onto a confidential limb with one of his closest friends and confidants, Lew Swyer. He also talked with an equally close and respected ally, Jim Drislane who, though always a ready promoter of Whalen's fortunes, was less than enthusiastic this time. Finally, persuaded on timing and feasibility, the sagacious Drislane counseled, "Go for it!" and advised the visit to Corning as the most practical first step. From that hour, Whalen was—in his own retrospective view—"aggressively seeking" the Council presidency.

With his eyes open, assuredly, Whalen had voluntarily stepped to the very edge of this swamp, expecting that he figuratively could walk across its surface. But Pipsisewah-like, a potential trap awaited, just as a potential price was to be paid by anyone who dallied too long and too heartily. The Council's former president, Richard J. Conners, widely and warmly respected as a circumspect individual, nonetheless paid the price when he sought election as Representative in Congress. He had been associated with the Council as a member and its president for 25 years. His opponent wrote in some campaign broadsides that in this quarter-century the Council had always voted unanimously for whatever they were instructed to do. "Don't send LBJ another yes man," the pamphlets urged.[7]

* * *

Erastus Corning never did anything accidentally. So testified Rutnik, the attorney who knew Corning so well.[8] "Corning very rarely made a decision he had not carefully thought through. He did not act intuitively or merely on the basis of loyalty."

Corning would not have given the Mayor's job to someone he really liked, a friend. He needed someone who would be a lightning rod, able to absorb the intense dislike that would be created by the policies that he'd need to put in place.

The successor couldn't be a "nice guy." Corning knew that the city would need a Mayor who could avoid the difficulties loyalty would mean as he tried to get rid of people who should be retired, for example. Replacing people with computers, perhaps.

For the job that had to be done, Whalen was the best choice, for both positive and negative reasons. His Irish roots were a big plus in providing a warm bath of sympathy from a major portion of Albany's populace. So was his status and reputation as a devoted family man. And he had good advisors—not only in Swyer and Drislane, but also notably in Steve Fischer, Bill Hennessy, Carl Touhey, and Alan Iselin.

In short, Corning really knew what had to be done to fix the city he'd led down a very long garden path—but, as Rutnik implied, "he didn't have the stomach for it"—actually swallowing the remedy. "Tom did the job Erastus set him up to do. And he paid a price, as Erastus anticipated. Corning expected to die with his boots on—never giving up his office as long as he lived. So choosing the individual who lawfully would be entitled to the office meant that this individual would in fact be his successor as Mayor. This was implicit." Without regard for just when, Corning really *was* selecting Albany's next Mayor.

In effect, Corning himself gave life to this proposition. Commenting late in his final campaign on the party's "Team for the Future" advertising, he admitted that it seemed to lend credence to speculation about his successor having been subtly identified. And lending strength to this vagueness about Whalen and the mayoralty, he flatly denied a parallel prospect in his political office, the party's county chairmanship. "I've never looked at him (Whalen) as a political successor," Corning was quoted publicly, which very reasonably can be interpreted as tacitly letting it be known that indeed Whalen had been "looked at" as a mayoral successor.

In an early meeting between just the two of them as they reached an understanding on Whalen's joining "the team," Corning went far toward acknowledging he might not last for four years because of either his own death or a decision to resign, presumably rather late in the term, thus giving Whalen an opportunity to run in 1985 as an incumbent Mayor. But he also tantalizingly dangled the possibility that, after all, he might choose to run once more that year. Little wonder, then, that Whalen later saw fit to observe, in a more general context, "I never knew what he was thinking. He was an enigma to me. He would say one thing but then do something quite different."

The whole matter of Corning's level of expectation is significant because of the leverage his firm choice of Whalen as the next Mayor—had it been widely known and accepted at the time—could have exercised on the dissidents who later refused to be persuaded of the legitimacy of Whalen, the outsider. For a few quite understandable reasons in 1981, Corning never was really forthcoming. But he thus weakened Whalen's governing and political positions immeasurably. And in the months of his decline in 1982-1983, Corning still withheld a public endorsement of the man who was in the very act of taking over his job. Again, the reasons were his own, but this time they were much less plausible, certainly at the expense of both the successor and the city.

The fact that Whalen, Corning's ultimate choice and ultimate successor, did prove to possess the insights, the tools, and the courage to remedy the fiscal ills Corning was bequeathing is strong testimony that he was selected for exactly that promise. Who else could have tackled the dire problems as he did—and triumphed? Score one for Erastus Corning's broad comprehension of what his city would require in the deluge. Whether Corning was capable of envisioning the successor's undoing of two long generations of ingrained beliefs and behavior—that's quite another matter.

An astute observer very much but very discreetly on the scene, Bill Keefe, the Mayor's executive assistant, had viewed Whalen as a Corning protégé because he'd "more than once" visited the Mayor in his office. En route, he came under Keefe's cordial but measuring gaze—even though he wasn't (in Keefe's opinion) the only candidate for the Council presidency. "Several oars were in the water." Before long, however, Keefe decided, "No question—Whalen is the guy. The question is really, how and when he got there." He considered him "a good choice—a bright young guy," but was convinced Corning hadn't regarded his selection as "the automatic successor."

* * *

Such words of reassurance—"honest," "integrity," "very good for you" as he heard from Holt-Harris—obviously were among those Corning wanted. Within days he had made another of his terse calls and Tom Whalen again materialized in the Mayor's office. Their conversation further satisfied Corning that he'd hit on just the man to add confidence among the uptown voters when the Democratic ticket went on the ballot that fall.

But, unquestionably, public confidence was far from the sole reason for his need to dump Giblin. And, then, to choose a more suitable replacement—one from within the party, surely, but with professional repute and community involvement, a good name.

With further advantage, Whalen shared a common heritage with a larger part of his constituency than had been true of any of the city's Mayor's for a full century.

Slightly more than one out of every four Albany residents in the 1980s (26%) were descendants of immigrants from Ireland.[9] While that figure may not appear overwhelming, its significance is pointed up by the fact that only Boston's fabled Irish population was relatively more numerous (26.8%) than Albany's among all the cities having ancient and traditional Irish immigrant populations. (By the 1990 census—according to a readout that Whalen obtained and pondered—Irish stock in Albany stood at 23% of the population.)

Another populous group of "first-wave immigrants," also descended from mid-nineteenth century arrivals, were Albany's Germans. By 1980, nearly one-sixth of the city's residents (15.7%) were of Germanic stock. Their influence had diminished, however, as a result of their former land's role in two world wars. The second wave of European immigration had given Albany a substantial proportion (14.8%) of descendants of Italian lineage. Over a period of many years, rivalries and jealousies associated with Irish dominance developed. Ultimately, that dominance was lessened, especially after Daniel O'Connell's death. Descendants of immigrants from Poland, also in the second wave, accounted for a relatively slight 7%. A third wave reached Albany from other American cities and states and from elsewhere in the Western Hemisphere. African-Americans, who had been counted at 4% as late as 1950, now accounted for almost exactly one-sixth of the city's residents (16.1%). Persons of Hispanic heritage represented only 2%. In 1990, the African-American portion of the citizenry, according to Whalen's figures, had increased to 20% and the Italian population had reached 17%. In these demographic shifts, one larger statistic stood out prominently: Albany's overall population decline over the two previous decades had been halted and stabilized in the Whalen years. The reversal of a widespread cynicism about the quality of life in Albany, and the gradual osmotic effect of optimism, confidence, and pride may need to be credited with a genuine physical result.[10]

Altogether, these six ethnic groups made up nearly five-sixths (81.7%) of the Albany population at the opening of the 1980s. The city's long tradition of WASPish Mayors had been sorely out of kilter with the backgrounds of the people who elected them so regularly. Those Mayors' lineage descended from the United Kingdom, and their Baptist, Presbyterian, and Episcopalian faiths were hardly representative of the national traditions or religious tenets of a great majority of the citizenry.

In a considerable sense, they governed by sufferance, through a rather condescending policy in which the Majority granted these privileged opportunities as a matter of cynical political expediency.

Corning's selection of Whalen, who entered City Hall at a time when he was scheduled to shortly become president of the Friendly Sons of St. Patrick, went far to put an end to this ethnic oddity.

Corning's somewhat faltering double negative, "I'm not sure it isn't time for a change," suggesting an underlying vein of righting ancient error, had become committed policy, a vital element of all that followed.

* * *

Ten weeks after giving Corning his reaction to a Whalen candidacy, Holt-Harris stood off to the side and heard the Mayor announce his addition to the ticket, finding a variety of ways to explain his choice without really clarifying anything at all. Whalen, he said, stood out as "the most experienced in public life and community affairs" among those he might have considered designating as the running mate. When asked his thoughts as to the new candidate's potential as a future Mayor, he conceded that this "did occur" to him in the winnowing process.

Whalen himself stood in the fourth row on City Hall's steps, next to Bill Keefe, and also offered nothing significant to affirm or deny reporters' probing assumptions that he'd become heir apparent.

Later, he complained within Corning's earshot of the newspapers' careless spelling of his name as "Whelan."

"No reason to be concerned," Corning replied. "I still get introduced as Mayor Thacher." (His predecessor had left office 41 years earlier.)[11]

NOTES

[1] Giblin, then 66 years old, was a prototypical product of Albany's political system, where he had not so much worked his way up as he had remained in place—the Fourth Ward—and let all else descend around him. As a salesman for the drug firm McKesson & Robbins, he "got around," which fitted ideally with his efforts as a committeeman in North Albany for the better part of a half-century. This duty earned him important status as the ward's leader for the party as well as Commissioner of Jurors for the coun-

ty. And when Alderman Dick Conners advanced to the Council's presidency Giblin took over his seat for the next 17 years. After Conners left in 1976, Jimmy Giblin was second in line to succeed him. Only a brief hiatus intervened before he moved up again in the tight hierarchical pattern. But he'd been Council president less than three years when he received Corning's coup de grace. Giblin, a modest man who sometimes had seemed appalled by the implications of his high position, accepted the verdict without question, much less anger. He stayed on as ward leader for several years, and so became an important figure for Mayor Whalen. Whalen spoke of Jimmy Giblin fondly, especially remembering one of his homely declarations: "Everyone knows where I stand! I didn't say 'yes' and I didn't say 'no'!"

[2] He had at least one strike against him—a well-aged but not-insignificant instance of deviation from the party line. During the 1971 public outcry calling for the creation of an elected school board with fiscal independence, Whalen signed a petition supporting that cause. Not much time passed before Corning was made aware of this apostasy and almost as quickly made sure that his annoyance became well known among the Loyalists. Eventually, word of the Mayor's displeasure seeped back to Whalen, which would have been just one of Corning's objectives. Not only did Whalen still remember the incident three decades later, but the Tories were reminded of how sweeping could be the Organization's survey of their behavior. (As Mayor, Whalen had second thoughts about his earlier position, as budgets and taxes escalated under the board's policies. Though separate from his budgets and the City of Albany's record-low tax increases, he believed that the money being demanded for schools unnecessarily imposed a burden on residents and diminished the pluses of his administration's prudence.)

[3] Richard J. Daley of Chicago had preceded Dan O'Connell to the grave by two months, and mayors such as Frank Hague of Jersey City, James M. Curley of Boston, and Thomas J. Pendergast of Kansas City were long gone. Even latter-day boss-mayors like Frank Rizzo in Philadelphia and David L. Lawrence of Pittsburgh were passé. Moderates with social consciences and reform programs were Lee in New Haven, Hartsfield in Atlanta, Shaefer in Baltimore—governing through broad coalition rather than narrow factionalism, by consent rather than dicta despite strong opinions, progressive ideas, and vigorous, decisive leadership. Joseph S.

Clark's reform record as Philadelphia's Mayor (1952-1956) helped to win him two terms in the United States Senate thereafter. (Author's note: I owe a personal debt to Democratic Mayor/Senator Clark, who was an important mentor for me in Washington.)

4 Author's Note: This view, related to me in an interview, was first published in Capital Region magazine, May 1987.

5 Among the wildly conflicting theories as to why Corning replaced Giblin with Whalen in 1981, one insists his purpose was simply to make sure Charles Touhey wouldn't be elected Common Council president. Carl Touhey's son had made a decent showing in losing to Giblin in the first spirited contest for the office in three-quarters of a century. Corning, according to this theory, expected that Charles Touhey would try again and, having learned a lot as a candidate, would make a more effective fight of it—and be ready to commit a great deal of money. The Democrats would need to counter him with a first-rate candidate.

Accordingly, Giblin would have to be moved aside and an able, more reputable Democrat recruited with the sole goal of defeating Touhey and securing the party's hold on a psychologically important though second-level office. Whalen, having performed a somewhat similar task for the party a dozen years earlier, was seen as an electable campaigner. (Coincidentally, he was by now actually interested in the comparatively obscure office.)

But the scenario went haywire. Touhey did indeed run and did spend quite freely with his own funds—nearly $50,000—but against Corning. Candidate Whalen was home free.

6 The first obvious outcome was an unexpected invitation— one of those unrefusable offers—to be the toastmaster at the forthcoming annual Aldermanic dinner where every Democratic politician, publican, and penitent was a must-show. The invitation, of course, was Corning's to dictate. Whalen had been a regular attendee for several years, though as the affairs grew in size and more beery than intimate or companionable he found them less enjoyable. (As Mayor, he came to dread his enforced presence there.)

7 Author's Note: I was the opponent. The year was 1966. I considered the comment appropriate and effective.

8 Rutnik was "a supporter of yours for a long time," Kinley mentioned to Whalen after he took office, adding the suggestion that the Mayor "use Doug for some things that he can be helpful

on—without his mother-in-law." (Kinley, one of Polly Noonan's allies, was tacitly conceding that Whalen had a problem with her displeasure.) "A lot of job-holders received their jobs because of Doug's help," Kinley noted, apparently hinting that this activity could be one avenue of Rutnik's potential for help to Whalen. Rutnik's close ties to Corning undoubtedly had been helpful indeed in placing job applicants. Kinley's proposal could be construed as implying that those grateful job-holders' view of Whalen might be improved by a word or two from their benefactor. Whatever influence he had at the time with Mrs. Noonan certainly never worked to Whalen's benefit.

[9] The data on this page are extracted from tables in Steven P. Erie's book, *Rainbow's End: Irish-Americans and the Dilemmas of Urban Machine Politics*, University of California Press, 1988. In one passage the book broadly implies that in post-Corning Albany some Democrats were lying in wait for a Loyalist to rescue City Hall. Professor Erie had visited Albany, one of eight heavily Irish-American cities he studied. His interviewees seem to have suggested that the Whalen administration was only an inconsequential stopgap. "The Albany machine," he wrote, "entered an interregnum phase" upon Corning's death. ("Interregnum" applies to a non-functioning government or a vacant throne; it is not truly applicable to a "machine.") Though his emphasis was on "the machine," Albany's history, which so closely entwines party and office, renders obscure a proposed division between government and political machinery. No direct reference is made to Mayor Whalen or to developments in the early years of his administration.

[10] Another cause could have been the improved caliber of the police force. For years, its questionable reputation had included widespread notoriety for disregard of civil liberties. Now that callousness and brutality were no longer accepted as normal, the city could be not only more agreeable for settled residents but more attractive for newcomers.

[11] Corning might not have been so glib if he had lived to read a *New York Times* writer's careless reference to him as "Augustus Corning" several years later. (Coincidentally, Corning had once likened himself to Augustus Caesar, presumably because of the long reign of each of them. He refrained from comparing his tenure to that of King Solomon, who likewise served four decades.)

Double H:
An Advisor's Brand

Having served Corning faithfully for 30 years as Harry Hopkins did for FDR, his hero/chieftain, Jack Holt-Harris hardly could expect an exact association to evolve with Whalen. Nor did he achieve it, even though their own relationship was distinctive and as inescapable as his hyphen. It extended for a further decade his unique capacity as a mayoral intimate.

Corning, who more than once had sought both men's special counsel in critical days, all but assured their future ties. Most recently, both had served in his informal six-man liaison team that lent some plausibility to his fading grasp on his office and to Albany's petri-dish culture in which it thrived.

As a result Holt-Harris melded from Corning confidant and nuncio—a receptive though balanced sounding board and a friendly though objective counselor—to become a special advisor to Whalen, one of broadly excellent repute, superb connections (including his respected relationships within the Organization), and keen political savvy. He could draw on extended experience with the fallen lions—O'Connell as well as Corning, although those friendships inevitably were very different—for an independent critical judgment to which both Mayors hearkened. Seven years younger than Corning, 17 years older than Whalen, he varied his place at the table accordingly. Three decades of placid involvement in the O'Connell style of politicking, campaigning, and governing had endowed him with insights and an even deeper perception of the Corning psyche.

His secure perch in the upper echelon of civic and social life supported his confounding credibility that washed away virtually all compromising stains of knuckling to the Boss, to whom he (of Welsh descent) was "The Dutchman." He was, after all, a man whose prominence largely was based on doing O'Connell favors and doing O'Connell's bidding. But he escaped, somehow, even the cynical taint with which the idolized Corning had to live.

And in a city fraught with legal talent, Holt-Harris was a heavyweight.[1] His very successful practice attracted a ranking clientele. As a name partner in one of Albany's most influential and sizable old firms, he ranked as a powerhouse above most competition. He commanded a reservoir of respect among the profession and when he came to court he could sense—as did others—the high and perhaps indulgent regard of the judges with whom he had mingled so jovially in first-name informality.

In City Hall's corridors as well as in its chambers, his passage glistened with smiling banter. His unfailing cordiality bespoke a surety of place, a confidence fitting to his acceptance in an elder statesman's role while still in his early forties. Where power resided, whether in courthouse or clubhouse, conference room or drawing room, "Jack" was very visible.

* * *

Holt-Harris had met Corning while in his early 20s, shortly before World War II. He brought to their early acquaintanceship and later comradeship a background that was by no means comparable. He was a Cornell law student when they met, still looking toward a career. But Corning, with two children already and five years' experience in the Legislature, was well launched in political life under Grade A auspices and almost ready to become Mayor for life. Holt-Harris had only just selected a profession; Corning's inherited family business/political connections would continue to prove to be credentials enough forever.

Both were Ivy League products, but as the only child of a nurse and an old-style physician who made house calls from his office in the family's series of row-houses downtown, Holt-Harris was schooled at Albany High and had reached Cornell's undergraduate arts college by winning a scholarship in a city-wide competition.

Holt-Harris's serious studies in courses such as Logic and other academic heavy lifting, contrasted with Corning's arty dilettantism as a prep-school and Yale student. Well over a half-century later, he spoke with enthusiastic recollection of probing, intellectual exchanges in the lecture hall with some of his professors.

Fifteen years after their first encounter, the contact with Corning resumed and began to mellow into very close and enduring friendship. Soon after he became a Traffic Court judge—a personal O'Connell selection from among numerous ambitious young lawyers—he began receiving invitations to stop by the Mayor's office after his court sessions. From that stage, the *ad hoc* conversations became daily occasions.

He grew to envy Corning's breadth, his "catholicity of interests." Corning's extensive reading helped make him a rewarding conversationalist.[2] And, almost equally, Holt-Harris admired the light touches of humor which matched his own inclination to quip and jest. For a quarter-century and more, in the younger man's awed opinion, he was treated to "a remarkable relationship" with a most unusual politician.

For his own part, he relished lounging back to tell stories (including his own involvement in one significant occurrence after another, as a restive Whalen often noted). This habit had been a relaxed and popular corner of his friendship with Corning, much less so with the more goal-focused successor. What a fly-on-the-wall best-seller he could have narrated!

With his court appointment, Holt-Harris's real political career had begun. His courtroom was filled with everyday

Albanians, mostly those guilty of one traffic infraction or another but hopeful of a merciful justice. The opportunity for little favors was immense. Otherwise, the court was a speck on the judicial system overall, beneath the note of chief justices and professors of jurisprudence.

But Traffic Court did force him into close touch with reality, on a par with an Organization credo: Do unto others what they will remember in November. This meant awareness of the little guy's eternal problems, fiscal pinch, hopeless dreams, or hapless dejection. Holt-Harris, who'd grown up on his penitents' same brick streets and had shared their spelling books, thus made a significant contribution in the O'Connell-Corning perpetual strategy of reminding Albany's citizenry that the Organization really was on their side.

That he was capable of an analytic comprehension of exactly what was afoot on the grand stage even while acting out his own obliging role—and then delivering that knowledge to aid Whalen's counterforce—testifies to a brilliantly adaptable character. The continuity of his sage counsel was an invaluable commodity Whalen respected and heard responsively. Holt-Harris's security enabled him to say "No" or "I wouldn't do that," or to demand "Why?" This quality was as prominent in his relations with Whalen as apparently it had flourished with Corning. His accepted status as a bona fide insider was exceedingly useful in gaining credibility within the Organization. Intent on trying to "hold things together" in the party and to assure that it could "maintain its significance" throughout the county after Corning's death, he volunteered an active role in peace-making among the factions, offering mediation or arbitration as the occasion might arise.

"His advice always was sound," in Whalen's view. "He was ready to criticize me—to my face, of course—if he thought I was off base on anything. He'd tell me what I'd done wrong when I led with my chin.

"But he was my defender within the party—thoroughly supportive. He intended to be helpful, and he was."

Very much aware of the respect approaching awe won

by his long years with the party's chieftains, Holt-Harris retained a strong sense of primacy well after their departure. It was he who had the words to convey title: "Now you are your own man." And he fully recognized his own value to Whalen, remarking that he "kind of adopted my presence," and seeing "prestige purposes" as a reason for Albany's new Mayor to seek him out. He made himself accessible for either private counsel or to chair the most significant of all the volunteer groups Whalen gathered within the mayoral fold (or even to run an errand, when the purpose was to smooth a Corning connection).

"Many things were militating against our establishing the association we had," Holt-Harris believed, citing particularly the considerable difference in their ages (he was ready to enter Cornell when Whalen was an infant). But, he would add, "I admired him, everything he did. I was anxious for him to succeed." And Whalen invariably was unstinting in his appreciation of the older man's ready guidance. As a counselor, however, he ranked him a notch below Swyer and Drislane, at least because of their long history as his mentors.

* * *

Commissioned by Corning in the early summer of 1982 to create and lead a multi-faceted group in the months of his disability, Holt-Harris's executed the burdensome duty with distinction. In chairing the small, unofficial gatherings of Corning allies—"the Regency"—for almost a full year, he carried the Mayor's wishes to his colleagues there, but also interpreted the state of the city to its absent chief—with wide discretion in each respect.

He was available to Whalen and McArdle as they struggled with day-to-day issues in this interim period, but was scrupulous about never intruding in the city government's workings.[3] And without office in the party—though with superior stature in the eyes of the members—he exercised a principal influence in calming the potential turmoil, including the implicit charter to tame some of those with free-lancing instincts.

Far more than any other advisor of Corning's, he maintained personal contact with him and watched his friend diminish from a physical state that Holt-Harris already recognized as hopeless. Throughout the trying private experience, he maintained a public stance directly focused on Albany's prospects for emerging from its extended travail as a viable entity.

And when the city once again had a full-time, functioning chief executive, he stood back, encouraging the man who was taking on the mantle of full responsibility. Corning's trusted friend had come through the classic emergency in a style that few could have matched. Granted a unique opportunity, he rose to the occasion with extraordinary skills and impersonal outlook as well as dedication.

NOTES

[1] Clubbily, Albany's own law school (under a university umbrella based at Union College) each spring produces a fresh supply of about 200 new attorneys, many of whom traditionally remain in the immediate area. When Holt-Harris took his law boards after Cornell about 400 lawyers were clumped around State Street's hill. By the time he ceased active lawyering, Albany had some 1,200. (Whalen was only the second Albany Law graduate to serve as the city's chief executive.)

[2] But to spread this talent he lacked much of a social life, though Holt-Harris described Betty Corning as "a great gentlewoman" who would be, he assumed, naturally hospitable. When the Mayor with increasing frequency invited his friend to share a meal, they ate at "the club" (Fort Orange; see Leo O'Brien's reference in "That Old Gang of Mine"), not at his home. At first, this surprised

Holt-Harris but he came to accept it as a necessary bow to domestic tranquillity, presumably a concession to a wife's haughty contempt for politics or, perhaps, disdain for the husband's associates in that very major segment of his real life. Another reason, of course, could have been the content of their conversations, which might well have been more efficiently—or agreeably—discussed only in dialogue. A *Times Union* story during the 1982-1983 "Regency" stated that while it was "rare" for Corning to invite "someone who was politically active to his home for dinner," Holt-Harris purportedly "was there for dinner often," a reference wholly at odds with Holt-Harris's own account.

    3 He did, however, chair two major "strategic planning" committees at Whalen's request (1984-1985 and 1988-1989). They drew up recommendations for goals, policies, and programs for the administration to adopt, and later evaluate its performance on these issues.

Add for an Ad:
Albany's Future

The V-B Printing Company's typographers already had set the type:[1]

CORNING-WHALEN

in outsize heavy lettering, set above a row of a half-dozen stars, the Democratic emblem, and beneath that a less-subtle reminder with sweeping strokes in the type known as Brush.

VOTE THE DEMOCRATIC TEAM

The copy for handbills, posters, bus placards, perhaps also for blown-up display on billboards was now ready for review by the top candidates in the 1981 election and by their advisors. The message was plain, blunt, traditional.

At his desk downtown, the Whalen of Corning-Whalen scanned the proof. A thought struck home; he put the sheet aside and mulled this idea before returning to it at the end of the workday, giving it renewed attention. Already he'd provided strong suggestions for the ad's format, even its language. He had long thoughts surrounding

the temerity of seeing his own name beside
that of Erastus Corning.

In the lower-left corner, he wrote, "How
about adding," then drew an arrow point-
ing to five words that he lettered in his distinctive handwriting—almost Spencerian—
across the bottom just below the printer's
union "bug":

A Team for the Future

* * *

That, of course, was not the end of the story. The junior partner hardly could expect to dictate the entire script for
the big show. His edited proof went up to City Hall, to the
team's leading man.

In the margin, Albany's Mayor scribbled *OK*. He added
his initials, a quick angular *E* blending into a single upward
stroke that constituted the *C*.

(One must wonder at his thoughts as he initialed that
approval of the recruit's revealed turn of mind.)

* * *

The recruit had, in a sense, upstaged the commander in
chief, even while gaining the chief's approval. He had put his
own stamp on the campaign unmistakably, although few voters would have cause to realize this. His quiet "How about
adding"—an affirmative, minus a question-mark—was appropriately tentative and deceptively deferential. Nevertheless,
he had not merely asserted a role in giving character to the
campaign beyond a single shopworn label; he had inserted
himself into the mix in a significant way with a significantly
public result.

But most importantly, the addition of the word "future"
brought into play a concept with subliminal impact far deeper

than "Don't forget to vote" and "Put these guys in office." Tom Whalen—whether or not he fully intended that impact—had raised the horizon for these candidates in this campaign, had signaled that he should be reckoned with as candidate and prospective officeholder, and subtly established the idea that the newcomer could be expected to be an essential part of the future. Psychologically, not many Albany voters would have linked "future" with a man already in office for 40 years. Rather, he might be seen to have a storied past, but subliminally the message, as edited, conveyed the concept that the new man represented a current change—*healthy* change?—one that could be associated with further change—progress?—and the city's future.

The message got through, even more acutely than its author would have predicted.

"The billboards proclaim it. The buses trumpet the message," wrote Nancy Connell soon after Corning announced his running mate. "The Democratic slate . . . is the 'Team for the Future.'"

Taking into account Corning's age at the time (71) and the "inevitable speculation" on Whalen's potential for even greater influence, she pointed out that "In this case, the past is not the measure of the future." It represented, "for once, more than a slogan." And the new candidate was "in line to take over City Hall if the mayor should fail to serve a full term." It was precisely one year before Corning walked out of his office for the hospital bed he was never to leave.

In an interview during the campaign, Corning agreed that the advertising could be viewed as supportive of predictions that Whalen's role was indeed the wave of Albany's future.

* * *

And sooner than Whalen or anyone else might have safely been able to predict, he became that future.

Tom Whalen was neither reading the future nor defining it in the ultimate sense that came to pass. Subconsciously, he may have had in mind Corning's recent private suggestion to him that he might resign sometime before the end of the forthcoming term in office. But it was indeed a remarkable instance of a foresighted—though vagrant—idea that eventually proved out as neatly as a theorem in geometry.

* * *

Late in their months-long run-up to the November election, Corning and Whalen got together on a joint campaign effort. They taped a five-minute radio spot commercial which, as it turned out, served largely to emphasize their wholly different and individually distinctive personalities and qualities. The contrasts were compelling.

Corning, in a rather high-pitched voice—while precise, strong, and clear, especially for a 70-year-old man with breathing problems—was dismissive in manner, bordering on the authoritarian. His New England educated, cultured voice was assured, suggestive of "taking care of you," but lacking any indication of deep feeling.

Assigned a lesser role naturally enough, Whalen offered a local twang, carefully delivered, possibly more than customarily rehearsed. Whereas Corning touched on at least a dozen topics, Whalen's script was less substantive, with more traces of a hometown boosterism. And while he twice repeated that he wanted to be "part of the team" or of "the leadership," he was surpassed by Corning's reference to his own experience in office and declaration that "I love the work."

The "team for the future" clearly had some rough edges to iron out.

❧ ❧ ❧

NOTE

[1] V-B Printing Co., Inc. had done a half-million dollar business with the city ($504,962) in that same fiscal year and the two previous years (1978-1981) V-B Printing was a law client of one of Whalen's partners. Whalen had acted as personal attorney for a principal in the business. But as an Organization outsider he never had any influence over such an arrangement as the city had maintained with the company. This company and the income it received from the city treasury were included by the State Comptroller in his 1982 report which cited "instances . . . in which bidding requirements were not observed." Within two years, the printery was out of business, thanks in part to the Whalen administration's policies and procedures on competitive bidding.

Part II:
Precepts
and Preparation

Introduction

Tom Whalen would say, much later, that he'd come to Albany's government with the makings of a rough idea in his head for shaping its future. This was a year and a half before he became Mayor.

In nearly a half-century among its people, observing, learning, considering, he'd found conclusions—tentative and tenuous as they necessarily were—that were destined to guide many decisions and policies once he'd been handed final responsibility.

He'd witnessed how the city functioned and malfunctioned, how its operations were improperly mingled with partisan political gain. In a limited way, he'd served the controlling Organization and accepted some of its benefits. Through personal experience he could understand the adverse impact of O'Connellism on the city's individual residents and on its commercial interests. All this conferred valuable insights on which he could capitalize when conducting its official business and establishing its new standards.

Preceding these assets gained as a result of his professional career, however, were the years at home which had fostered personal precepts and perceptions that were to be equally important in determining his approach to governing and girding his fortitude through many difficult days.

From his taking on of unusual familial duties at the age of 9, to his preparation for an exacting livelihood, and to his sharing of community affairs as a volunteer, Tom Whalen's half-century 1934-1983 played a substantial role in fixing his sights on goals characterizing his later success in establishing what would be called an All-America City.

Man of the House

"Now you're the man of the house. I'm depending on you to take care of your mother and the others."

These were the parting words of Thomas M. Whalen, Jr., to Tommy, his sturdy 9-year-old elder son in the early years of World War II.

At age 36 with four children ranging from 11 to a 2-year-old toddler, he had volunteered for Army service soon after Midway and Guadalcanal, North Africa and Sicily, all verifying the long warfare yet to come. And when the day arrived for his departure, he felt able to look for a sense of steadfastness from Tommy.

The father's trust was a burden that the boy received very seriously, and for the duration he did his best to be of help. But the responsibility for raising the family was Mary Whalen's and she carried it diligently for nearly three years.[1] She had not been happy when her husband informed her quietly one night, "I've got to go. It's just something I have to do."

She heard the long-dreaded words in the kitchen in the house on Ryckman Avenue, where they had moved to accommodate the growing family. All the children were in bed, but the kitchen adjoined the two boys' bedroom. Tommy could overhear, and he always remembered his father's determined voice that night, as well as the admonition he received on the day for goodbyes.

"My mother and I became very close during those three years," he recalled, "and it was a marvelous experience for me." But it was exciting, as well, to have a father who was an officer in the Army, detailed to important missions with the British Eighth Army, and writing home about close-up contacts with Field Marshal Sir Bernard Montgomery and Pope Pius XII. Promptly on his father's departure, Tommy acquired a large scrapbook and faithfully filled it with mementos.[2]

* * *

Tom, Jr., put in a dozen years in the Department of Audit & Control before his Army duty. Commissioned on the strength of his fiscal skills and assigned to the Allied Military Government, he first went with the Fifth Army under General Mark Clark but later was seconded to the British Eighth Army under Montgomery. Major Whalen returned to Audit & Control upon his discharge in 1946, taking the title of Director of Investments and Cash Management. Under five Comptrollers—Democrats and Republicans—from Morris Tremaine to Arthur Levitt—he was a non-political professional in a highly demanding occupation, though he always maintained numerous political contacts. Erastus Corning and other Albany County Democrats regarded him highly and considered him a friend in a very sensitive environment. Before he retired in 1979, New York State's 1975 fiscal crunch—the end of "Wine and Roses" in the government's policies—had overtaken the state.

When the time came that year for the customary spring borrowing to tide the treasury over a low point in cash flow, New York City's big banks were declining to buy the state's obligations as they customarily would have done. Tom Whalen successfully persuaded lenders elsewhere in the country—and thus "saved the day for New York State," in the grateful words of Governor Hugh Carey.

Because both Whalens had studied at Manhattan College, this eventually meant a career-critical association for

Tom III with a major Albany law firm. In college, his father and Edward S. Rooney had become good friends. After graduation, Ed Rooney promptly joined the Cooper Erving law firm, and by the time young Tom was ready to look for employment three decades later, he was senior partner and also president of the First Trust Company so closely tied to it.

"Dad arranged for the interview that led to my joining the firm," Tom III had recalled. "Apart from their acquaintance at college, they had frequent reasons to meet in the city's banking activities. Getting that first interview just as I was about to graduate from Albany Law School in the spring of 1958 made a great deal of difference to me, and it was typical of the helping hand I always had from Dad."

Tom Jr.'s fiscal conservatism was a quality handed down to his older son. The father's policies "rubbed off"—as Tom III put it—and eventually served well as the son introduced reform measures to correct Albany's dire financial straits. He invariably emphasized this when credit for his own performance was mentioned. "Right up until the end we were in pretty regular communication. I would bounce things off him, and it always was very helpful to me. I greatly valued and respected his comments and his advice."

NOTES

[1] Mary Elizabeth ("Pat") Broderick, one of three children, was born in Massachusetts in the Berkshire County hill town of Dalton in 1909. Her father, Patrick, was a General Electric foreman in Pittsfield and her mother, Elizabeth, was a Parker descended from a hero of the American Revolution. Mary received a full scholarship to the Ursuline Order's College of New Rochelle. It was one of the college's sternly social weekends that she met handsome Tom Whalen, Jr., a Manhattan College basketball star and business

administration student. The acquaintance blossomed and they married soon after her graduation in 1931 just as the Great Depression approached its depth.

The young Whalens moved to Albany, soon locating on Pinewood Avenue, in a middle-class neighborhood between New Scotland Avenue and Hackett Boulevard. "Pat" gave birth to their first child, Mary Patricia, at the time her husband began his career of over 40 years at the State Department of Audit & Control.

Thomas III, the second child, was born at the Brady Maternity Hospital early in 1934, during the most stirring days of Franklin Roosevelt's New Deal. The FDR-inspired March of Dimes dates from that same month.

Another daughter, Carolyn, and a second son, Michael, arrived within the next few years, a period when the family moved twice—in each case to more upscale housing—first on Ryckman Avenue and later on Brookline Avenue.

2 After the war, a new scrapbook quickly bulged with photos, clippings, and similar trophies of major league baseball, particularly the New York Yankees.

Fun & Games . . . and Reality

In a land that's jaded today by politicians' stunts, Charlie's Circus might not seem a huge deal, but six or seven decades ago Charlie Ryan was off to an early start—and he wasn't even running for anything.

Franklin Roosevelt's New Deal was in its first throes of trying government programs such as the NRA and CCC and PWA to pull the country from the depths of Depression, and the film industry was doing its best to divert gloom by starring its Groucho and Harpos, its Bing and Bobs, and its W. C. and Maes. "Make 'em Laugh, Make 'em Laugh, Make 'em Laugh" hadn't yet been composed for Donald O'Connor, but lightening the national mood could be a goal in itself.

Charlie and his brothers—perhaps "The Three Ryans" would have been apt billing—never were known as comics. But Charlie's Circus was a big hit, season after season, in a boulevard segment of very middle-class Pinewood Avenue, close by Hackett Boulevard, so named to honor Albany's recently martyred Mayor.

And one of the circus's best parts—it was all free! The clowns, the rides, the cotton candy, the Midway sounds and smells all were grand. True, there was a material side, too, for Charlie was assigned important jobs after he—along with his mother and brothers—had won Dan O'Connell's affections and trust. Among his responsibilities was keeping his ward in line as its designated leader, and he hustled to make certain his constituency was well satisfied. He employed the O'Connell tradition of distributing jobs and, when necessary, also hand-outs. Plus all the favors—often enough, cash—to prod the electorate into regularly performing as expected. "Make 'em laugh" was an easy component of "Keep 'em happy." So Charlie had dreamed up Ryan's circus. It occupied the center island of Pinewood between two paved lanes, and it became a big, happy draw year after year, a genuine family affair. Boys on bikes arrived from countless side streets, mothers took off their aprons and curlers to bring the smallest children, and shirtsleeved dads never were far behind with slightly older moppets.

One of the regulars was Charlie's neighborhood friend on Pinewood, Tom Whalen, who showed up with Tommy on sunny weekends and warm early evenings.[1] And so Tommy, then just past toddler stage, first met one of the linchpins of the whole "O'Connell machine." A force in his own name, known to share O'Connell secrets and therefore a corner of their power, Charlie Ryan was a marked man anywhere in town.

Circus expenses were paid from a roll of bills, out of Charlie's pocket wherever the cash may have originated. Not quite the greatest show on earth, and its proprietor admittedly was hardly a Barnum, but it burnished the Ryan legend over the several years when it excited his ward and others too. For Depression-era Albany, the free circus all but ranked with Chicago's Century of Progress.

* * *

So this was young Tommy Whalen's introduction to the legendary Charlie Ryan. Charlie himself hardly could be expected to have made much of an impression on the youngster. But the families' association over the years when Tommy was growing up and maturing inevitably created a degree of intimacy. When Whalen took over for Erastus Corning, with whom Ryan had been competing and feuding for years, the old man could be pardoned for dreaming of a political rebirth.

How that relationship actually developed is another story, to be related later in this account.

NOTE

[1] The Charlie Ryan-Tom Whalen, Jr., friendship actually dated back to the 1920s, as students together at Manhattan College, and they later had become colleagues as state employees (though in different divisions) in Audit & Control.

Beyond Lessons, Learning

Manhattan College, which he entered in 1951, was a lifetime's intellectual landmark for Tom Whalen. Because of his father's successful experience there, it had been his only choice. And because of its import in these respects, it deserves unusual attention here. Its precepts and its professors unmistakably shaped his journey to the career that followed.

The experience of attending college in New York City was as exciting for him as for so many generations of talented young people. But daunting it was, too, in its challenge of forced intellectual growth against a backdrop of attractive opportunities to which the Big Apple invited a 17-year-old away from home for the first time. A late bloomer, Tom nearly flunked out in his freshman year before he began to satisfy the time demands for his study.[1] After his very rocky start, his marks improved progressively in each of his succeeding years.

Though, as ever, the city offered its traditional escapes and escapades, it was the four academic years that were the more effective in opening a path into the future. He always had in mind the special challenge in entering the school where his father had been an outstanding scholar-athlete two decades earlier. An inspiration, yes, but a bit intimidating as well.[2]

These collegiate years were, in the wider world, a period of controversy, change, and conflict, even of a national trauma: of the Korean War, McCarthyism, the "I Like Ike" Republican resurgence and soaring Stevensonian oratory, JFK's "Profiles." In Albany, Thomas E. Dewey departed and Averell

Harriman's Democrats arrived. Not yet at what was then the legal voting age throughout his undergraduate years, Thomas Whalen declined to be diverted by the passing parade; he put his head down and dug in, giving stern priority to the tasks immediately before him—focusing on business administration principles and certain other studies, gaining peer respect and honors, working overtime at campus jobs and filling in his summers at exhausting manual labor.

But it was the nature of the college, its professors and the high expectation they held for all who came to draw from them, which made the outcome worthy of the task.

Founded and operated by the Brothers of the Christian Schools, who describe their tradition as embracing excellence in teaching, respect for the individual's dignity, and commitment to social justice, Manhattan College clearly leaves an indelible impression on its students.

"The ethical standards the Christian Brothers sought to develop remain with me to this day," Tom Whalen wrote, nearly a half-century after he enrolled as a freshman. "It was more than the traditional values of the church. Much of it related to participating in a meaningful way in a modern society—and doing so with integrity, regard for truthfulness, and hard work.

"Not only were the Brothers committed to incorporating these values in their teaching. I found that many of the lay professors wove those principles into their instruction.

"We boarding students were very closely knit. And the Brothers kept a stern watch over us. The rules were strict. Evening study was mandatory. 'Lights out!' came at 10:30, and to leave your dorm, or to go off-campus, permission was obligatory.

"And though all this sounds outdated, I realize that, especially as a freshman, I needed the imposed discipline in order to survive the transition from life at home in a relatively small city. Some of the fellows from the outlying areas made the transition, but others didn't."

Because Manhattan's red-brick Georgian-style dormitories were segregated according to class-level, Tom lived in a new one each year. As a junior and senior, he was a student prefect, earning free room and board for the responsibility of overseeing classmates. The assignment was to keep a close watch on freshmen in their dormitories—to make sure they were in their rooms by 7:30, and that they adhered rigidly to "Lights out." This meant a range of duties, including keeping track of "late permissions" and Sunday evening arrivals from home. There was a strong tradition of discipline in Manhattan's official code. Thus charged with helping to enforce the college's standards of behavior, he gained the advantages of resiliency and maturity, exercising the dual roles of student and quasi-staff member. For tasks said to require "an open mind and a sincere heart," he received the material advantages of his dorm room and a very modest stipend—but also status on campus and résumé-building evidence of prob-lem-solving, teamwork skills, and leadership potential.

At evening meals, he was behind the counter in the cafeteria. Class president in his junior year, he earned election to Pen and Sword, the college's most prestigious honor society, where membership was a much-desired campus goal that rec-ognized leadership qualities but not necessarily academic accomplishments. After his skin-of-the-teeth academic record as a freshman, in each of the next three years he was a Dean's List student.

Part of his athletic career was blighted, however, for Manhattan had abandoned football as a varsity sport. He referred to himself as a nondescript member of the baseball varsity. As an outfielder and third baseman, his skills in the field surpassed his achievement at the plate.

In spite of his varied interests, he recalled that, "The course I best remember with fondest of memories was The Humanities, which I enjoyed and benefited from so greatly that I enrolled in it all four years. The professor was a great teacher, Howard Floan, and he led us into classical literature, an experience I genuinely loved. Through those four years, we progressed from Greek classics to twentieth century American novelists."

Further testimony on these values is offered by Whalen's classmate and friend, L. Jay Oliva (president of New York University, 1992-2002): "My Manhattan College education is with me every moment of every day. . . . We gained a unique perspective on Western development and a deep sense of history."

The School of Business, where Tom majored, as his father had, is ranked by Standard & Poor's as one of the countrys principal undergraduate sources of managerial and financial leadership. Among the nation's liberal arts colleges, Manhattan is known as a leader in offering that specialty. In combination with the discipline of a law degree, the business emphasis was eminently useful for the Whalen career, including particularly the requirements of managing a city and developing its standards.

His four years (1951-1955) at Manhattan, close to the northern end of the West Side IRT subway,[3] served effectively in opening up what turned into a lifelong attraction to classical music and the opera. He had been spurred into aggressive attention to New York City's cultural advantages by his mother's final admonitions in surrendering her son to the big city.

Uncharacteristically for most students, he did take note of the opportunities and quite frequently patronized Carnegie Hall concerts and the Met in its old opera house just off Times Square.[4]

"If you look at that impressionable young person, on the one hand, and opportunities that were there to be seized, it was major," he summed up his adventure in the city's cultural thicket. If in this activity he could be considered an atypical collegian, he was also cutting against the ingrained habit of most. Students in specialized areas (such as business) are so often exposed to little study, or none, in the liberal arts and sciences. The result, as one observer has pointed out, may be a graduate who is competent in a limited field but poorly prepared for comprehension and appreciation of the arts or philosophy or for an informed understanding of public life.

Tom's immersion in his humanities classes presumably

was an intimation of his personal tastes. This clue was verified many times over in his adult life. The verification is to be found in his enjoyment of music and other performing arts or his self-designed reading programs including his auditing university courses even while holding public office, and similarly his turning to teaching college-level courses later in Albany at the College of Saint Rose and in Ireland at the University of Cork. And, of course, the obvious commitment of his administration to strong funding and creative leadership advancing cultural aspects in the city's life that had not existed or thrived previously.

NOTES

[1] At Vincentian Institute, the main influences—both pro and con—for teen-age Tom Whalen had been athletic rather than academic.

Brother Marcian—redheaded like himself—who was the athletic director and also a teacher, provided a confidence-building attitude. The football coach, Walter Scanlan, however, "didn't think much of me," and Tom's varsity aspirations languished. Only when he was a senior did a new coach, Bill Boehner, arrive at VI and put the 16-year-old boy on the first team.

"At the beginning of fall practice, he pulled me aside," Tom remembered, "and he said to me, 'All that is behind you. Now show me what you can do as a quarterback.' The confidence he gave me had a major effect on me."

Characteristically, he found ways to keep occupied in advantageous ways. For 55 cents an hour—"which was very welcome"—he worked as part of a janitorial crew at school on Saturday afternoons and after classes on Fridays. This was just before and after his seventeenth birthday. Vincentian was "a very full part of my life as a teenager," in his recollection.

[2] His father was very well known to some of Manhattan's

teaching Brothers.   When Manhattan's athletic teams came to Albany, Tom Whalen, Jr., invariably was on hand to cheer them on—and usually was in the center of a group of Brothers. Tom III was president of the Capital District Chapter of the alumni association in the 1960s.

[3] Despite its name, the 47-acre campus is located in the Riverdale section of the Bronx, on heights above Van Cortlandt Park and bordered on the west by the Hudson.

[4] We must note, too, that in those years, the Bronx also was home to Casey Stengel's long series of championship Yankee teams. In 1951, both Mickey Mantle and Willie Mays were, like Tom, New York rookies.

The Critical Choice

The communications giant once known as New York Telephone lost a fine prospect for a manager-in-the-making in the days of monolithic rotary dialing, picturesque area-exchange identities such as Hemlock or Ivanhoe, and five-cent calls from a booth with a seat in it. Its management recruiters had a promising candidate, Tom Whalen, on their line.

At the time—the spring of 1955—their apparent competition for hiring the 21-year-old college senior was Metropolitan Life.

But both prospective employers let him get away. In the countdown to decision on just what to do next, the careers offered by the recruiters seemed to create a *je ne sais quoi* residue of uncertainty. Were either of these what he really wanted for a lifetime's occupation?

Pat Whalen finally resolved her son's indecision. "Why don't you think about law school?" she asked, with a mother's keen sense of timing, during the Whalens' breakfast one morning when he was home from Manhattan for spring break. By the end of that day, Tom—who had liked his exposure to Business Law at Manhattan—had filled out an application at the neighborhood law school, the one they both would have had in mind. In fact, for many years, Albany Law School's admissions office had looked to Manhattan College as one of its most reliable feeders.

Being admitted in a class of 150 was no big problem at that time even for a student who had finished with less than a prime grade average in earning his Bachelor of Business Administration degree. The big question for every one of the 150 was: Who would prove to have the staying power? Their numbers were reduced by one-third in just their freshman year, and only 81 survived to graduate. Tom Whalen, despite another middling academic record, was safely among the 81. He consistently stood in the upper 16-to-20% of his class, a very respectable showing though far from spectacular. His relative standing improved in each of his second and third years, and he ranked thirteenth in the graduating class, with a three-year average that merited an overall "B." Half of his grades had been the numerical equivalent of a "C." Of the others, three-fifths were "A" and the remainder were of "B" rank. His efforts in two subjects—Administrative and Labor Law—were good enough to win prizes. He had difficulty with the bar exam, which he'd taken too lightly on his first approach, but subsequently he buckled down to the realistic review requirements.

But the young man's entrepreneurial and political appetites gained him recognition that far surpassed the outcome of the lecture hall's memorizing demands and of the irksome quizzes.

His varied outside activities seemed to claim precedence for his attention. He maintained two time-consuming causes, one of which gained him much wider experience than was available in Albany, and the other provided the wherewithal for his $800 tuition payment each year.[1]

* * *

After observing during his first year how the Law School's machinery cranked and clanged out its products, he experienced a challenging vision of a potentially rewarding spin-off from his studies. And then he proceeded to carve out a unique enterprise.

In status and reward, it was, fortunately enough, several cuts above the backbreaking summer laborer's jobs or the humble tasks of cafeteria busboy/dorm monitor he'd shouldered in school and college.

Beyond the seemingly endless hours of preparation demanded of any budding lawyer—the requisite inquiry into Torts, Property, Procedure, the whole nine yards—he'd now dash ahead through assigned texts' cases. He digested all the complex cases, describing issues involved, citing courts' rulings, and explaining their applicability in creating new law.

Reproduced, these soon were respected and renowned among his classmates as "Whalen's Cans," and attained instant popularity, especially so in reviewing for Finals. Each "can" sold at an acceptably modest but decently profitable $4 or $5 per course. ("Cans," a not unfamiliar term among students, seems to derive from a concept of neatly condensed and packaged facts.)

Midway along in producing his homemade trots, Tom Whalen received a summons from the dean, Andrew Clements.

"Just want you to know that we're on to what you're doing," the dean quietly informed him with an impressive show of sternness moderated by a slight smile that could be construed as an unduly benign blessing from Albany Law's lawgiver. Neither dean nor faculty ever got around to following up with action in restraint of trade. Perhaps their do-nothing policy represented merely realistic application of First Amendment privilege—or an untraditional, forgiving view of it as just another student's creative escapade.

In relating it all almost a half-century afterward,[2] Tom Whalen's eyes gleamed at this recollection, as they did for his tales of helping to pull together a half-dozen friends in a "study group" for boning up on each course. Starting in April before exams, they met for four or five hours evenings, drilling each conspirator in turn until fully satisfied everyone truly understood the principles in every case. Whenever one of the mates stumbled over some issue, everything stopped until his colleagues felt assured that he was up to speed.

"And you know," Whalen exclaimed many years later,

seeming to surprise himself by the insight, "I think that may well have set the stage for the 'group concept' I worked out as my administrative style in office!"

* * *

Meanwhile, he diverted more of his energetic ambition into a side issue, the agenda of the American Law Student Association, an ABA affiliate with membership from every accredited law school. By his senior year, his zeal had made him well enough known among these self-selected leaders to win him election as the association's executive vice president. He smothered early hopes of winning the presidency and accepted a deal as second banana. Then he plunged into the time-consuming responsibility and ended the year with recognition as "Outstanding National Officer," a satisfying notch on a growing résumé.

Other dividends, as well, were declarable: Exposure to unfamiliar faces and accents among other Americans, and to organizational processes giving "an extra dimension" which later would buttress a career that could have been more circumscribed and confining.

Because ALSA itself carried a certain cachet, Whalen's role in it added a nice distinction on campus, but the ornament didn't hang very high on the Law School's tree: He was assigned a cubbyhole office near the boilers. Ignoring the putdown, he persisted in carrying on a hands-on oversight of key officers in every district. (The association's districts coincide with the federal judiciary's.)

Despite the many hours that association work obligated, he found his final year of studies advantageous, capitalizing on—he recalled—"a good foundation in the first two years," when academics needed to prevail over showcasing.

His performance in the association was astute and well-executed. Representing a regional institution which the commandos from Harvard, Stanford, and other ranking law factories could dismiss as an upstart, he turned in an impressive report card.

* * *

Thus prepared and situated for practicing law (after a year's military duty), he found his opportunity in an offer from one of the city's leading firms, at $50 a week.

NOTES

[1] Living at home again throughout this period, his other expenses were nominal (and he had hard-earned summer-job income as well). His two-mile commute was in a classmate's car. At 8:15 each morning, he met Matt Mataraso at the Western Avenue corner of Brookline and rode to school in style in his friend's Morris Minor. (Many years later, Mataraso was a staunch supporter and dependable advisor despite a frequently differing outlook in political positions other than Whalen's own issues and policies.)

[2] As a member of the Law School's Board of Trustees since 1986, Whalen in 2002 was completing a three-year term as the board's chairman while also heading the annual fund and capital fund campaigns. In 1994, his board colleagues had conferred the Trustees' Gold Medal Award in recognition of his service to the school. He had served as the alumni president previously.

A scholarship fund honoring his memory was inspired by one of his clients, Morris Silverman, who became its initial donor. Whalen represented "Marty" Silverman in negotiations for numerous aspects of development of the University Heights academic complex, which began with acquisition of property adjacent to the law school in order to make possible an expansion of its facilities.

Between the Wars

When the North Koreans crossed the Yalu and
Harry Truman responded by putting American GIs into a
"police action," Tom was a high school junior. By the time
Lyndon Johnson was dispatching troops to Southeast Asia,
Tom was over 30 and a family man with three children.
(The youngest was born in the week the Senate approved the
Gulf of Tonkin Resolution, steppingstone to the prolonged
conflict that followed. This son was a sixth-grader before
the war officially ended.)

In the meantime, having entered the Army as a
volunteer in 1958 after gaining his law degree, Whalen
ended up as a private at the Army's Finance Center at Fort
Benjamin Harrison in Indiana. Under terms of his
enlistment, he served seven years in the National Guard as a
lieutenant produced by the officer candidate program. His
guard duty was principally as an aide to the commander,
General John Baker, who also was chief of staff to Governor
Rockefeller.

Patrons for a Practice

At a sandwich shop on Watervliet Avenue near Lew Swyer's office—a drably unfashionable part of town—Lew, Jim Drislane, and young Tom Whalen often sat down together at lunch, not so much for the meal as for the opportunity to chew over business, politics, a miscellany of speculation and gossip—and more business. It was another very important connection for Whalen.

For an up-and-coming lawyer, tangible advantages opened beyond the relaxed pleasantries of these sessions with the two older men. Out of their early conversations came a very worthwhile business arrangement: Lew Swyer, a contractor and developer, had acquired property in the former New York Central's West Albany yards not far distant from his own office. He projected an industrial park in the extensive area that once had been the railroad's Albany shops. For Albany Industrial Development, the not-for-profit corporation that the Swyer-Drislane interests formed to successfully create the park, Whalen took on all the very substantial law work.

That wasn't the only benefit he derived, for his responsibilities brought him into close contact with many in the area's business establishment. The corporation's board included a majority of the directors of the Greater Albany Chamber of Commerce, where Drislane was president at that time. "A great opportunity for a young lawyer like me," Tom Whalen recalled. "This was at a time, remember, when the last thing in the world in my mind was a full-time public office, much less as the city's Mayor." He was considered eligible for the assignment because he already was involved in the Chamber, having persuaded his senior partners to pay for the law firm's membership, a quite rare affiliation for lawyers at that time.

"It was a professional relationship we had, but also a personal and social one, with both Lew and Jim. I could seek their counsel freely. For instance, if I had questions in my own mind about a case I was working on, I would look to Jim for another opinion. All this was very, very helpful to me."

Drislane was then "one of the most respected practitioners in the Capital Region," in Whalen's view. (He later joined the Cooper Erving firm as a senior partner in 1980.) "He was very well known among the profession."

"And he was known for his integrity," Whalen recalled, "and for being very tough—he was not flexible at all in his representation of a client until in the client's interest he had no option. It was his integrity, in fact, that had caused Lew to be attracted to him as a business partner as well as a client.

"His activity in the Chamber was typical of the manner in which he reached out into the community in ways that most lawyers don't—and this was extremely helpful to his practice."

Within the party, he was regarded as a Democratic lawyer who rarely was visible but "who'd be around at election time." It was in this independent mode that he became a partisan of Whalen's early in his first campaign (for City Court in 1969) and again for his candidacies in 1981 and 1985. His health was failing rapidly in later years. He and Lew Swyer, who also was very ill, took little outings together.

Swyer rode as Drislane's passenger to Crossgates Mall so both of them could find an opportunity for sheltered exercise together, slowly pacing the broad corridors and sometimes pausing to consider shop window displays. As mordant fate decreed, Jimmy Drislane died exactly three months before his friend, in early fall of 1988. Tom Whalen composed and spoke memorial tributes for each.

Lewis A. Swyer, much more of a public figure than

Drislane, "had great instincts on social justice," Whalen said in recollection, "and on what a society is all about."

"I had tremendous respect for Lew's integrity. He was, incidentally, quick on the draw—one reflection of his very acute mind. If he felt that someone had wronged him, of if he was distressed by some other kind of behavior, whether or not he was personally affected, he would dash off a scathing letter. But Jim often would then say, 'Give me that letter—and I'll mail it tomorrow.' But before then Lew would call to tell him, 'Don't mail that letter!'"

For reason that he kept to himself but probably were basically designed to avoid possible damage to his business interests, Swyer never became directly involved in elective politics, although he invariably had strong opinions and personal support and though he was often mentioned as potentially an appealing candidate.

As long as he remained a possible opponent, Corning was said to bad-mouth him at any opportunity. Swyer's closest friends considered that the Mayor, apprehensive of the Swyer reputation and popularity, hoped to discourage any idea of a challenge from such a formidable source (as he received, for example from Carl Touhey in 1973).

A brilliant aesthete with wide-ranging and engaging artistic interests, he had made his fortune by opening the earth and impressively piling concrete and steel, bricks and mortar onto it. His concerns were innumerable, his contributions many, his turn of mind provocative, his citizenship broadly exemplary.

Assuming roles both aesthetic and material as a principal in the development of the Saratoga Performing Arts Center, Swyer involved himself so deeply in promotion of drama, dance, and music in the Capital Region that eventually one of the theaters in The Egg at the Empire State Plaza was named to honor his memory. Over a quarter-century, few Albanians were as respected.

In the busy celebratory year of the Tricentennial, for which he'd accepted much responsibility, Swyer was diagnosed with a cancer. Hospitalized much of the next two years, he wrote uncomplainingly of his new-found "time of rest and contemplation" but in periods of discouragement he likened his situation to being "incarcerated part-time in the Tower of London" or even to "going through purgatory."

To the limit of his capacity, he worked on funding for a shelter for homeless youths. When able, he took occasional walks, describing his own enjoyment—characteristically—in gaining a "different perspective about the city, its personality, and human value."

From his hospital bed on December 20, 1988, Lew dictated a long letter to the Mayor. "Since you have become Mayor," he wrote, "there are opportunities that I feel are available because of the timing, the forceful commitment you make to those things you feel strongly about, and because of the strength of your position in an office that is fortified by the fiscal stability that you have attained.

"The door is opened," he added, "to unlimited possibilities."

He valiantly spoke of having regained enough "vigor and vitality to address some of my dreams and aspirations for the future I believe can be accomplished only through your interest and efforts."

Before closing, he added a few lines of even more personal testimony: "I take great pleasure in your accomplishments and all of the good things that are happening in the city. For perpetuity and for what Albany may become in the future, I take even greater pleasure in thinking that my good friend, Tom Whalen, has been responsible for it."

Separately, he sent the Whalens a note of appreciation for a Christmas card: "It brought me a number of extra heartbeats of pleasure and sentiment because of our friendship of so many years."

Though he had written of hopeful expectations to be at home for Christmas, Lew Swyer died that day, not far away, in St. Peter's Hospital.

In Academy Park, a few rods from City Hall's front

windows, Lew Swyer remains in all weather seated on a park bench, one bronzed leg crossed in a posture of rest and contemplation, and with the ever-present fedora properly in hand. In accepting "The Lewis A. Swyer Community Renaissance Award" from the Friends of Saint Rose just before he left the Mayor's office, Whalen mentioned this striking memorial and observed, "There Lew sits, one eye on the park and one eye on City Hall and its future Mayors."

Man of the Hour

In the early spring of 1969, a pair of neatly interlocking ambitions came together in Albany's Democratic party to form a perfect dovetail. Four months earlier, the party had sustained five painful and totally unprecedented election defeats. In the meantime, an aspiring but disgruntled 29-year-old lawyer and party factotum switched allegiance to become the Republicans' candidate for a judgeship in the city, expecting to run against a sitting judge exactly twice his age. But the judge, Simon Rosenstock, who'd been appointed—rather than elected—three years earlier, had decided to retire. The Democrats would need the strongest possible opponent to take on the deserter, in order to help stanch the hemorrhaging at the polls.

Simultaneously, Thomas M. Whalen III, having just turned 35, was wondering whether he might have a future in politics. With the judge's retirement, a suitable opportunity opened up. And he discovered that the Democrats happened to be looking for a candidate with exactly his profile and statistics. He might be just the vigorous young man with impeccable credentials who could successfully come to the aid of his party. The attraction was mutual, but the party needed Tom Whalen more than he needed it.

A perpetual rival of Erastus Corning's, Eugene Devine, who was the five-term County Treasurer—and, more significantly, Dan O'Connell's personal attorney—hustled out to the boss's home on behalf of his young associate as soon as

Rosenstock let it be known that he would not run and Whalen privately mentioned his own interest.

Devine got to Whitehall Road first, successfully proposing Whalen as an up-and-coming fellow who could make a good run. Mayor or not, Corning could lump it. He came around without a public fuss, and ultimately let it be put in print that Whalen was "uniquely suited," with "rare qualifications" to be judge, and in any event was "by far the most qualified candidate."

"They all had their favorites for office," Whalen recalled much later, "and that year I was Devine's, not Corning's."

"What was at stake was political power and its dispersal," Fred LeBrun wrote later in the *Times Union*. "In this struggle, both candidates were merely symbols. From the beginning (it was) the race to watch."

Though the fit was ideal, the challenge remained: Could this particular candidate, innocent of virtually any political exposure, actually cut the mustard in November?

As things turned out, the answer transcended November 1969, for the testing and proving-out of Tom Whalen that fall bore implications of much longer-range promise for himself and for his city of Albany.

Without his successful entry into elective politics at this time (followed by his conduct of an office where discretionary judgment is everything), he could have been lost among the untested when a larger challenge emerged. And his appetite for a true candidate's tireless footwork and endless handclasps created a firm impression of an ambitious and electable politician.

* * *

"Make sure he is pictured whenever possible with the Mayor," wrote Francis S. Rivett in April, seven months before the November election in which Tom Whalen would first become Erastus Corning's running mate.

The state Department of Audit & Control's public relations officer was responding to a request from the new candidate's father. Himself an officer of the department, Thomas Whalen, Jr., was anxiously seeking advice on campaign strategy. He had turned to "Doc" Rivett, a seasoned reporter and editor whose earliest contact with the youngest Tom Whalen, nearly two decades earlier, had been as a *Times Union* sportswriter describing the Vincentian quarterback's long passes.[1] Obliging, "Doc" offered a six-point list of suggestions, closing with the caution that "He should not spin his wheels too much at this time." Instead, "After the first licks, a short and concentrated exposure."

This, along with much else of Rivett's counsel, was heeded. Not long afterward, sure enough, a photo was published showing Mayor Corning with candidate Whalen standing respectfully somewhat to the rear. Both were surrounded by apparently happy constituents of Corning's: Bishop William Wilborn, pastor of Wilborn's Temple Church of God and Christ; Ida Yarbrough and Mae Douglas, important board members of the Albany Interracial Council; and the straw who undoubtedly had stirred this drink, Arthur Mitchell. In the picture's caption, he described himself as "local church reporter," as well as promotion and public relations director for the "Mid-Hudson Herald," the occasional newspaper available to a black readership, where the photo was strategically published. Art Mitchell was a significant interpreter for the black community to Albany's political power structure.

Corning, while a co-conspirator in this particular photo-op, was not yet a strong partisan of Whalen. Just before the nomination he had received a message from Lew Swyer, Tom's friend and a very influential citizen, boosting the young lawyer. In return, Corning sent a two-line note: "I am glad of your thoughts on Tom Whalen being on the ticket." In truth, the Mayor wanted his own candidate for the court, not necessarily in opposition to Whalen—whom he didn't really know well yet—but rather as part of the constant in-fighting for status and preference within Dan O'Connell's small circle.

Whalen's very first photo as a politician, however, had

linked him with O'Connell. The 83-year-old boss was seated and the candidate stood nearby, hand outstretched and a rather tentative smile crossing his face. The photographer trapped a quite benign expression on O'Connell, one much more genial than the almost contemptuous poker face that revealed very little on those occasions when he turned out for a party caucus. His hat seemed jaunty rather than jammed down, his overcoat was neat instead of mussed in an old man's careless way. Whalen's well-wishers, viewing that published picture on the first spring morning of 1969, hardly could have been better pleased.[2]

* * *

In his nine years as an Albany lawyer, Whalen's responsiveness to the city's politicking had been meager. His emergence as a candidate in the spring of 1969, then, was unusual. Until this spring, he had seemed no better than a long shot as a successful candidate. He had persistently provided evidence of affiliation with people extremely close to the heart of that controversial Organization known for militant ways and ruthless means.

He was upwardly mobile in a law firm that historically maintained unusually intimate relationships with the party and (as later developments revealed) even made room for the Organization's own little tin box. Unabashedly visible were his friends and patrons—the longstanding familial connections with Charlie Ryan, one of O'Connell's most intense enforcers among all his brigands; the professional and personal association with Jack Pennock, widely cheered or feared for his exceptionally fierce partisanship; and the partnership/ friendship with Gene Devine, whose very name could raise political hackles but who carried his A-1 credentials like an armpit holster.

Other alliances aside, Tom Whalen owned the advantage of Devine's personal endorsement and upward boost when he began to waken politically. The awakening could well be considered surprising. Never was he known to have

publicly proclaimed any of the committed passion and emotion of John Kennedy's New Frontier or Lyndon Johnson's
Great Society. His personal history, dating from the first year
of Franklin D. Roosevelt's administration, showed no apparent
reverence for the New Deal's programs. Or for either the feisty
Harry Truman or the cerebral Adlai Stevenson, the principal
Democratic spokesmen during his years in high school, college, and law school and then early in his profession. He had
reached his late twenties before an inspiring Kennedy candidacy existed or an administration with the JFK imprint. (He
gave himself a "Kennedy Democrat" label later, but actually
defining the presumed acts or accomplishments behind those
words is difficult.)

And now he was halfway through his 30s.[3] Very
recently, however, important change had intruded on his perceptions of private and public life. The Viet Nam war controversy, nationally and locally, was raging at its height. His
younger brother, Michael, an Army captain in the Medical
Corps, was assailed daily by desperate and violently enraged
inductees whose physicals he was certifying for overseas duty
eligibility. Political assassination had flared twice more within
the year. The Democrats' national ticket had lost in November
while New York reelected its senior Republican Senator. For
the first time in its 50-year history, the O'Connell
Organization's slate of candidates had been badly defeated.
During that unprecedented debacle, Whalen, a committeeman,
had been submerged as little more than a spectator among all
those out ringing doorbells.

* * *

Beyond politics, however, a shattering event had also
altered Tom Whalen's world. His mother, greatly influential
his whole life, had died at age 59 during the winter.

She, the conscientious parent, and he, the grade-school
pupil, had seen the Whalen household through the years of
World War II. Her very considerable long-range effect on his

thinking was exemplified when she provided the decisive idea of his entering law school when he was floundering on choice of a career.

Now, a very few weeks after her death, a deliberate broadening of his own horizons—demanding in itself—might be all-but-equal to the cataclysmic change that had so rudely impacted his perspective of a placid world where events occur only as they should. This interpretation, of course, clearly assumes that a fostering mother would in spirit applaud a son's seeking out a new challenge, moving beyond what he had thought possible.

* * *

Qualifications were surely pertinent in the selection of a judge, but electability was the true issue in the 1969 contest.

The party had problems. One factor was that insurrection had broken out. A single instance so far, but a defection might turn out to be an infection. If an individual (Lawrence E. Kahn) who had gained trust within the highest councils could successfully break away, then who could forecast where apostasy might end? If he were to win, it would show young people that they could succeed by going outside the party. A Democrat running as a Republican, even though retaining enrollment as a Democrat, was a traitor who must be stopped, decisively defeated. A perceptive *Times Union* political reporter, John McLoughlin, commented that, compared with those Republicans who had won in the immediate past, Kahn was "a challenger with more potential for unsettling (Democratic) ranks than any of the several Republican upsets." This conjecture was interesting, even if somewhat fanciful. The Republican victories and gains of 1966-1967-1968 were actual, and Kahn's prospects in 1969 were still problematic. In suggesting the possibility of a Kahn victory, McLoughlin's analysis accurately said "it would tell all dissidents and would-be dissidents within the party" that Dan O'Connell "can be successfully challenged not only by Republicans but from within the ranks too." Such a hypothetical projection was over-reaching for the sake of a good story, so McLoughlin added:

"Conversely, Whalen's victory over Kahn—especially decisive victory—will tell these dissidents that party loyalty is not something to take lightly."

This all-out emphasis on the significance of one man's disgruntled defection is somewhat inflated in view of other important considerations. But it would have figured as one reason the boss was concerned enough to accept, on Gene Devine's say-so, Whalen as a citywide candidate—a young man who had avoided a climb through the ranks. It was gospel that a political aspirant had to be a journeyman Democrat, proving oneself through many years of loyalty and hard work before—maybe—being rewarded. As the candidate himself publicly conceded, "I have never held any elective or appointive position in government, nor have I run for office previously. This is really my baptism of fire."

O'Connell's willingness to accept this politically untried lawyer implicitly recognized the importance of offering a fresh, clean candidate. Implicit, also, was the suggestion that Corning's name at the top of the ticket would not necessarily be sufficiently strong to pull in just any candidate for the court.

The choice of Whalen to run for City Court, then, was dictated by factors almost irrelevant to himself. But it was equally true that he did possess many elements in his favor, most of all his being untouchable as to personal and professional reputation.

* * *

If the desire to discourage desertions had a share in the party's need to field a strong alternative in the Whalen mode, another tide was at least equally strong. It was a tide that had been flowing in the wrong direction, namely the series of defeats and close calls for Democratic officeholders and other candidates. In alarming numbers, voters had been turning away from old-line Democrats. *What had happened to the boss's wisdom?*

The backdrop for this unprecedented shift in Democratic profile and strategy extended back three years in Albany County's political history. In elections during that time, the O'Connell party had lost a Congressional seat, a State Senator, a pair of Assembly members, and the District Attorney, and only narrowly won a hotly contested election for County Clerk, a position long held by a member of the O'Connell clan. The Republican gains had picked up momentum in each successive year.

As it happened, Larry Kahn had been an unwitting tool in the Republicans' pre-1969 resurgence by ineffectively managing Dick Conners's campaign for Congress in 1966. Together with the candidate, he had turned a trick famed in a phrase of wry irony: they snatched defeat from the jaws of victory.

Thereby they had opened the door to succeeding triumphs by the opposition party. Nonetheless, Kahn seemingly had remained in the good graces of the boss and he held on to his political job—as an assistant corporation counsel, a part-time lawyer for the city government—for more than two additional years.

His dismissal from the patronage job was abrupt. "In January of 1969 he either left or was ousted from his spot in the Democratic sunshine, depending on who tells the story," John McLoughlin wrote, noting the disparity in the scuttlebutt.

Within days, he called a press conference to declare himself the Republicans' candidate for City Court. He was in the race for two months before the Democratic ticket was firmed up with Whalen selected as his opponent.

* * *

As the Whalen campaign developed, more and more Rivett advice was followed:

"Select a campaign director," he had urged. "Someone

with whom the old- timers can identify even though he is not one of them." It is perhaps portentous that even at this early stage in the Whalen political career he became accurately tagged as the outsider. The advice about the campaign's direction, also well taken, resulted in one of Whalen's mentors, Jim Drislane, taking charge of detail. He eventually assumed a major role, a source of severe irritation to Devine.

"Line up various committees for TMW," Doc Rivett counseled, suggesting groups of lawyers, of Manhattan College alumni, of fellow graduates of Albany Law School— and, of all things in the O'Connell fiefdom, "Independents for Whalen."

In fact, a "Tom Whalen Citizens' Committee" was formed, with over 20 members, half of them lawyers, and a few businessmen. Larry Burwell, influential executive director of the Albany Urban League, said it was the first time he'd been willing to "stand up politically." He was important to the Whalen campaign, which worked diligently in the minority community. Art Mitchell—who had managed third-baseman Whalen on the Twilight League's Black Sox team—was recruited for the committee.

Whalen's extensive—and quite intensive—effort offers not only substantive evidence of a dedicated campaigner but, additionally, insight into the mechanics and commitment of even a candidacy for an office which supposedly was off-limits for strenuous combat.

Keyed to the Burwell announcement, Whalen's campaigning started in earnest in the first week of July—three months before political activity ordinarily would get under way, as reporter Dave Nathan pointed out in a *Times Union* story.

From within the party's interior came the volunteered help of two of its mainstays, John Treffiletti, the major produce wholesaler, and the real estate developer Ruben S. Gersowitz, the Fourteenth Ward's leader. Among the principal backers of this first Whalen candidacy, they were solid supporters a dozen years later when he ran for the Common Council presidency, then remaining as steadfast interpreters of his progressive course.

Eventually, Whalen and his campaigning were all over the city. Billboards went up. He was principal speaker at the Temple Israel Social Club; whoever arranged that engagement surely was acclaimed within the campaign for having enabled him to strike at the heart of the Kahn turf. Speaking to the Central Avenue Merchants Association, as a reporter wrote in the *Knickerbocker News*, he "demonstrated a looseness and a style which the audience found appealing." The smiling candidate "seemed to enjoy himself." This was despite a heavy cold, which Corning, showing up at the same event, happened to share.

At an affair arranged by a union local, Whalen gave a preview of one of his themes expounded many years later in City Hall: He called for a "politics of participation," declaring that he was finding people were eager for opportunities to become involved in political and governmental activities. Essentially, of course, this ideal was very much at odds— ridiculously so—with the entire tradition of the party under Daniel O'Connell. Within the party, this expression of independent judgment was ignored as irrelevant or tolerated as nonsense that later would be expunged by the realities of genuine political experience. But it stands as the first recorded instance of the essentially independent-minded Whalen.

The law partnership linking Whalen and Devine— actually much personally closer than their detractors realized—was seen by Republicans as a hot seat for Whalen if elected judge. Because Devine was the Albany Housing Authority's chairman (in addition to his elected position as County Treasurer), and AHA stood out as the single most active litigant in City Court, the opposition intimated that Whalen wouldn't be impartial in these cases. (Oddly, the Democrats' progressive wing at the time—the New Democratic Coalition—demanded that Whalen answer questions with identical implications.) Responding to this inferential quizzing, Whalen went so far as to publicly acknowledge

being "very close" to his partner and he also voluntarily men-
tioned having "talked politics from time to time" with
Devine—who was labeled "a notorious political figure" by
Walter B. Langley, the county's new Republican State Senator.

The association would not "taint my ability to administer a non-political court," Whalen maintained.[4]

* * *

A judgeship candidate could have no campaign—as
Whalen repeatedly reminded any interested citizen. Protocol
precluded activity that did not directly bear on the candidate's
qualifications for a judge's responsibilities. But of course a reasonable facsimile of a campaign had to be mounted, and both
candidates pushed the fringes of their respective statements of
credentials.

And all their effort was invested in obtaining a job
which offered a salary of $4,500, nominal even before the major
inflationary pressures that were to follow.[5]

The City Court's bargain-basement compensation was
justified, in part, by the schedule of the court's three judges.
Each sat on the bench only one month in a calendar quarter—
four months a year in total. As Candidate Whalen explained to
one audience when he was asked if he would devote full time
to judicial duties, "When I am on the bench—once every three
months—I will devote my full energies to this position. When
I am not participating in court proceedings, I will continue as
a partner in the firm of Cooper, Erving and Savage."[6]

A civic organization asked both Whalen and Kahn:

"Is this a stepping-stone for other political ambitions?"
It was a question worthy of Clintonian interpretation and definition. The one-word answer from Whalen was "No." Kahn
used 47 words to deny such ambition. The key words among
them were "My only desire now. . . ."

* * *

The non-campaign for the judgeship provided some intriguing insights.

A two-fold brochure prepared by Whalen's Citizens Committee emphasized stature in practice of the law, declaring Whalen "one of the area's most brilliant attorneys . . . uniquely qualified for the City Court judgeship . . . a partner in one of Upstate New York's outstanding law firms . . . has appeared in all courts in the state . . . admitted to practice in the United States Supreme Court."

At times, newspapers reporting on the campaign seemed to suggest that the Whalen-Kahn contest was over-shadowing the mayoralty race between Corning and his oppo-nent, Albert S. Hartheimer. Such an impression was erroneous, for Al Hartheimer waged an intelligent, vigorous, and worthy campaign, especially in comparison with some previous Republican efforts.

But the drama of a disloyal Democratic insider fasci-nated the press. Whalen, termed "one of the more attractive personages" the Democrats "could possibly have offered the voters," was seen by the editors as a suitable foil for Kahn's abandonment of the party where he had prospered.

The Whalen campaign calendar was filled throughout the two months leading up to the November 4 voting; rallies, meetings, clambakes, church picnics, parties, teas, street tours kept the candidate hopping. In October, he averaged a couple of engagements every day except for three open Sundays.

Repeatedly, the minority vote was actively courted. During a walk with ward leader Homer Perkins along a half-dozen Arbor Hill streets, he expounded to a reporter, "The voter is sophisticated enough that he wants to know who is running and talk to him." At the time, Whalen was president of Clinton Square Neighborhood House on North Pearl Street, where the clientele was largely of minority residents. For Art Mitchell's ethnically oriented programs on WABY, Whalen was interviewed three times in October alone.

Lawyers—175 of them—signed up for the Whalen committee that was Jim Drislane's inspiration. Several Albany

Law School students worked in the campaign. A recruit was spontaneously found in a meeting attended by 27 students at the College of Saint Rose. He was Kenneth Ringler, a Siena student from an Albany Democratic household who was so impressed by the Whalen presentation that he promptly volunteered.[7]

At his Saint Rose talk, the candidate declared that "Positions like this should not be decided by popular vote; the public has no real way of knowing who is best qualified. "Asking the electorate to pick a judge," he added, "is like asking the electorate to pick the chief of surgery at Albany Med."

"The Democratic Party is far from perfect," he conceded at another point. "But the office of City Court judge is not a platform for reforming a political party. I am a lawyer running with the backing of a particular party for the position of judge. I am not attempting to save that party," The message had eerie overtones of the position and policies he would actively accept and employ more than a decade later. But regardless of his view, it was quite apparent that others regarded him as a man who could indeed "save the party."

Doc Rivett's advice was generally followed. But the "short and concentrated exposure" Whalen-Kahn contest that he counseled was far from concentrated, though more heated in its latter stages. Two weeks before Election Day, the *Knickerbocker News* said that Whalen had belatedly "come to roll up his sleeves"—after appearing to dawdle—and to "seek the office with vigor." Such an estimate of his earlier effort was well off the mark.

Kahn actually remained a Democratic committeeman even while a Republican candidate—a point he sought to emphasize. Although he could not make use of the party's name and logo, his advertising featured the Democratic emblem, the star, whenever possible. One ad embroidered his name with 141 stars and scattered 330 more around the page. But when he began combining the label of Democrat with the party's symbol, Whalen went to court. Just before a ruling was due, Kahn suddenly abandoned that advertising.

The Republicans thought that their capture of the Democratic deserter was magical. At a bumptious mid-October fund-raiser, Nelson Rockefeller pumped up an optimistic dinner party by likening the reborn Albany Republicans—still high from the previous year's quaff of successes—to the New York Mets, the Cinderella team that had just won the World Series. He hailed Joe Frangella, the county chairman, as another Davey Johnson, the Mets' manager. Frangella had engineered the subversion and recruitment of the Democrats' young star.

A published estimate of Kahn's campaign spending was $40,000, or 50% greater than the office would pay altogether in its six-year term. The Whalen campaign, under the determined but conservative guidance of Jimmy Drislane, spent not much more than half of Kahn's budget. Inasmuch as his campaign had no organized fund-raising effort on his behalf, the budget for expenditures was provided from the County Committee's customary resources. After the voting, the campaign's treasury owed a few hundred dollars to vendors. Visiting headquarters, Whalen mentioned this to Jimmy Ryan, the committee's treasurer at the time. Ryan left the room and returned shortly with cash covering the bills.

Whalen was successful in coming up with an issue that made sense in relation to the office. The catch was: Could he get it across to the audience for whom it should matter most? The idea needed to be repeated to all who might listen.

City Court has a special section—Small Claims Court—where persons seeking minor amounts of cash or damages (the limit at the time was $300) can represent themselves without a lawyer's involvement. There, as the candidate described it in language resembling an echo of the old frontier, "An individual can seek his own justice."

Small Claims sessions were held on Wednesday mornings and, as Whalen pointed out, people "most likely to use this court are working individuals." His idea was to move the sessions to Monday evenings, arguing that this "would provide an opportunity for them to appear before the court in their

free time instead of having to take time off from jobs in order
to appear in the morning." Whalen, having acquired considerable workaday experience as a laborer, had gained insight into
the consequences of enforced job absence.

His proposal, in theory, would appeal to the electorate
at large as compassionate and progressive. Some skeptics
wondered whether opportunity to settle their arguments after
dark had much chance of becoming a hot issue among the presumed beneficiaries, those suing or being sued over relatively
trivial sums and squabbles.[8]

* * *

Both the *Times Union* and the *Knickerbocker News*
endorsed Kahn. The editorials cited Whalen's association with
Cooper Erving as a strong negative factor: "A local law firm
that is tied about as closely as one can be to the Albany
Democratic organization" (*Times Union*) and" An old, old
Albany law firm that has had an old, old friendly relationship
with the Albany County Democratic organization"
(*Knickerbocker News*). This editorial added, with more than a
touch of insinuation:

"Even as the Democratic Party presents, with unsullied
hand, yet another of its sons as candidate, concern is proper
over what, if anything, the hand the party keeps concealed
behind its back is doing."

The *Times Union*'s endorsement was somewhat more
restrained, denying that it "intended to reflect . . . in any manner on either the personal integrity or the professional capabil-
ity of Thomas M. Whalen." The editorial noted, however, that
his goal was to "ensure that an openly anti-organization
Democrat" (Kahn) "does not defeat an organization Democrat"
(Whalen).

The *Times Union*'s campaign summation on Halloween
used 600 words to describe selection of a City Court judge in
almost doomsday terminology: The choice between Whalen
and Kahn was termed" an important issue for the future of the

city ," since what the candidates represent "is at stake—one represents the prospect of continuation of the old order and the other represents a further break from it." With a simultaneous contest being waged for Mayor, this language can be regarded as overkill. But it clearly reflected the significance generally placed on the judgeship vote.

* * *

Whalen's race as "the Organization" candidate was run in the shadow of nearly 50 years of the Democratic party's dominance of Albany politics and government— with voters' habits and expectations prevailing accordingly. For 34 of those years, Erastus Corning had been in public office, 28 of them as Mayor, by far the city's preeminent candidate and officeholder.

As the decade of the 1960s opened, he had already completed five 4-year terms. In 1961, he was reelected for a sixth term with a 33,650 majority and was elected again in 1965 by 34,836. But some of the old habits and expectations were in the throes of change.

Immediately after the 1961 election, destruction of some 3,500 dwelling units had begun under the auspices of that occasional Eagle Street resident, Nelson A. Rockefeller. The population of Albany decreased by nearly 15,000 during the 1960s in part because of the demolition of those 98 acres of humanity and the concomitant exit to the suburbs by impatient Albanians eager for a better life in a healthier community.

Further, returns in the three annual elections immediately before 1969 had shown a remarkable resurgence in the opposition's totals in comparison to votes for Democratic candidates.

In 1969, Daniel P. O'Connell—varying his annual brush-off ("The Usual") to reporters' requests for predictions— forecast a 35,000 margin for Corning.

The Mayor actually was reelected by 22,663, or less than two-thirds of the optimistic bluster—or derision—in the forecast.

O'Connell's stubbornness inadvertently revealed not merely his habitually arrogant inflexibility but, this time, a very considerable error. And also an apparent readiness to ignore a major tide that had been flowing throughout the 1960s in the city he bossed. To have suggested that Corning would improve on his majorities in his most recent elections despite a newly activated opposition party in a city suffering a major population decline, was bordering on the irrational. Boastfully tough and crankily crotchety, yes, but sensible, no. It was an invitation to embarrassment, ridicule, and insurrection.

For some, the cumulative effect of the changing demographics and voting patterns raised legitimate questions as to whether O'Connell was out of touch with the times. He apparently failed to take into account the fact that Rockefeller's wrecking ball had chased one-fifth of Albany's previously normal Democratic vote out of the downtown area and, often, out of the city. And, further, whether he was truly as much in control of the party, the city, and the county as tradition and lore maintained.

* * *

The interest inspired by the extraordinary nature of the Whalen-Kahn competition was evident in the fact that 225 more votes were cast for them than for Corning and Hartheimer combined.

Whalen more than doubled Kahn's vote despite the opponent's spirited and relatively expensive effort. Whalen's 35,961 votes (68%) represented a 19,072 majority over Kahn's 16,889, and that winning margin was a better showing than had been made in the city by any Democrat only a year earlier, except for Eugene Devine's and Hubert Humphrey's.

For a judicial office, the contest had been unusually keen, the non-campaigning campaign active and sharp. An overconfident Democrat lulled by O'Connell's complacency could have been overtaken by Kahn—just as, for recent instance, complacent Dick Conners (managed by Kahn) had been overwhelmed three years earlier. Democratic candidates' margins in the city had been reduced by up to 50% and, in some cases, by substantially greater amounts. Nevertheless, their watchword—reputedly voiced by O'Connell himself—continued to be, "We *stand* for office, we don't run." Luckily for Tom Whalen—warned by the experience of 1966, 1967, and 1968, and with Jim Drislane's determined shepherding—he *ran*.

"A surprisingly easy win," as a reporter expressed it, was the result.

The returns evoked rounds of applause from party-goers—campaign workers led by Drislane—at the Whalen home, tuned to Channel 13. When it was official, the winner and his father put in an appearance at headquarters downtown, then came back to wind up the party on South Pine Avenue well past midnight. In the morning, a headline described Tom Whalen as jubilant.

* * *

Whalen's victory became an undeniable factor in his subsequent career in higher public office. At the very least, it demonstrated that he was an electable candidate despite his lack of experience at the time. And, viewed in a larger perspective, it cast a long shadow toward goals and triumphs to come. To many, he was now a marked man within his party, and a widespread assumption grew that he was being groomed for important office.

After the election, an individual identified as a "Democratic stalwart" was cited by the *Times Union* as having argued during the campaign that Whalen was "the only man in this city who can beat Larry Kahn."

And with greater hindsight, a prominent Democrat much later asserted that ever since the 1969 success Whalen was generally viewed as the eventual successor to Corning.

The electability that he demonstrated at the age of 35 turned out to be the only time he was called upon to run a serious campaign even though he won three more elections.

When he was elected to the Common Council's presidency in 1981, he had no opponent. In his first contest for Mayor four years later (as an incumbent) he took 92% of the vote. And for his 1989 reelection he again had no opponent. In the two mayoralty elections, it is fair to say, he had considerably more popular support from the city's voters-at-large than from his party's own functionaries. This, too, was an omen.

NOTES

[1] A highlight for both Whalen and Rivett in the 1950 renewal of Vincentian's rivalry with Christian Brothers Academy was "one of the strangest plays I've ever seen," still vivid in the reporter's recollection a half-century later. Whalen, one of VI's quarterbacks, was on the bench in the fourth quarter, with his team leading 19 to 7 but now trapped on its own one-yard line on third down. Bill Boehner, VI's coach, called for Whalen to go back into the game—not in the backfield but to snap the ball from the center's position. He fulfilled the coach's instruction perfectly: a pass high and long, out of the field of play. The ball ended up in the bleachers. Though the play gave CBA two points, as Boehner planned, it brought VI out to kick from its 30-yard line, a strategy that pulled VI out of immediate peril. But the advantage was nullified almost immediately, by a CBA touchdown. Vincentian held on to win, 19-16.

[2] In December 1996, a *Times Union* review of 75 years of the Democratic party's primacy in Albany reused this photograph. It was the only picture of Whalen in a large display of politicians' likenesses. His subsequent mayoralty and the immense Whalen photo file accumulated in those years were inexplicably ignored by the newspaper.

[3] And now the Whalen family was complete. The fifth child, Jonathan, had been born some six months earlier, in October

1968. His siblings were Matthew, born September 1966; Mark, August 1964; Thomas, April 1963; and Laura, July 1961.

[4] In subsequent years the record amply bore him out.

[5] There is, of course, no connection between reality and the following anecdote which columnist William Safire once used to slyly introduce another topic in one of his twice-weekly commentaries. As he related it, "The story is told of the corrupt Albany judge who called opposing counsel into his chambers and said: 'Plaintiff slipped me $5,000 to throw the case his way, and the defendant gave me 10 to deliver for him. How's about another five from the plaintiff and I decide the case on its merits.'" Apparently in some circles Albany judges have over the years acquired some of the fame long and also undeservedly held by Philadelphia's lawyers.

[6] During his six-year term, Judge Whalen rotated with his colleagues—Harold Segal and Evariste Lavigne, when he took office, and later John Yanas, Morton Lynn, and Leonard Weiss—in sitting for a full month every third month. And on every fourth weekend, each judge presided in the city's Police Court.

[7] Ken Ringler became not only an active volunteer for the campaign but later a close friend whose Republican persuasion (developed years later in the suburbs) did not mar a personal attachment that persisted for some three decades. Contemporaneous with the Whalen mayoralty's last term, Ringler was elected twice as Supervisor of the suburban Town of Bethlehem. He and Whalen retired from office on the same day, New Year's Eve of 1993.

[8] Campaigning aside, the idea did move ahead. The court's sitting judges gave their assent to a tryout for the innovation; then, with Richard J. Comiskey of the Administrative Board of the Judicial Conference, Whalen helped shepherd the proposal through the board and gain approval for it. When put into effect early in 1970, the Monday evening schedule attracted a couple of dozen cases each night the court was in session. Soon it was deemed to be a highly successful idea which did in fact save time and money for a certain sizeable clientele. Because he had followed through on the campaign promise, he gained a newspaper's commendation: though "the election promises of politicians are ever the butt of post-election jokes, we have an exception right here in Albany in which a politician made a promise and kept it."

Conflict and Confrontation

In the middle of the election campaign of 1969, an untoward event overtook Albany—the sudden death in mid-August of Gene Robb, the Hearst Corporation's publisher of the *Times Union* and *Knickerbocker News*. For years, he had been yearning for some Albanian to stand up and "take City Hall."

A forthright Nebraskan who exemplified the observation that "For years, Nebraska watched many of its youngest, best, and brightest go elsewhere," Gene Robb had been identified as a brilliant member of Hearst's legal staff. He arrived in Albany in 1953 upon receiving his first publishing portfolio, the *Times Union*, from the empire's upper echelon.

After educating himself about the city's mores and idiosyncrasies for a half-dozen years, Robb finally felt secure in innovating a policy of outspoken editorial comment based in more vigorous reporting. The combination brought him and the papers into frequent conflict with the O'Connell/Corning organization and city administration. (Through Robb's leadership, Hearst acquired the *Knickerbocker News*, an afternoon newspaper, from Gannett in 1960.)

"Those were the days we came toe-to-toe with the Albany political hierarchy," in the view of Duane LaFleche, city editor of the *Knickerbocker News* in that period.[1] He attributed the warfare to "the courage of a remarkable publisher."

The strife began promptly when the *Times Union* undertook genuine coverage of a spirited local race—a rare element in the paper's attention to local politics at that time. In the year of the Kennedy-Nixon election campaign, a Republican attorney, Irving Waxman, was running against the Democratic Congressman, Leo W. O'Brien, a former *Times Union* reporter and an O'Connell fixer. The boss sent Corning to Hearst headquarters to object to the unexpected introduction of some honest newspapering, but the complaint was merely passed along to Robb to handle as he saw fit. He stood pat (and refrained from exciting the *Times Union*'s new editor about it until two years had passed).[2]

In that campaign, incidentally, the *Times Union* endorsed O'Brien, editorially, but the *Knickerbocker News* endorsed Waxman, with the publisher determining the choices in order to maintain what he saw as necessary—a show of "balanced" support in spite of the Democrats' overwhelming majority. (Corning had denounced such balancing as "phony" and a "sham" that was absurd.)

As differences grew wider and more heated, O'Connell ordered legal advertising withdrawn from the daily newspapers and placed instead in a country weekly (for the county's advertising) and created a strange little sheet masquerading as the city's journal to carry its advertising. The penalty to the newspapers amounted to about a quarter-million dollars in lost revenue each year—but the publisher made no move to retrieve that income through compromising his newspapers' independence. During that period, Robb's Capital Newspapers reputedly were one of only two profit centers in Hearst's newspaper holdings.

* * *

As the *Times Union*'s executive editor, I was subpoenaed by an Albany County grand jury to appear one March morning at 10 o'clock. The subpoena was, in fact, served on me at my desk at exactly 10. Clearly, the timing was arranged so that I would have no chance to obtain a lawyer's advice in any respect. I was examined by a prosecutor at length, under oath,

before the grand jurors. His questions demanded my explanation of the separate meaning of each single word in an editorial that had criticized members—the Republican members—of
the county's Board of Elections for their lackadaisical approach
to their responsibilities in protecting voters' rights. I was called
to testify once more on the subject; no damage occurred,
though the shadow of a trap—potential perjury accusation—
always was in the background and the flagrant attempt to
intimidate was only too obvious. I was counseled on those
subsequent occasions and similar ones by Mr. Waxman and by
Samuel E. Aronowitz of the firm of O'Connell and Aronowitz,
the newspapers' lawyer, who appears elsewhere in this
account. I was advised of my potential vulnerability to entrap-
ment on any of four trumped-up allegations.

Later that year, Mr. Robb and several editors were summoned before the grand jury to explain one or another of our
sins—"pilloried by a grand jury composed of political hacks,"
said Duane LaFleche.[3] We editors were advised by our respective lawyers to refuse to sign a waiver of immunity, at which
point we were excused from testifying—but Gene Robb signed
and testified for a very tense hour. The immediate goal probably was to find someone contradicting himself or another person, thereby setting up the presumption of perjury. The long-
range objective was to discourage the Albany newspapers
from vigilant reporting and vigorous commentary. "I never
heard of a comparable situation in the United States," Mr. Robb
said, in underscoring the gravity of the O'Connell/Corning
assault on the freedom of the press.

* * *

Soon after Mr. Robb's untimely death at the age of 59,
the newspapers were ready to move several miles from their
plant on Sheridan Avenue in downtown Albany, as he had
planned. The strategically selected location in Colonie near the
junction of the new Northway and Albany-Shaker and
Maxwell roads, was right at the head of Wolf Road, which was

soon to undergo vast development. Disputes with the Democratic hierarchy were "a most substantial factor in the move . . . out of the mainstream," in LaFleche's opinion. But the precipitating cause was action by Erastus Corning.

The initial impetus for the move was a November 1964 strike by the Newspaper Guild during which the papers were published on schedule for 18 days because the mechanical "craft" unions honored their contracts with the publisher. But the papers could not be distributed widely because of Guild picketing in front of the plant's loading dock, which fronted the public sidewalk. Despite a court order, Albany police would not remove the pickets from blocking this vital entrance to the plant. Gene Robb, blaming the antagonism of the Corning administration, vowed that his papers would not be victimized in that way again.

The move out of the city five years later was significant not only for that straightforward purpose. Even more significant was the disappearance from Albany's boundaries of the periodicals that presumably were there to record the city's pulse. In commercial terms, the move turned out to be a vast blessing for the corporation, for it centered the enterprise physically athwart a rapidly growing business and residential area. The newspapers were now geographically positioned to permit coverage of other cities as adequately as Albany's, and to exploit their advertising potential. One long-term effect, however, was to diminish the newpapers' focus on Albany (presumably their central, home city) as they greatly increased attention to other cities and suburbs in search of the added circulation that would enhance their value as an advertising medium.

But if Albany's loss of Gene Robb's plant was to have long-range effect, the loss of the man himself was at least as important. For the decade of the 1960s his zealous leadership was the community's critical ingredient. The absence of his prestige and influence, created by respect for his integrity, independence, and determination, unfortunately would make a substantial difference, in the years ahead, in Albany's response to its opportunities and its challenges.

Gene Robb was a statesman, too, in the world of journalism and publishing. He had served as president of the American Newspaper Publishers Association, a distinction in itself, but his interests and influence found many outlets. He had prepared for his career with studies leading to degrees from the University of Nebraska, Princeton University's Woodrow Wilson School of Public Affairs, and George Washington University's law school. In the Hearst Corporation's hierarchy, he ranked as a vice president and director. His dedication to his profession (begun at an early age as a reporter for the *Lincoln Star* in his hometown) might be summed up in one of his calls for its striving toward its constitutionally protected destiny:

"Newspapers can, must, and will continue to appeal to people who think and act—rather than to those who simply sit and watch." A profound thinker, he himself was an activist in the greatest sense of that term.

Gene Robb effectively fit a description once applied to the late Lord Rothermere, publisher of London's *Daily Mail* and other newspapers:

"He was the quintessential publisher—passionate for his papers, robust in his views, and commercially courageous."

NOTES

[1] Duane LaFleche's career at the *Knickerbocker News* extended for more than 35 years. After joining the reportorial staff in 1942, he served for many years as the city editor before becoming the editorial page editor for more than 10 years before retirement. On the city desk, he was noted for having trained numerous young reporters who went on to journalistic careers at metropolitan newspapers or elsewhere in the media. He instituted active coverage of

the arts by his newspaper, inspiring this with his own reviews and criticism. The Albany League of the Arts presented its prized award for his contributions, which included advancing the concept of the Saratoga Performing Arts Center.

2 Corning made at least one other fruitless trip to the Hearst headquarters. He showed up at the office of Richard E. Berlin, the Hearst Corporation's president, shortly after Gene Robb's death. Speculation on the publisher's successor focused on two men, both of whom held executive positions at the newspapers. One of the aspirants was Robert J. Danzig, a 38-year-old native Albanian who had worked his way up from a stockroom clerk in the circulation department. The Democratic leadership saw Danzig as being too close to his mentor, Robb, and assumed—quite correctly—that he would have absorbed many of the late publisher's strong principles and precepts. Corning made the case against Danzig, implying that the party's disfavor could mean deeper inroads in the newspapers' profitability.

The interview was properly polite; Berlin made no comments or commitments. But a few days later, Danzig got the job. He was publisher for eight years and then became Hearst's general manager for all its newspapers. He retired in 1998. The authority for the references to Corning's visits to Hearst headquarters is the late Lillemor (Lee) Robb, wife of Gene Robb.

3 Author's note: Feelings as a result of all this ran high enough to serve as the genesis for my personal decision three years later to challenge the Democratic organization as a candidate—a successful one, as it turned out—against an Organization man, Richard J. Conners. Because of my own exposure to the harassment and its hazards, I was angered by failure of the Albany County bar to protest the egregious use of a grand jury and prosecutors in the attempted intimidations. Since Albany's lawyers were overwhelmingly affiliated with the dominant party, I resented their meek acquiescence in the harassment. Ironically, these incidents were occurring at the height of the inspirational, idealized national leadership of President John F. Kennedy, who was lionized locally. Tom Whalen was among Albany's silent majority in this instance. To whatever extent he became aware of the running controversy, he never had an active part of it; he was not yet a party committeeman. At that time, I knew of him only as a friendly neighbor with a growing brood in the next block down our street. Our cordial acquain-

tance was many years in the offing and much was yet to occur in numerous perceptions and events during those years.

"A Lesson in Humanity"

"The human experience in all its unhappiest emotions
anger, fear, revenge, hostility, greed"—
as played out several hundred times a year was "marvelous
education" for a lawyer sitting as a part-time judge in
Albany's City Court.

"A people's court" was Whalen's view of the modest tribunal,
where at first hand he was presented with a "very
educational opportunity" that few private citizens would
ever find occasion to share—"a lesson in humanity."

"It was a wonderful learning experience in terms of
the workings of the law, the judiciary, and human nature,"
he said of his six years on the bench, in an interview with
D. Michael Ross for the Albany Law School's magazine.

Customarily, with nearly two dozen cases on the
calendar each morning, the judge presided over eight or
ten pairs of indignant and strident litigators, plaintiff
righteously confronting recalcitrant defendant, typically an
irate landlord pressing a delinquent tenant—or with roles
reversed.

City Court's three judges alternated on its bench
year-round, each serving a total of four months—plus
hearing Small Claims Court quarrels and misunder-
standings, sitting in Police Court every third weekend, then
filling in when Holt-Harris was absent from Traffic Court.

The Devine Connection

Whalen's intimacy with one of his senior partners, Dan O'Connell's personal lawyer, extended far beyond the law office where, as Whalen described it, "He took me under his wing."

Tom and Denie Whalen, two decades junior to Gene and Phyllis Devine, occasionally were entertained at dinner at Jack's or Keeler's downtown or at the Wolfert's Roost club. In his late 20s and 30s, Tom strolled of an evening the four blocks westward to 88 Euclid Avenue. There the men would sit leisurely for hours of rambling talks around the table in the kitchen of the Devines' big white Colonial. They would cover subjects from the pennant races to political developments either national or, more likely, closer to home. And often, naturally, some pending case at the firm. The walks back home seemed enriched by visions of wider horizons, imbued with excitement and promise.

With his extensive legal experience, his long-standing public elective office, his bank directorships, his stature and repute within the party, Devine offered valuable insight and contacts. Politically, he was very close to the top. A classic photograph of Dan O'Connell, taken in his eightieth year, reveals him in the dim light of a party committee's meeting, casting larger-than-life menacing shadow. Immediately beside him, the round, beaming face of an acolyte is also caught by the camera. It is Devine's. Just a year before the Whalen 1969 candidacy, running for a fifth three-year term as County Treasurer, he had been the only prominent Democratic candidate in Albany County who survived the party's debacle at the 1968 polls.

In those days, to have Eugene Devine as a sponsor was—as often was said of him—"really something." A winner even in a disastrous year when the rest of the ticket was going down ignominiously, he could stand off Erastus in a show-down, could quote Nelson's innermost complaints about a frustrating deal, could open Dan's door unbidden, and could provide behind-the-hand counsel even when the old tyrant was surrounded by his own judges.

Devine's push behind Whalen at the base of the greasy pole was easily enough to win the only primary election imaginable in Albany in 1969—the contest for the boss's approval. And, though the protege's record lacked the many years of low-level servitude commonly demanded of politically ambitious Albany lawyers, Devine had no cause to view him as the man who eventually would break the Organization's heart. Every sign subscribed to the proposition that Tom Whalen was safe.

After his 1969 success in helping to get Whalen elected to the City Court, Devine had another inspiration two years later: Run him for District Attorney. In this, Devine may have had special motivation, for he was in a tight race for reelection to a sixth term and he could benefit from a strong new vote-getter as a running mate. But Whalen demurred and then held out even after an audience Devine insistently set up with O'Connell. "An offer you can't refuse" was not unknown when face-to-face with the boss. Whalen's may not have been a pointblank refusal but the effect was the same: No thanks. And he not only got away with it but his stock rose among those who'd never found the courage to stand up; this would have included Corning, whose one evident instance of disobedience was an unseemly personal relationship that O'Connell frowned on. Altogether, Devine's failed effort to recruit his younger partner may have inadvertently been a real boost for Whalen's political stature and future.[1]

In that 1971 election, Devine did have a very close shave—after relying, inevitably, on the Organization's old tactics. The "complete" returns showed him as the loser by a few hundred votes, and only the traditional miracle of the recount saved him from defeat with a winning margin, finally, of 255 votes. Whalen recalled hearing of an understanding within the Organization that, in fact, even the recount had failed to provide enough change and consequently Devine really lost the election. This turnaround closely paralleled Dan O'Connell's experience in 1919 when one vote tabulation after the polls closed showed him a loser in the contest to elect the city's Assessors. But the next day enough additional ballots were "discovered" to elect him by 163 votes. (Devine's eventual running mate for District Attorney, Tom Keegan, was soundly defeated.)

A controversial issue was Devine's role in cancellation of Albany County's sale of $70 million in Empire State Plaza construction bonds, thus assisting a Democratic ploy in a fiscal/political falling-out of Corning's with Nelson Rockefeller.

* * *

Gene Devine was to play a critical role—not as the leading man but rather as a bungling Pink Pantherish tragicomic—in a scenario featuring certain Organization operatives.

The scene: the Cooper Erving Savage law firm where he was a senior partner (and which Whalen had joined in 1959) maintained its offices on the uppermost floors of the picturesque bank building numbered as 35 State Street though it wrapped gracefully around its Broadway corner.

That building includes an unpublicized, invisible adjunct—a large vault that lies beneath State Street. The vault was to become a colorful part of Whalen's advanced education in Albany's traditions and its political manners.

During the law firm's long tenancy—more than 80 years—it made use of the vault for storage of files that had to be retained over long periods. Obviously, occasional weeding

was necessary, and early in his career Whalen was detailed to
determine what might be discarded (and where valuable but
forgotten documents might exist). Long-outdated files were
sifted and evaluated. In some instances, documents were
saved, to be offered to the Albany Institute of History and Art
for their potential value in illuminating corners of the city's
past.

Properly disposing of such records was a serious matter for the law partners. To pass title to the papers, a formal
ceremony was conducted in the firm's circular library far
upstairs. "The whole weeding process went on for years and I
painstakingly went through each file to determine if any held
historical value," Whalen recalled. "I was able to find a lot."
The Institute's annual report occasionally took note of this,
reporting acquisition of "ancient archives" from Cooper Erving
Savage that "added depth to the Institute's unique working
research and reference library."

In the course of winnowing, Jean Savage, the widow of
one of the firm's name partners, B. Jermain Savage, was deferentially involved because she was, in effect, the last remaining
link to the existing partners' antecedents. Like Ed Rooney, his
successor as the most prominent partner, "Jerry" Savage was
also president of the First Trust bank downstairs.

"Mrs. Savage and I became good friends," the Mayor
related, " and for several years I would visit her regularly in her
apartment at 248 State Street. She was a wonderful lady."

Whalen and other lawyers—with slight exception—
were made to understand that one section of the vault was off-
limits. They were aware of scuttlebutt that some of the
Democratic party's money was kept there—seemingly within a
bank's auspices but not in its own vault or, actually, in its possession at all.

It was here, one day in 1972, that the incredible
occurred, according to reasonably credible lore.

The time was immediately after a classic mistake by
Devine, whose lofty political status and his eminence among
the Roman Catholic diocesan laity meant that when the clergy

needed an ambassador he was a likely candidate. That enviable status led directly to one of the most revealing episodes in Albany's gaudy political chronicles.

Bishop Edwin Broderick, new to the diocese in 1969, was viewed by some in his flock as overly compassionate in his occasional advocacy of unpopular movements, such as one that was agitating the populace soon after the bishop's arrival in his see; namely, the right of municipal employees to organize and gain union representation. By 1972, he had interested himself in the frustrated demands of Albany's firefighters to win the city's recognition of their bargaining power, an idea anathema to Corning and O'Connell, who sought to deny the whirlwind by shutting a damper.

He persuaded Devine to argue the firemen's case before O'Connell, not only urging that the boss grant the union status they sought, but in effect that he humiliate Corning, who was very publicly opposed to unionization.

The response was prompt, brief, and forceful: "Mind your own business," Devine was angrily told, "and tell your bishop that, too!" Or words to that effect.

When the story was inevitably laid out for public display, the Mayor and the entire Democratic establishment were irate—aghast, too, at the credulous, devious effrontery of Broderick, and joyously vindictive toward Devine's part in it. Devine was immediately *persona non grata* to Corning, who had never regarded him highly. It was a prime example of the "fishing behind the net" behavior that Corning abhorred and frequently denounced.

The shame of being caught in such a caper was bad enough. But there followed shortly a more specific example of Devine's fall from grace among those around Dan O'Connell.

* * *

By doing Bishop Broderick's bidding, speaking up on behalf of the firefighters, he had violated the O'Connell code.

No matter how high he had risen, he no longer was deemed trustworthy.

To 35 State Street, down to its basement level, and into the vault came Dan O'Connell's nephew-in-Iaw, Donald Lynch. He was a functionary of the Democrats' county committee, and enforcer of his uncle's wishes and whims—and accordingly respected with that degree of salaami accorded to people who carry menace in their manner and even in their toothpick pockets.[2]

Donald Lynch also carried a brown paper sack that afternoon, a grocery bag that previously had held such commonplace items as lettuce and potatoes and condensed milk. Once in the vault, he began to fill the empty sack with a long series of moderate-sized bundles, for he was packing up $250,000 in cash, the party's current nest egg.[3] Very pointedly, Devine was being formally relieved of its custody.

Goal accomplished, back upstairs the messenger went, out the door into the daylight, and up State Street, grocery bag securely clutched in one arm's grasp, like a Kennedy headed for a touchdown in a game of touch football.

The authority for the scenario was Eugene Devine himself, who said he had witnessed it all.

Devine's health, undermined by a rather flamboyant life style, deteriorated early, and two weeks before the election that closed his final term of office he died, aged only 61, in late October of 1974. It was several years too soon for him to witness the culmination of his protégé's career in which he had played such a decisive early role. But he would have enjoyed the protégé's achievement of gaining Erastus Corning's office—if not necessarily pleased by the style and philosophy of government that prevailed thereafter.

The party's cash reservoir was thus preserved for whatever purposes the chairman might have in mind. The timing was years late for its distribution in units of five dollars each, the old Albany tradition. Other division would be determined, quietly so. The source, too, was obscure—contributions that could not pass inspection, presumably. Goodwill offerings from vendors, some would say—goodwill but not necessarily voluntarily offered.

NOTES

[1] Whalen later rebuffed yet another election prospect. He was one of those "mentioned" in 1976—after Devine's death—as a candidate for the State Assembly when Tom Brown decided to quit after three frustrating terms. But he was not at all interested. Upon hearing his name in a radio newscast, he called the Whitehall Road house where O'Connell was sequestered in his last months, and asked for a few minutes' interview. He went and made it clear to the old man that he would not be a candidate. His forthright action, however, again attracted attention, for the next year both Corning and Pennock called on him for help in their campaigns. These calls to action ended a long withdrawal from the political scene. The 1976 nomination and Assembly seat eventually went to Dick Conners. An office suitable for Tom Whalen's talents and interests was still five years distant.

[2] Whalen had heard much earlier from Lynch what presumably was intended as sage advice to a political greenhorn: "You've got a wonderful future. But you ought to be on the team! Play ball!" Lynch didn't bother to add, "Or else." Whalen shunned the advice, but he remembered the chill of it. Lynch had a handshake that could be painful; it matched a cocky stance and a demanding stare that proclaimed, "We're in charge. Do as you're told." He might well have fitted the movie role of a George Raft. His piercing eyes dominated a strong-featured, leathery face always heavily tanned. In his absence, he was sometimes referred to as "The Snake."

A Montanan from the tough town of Miles City, Lynch gained a new uncle who provided a title and legitimate income, making him Deputy County Treasurer when he was an unproven 26-year-old straight out of Albany Law. At 30, deemed ready to go before the voters, he was elected County Clerk for the first of five terms. He then took over from Leo Quinn at the party's headquarters, a year after SIC investigators criticized what they called excessive profits from his sideline—buying up tax- delinquent properties on the cheap.

[3] Another good story deserving of a slightly closer examination. One-hundred bills (of any denomination, of course) weigh .22 of a pound—a convenient aid in calculating such a commodity's bulk vis-a.-vis its portability. So, if the package that Donald Lynch was said to have carried up State Street had consisted of dollar bills, he'd have wanted a helper or two, for $250,000 in singles would weigh about 550 pounds. In familiar $5s, the burden would have been somewhat more manageable—about 110 pounds, but at that weight still not something to tuck under one's arm. If the bills were $50s, he'd have an 11-pound bundle. But in C-notes, he'd have been carrying a comfortable 5.5 pounds. So a mix of $50s and $100s would have been a feasible load. Any sizable proportion of smaller bills (in $20s, more than 27 pounds) would not have worked out well. Yes, he could have done just what was described—that is, if the Democrats preferred their cold-storage cash in large denominations. Not quite so handy in certain respects, but obviously more portable.

A Time to Part

Within an abbreviated period measurable almost in weeks after Dan O'Connell's burial near his brothers and Leo Quinn, in 1977, a bitter contest that had been unthinkable in his lifetime exploded among Albany Democrats.

An insider-of-insiders in the O'Connell era, Charlie Ryan, one of the famous twins whose reputation almost surpassed legend, was a principal challenger. Among the favors he had collected over the years was the privilege of sitting as the party's representatives in the county Board of Elections. That responsibility's obvious potential for discreetly doing unto others earned its incumbent great respect—though the fealty would last only while the job existed. Simultaneously, his brother Jimmy who had been running the party's headquarters, doling out patronage at broom, shovel, and mimeo levels, decamped for Florida. Heir to the ironfisted power of Leo Quinn and the insinuating grasp of Donald Lynch, he had controlled access to and dispensation of the Organization's finances.

But all this counted for very little in the face of the counteroffensive by Erastus Corning, who had succeeded O'Connell as county chairman.

Charlie Ryan was removed from the Board of Elections and its $10,700 salary, and soon was deprived of an unpaid but nonetheless significant and sensitive post in the Democratic hierarchy—the office of treasurer of the county committee.

Whalen, lacking even a committeeman's status within

the party, was uninvolved in this uneven struggle, and was just as subdued in other Ryan rebellions. It appeared evident that he had fundamentally made the decisions that he was an Organization man and was ready to play on Corning's team.

And when Ryan tried an end run, seeking the party's nomination for Common Council president—on Corning's own ticket—he was buried in the September primary by the Organization's choice. Ryan won only 29%. Long a feared name in the party and figure in the city, he was now officially a has-been.

* * *

In mid-June of 1983, in one of his first public appearances, exactly two weeks after taking office, Whalen was a speaker at Ryan's seventy-fifth birthday party—a huge affair assumed to have heavy significance in the party. It would have been easy at that time to construe his appearance as a bold political announcement, for Ryan and Corning were political rivals and enemies to the end. And Corning, Albany Democrats' hero, was barely in his grave. No apparent damage was done to Whalen's credibility despite his generous compliments for Corning's old foe.

"In the great traditions of Dan O'Connell and Erastus Corning," Mayor Whalen exhorted the diners, "let us all join together in continuing the strong, vital, and united Democratic party, the party of the people."

He recalled that Mrs. Ryan, having seen him fall from a carriage onto his head as a baby, knew then "that I would want to be Mayor of Albany."

* * *

But Whalen apparently knew instinctively, as he analyzed his course of action later, that Ryan would not be the right person with whom his name and repute should be asso-

ciated. In spite of the two families' long friendship, he concluded that he couldn't expect that Charlie would "do the right
thing" in the tangled world of politics and government in
Albany County. This judgment was proven entirely accurate.

A Jinxed Judgeship

Tom Whalen's parents and his Whalen grandparents, with their roots deep in Troy, were intimate friends of James T. Foley, a prominent lawyer there who in 1949 had become a federal judge at 38. President Truman had appointed Foley immediately after he started his second term, at least partially in recognition of unusually energetic campaigning on his behalf. Somewhere in the background was Foley's friendship with Daniel P. O'Connell, so similar in certain ways to Tom Pendergast of Kansas City, Truman's own early patron.

Foley was so close to O'Connell that he read to him on a regular once-a-week schedule and cooked their evening meal that day. "I heard Dan tell Erastus many times that the Organization should be good for a hundred years," he once wrote in a note to Whalen.

Whalen tried some cases—bankruptcies, commercial litigation, at least one criminal case—in Foley's court. "One of the finest, most compassionate men I've ever known," with "a manner to which all judges might aspire," was Whalen's estimate.[1]

This regard clearly was warmly reciprocated, for when Foley decided in 1980 to take senior status after 30 years in the judiciary, he quickly urged Whalen, at 46, to seek appointment to the seat he would be vacating. O'Connell had been far out of the patronage picture for three years by then, but Foley's highly unusual association with him for more than three decades carried weight seemingly transferable to Whalen's advantage. He had impressed the judge in several cases in federal court.

Foley escorted him to the Second Circuit Judicial Conference held at Buck Hill Falls, a retreat in the Poconos, and introduced him to the circuit's other judges, prospective colleagues he might be working beside. Foley's enthusiasm did seem to place the cart well ahead of the horse. Whalen met with a screening committee set up by Senator Daniel Patrick Moynihan. Corning, in his role as county chairman, cooperated with a rather moderate endorsement.

But then fate, in the form of Ronald Reagan's ardent presidential quest, intervened. Sensing a Reagan victory and a majority in the Senate, Republicans put a damper on further judicial confirmations. All manner of alignments and allegiances were tested in the episode. National and New York politics turned everything upside down. Along with these many changes went Whalen's evaporated opportunity for a federal judgeship in 1980. By the next spring, he had decided to seek elective office in Albany.

* * *

It was a jinxed 13 years later when a parallel frustration took place. Whalen announced in early 1993 his decision not to seek reelection that year. Four months later, Moynihan appeared in City Hall's rotunda to declare his intention to send the Mayor's name to the Clinton White House for nomination to a seat in the U.S. District Court.

Interviews with scores of Albanians were conducted in keeping with protocol to assure a nominee's probity, and Whalen's name was referred to the Justice Department's clearinghouse for judicial appointees. It never emerged from there after Whalen submitted to an interview with an all-female screening group whose questions he construed as unfriendly. His conclusion was that the hostility that had existed between him and some Planned Parenthood activists had been effectively conveyed to Washington.

Meanwhile, the last-ditch Old Guard opposition in Albany found an opportunity to try to settle old scores. A delegation hurried to Washington to put in a bad word where it might hurt most. Back home, they boasted of their efforts, but this probably was a case of overkill, for evidence strongly indicates that the female contingent's vindictiveness had been enough to preclude the necessary action by the President. The fact that Moynihan was in Clinton's doghouse because of his position against Hillary Clinton's health care proposal undoubtedly was a further deterrent, sharply limiting the Senator's leverage.

Whalen had now experienced one of the sharpest of a mayor's perils—vexing and angering a variety of pressure groups merely by making decisions—some of them bound to be misunderstood—that his position and his judgment required of him.

After waiting more than a year for the situation to clear up, Whalen asked Moynihan to withdraw his nomination so he could get on with his life. It was a disappointment at that time, but by this time he was deeply immersed in his efforts at the Rockefeller Institute on behalf of intergovernmental coordination, a project for which he'd become an ardent advocate and missionary.

NOTE

[1] When Foley died in 1990, not long after swearing Whalen in for a new term as Mayor, his friend delivered a heartfelt memorial address to a gathering of the judiciary and lawyers. Foley would have made "an ideal—and successful—candidate for any elective office" because of his positive approach to others and his "high sense of civic responsibility," Whalen told an audience of lawyers and judges. He was "humbled" to be "among the benefici-

aries of Jim Foley's friendship, his patience, and his tolerance," qualities for which, along with fairness and kindness, the judge had vowed to strive.

"A Great Loss, Indeed"

Whalen's frustrated request to Moynihan in late 1994 to withdraw his name from consideration for the judiciary brought a pained response from his sponsor.

"If you feel you can no longer suspend your career," the Senator wrote, "I quite understand. I will communicate your decision to the President. . . . I am disappointed. You have been very patient over these many months. And sorely tried. I fear we have a system for selecting judges that takes too long and asks too much. For your perseverance, you have my great thanks. . . . Your decision will deny New York the talents of a truly fine jurist and a superb, accomplished public man. This is a great loss, indeed."

During that year of patience and perseverance, a book, The Confirmation Mess, by Stephen L. Carter, included virtually a direct (though unintended) commentary on the Whalen nomination: ". . .Very little that is discussed in contemporary confirmation debates has much to do with qualification. . . . We talk little nowadays about a nominee's qualifications. Instead, today's hearing are mostly about disqualifications. When controversy erupts, we spend little time letting the nominee and . . . backers (and supporters) make the positive case, and a great deal of time arguing the case against." (Basic Books, 1994).

The Bird's-Eye View

Learning "a lot of things over a long period" was a key element in Whalen's background for public service in a highly politicized setting. The bottom line appears to have been a realization that, as he said, "the city cried out for so much."

Starting in the early 1960s—not long after he became a practicing lawyer and even closer to his becoming a family man—he was subconsciously registering bits of revealing data and lore which "stayed in the back of my mind."

Some of these fragments came floating by from the people and institutions he encountered in his profession. His access to Eugene Devine contributed glimpses of Albany's political realities, as did his subsequent few years' work as a committeeman carrying out the Organization's assignments. "I had to be in the Organization, earn my stripes, in order to become a participant. I learned what the atmosphere was." But he consciously sought to avoid commitments to these politicians, thereby averting situations "where they could lay claim to me." As a result, despite having been chosen by Corning, "I was pretty much an unknown quantity to everyone" upon coming to office.

"I was getting to understand how the city was run—the assessment practices, the add-on contracts, the patronage, the importance of county committee headquarters.

"And I was thinking about all these things—while making my way to court, walking along a street, returning to the office at lunch." He'd think about having witnessed—as a luncheon guest in Erastus Corning's club—the Mayor with some pals at the grill room's long table, chatting for an hour with the males who had hastened to be on hand, regarding themselves and each other as important in the city's super-structure as Tarzan's apes deferred to him in the jungle's tree-tops. And, young Tom Whalen came to realize, whatever sub-stance lay in their conversations died when Corning would depart gracefully, make his patrician way back to City Hall, and invariably forget about any potentially useful ideas and proposals he'd just heard. (And when the time came for Erastus Corning to consider Tom Whalen as his successor, he might well have thrown onto the scales a recollection of having seen him in good company at the right places—without an inkling of what might have been the younger man's thoughts in those circumstances.)

More charitably, Whalen also could profit from seeing at first hand how "the other half" lived and how selflessly vol-unteers labored at causes. At a North Pearl Street neighbor-hood house, and in other civic groups, he turned into one of the do-gooders despised and derided by most of his Organization associates.

Such contrasts and frustrations "weren't eating at me— I can't say that I had an itch to accomplish some particular thing," was Whalen's recollection.

"But I certainly did get a bird's-eye view of what was going on. It didn't require a genius to know that remedial steps were needed. And, just as apparent, they'd take time if that process was begun. And more time to lift people's spirit and their expectations."

* * *

But his route to these late choices didn't come quickly or easily. For years—most of the quarter-century between his return to Albany from college in 1955 and his joining the Corning ticket in 1981—he had vacillated in making a political choice. Meanwhile, some evolutionary—and a few revolutionary—developments had sharpened the opportunities for dissent. To these, he was not immediately responsive.

"I was disenchanted with the Organization," he recalled, adding, "And yet I was mesmerized by its power and how it really pervaded so much of life in Albany County.

"Although I was certainly interested in what was going on around me, I wasn't much a part of it. I was a busy young lawyer, trying to establish a practice, with a growing young family."

Nonetheless, the thoughts that he quietly was giving to a variety of programs and policies produced a notable, final result: The dispatch with which he was able—and willing—to take on the city's besetting problems as soon as responsibility and power were in his hands is ample testimony to his recognition that, governmentally, Albany was not beyond rescue.

So finally, when the time for accepting that responsibility arrived in mid-1983, he was ready to act decisively for honest, moral administration, repeatedly adopting policies harmful to many of his erstwhile associates, among others. After years and years of temporizing he saw his duty and performed far beyond expectations.

Might he have been an effective agent for reform if as a "busy young lawyer" he'd chosen earlier to start speaking out, even if only for a more efficient manner of governing?

Who can know the answer, or whether the result might have taken him further, faster?

Of one thing we can be sure, however: In 1981, he would not have been Corning's choice as running mate. He never would have become Albany's Mayor by that route.

Whalen would learn in unexpected ways within the Corning relationship. As president of the Common Council, moving it toward an enlarged function in the city government, he unguardedly spoke up on a controversial issue—and quickly found that his new proximity to Corning didn't necessarily include a right to his own opinion.

In the early months of 1982, before the Mayor's long hospitalization began, "Corning wasn't always all that happy with me. I'm thinking especially of one time he called me on the carpet. He demanded—loudly—'What do you think you're doing?' Then he told me 'You don't know what you're talking about!'

"The specific issue was an idea for developing a section of the Pine Bush. A reporter had asked for my view on a development proposal and I pointed out some weaknesses from an ecological standpoint. Corning, who ordinarily took a conservationist's position, in this instance was interested in assisting development. So I learned! And I also learned again that his City Hall really was a one-man shop."

* * *

Upon arriving in the Mayor's office—now "able to do what I wanted to do"—Whalen could "call upon an accumulation of facts governmental and political. This was all extremely helpful." But, "A lot of other people had the same information; I was not privy to knowledge others didn't have." This, of course, is not wholly accurate, for not everyone had a Gene Devine as a partner, an Ed Rooney as a friendly booster—or Thomas Whalen, Jr., as a uniquely dedicated consultant.

Part III:
The Long Year

Introduction

The significance of Corning's indisposition in mid-June was easily misunderstood early on. The timing would have suggested to an earlier generation that perhaps he merely was suffering from a summer colic, the kind that folks would get from mixing a handful of cherries with a tumbler of cold milk.

A fixture as permanent in his own firmament as a Bob Hope or George Burns, he surely would bounce back right away. He would dismiss adversity with his strong backhand as readily as he'd always slapped away critics' carping. Understandably, his current complaint seemed dismissable in an eight-line news paragraph.

But the significance, far from superficial or transient, was compounded of many layers. The fact of his absence from his desk, immediate and obvious, eventually would be superseded as the layers unfolded to display how untidy was his management of Albany's affairs, how hurtful that untidiness had become, how truly he had forfeited his sentiment-charged status as the irreplaceable man, how quickly a freer hand could generate recovery, and therefore how false had been very much of the legend and myth on which the city had subsisted. And how grave the error of having intrinsically linked a political party's fortunes with efficient conduct of official business.

The product of these revelations was to be a decade filled with unpredictable resurgence of Albany's health fiscally, socially, culturally, psychically. All this was to be achieved under the firm—not to say *stern*—hand of Corning's successor,

whom he had personally chosen in a late—almost too late —
burst of prescience.

The chapters which follow explain and interpret the
347 diminishing days marking Erastus Corning's mayoralty—
and how Whalen guided the transition to successful and stunning reality.

The Badly Tangled Web

In mid-afternoon of the last Monday of September in 1982, Whalen took a call at his desk on the sixth floor of the Bankers Trust Building downtown. Vinnie McArdle was calling from his own office farther up State Street where the city's Law Department was isolated in a private office building nearly a quarter-mile from City Hall.[1]

Vinnie, who was, like Tom, a Vincentian Institute and Manhattan College athlete, had starred as a distance runner on the track team. His long legs had carried him to several notable victories and won him a plaque in the college's sports hall of fame. After Albany Law School and establishing a practice, he had worked as one of the city's part-time lawyers under the Corporation Counsel for several years. Then, in 1980, Corning had demonstrated his confidence by promoting him to the top job. The resulting Whalen-McArdle association after Whalen's entry into city government was another instance of chance intervention by family connections. Their fathers, also Manhattan graduates and holders of prominent positions in the State Department of Audit & Control, had maintained a long-established friendship.

Through the nine months in which Tom had held the Common Council's presidency, he and Vinnie had been drawn into occasional contact on the city's business. Since June, with Mayor Corning's hospitalization, they necessarily were in touch much more frequently. And greater collaboration lay ahead. "No one could have been more loyal" to Whalen than McArdle was at this time, Holt-Harris said.

Vinnie's call was relaying a summons from Corning. He wanted to see them both on Tuesday morning. A glance at his calendar showed Tom that he would need to do some shuffling of appointments, but the Mayor's request was a mandate. He'd be there.

* * *

In a pleasant, sunlit corner room, lying so that he could look southwesterly out leafy New Scotland Avenue,[2] the Mayor informed the two men—both of whom he had personally selected for their present positions—that they were to begin preparing the city's budget for 1983. He was initiating the process many weeks earlier than he customarily buckled down to the task. The reason, he neglected to explain, was his quiet plan to leave town shortly.

His directive was communicated in handwritten notes, for he had great difficulty in talking. He was on a respirator, but Whalen was quoted later as having noted that he was "in good spirits" and "very enthusiastic."

Corning's announcement represented a very major concession on his part, for his personal style of municipal budgeting was at the heart of his control of the city's government—and of the city. Idiosyncrasies unique to him and exclusively convenient to his whim were about to be unveiled and—to an unknown degree—dismantled out of his sight, out of his hearing, though not (he must hope) out of his control. Fate was rapidly loosening his fingers' grasp on Albany's pulse, which was slowing in tune with his own. At that hour, an historic retreat by an aging oligarchy had irresistibly started. *Change*— that dreaded word and idea—was on its inevitable way to Albany. And by virtue of Corning's own judgment in a sensitive personnel decision a year and a half earlier, the principal architect of change was destined to be the lawyerly, athletic, family man now seated respectfully—though with certain silent misgivings—on a straight chair between the windows of the old man's sickroom.

Whalen construed the assignment to be "a demonstration that Corning expected that I would play an important role during his period of hospitalization, whatever that period might be." As "that period" became a full year of steadily diminished capacity, it clearly confirmed Corning's bald, self-centered view of his high office. And unflatteringly suggestive, too, of reasons why he successfully insisted that he would not leave the office alive.

A week after handing over the budgetary responsibility, Erastus Corning forevermore departed Albany for a city foreign to his nature—and probably contrary to his own best interests.

* * *

What did the Mayor know, and when did he know it?

That is, at what stages in his tortuous decline did Erastus Corning confront a prolonged series of unavoidable facts and inescapable conclusions about the downhill progress of his ailments, the likelihood of continuing inability to carry on his sworn duties as Mayor of Albany, and—finally—the inevitability of the outcome? Friends testify that, so long as he retained consciousness, he was adamant in a conviction that he would return from Boston to Albany and City Hall. From the best vantage point, Holt-Harris saw that "No matter what the realities were, he believed he would be coming back."

Undoubtedly, his awareness was blunted by denial, by whatever few encouraging signs might have seemed visible along the descending slope, and even by the progressively evasive—and calculated—deceptions woven into the tangled web of reports on his health and his capacity to govern his city.

It's not difficult to find a certain ethical parallel between Franklin D. Roosevelt's illness when he sought and won a fourth term as President in 1944 and Corning's ailments when he was elected for the eleventh time in 1981. Roosevelt survived five months beyond his reelection; Corning lived on for 19 months after November 1981, but they were increasingly miserable months during most of which he was incapable of doing the job he was elected to do.

The issue here is, should either "indispensable man" have run that last time? A telling sidelight is that both showed awareness of their infirmities by deliberately shunting off the men in line to succeed them, and selecting unexpected replacements: Harry Truman for Henry Wallace and Tom Whalen for Jimmy Giblin.

By that act, Corning conceded some degree of uncertainty about completing his eleventh term, which would have run through 1985, when he would be 76—not an unduly advanced age, but he already was living with unmistakable hints of his own mortality. Degenerative disease—first emphysema and then arthritis—that had slowed him down, hobbled and embarrassed him, was soon to incapacitate and humble him. Respiratory troubles began two decades earlier, in 1963, when emphysema was diagnosed. He immediately abandoned his long addiction to Kools. But promptly another affliction beset him. An arthritic hip created great discomfort, resulting in a limp. Soon he stopped leading Albany's traditional biggest parades, those for St. Patrick's Day and Veterans' Day, where the disability would have been so apparent. After his tenth election as Mayor, in 1977, hip-replacement surgery kept him inactive for more than a month.

That final term at the beginning of 1982 started inauspiciously as the Mayor's health prevented him from taking part in a public ceremony marking an unprecedented term in office. With only a few hours remaining before the new term was to begin, Corning called Whalen, who heard a throaty rasp inform him that he should "find Mike Gabrielli and arrange for him to swear you in."[3]

"Then," Corning continued, "you will swear in the Aldermen. I'm just not going to be able to do any of it. I'll take the oath here" (at home).

Whalen carried out the emergency plan as Corning had contrived it. He saw Corning's recommendation of a judge from the State's highest court as a well-meant compliment, an effort to avoid tying Whalen to one of the Organization judges as Corning himself always had been. The media didn't bother to report on the event. Corning's own new term was begun in virtual seclusion. It earned little more attention. He was sworn into his new term in bed at home, while downstairs a small group of quasi-intimates milled about, politely avoiding the temptation to speculate about the possible meaning of this charade overhead.

During the winter he took an extended vacation in Florida, most unusual in his personal history, for even on the lonely hermit-like fishing trips to Maine that he favored, his absence from Albany frequently was merely overnight. He preferred to be in City Hall because he could not ever trust the judgment—or other qualities—of the followers assigned to nominal duties as his department heads. They knew too little about the arts of administration—or about his administration—to function efficiently on their own. And by virtue of his being eternally on hand, they need not learn too much.

As his condition worsened later in the spring, his physician, the venerated Dr. Richard T. Beebe, a specialist in internal medicine, was increasingly concerned. One June morning he felt so ill in the Mayor's office that he walked out and went home before noon. By nightfall, Dr. Beebe ordered him into the Albany Medical Center Hospital, where he would be only steps away from the doctor's own offices. Corning by this time had completed barely one-tenth of the term to which he had just been elected.

From that day—Tuesday, June 15, 1982—forward, he never was out of hospital care (save for two hours of freedom in mid-July). Albany's two newspapers caught up with this beginning of the year's biggest story only on Thursday, in brief, bottom-of-the-page paragraphs. They alternatively anticipated that Corning would be hospitalized for "a few" days or for "several" days. In fact for the next 347 days, his knowledge of the outside world was so circumscribed as to parallel the description in Oscar Wilde's "Ballad of Reading Gaol"—"that little tent of blue which prisoners call the sky."

And so began, perversely, one of the very most significant periods of Corning's mayoralty. Without adequate attention to its detail, no story of his life or career can be complete. The 50 weeks of his terminal illness increasingly thrust responsibility on the man he had just put in place, probably having had in mind his own cloudy status. He would cling to his office to the very last. But his inability to perform most duties meant that his stand-in—quietly recognizing and accepting the onus—thereby began certain governmental changes that forestalled ultimate disaster but also provided a base for the long-overdue reforms that were to characterize the Whalen decade.

Some have called Corning's selection of Whalen as his best single act in his own 40 official years. ("Mayor Whalen may well be the best and most interesting thing to happen in Albany" in all the years of the O'Connell-Corning hegemony, wrote a political scientist, Richard H. Kendall, in 1986.[4]) To whatever extent these ideas may be true, Whalen's success as Mayor firmly took root in the 50-week prelude, more impressively so as its days passed. He could be effective in the long term because he'd stepped forward in the short term.

Corning's conduct, including his retreat into non-performance, is a haunting story in itself, as related in this section. "Uncertainty, tension, and foreboding prevailed," Whalen wrote of this period several years later.

* * *

Less than a week after Corning's hospitalization began, the Democratic state convention—critical to the hopes of Mario Cuomo, whom he stubbornly favored for Governor—opened in Syracuse.[5] Cuomo desperately needed to demonstrate sufficient support there to earn his way into a primary election in September combating his Nemesis, a man who had always defeated him.

Imagine the very frailty of Erastus Corning's protests as he railed against the confinement that would keep him from the convention's floor and its smoke-filled rooms. His absence

came at the crux of his willful odds-against effort for the man
he had come to know and respect during Cuomo's eight years'
residence as a tenant of the city, in the stark quarters of its deteriorating old Wellington Hotel (first as Hugh Carey's Secretary
of State and then as Lieutenant Governor).

Perforce, Corning was absent from that imperative
scene, his voice and maneuvers and counsel missing and
missed.[6] But Cuomo, the underdog, did receive enough delegates' votes to qualify for a primary against Ed Koch, who had
repeatedly won in their past rivalry in New York City. So the
large block of votes Corning controlled in Albany County
would be very significant, signaling ten weeks of high-octane
output by the cadre which would look to the absent Mayor for
both strategy and tactics. (In neither primary nor general election did Whalen take an active role.)

By early July, Corning had to conclude that "the few
days" would instead be a considerably more prolonged stay
than the three weeks they already had proved to be. An old
saw in medicine is that a patient will "enter for observation and
die of complications," a euphemism for the realities of the profession's own, not-infrequent impotence. In Corning's case
that summer, the complications included those piling up from
the innumerable interests and responsibilities that, as a bedrid-
den patient, he just wasn't able to handle. By this time, the
deficit of his government's operations had swollen to $8 mil-
lion for the year, though Corning had predicted, at the outset,
that operations might even produce a small surplus or, at
worst, a slight deficit. In the face of such bad news and its
implications, his instinct was to retain full control despite his
anchor away from the action. At first he "insisted on answer-
ing every piece of mail he received," as before, Bill Keefe
reported. After Whalen substituted for him in officially wel-
coming Queen Beatrix of The Netherlands on her visit, the
Mayor immediately sent a note thanking him for "a marvelous
job." He carried on the semblance of being in touch by constant
use of a telephone until his strength surrendered to the stresses of each day. But soon Dr. Beebe declared "Enough!" and

ordered the bedside phone removed. There were to be no incoming calls, and Corning would have to travel to a pay phone down the hall to make his less-frequent checks on the people who worked for him. His complete dominance of the city's government was compromised, as were his political controls or influence in city, county, and state. Accordingly, he was forced to think about an effective yet discreet way of keeping in touch, getting and dispensing information and counsel, in general ensuring that his will would be done.

Nearly a month from the day he left City Hall, he designated a small knot of associates to act for him—the "Kitchen Cabinet," as it privately came to be called in a throwback to the days of Andrew Jackson, when private counselors for a public official were given the label. A more apt term is *regency*, for its counselors were indeed acting "in the absence or disability of the sovereign" who, in this instance, was both absent and disabled.[7] Is it unreasonable to define Erastus Corning historically as sovereign of Albany?

For his liaison with reality, he started with two incomparably trusted and trustworthy men, one as anchor of credibility and the second a thoroughly reliable, respected friend. Eighty-year-old Francis Bergan was an O'Connell-era patriarch and judge. John Holt-Harris also impressively conveyed judiciousness. Both were, beyond question, faithful adherents respectful of his office and his command. Holt-Harris, who undoubtedly knew Corning better than anyone in Albany—"a special relationship," it was understood—assumed active leadership although, 15 years younger than Bergan, he was also junior in most aspects of respect and authority.[8]

Drawing on the strength of this well-matched pair, Corning constructed his all-but-invisible circle of ambassadors and missionaries. Not one of the five closely knit, tight-lipped male lawyers he initially chose held an elective office and only one was an employee of the City of Albany.

And virtually invisible they were, for the counselors went their solitary ways about Albany for all but a single hour each week. When they came together it was in a locale ordinarily inaccessible to the working press.

Essentially, what Corning delegated was on-the-scene oversight of Albany County Democratic politics. The Regency offered only scant awareness of, or bits of guidance on, issues that enmeshed the floundering municipal government. But to a considerable extent, the weekly conversations around the breakfast table under the clock in the recesses of the Fort Orange Club tended to revolve on relations with Albany County, patronage liaison with State government, passing on the credentials of job-seekers in the city and county, or unknotting tangled relationships with the city school district. The sessions were inaccurately described later by the *Times Union* editorially as having "effectively governed Albany."

That the sessions were less than comprehensive is supported by their setting: the ambiance of a club's dining room rather than an office—and by the practical time limit placed on them, about an hour a week before the start of the business day. At most, the conferees could spare an extra half-hour on occasion; all were busy men of affairs.

Among their colleagues, Albany County was represented by Robert Lyman, its official attorney, an appointive position, rather than by the elected County Executive, James J. Coyne. In fact, an undue portion of the deliberations concerned Coyne's conduct of his office. McArdle, in whom Corning placed much confidence for judgment, discretion, and loyalty, sat in for the city government at the outset, but he was an appointee with only unelected status and no claim to rights of succession. And one more member was necessary: Douglas Rutnik, the young lawyer with a key connection and with whom Corning shared so many confidences and who thereby knew so much that was inaccessible to others. He could bring to the table certain insights and opinions as if reading the Mayor's mind. His appointment was also in recognition of the ever-present Polly factor, with Doug as a most useful bridge to his then mother-in-law.

The meetings began in July soon after Cuomo opened his uphill race for Governor. They continued through the September primary and the November election when other statewide positions and numerous local offices were being contested. They were instrumental in translating Corning's wishes throughout the transition to a new state administration with all the questions of potential patronage and, finally, to the earliest months of a new Democratic Governor. For such a politically oriented group, these were heady days.

* * *

But Corning had bypassed or overlooked Whalen, potential heir to the Mayor's own chair. The omission offers evidence of his main concern: Albany County's political climate, contrasted with the degree of his emotional involvement in his city's government. Altogether, it also testifies to Corning's innate rejection of even the idea that anyone would soon be in a position to take over from him, dead or alive. (Similarly, J. Leo O'Brien, heir to Corning's other position as chairman of the Democratic county committee, was excluded although later the members occasionally invited him to sit in, his presence at such times underscoring the political emphasis.)

For nearly three months, Whalen's exclusion continued. Frustrated, he finally visited Holt-Harris. As the person who someday might well take on the mayoralty's responsibilities, Whalen complained, he should be in on the deliberations. Unsurprisingly, Holt-Harris had been mulling the same thoughts. (Later, he even recalled the initiative as having been his own.) "I had a conversation with Erastus just after he went to Boston," as he described the outcome. "He had overlooked the need for Whalen to be part of the committee he'd selected to oversee things in his absence. I told him it was crazy not to include Tom because he would be the next Mayor. I said it just that way. Erastus certainly didn't disagree with that flat statement (as well as with the idea of adding him to the committee). In my mind, there is no doubt at all that Corning was picking his successor, and it was a political decision."

Coincidentally, this development occurred almost

simultaneously with his designation to share preparation of the new Budget. With several years' perspective, Whalen arrived at the conclusion that this month of October had been truly a fulcrum in his public career.

As the only elected official included among the Corning advisors, he otherwise would have taken office as Mayor deprived of many invaluable insights into his job, and would have lacked on-the-job experience with Corning's key men. He plunged headfirst into the discussions, to the early annoyance of some of his colleagues, not all of whom had been eager for his participation. The ancient maxim for political candidates undoubtedly was in his mind as he spoke up: "You have only one chance to make a first impression." He was not going to be only a spectator in this critical testing. Whatever negative reaction existed probably reflected the attitude of Polly Noonan, whose tolerance for anyone touching the hem of Corning's garment was zero. Under the circumstances, Whalen—as the prospective successor—inevitably bore the full force of her wrath then and thereafter.

The Regency's focus unabashedly was disproportionately on Corning's political concerns. Whalen, who rounded out what Holt-Harris liked to call the "Select Six," was left largely to his own devices, almost ignored and somehow sheltered by the fiction that Corning was still doing the Mayor's job.

Discretion in even letting the Regency's activities be generally known prevailed for nearly nine months. Belatedly, in April Bob McManus finally learned enough about it to publish an account of its existence.[9] "We had an obligation not to get out front," Holt-Harris explained later, presumably meaning that Corning's unique idea for trying to carry out his responsibilities would best be underplayed. Clearly, the less attention paid during the crisis to these makeshift arrangements the better.

* * *

Soon after Corning was admitted, bulletins from the hospital staff had begun offering optimistic dates when he could be expected to return home, though he spent weeks at a time in respirators in intensive care units. Bold announcements heralded an actual departure from the hospital on the thirty-first day. He was going home for a restful weekend before returning to his desk and resuming his official tasks, perhaps on a somewhat reduced schedule. All was positive, upbeat, confident. Erastus Corning would be as unbeatable in life as in elections.

The official version of Corning's departure from the hospital's round-the-clock care at 11 a.m. on Friday, July 16, was predicated on assurance that he was ready to resume his duties at City Hall shortly. However, according to this version, he suffered an asthma attack during Friday night, several hours after leaving the hospital, and returned there between 8 and 9 o'clock Saturday morning. This version was widely published. Sunday morning's *Times Union* report, for example, stated that Corning was admitted to the hospital's intensive care unit *"early Saturday, less than 24 hours after he returned home,"* and that he was "taken by ambulance to the hospital's emergency room *at 8:45 a.m."* These statements were repeated the next year in obituary articles—all except John Maguire's account in the Schenectady *Gazette*, which pointedly included a very intriguing statement. Its significance was easy to overlook. Maguire, regarded as Corning's favorite reporter—in fact probably one of the two or possibly three he really liked or trusted since Leo W. O'Brien, a former reporter, was elected to Congress in 1952—wrote a personal account that contained a detail every other reporter had missed in chronicling the Mayor's difficult final year. His account included these two sentences:

"In 1982 . . . Corning was admitted to the hospital (Albany Medical Center) in June for treatment of his persistent emphysema and bronchitis.

"He left the hospital after a month, *but returned just two hours after being released, spirited in the back door of the medical center."*[10]

Two large questions necessarily intrude:

First, what could have been the errand that apparently made it imperative for Erastus Corning to be able to escape from confinement and then promptly return?[11] Quite clearly, the cover story of an anticipated long-term recuperation at home and in his office may well have been only a ruse. How many people knowingly conspired in the deception is an open question. In the next ten months before his death, Erastus Corning never again was away from instant medical attention.

Second, why carry out what seemingly was an elaborate charade for public consumption—beginning with creating an expectation that he would be home—and then working— for an extended period; and concluding with a contrived deception about the time of his actual return to the hospital— and a maneuver to "spirit him in the back door"? If a patient is so desperately ill that he must be hospitalized immediately, any rationale for such maneuvering falls apart.

The answer to the second question plainly relates to the unknowable answer to the first.

As a writer specializing in health reporting, John Maguire had a long background of extremely good contacts at Albany Medical Center. As a careful, meticulous reporter on friendly terms with Corning, he had no conceivable reason to manufacture an inaccurate account. Newspaper and book, journalist or author, all have universally accepted the official version of the overnight visit. Only one writer has it the other way. (Other individuals familiar with the events of that day have confirmed that Maguire's account was accurate.)

Every unanswerable aspect of the entire escapade contributes to the aura of intrigue that characterized so much of Erastus Corning and his indefatigably erratic administration of Albany.

*　*　*

Hardly by design but nevertheless a masterpiece of accidental timing, a restive *Knickerbocker News* reporter, Bob

Ward, wrote an "open letter" to Corning that was published on the day after his exit from the hospital and sudden return. The letter was an unusual device for an expression of exasperation and concern by a reporter who covered the public office.

"You haven't been doing a good job," Ward complained. "You haven't been doing a good job of keeping finances in order the past few years."

Declaring his worries about the future of the city's tax rate because of that record, Ward reminded Corning: "You're not going to be around forever and whoever replaces you isn't going to know anything approaching your understanding of city government and the people here."

To another reporter preparing a story that would be headlined "City Hall at a standstill," Comptroller Jim Brunet, an elected official, offered an unintentionally devastating comment: "Sooner or later, I'll have to make some decisions myself." Corning's essential role in his government's workings couldn't have been more clearly stated. It was one of those ill-fated wisecracks better stifled in the joker's throat. Nevertheless, the gaucherie underlined the indelible fact that because of his own style of managing the city without adequately delegating and consulting, Corning had dug the pit deeper for those charged with carrying on when he was out of dictatorial control.·

Corning met with a few reporters once, in early August, saying that he intended to tell his department heads that they should begin solving their own problems instead of seeking his solution. Such hugely innovative instructions were not issued in his remaining days and, all but certainly, he would never have put into effect any real dispersal of responsibilities. To Holt-Harris the idea was laughable. "You've got to rely on yourself," Corning's warning to his commissioners, was generally interpreted to mean that he was foreshadowing a long-range expectation that he'd be less involved in day-to-day operations upon his return to active duty. But its true significance was much smaller. He was simply signaling that he would be unavailable for much decision-making in the indefinite but short-term future.

The unexpected, however, did intervene to devolve responsibility onto others' shoulders. Gathering prerogative around himself—regardless of just how well the duty was discharged ultimately—was basic to his conception of his office. To Corning, that office represented the essence of Albany and, as his closest friend colorfully interpreted his view, "Albany was the warp and woof of Erastus's being."

"He loved the city and completely enjoyed his role as Mayor," said Holt-Harris. "He was uncomfortable if he was more than 10 miles from home; that is, from Albany. When he'd go fishing, he was on the phone to Albany more than he was on the pond.

"Furthermore, he conceived a political difficulty in delegating some of his chores. He believed that for every person who might relieve him of some of that workload, there were many others, each of whom would feel that he should have been the chosen one. So, the wisest course—he was convinced—was simply to keep a grip on the reins."[12] Holt-Harris felt certain that, despite Corning's remarks while hospitalized, as a functioning executive he never would have permitted a latitude of discretion on the part of his underlings, for whom he felt neither regard nor respect, with very few exceptions.

It would not be Corning's style to take the time and trouble to contemplate how a successor might choose to carry the load, but if he did give it a thought his most likely response would have dismissed the matter as beyond his personal interests.

In fact, of course, the successor promptly—and very effectively—set about following a broad policy of spreading numerous areas of delegated duty and responsibility. The two men had diametrically opposite approaches to management.

"*L'etat, c'est moi*" continues in eternal conflict with "Government of the people, by the people, and for the people."

❧ ❧ ❧

NOTES

[1] The reason for the isolation was pure old-Albany politics, dating back to early years of O'Connell-Corning decision-making. Mayor William S. Hackett (1922-1926) was also president of the City Savings Bank, which needed tenants in its leased office floors above the bank. The problem was easily solved. The city's lawyers were exiled from City Hall and put to work in the 100 State Street structure. They remained there for 60 years, until Mayor Whalen quickly reversed the old decision and made room in City Hall for nearly two dozen lawyers and staff, thereby saving the $16,000 rent. Their new location was handiest to the Mayor's office of all the city departments, and to further facilitate communicating a new doorway was cut through the wall separating the Mayor's suite from the counsel's.

[2] Author's note: That setting comes clear to me, in retrospect, for I was also a patient in the room, not long after his occupancy. Its history was repeatedly pointed out to me by the hospital staff.

[3] Associate Judge Domenick L. Gabrielli, elected in 1972 to the Court of Appeals, was a York Stater from remote Bath in south-central New York close to the Pennsylvania border. A graduate and trustee of Albany Law School, he was known as "Mike" to both Whalen and Corning. Occasionally, he sent Whalen newspaper clippings of presumed interest. A few times each year they shared a meal. In a note after an informal visit, he wrote that "Dot and I are very, very proud of you." Judge Gabrielli was one of three members of the high court particularly close to Whalen. The others were Chief Sol Wachtler and Judge Joseph Bellacosa.

[4] Essay, "Political Tradition: Life Among the Dinosaurs," in a Rockefeller Institute brochure, "Experiencing Albany: Perspective on a Grand City's Past."

[5] Simultaneously, the Cornings' fiftieth anniversary occurred (June 23). One published account of that period (in *Mayor Corning: Albany Icon, Albany Enigma*) places the Mayor at a dinner party where he spoke of personal reminiscences. But on that date he was in intensive care, on a respirator and fed intravenously.

[6] In his place, the Albany County delegation's official leader was Pamela Noonan Montimurro. Five months earlier, she had been appointed by Corning, as county chairman, to become a mem-

ber of the Democratic State Committee representing the 104th
Assembly District. She resigned from the committee in April 1984
on the recommendation of the Governor's Board of Public
Disclosures in order to avoid a seeming conflict of interest created
by her $43,363 position as the State Tax Commissioner's special
assistant, one of the very few mid-level patronage positions allotted
to Albany by the Cuomo Administration. Meanwhile, her mother,
Polly Noonan, had been appointed as a vice-chairman of the State
Committee.

  7 A much earlier "Albany Regency" had several parallels but
also notable distinctions. In the 1820s, Martin VanBuren, some 15
years before his presidency, created a group of supporters "bound
by party loyalty, regularity, caucuses, and patronage" and "directed
by an inner circle of trusted lieutenants that functioned as a coordi-
nating board. . . ." Van Buren's Regency, however, was much greater
in scope than our 20th century group: a "unified, statewide political
apparatus" which employed such techniques as "subsidized newspapers to set the party line" and "practical mechanisms to mobilize
voters." The analysis is included in an appreciation of the Albany
Regency in a 1997 book, *Martin Van Buren: Law, Politics, and the
Shaping of Republican Ideology*, by Jerome Mushkat and Joseph G.
Rayback (Northern Illinois University Press). ("Republican" in this
usage refers to a concept of governance rather than to a political
party.)

  8 Judge Bergan, who was "the soul of good judgment," in
Holt-Harris's opinion, had a remarkable career in the law. As a
retired Associate Judge of the Court of Appeals, he was one of the
very few New Yorkers ever elected unanimously to state-wide
office. (He had been endorsed by all parties: the judges on the
state's most eminent bench were elected, rather than appointed, at
that time.) A native Albanian, he received his law degree at 21 (from
Albany Law School) and while still in his 20s he was chosen by the
Organization to run for City Court. He was rewarded with the
party's nomination to the State Supreme Court's Third Judicial
District in the same year Erastus Corning's political career began.
For 28 years, he sat in that court and its Appellate Division.
Meanwhile, he enrolled in some college courses and obtained his
A.B. at 44. During his nine years in the Court of Appeals, he had
numerous other interests: vice-chairman of the convention that con-
sidered overhauling the state's constitution; chairing the trustees of

Albany Medical College; and lecturing at the law school. His devotion to books and enthusiasm for libraries led him to the chairmanship of the Albany Public Library for many years and to organizing and chairing the Upper Hudson Library Federation. In retirement, he wrote a history of the Court of Appeals.

[9] Years later, in Holt-Harris's obituary and in an accompanying editorial, the *Times Union* compounded this untimely reporting with references indicating that entire assignment of the Regency group had originated in April, nine months beyond the time it started functioning.

[10] The italicized emphases were not included in the Maguire story or in the subsequent reference to the time.

[11] Author's note: I have been credibly informed that a residence other than his own was on the Corning itinerary that day.

[12] "Every time I create an appointment, I create a hundred malcontents and one ingrate" (Louis XIV).

From Here to Austerity

To tackle Corning's assignment to prepare the Budget, Whalen took the lead in gathering up helpers in City Hall—McArdle, of course, plus the Treasurer, Ray Joyce, and the ailing Comptroller, Jim Brunet, often spelled by his deputy, Charles Hemingway, who was soon to succeed him. Handed shovels, everyone doggedly dug. It was a backbreaking job. All were innocent of budget-preparation experience, and Whalen commented later that "None of us knew what we were doing." What they were given to work with was a foot-high stack of outsized computer printouts. Nothing at hand could indicate any effective process. Some published accounts misleadingly reported that Corning had given them a virtual road map of procedure. It was, in truth, all hopeful trial and error.

Meeting in Joyce's office, tucked away within the embrace of a bow window in a far rear corner of City Hall, the budgeters had to contend not only with the city's straitened finances but also with the much larger heritage implicit in the Corning legacy. Compounding the hugely complex problem was the severe recession—the worst since the Great Depression—which clutched the entire nation in its grip. Its vise constricted fiscal alternatives and projections for the last two difficult years of Corning's life. And its overtones were part of Whalen's confrontation with reality. He would be challenged to find the effective means to end the crisis and summon the stamina and determination to see it through.

Though to inquiring reporters they gave the politically

obligatory answers as to the Corning role—they claimed they were doing it "under his direction"—in fact, they succeeded in establishing very little useful contact with the Mayor during the six weeks that they labored over shaping the budget document. Such an assignment was unprecedented. The Mayor had involved only himself in budget-drafting for endless years. He worked habitually without benefit of a director who would normally draft a budget proposal and ride herd on its execution.

Corning had no plan in his budgeting. Fiscal projections, based on hope and bluff, were *ad hoc*. When they chanced to work out well, it was to be attributed to happenstance. His annual budget document consisted almost entirely of big computer-printout sheets with virtually no narrative in explanation.

Customarily, he did not buckle down to his solo performance in budget-making until mid-autumn, after the new fiscal year had actually begun on November 1; then, near the end of the calendar year, his draft would belatedly be sent up to the Common Council for automatic approval.[1] (Meantime, the city would be expensively borrowing through short-term notes in order to pay November-December operating expenses.) Altogether, as Jack Holt-Harris observed later, "The budget was whatever was in Erastus's head at any given time."

A professional budget expert, Harold Rubin, who had a long tenure as chairman of the influential Council of Albany Neighborhood Associations, scoffed that a Corning budget was "essentially an appropriation bill" lacking such desirable detail as explanation of changes. "The annual budget document was an embarrassment." Rubin, a ranking career expert in the state's Division of the Budget, where governors' programs and proposals are vetted against the facts of life imposed by the realities of revenue projections, was exceptionally well informed about the nature and shortcomings of such budgeting as Corning indulged in.

* * *

The stresses of budget-drafting were multiplied by asterisked information that unfolded on the table, beyond the control or wishes of the drafters. These were the hard facts that would likewise have confronted Corning himself if he had been fit to work. The asterisks serially showed them that:

Existing contracts with the uniformed unions required raises to be put into effect in the year ahead. Nothing could forestall this additional drain. And the city was on notice, as part of the State Comptroller's strictures, that no longer could Albany expect to get away with borrowing bags of money to pay for unbudgeted overtime, as had been the improbable practice for years. Extra-hours compensation now had to be anticipated and written into the annual budgets. The days of quietly deferring such major operating expenditures well into the future were over. It added up to a costly shift toward candor vs. stealth in accountability, obligatory if Albany was really going to clean up its act.

The toll that these new circumstances exacted was nearly $6.5 million. The raises amounted to 85% of all the new spending for which the budgeters provided. Without enlarging the overstuffed manpower of either the Police or Fire Departments, their funding for 1983 necessarily went up, by $3.63 million and $2.83 million respectively, beyond the amounts budgeted for 1982. The Police Department's increase was 44.6% and that for Fire was only somewhat less at 40.7%.

Given the prevailing conditions of Albany's finances and the constraints that the city was forced to face, these figures represented a huge hurdle with which to start their efforts. To begin all the calculating and negotiating so deep in the hole was immediately a major challenge mandating greater stringency in all other areas. Belt-tightening? A more apt and more colorful simile would have been the mightiest of tugs on the corset strings!

The amateur crew finished the draft by early November. It proved to be a conservative plan—"austere," Whalen termed it—with a 2.86% increase in expenditures, somewhat below the recent inflation rate.

Their handiwork eked out increases for all but one of 20 broad categories of budgeted items. But the increases were largely nominal—9% more for waste disposal, 4% for waste collection—or just marginal (up $1,000 for Central Data, $9,000 for Planning). The sole item receiving less money was a gamble on the cost of snow removal. "The cupboard is pretty bare," said Whalen. "We figure we have bareboned it!" But the total of $70.2 million meant a 7.3% increase in taxes, which for property-owners amounted to an additional $6.51 per $1,000 of assessed valuation.

They held their breaths as they submitted their results to Corning. Holt-Harris and Keefe, delivering the bulky document to his bedside 36 hours after Election Day, reported that they had found the Mayor elated (but primarily involved in thoughts of the significance of the Cuomo victory for Albany and for himself). A terse covering note from the Albany team asked that he return the budget to its creators by the next week. The temerity in this onerous deadline apparently was attributable to the group's recognition of the pressures Corning himself had always brushed aside but which were to be involved in taking the budget public. Especially troubling was the vision of putting it in front of the Aldermen, who were unaccustomed to the privilege of actually looking critically at anything so basic to the city's governance. The budget came back from Corning—on time—with only minor tailoring in a script as shaky as would be expected from the occupant of a hospital bed.

Before the document was made public on November 15, a two-page narrative was prepared, credited to Corning, who had never provided one in 40 years. It was a novelty, a big hit, as reporters described it glowingly. For the first time, also, department heads were asked to comment at a Council finance committee session. The finance chairman referred colorfully to the exercise: "It's going to be a little like a woman having her first baby. It's going to be a little tough." Some citizens who were budget critics in previous years now were mollified that a public hearing was held on November 22, well before the

Council's vote to approve. The timing alone was a startling innovation.

A few thousand dollars were subtracted by the Aldermen from the spending proposal in the draft. In the roll-call, one negative voice was heard from Nancy Burton, the Democrats' outsider in the Council, who reluctantly voted "No" even though, she conceded, the budget was "100% better than last year's."

Comptroller Ned Regan, voicing the State's official opinion, significantly offered slightly more than faint praise: "The best budget in years." He didn't specify how many.

* * *

A positive but oddly disconnected editorial in the *Times Union* welcomed what it viewed as "a revolution of sorts." A reader could gather in its language that the new budget had "just growed." Neither Whalen, McArdle, nor any other city official was mentioned as having participated, much less deserving of credit.

The editorial saw the budget offering "long overdue" changes exposing some of Albany's "financial operations . . . to the light of day"—and also calling for "much, much more." Emphasized for gratified comment were the "relatively detailed format," the unprecedented explanatory message, the timing of the public hearing, and the readiness of "someone other than the Mayor" to meet the press for questioning.

The budget was seen "as a move, however small, away from the oligarchical structure that has characterized city government here and toward a form of government more open and republican" (meaning the citizenry's ultimate powers, and presumably including delegation of certain of them to a representative body).

There was a single exception to the anonymity of the editorial's praise and its impression "that Albany's officials are beginning to let people know more about where their money is going." The exception was the name of Erastus Corning, but the reference was notably backhanded: "Until now the budget was hermetically sealed in (his) head."

* * *

Throughout, a picture of an eager Corning giving directions and initiating change was provided to the media, to the degree that plausibility permitted—and sometimes beyond. Regularly, new, optimistic dates were set for his return to City Hall. Even allowing for the deception to preserve his reputation, this public display of the staff's work could have been the tip-off that by now the Mayor just wasn't up to all the demands of the job.

A cover story protective of Corning—given voice particularly by McArdle, but with Whalen seen as offering silent consent—made a series of claims on the Mayor's behalf: Purportedly, he had provided "pages of notes about the budget's final form," then the four men who really developed the budget had extensively used these as guidelines. Corning "hadn't made many changes" in their draft because they'd followed his "instructions." ("Guidelines" had morphed into "instructions.") But beyond saving important face for Corning—all this was still believable enough in the minds of a credulously uninformed public—the misleading credit ("He was the budget's author") could only detract unfairly from the weeks of exacting and exhausting labor by Whalen, Brunet, Joyce, and McArdle himself.

We confront here a classic effort to dress up Corning to fit a cosmeticized perception of what he was now capable of doing. This effort's net result was to credit him with performing more effectively in absentia than he ever did in person.

"It was his budget," McArdle summed up.

Harold Rubin, always an informed critic, decided the budget had been "produced largely by McArdle." A readily discernible difference in draftsmanship undoubtedly was very evident to him merely because of the form in which it was made public. Rubin did necessarily lack, however, firsthand access to the process which actually produced it, including the respective contributions of the four members who signed off on it. Comparing the new budget with those of previous years, in any event, he found it superior.

* * *

When the demanding budget process was complete, Whalen voiced a hope that department heads now understood they would have to be prepared to back up any requests for expenditures.

"But," he added, "things don't change all at once with one wide stroke of the brush."

To say the least, much lay ahead—as he apparently was learning. He had promises to keep, and many miles to go.

* * *

The city's nervous uncertainty in Corning's prolonged absence may not have actually been a determining factor in some keen editorial decisions at Albany's two newspapers during the early winter. But these were timely and useful in reminding Albanians of ways their government was squandering their tax dollars.

In December, a short but informative series of researched articles reported on "The Machine's Expensive Friends," the titling a poke at Corning's well-publicized expression, "I like doing business with my friends." In the series, the Corning administration's twisted ties with the party machine were well documented. Among the vendors who consistently received lush contracts without the need to bid for them were two ward leaders, Harry Linindoll, the pest exterminator, and John P. Martin, a plumber. A third ward leader, Ruben Gersowitz, managed the old Wellington Hotel, a city property, which ran a deficit of nearly $150,000, partially caused by services that were provided by the other two. A principal point emphasized that, in acquiring the city's business through unorthodox means, the vendors' charges were substantially above what genuine competition would have required. Both Whalen and McArdle assured reporters that they would be seeking ways to control the drain.

NOTE

[1] Corning had been Mayor only a year before the city's charter was amended to permit him to submit an annual budget as late as two months beyond the beginning of the very fiscal year it would affect. He never took full advantage of the leeway he was allowed, but traditionally he did hand in his fiscal plan weeks after each new year opened.

Defending his chronically behind-schedule budget, Corning contended that if Albanians gained access to it before the November fiscal year began, they would gain less knowledge of its provisions than they were provided by his "retroactive" budgeting, as he came to describe it.

Patronage and Pastimes

In late August, surgeons decided on the radical step of a tracheotomy—an opening cut into the windpipe—to ease Corning's breathing difficulties and to control the buildup of fluids in his lungs. Though presumably necessary by that stage of his debility, this created a profound impact, both immediate and longer-term, on his ability to function.

With a tube protruding from his neck, he was unable to really talk for the last several months of his life. To communicate, he resorted almost entirely to scribbled longhand notes. When, for appearance's sake, it became greatly desirable that he somehow contrive to speak, he would desperately focus all his energies to form sounds an acute listener could recognize as words. A Mayor who couldn't readily communicate his wishes was severely handicapped even beyond prolonged isolation from his office.

Corning reported that he was working an hour a day. Pictures taken on the occasion of his forlorn little August press conference and later revealed a bleakly frail, shrunken invalid.

When he departed for Boston in early October, he was strapped to a gurney, barely recognizable from his jaunty prime. His prediction then was that in the latter half of November he would be back at work in Albany, in the office "two to five hours a day, five days a week." In truth, however, there never was a possibility that he could return on such a schedule—or ever.

Communication with the Mayor was immediately

more remote, though one staff member offered the view that whenever circumstances warranted, "We'll just hop in the car and go over." Boston University Hospital, 175 miles distant, was relatively accessible because it was not far from the end of the Mass Pike, situated approximately between Boston's theatre district and the city's "Chinatown." A courier service was set up with Bill Keefe as the messenger and John (Dusty) Miller of the Mayor's staff as the driver.

Holt-Harris[1] usually visited twice a week. Each time he and Keefe reached Corning's floor, Keefe went into the room alone with messages, mail, and papers requiring an official signature. Then, also alone, Holt-Harris entered for several minutes of very private conversation. They needed to communicate in complete confidentiality on issue after politically queasy issue.

In their exchanges, Corning—largely through scribbled notes, often on the backs of envelopes—passed along his judgments and wishes. "Communication was very tough, but I did come back with pretty clear instructions as to what—politically—was to be done in Albany," Holt-Harris recalled. "And I transmitted these to our group" (his five colleagues in the Regency).

An unstated but important portion of his responsibility meant doing his best to ensure that anyone who somehow had Corning's ear—or who pretended to—couldn't successfully interfere with what he had learned the Mayor actually wanted. This caution was founded in actual undesirable occurrences, he commented.

Altogether, they estimated, they made some 50 round trips to the Boston hospital—totaling 20,000 miles—within the next few months. Ultimately, the trips became pointless because of Corning's inability to focus on anything other than his own pain and prospect.

Dr. Beebe and others associated with his care at the Albany Medical Center had been appalled by the Mayor's willingness to go to a Boston hospital. Such was Holt-Harris's vivid impression. During a private conversation in the last months of his life, he made a startling reference to this. He described the shock he had felt upon learning from Corning in 1982 that Polly Noonan, after a revelation in a religious experience, had deemed his recovery dependent on a physical rehabilitation program, had scouted for suitable facilities and found in Boston such a hospital, then had sold Corning on the idea, overriding the Albany physicians' reservations and preferences. Holt-Harris regarded the implications of this account so troublesome that he stipulated that it was not to be published in his own lifetime. He quoted Dr. Beebe as having declared, "We never should have let him go. We should have made him as comfortable as possible here and let him spend his last days here."

As a visitor to Corning's bedside in the fall, Holt-Harris was acutely distressed: "I could see that he was a dying man." Assuming that his recollection of those painful days is accurate, Holt-Harris's penetrating insight raises the issue of the quality of the Boston physicians' prognosis over the months. For whatever reason, Albany never heard the blunt facts from Boston. The hospital enrolled him in a rehabilitation program designed to help him adapt to his worsening physical condition. He was destined to linger far from home for 33 weeks. The bill easily could have touched a quarter-million. The cost to the City of Albany, in a different coinage, was far greater.

* * *

Another mayor, Kevin White, who had dominated Boston's politics for at least a decade, was very much in the news when Corning became a quasi-Bostonian. The coincidence was inadvertent but striking. Daily, Albany's mayor could read in *The Globe* about the travails of his counterpart's administration. White had just announced his candidacy for a fifth term, and *The Globe* was strong in its editorial opposition while its news columns were replete with scandals involving City Hall.

A federal grand jury investigating allegations of municipal corruption indicted a former official of White's redevelopment authority for bribery, simultaneously with Corning's becoming a regular reader of *The Globe*. As the federal inquiry broadened, peeking at White's campaign funds, accusations began to raise questions about delicate aspects of the Boston mayor's spectacular career.

The headlines now told of a "major federal inquiry into corruption" in Boston's government. Such news was sufficient to cause any mayor—even one who, back in Albany, had stolidly withstood investigator after investigator over the years—to re-read *The Globe*'s accounts. Far from the old familiar corner office, unable to feel confident of keeping his thumb on any untoward event that might erupt at home, Corning could be excused for ironic recollection of four decades when he was always on hand except for occasional two-day vacations—and now, who knew what might blow? His sessions with Holt-Harris aside, or the messages brought by Keefe, the scant meetings with Whalen and McArdle, the sentimental but stressful visits with Betty on one day and Polly the next—what could he truly depend on? Who was really minding the store as effectively as Erastus Corning's patented style of retailing civic affairs?

His isolation sometimes caused him to choose unbeaten paths. Underscoring his habitual involvement with the classic "cat in the tree" emergency, when a staff memo reached him conveying a $1,522 estimate for putting in 20 plants "for the bare spot in Washington Park," his recourse was to send it home, asking, "Bet, please look this over and let me know what you think."

Before Christmas, as Corning's physical woes mounted rather than mending as officially predicted, he had no difficulty finding news of Kevin White's downward slide. It was increasingly reminiscent of old Boston's pain in the four separate mayoralties[2] of James Michael Curley.

By chance when Corning hardly would have focused on it because of major surgery—one of Boston's most intriguing writers, the novelist James Carroll, published an essay which declared: "Kevin White thought he was too large for this city, but he has become too small. . . . Like the classic tragic figure, he incites in us pity and fear. . . . The final chapter has begun."

* * *

Only a mere hint crept into news accounts to suggest the optimistic predictions on Corning's health and recovery were sugarcoated or worse. Could it be that his own "final chapter" had begun? Albany's politically sensitive mores forbade such harsh language in public, but "No one expects that the Mayor will fully recover," was an incautious remark that found its way into a story just a month after he had moved to the Boston hospital.

Otherwise, month after month, it was up to the individual Albanian to read between the lines and recognize symptoms of a deteriorating, hopeless case.

To inspirit the long days, Corning was indulging an unusual hobby. Through Bill Keefe's regular visits, he began placing bets on horses at tracks all over the country. His involuntary bookie reported receiving cash in amounts of up to $200 at a time. The source of the ready money was not evident, nor was it ever explained.

His betting habit went on for many weeks, just about until he became so ill that focusing on the diversion became unbearably irksome. Then the scrawled jottings appeared no more and the tidy stack of bills went, at least figuratively, back under the mattress.

In a much earlier day, the elder Cornings—Edwin and Parker—had operated their "Upper" and "Lower" farms whose considerable acreage just outside the city enabled them to play a gentleman farmer's role when they pleased. This included the whimsy of breeding thoroughbreds, true avocation of landed squires.

Jim Coyne's published version of how things actually went in Albany politics and government recounted a long-ago conversation with Corning in which the Mayor had correctly, and somewhat surprisingly, revealed an exotic bit of racing trivia. But any real attachment to "The Sport of Kings" has never been uncovered—if it ever existed.

Most likely, those bets placed by an invalid Mayor, surviving offspring of the squires' generation, were no more than a pathetic avenue of escape from the dull, demanding, and depressing routines that had claimed his entire existence. His wagers equated to another patient's crossword puzzles or solitaire. They open a window ever so slightly but ever so tellingly on Erastus Corning's response to oppression by nurses and therapists . . . a grownup's version of what Robert Louis Stevenson recalled as ailing children's afternoon pastimes in "The Land of Counterpane."

* * *

In the September 23 Democratic primary, Cuomo had won an overwhelming 71% of the Democratic vote in Albany County. It was 78% in the city, which was better than Corning's own majority in his reelection a year earlier. The outcome was particularly pleasing to Corning, for Charles Ryan, Koch's coordinator in the county, would once again dine on wormwood and gall.

In November, Albany was the only upstate county to give Cuomo a majority (58.8%) with a 23,000-vote margin as he won the state by about 166,000. Erastus Corning's personal contribution to the majority turned out to amount to almost one-seventh of Cuomo's margin statewide.[3]

A day after the voting, a *Times Union* columnist wrote that "Corning is absolutely golden" with "extraordinary access" to the Governor-elect. A news story announced that he "can get anything he wants in patronage." In case anyone missed the point, analysts were certain that "Corning's legendary patronage pipeline into State government would remain open for at least four more years."

* * *

When Holt-Harris excitedly told him soon after the election that a feeler had come from Senator Alfonse D'Amato's brother, hoping to employ the Mayor as intermediary for a peace meeting "to reconcile all past differences" between the Senator and the Governor-elect, Corning gave it the back of his hand: "There is no hurry." He would find out "if Mario is interested." In passing, Corning added a politically gamy tidbit: "Lehrman (whom Cuomo had just defeated) and D'Amato are half-assed buddies." And, he cautioned, "I want that knowledge to get to Mario from me—not secondhand." (His reference contained no hint as to why Albany's leading Democrat would possess worthwhile gossip about a pair of downstate Republicans which would have eluded Cuomo, veteran of endless downstate intrigue. His pointed remark indicated, however, his implicit evaluation of D'Amato's trustworthiness.)

It was Cuomo, in well-meaning though indiscreet comments to the press, who revealed too much about the Mayor's actual outlook. Upon visiting Corning in the hospital three days after his election, he tried mightily to be upbeat. Employing some language essential to accentuating the positive, he said too much, apparently without realizing what his words were betraying.

"Sharp as ever, looks great; mood good; very, very happy about what has happened politically" (namely, the election victory) were Cuomo's reassuring expressions following a quarter-hour alone with Corning.

But, as so often happens, complications were lurking in the details.

"He had prepared a note for me to read," Cuomo reported. "I asked him not to speak but he spoke some words. I read the note and we exchanged a few words before I left." Here we inadvertently obtain a picture of a bedfast patient already hospitalized for five months. Realizing that he will not be able to actually converse with his distinguished visitor, he jots down—in a scene replete with pathos—a few things he wants to convey to this man he befriended and who now is in a position to somehow befriend him. Then he struggles, anyway, to get out "a few words." His visitor sees that he is "still learning how to manage speech" as a result of surgery performed three months earlier to alleviate his basic ailments.

The principal item that reporters and editors looking for good news could salvage was the Governor-elect's "prediction" that by the end of 1982 Corning would be well enough to return to Albany for Cuomo's inauguration. But their stories missed the essentials of the true picture. Cuomo had reminded Corning of the Mayor's sentimental "promise"—made many weeks before—to be present if and when he took office as Governor. But now the only response he could make was to "flash a hand signal" in agreement. On the strength of this wan gesture Cuomo told reporters that "yes," he expected that the Mayor would be on hand. This was the basis of his rosy "prediction," which received major page-one attention to palliate the nervousness of the city.

But on the same day a physician was publicly conceding Corning "still has a long way to go." He was reporting in a kindly, roundabout manner on a patient who had to scrawl a note in order to communicate with the Governor-elect and fall back on hand signals when the written word wouldn't suffice. And on New Year's Day, when inaugural cannon boomed on Capitol Hill and shook the windows of the Mayor's office, he was abed in his Boston prison with scarcely a visitor to relieve the discomfort and the tedium.

NOTES

[1] All three of these frequent travelers—Keefe, Miller, and Holt-Harris—died within a very few months of one another just before the close of the century.

[2] Based on this extensive experience, Curley could proclaim that "Mayoring is fun and exciting—but there's no future in it."

[3] Other results of the 1982 general election included Daniel Patrick Moynihan's reelection to a second term in the U.S. Senate (without help from the Albany organization) and Michael R. McNulty's election to the State Assembly in a newly drawn "river district" encompassing part of Albany.

"I and Only I"

Following the Governor-elect's brief visit, the Mayor had summoned Holt-Harris and Keefe back to his hospital room. The subject was primarily handling of Albany County's patronage through the Cuomo administration-to-be. Corning wanted specific understanding in Albany—and explicit attention to his wishes—about how the vital contacts would be handled. His instructions—that he would make all the political decisions ("*I and only I will decide*" were his exact words)—were to be delivered to nine people (in addition to a representative of the Governor-elect's staff). Four of the nine were members of the Noonan family: Polly, Peter, and Brian Noonan and Doug Rutnik. The others were Bob Bender, secretary of the county committee, a key man in most routine patronage appointments; Leo O'Brien, Watervliet's mayor and the county committee's first vice-chairman; Ron Canestrari, mayor of Cohoes; Edward (Ned) Guire, that city's Democratic leader and a trusted Loyalist; and Ray Kinley, the "operator" who, as Whalen often observed, "could do certain things Corning couldn't do." Council President Whalen was not included, if for no other reason than the obvious assumption that job-seekers would not be trying to approach him.

The impact as well as the intent of this mandated procedure was double-edged. Corning had designated what appeared to be a neat little inner circle of most trusted patronage confidants—and one confidante—who could feel complimented and knighted. But they were on notice, one and all—

especially one?—that he would tolerate no deals that he himself had not initialed or facilitated or approved. The hands
receiving this new secret grip were also hands that had been
tied. Corning could not trust some of his most intimate associates.

In a note written in his own hand later that month, he
described the essential qualifications for job aspirants hoping
to receive his recommendation to the incoming state administration's patronage dispensers:

"*Good, loyal Albany County Democrats.*" To emphasize
his point, he added, *or not.* "Nothing else," he wrote in an afterthought.

But he entered a complaint: "It is amazing how few
people really do go through their county leadership—(he
called himself the County Leader)—as standard."[1]

"It is so much the simplest and most practical as well as
keeping a lot of idiots"—he gave vent to his churlish dislike of
three dissidents, Howard Nolan, Jack McNulty, and Jack
Garry[2]—"from successfully fishing behind the net." The
expression was a favorite to convey a mix of annoyance, disdain, and distrust whenever another politician might dare to
cross him or to move outside the approved channels in seeking
some preferment.

"If I know of a particular job," he wrote in elaboration
of his outlook, "I may mention it, but it is Mario who fills the
spot. Once in a while, I may go one step further . . . for someone about whom I could have special, valuable information as
to really unusual qualifications."

Occasionally, some official duties supplemented political concerns, but his level of involvement cast a weird light on
his prior 15,000 days in office. As disclosed by memos to
McArdle late in the year, he appeared uninformed or disingen-
uous about practices that as chief administrator he had con-
doned for longer than most people could even recall. After
four decades without a capital budget, he seemed to be jolted
by Comptroller Regan's adverse report in November covering
four past years of the Corning administration's operations.

"What has happened to the capital budget?" querulously asked the man who never had one. He edged toward "trying out one or two" purchase contracts through competitive bidding, as though he considered such a procedure to be a novel and perhaps dangerous idea. (And there was, in fact, danger in it—danger for his own organization.)

"Corning's associates say the boss looks good," one headline proclaimed in early December. When he met for a half-hour with Whalen and McArdle, his breathing was controlled by a respirator, but for reporters afterward they used such positive terminology as "he feels good," "very enthusiastic," and "interested and excited." For Whalen, it was the first opportunity to visit with Corning in the eight weeks since the Mayor left Albany, a period in which the unprecedented drafting of the budget had been accomplished.

In the late fall, a Boston physician suggested that some projections had been "overly optimistic," and that Corning's return home "might be before Christmas; it might be after Christmas." In mid-December, the Mayor wrote that he expected "to be home before February."

* * *

Mario Cuomo opened his inaugural address on January 1 with tributes to three people: Matilda, his wife; Hugh Carey, his predecessor and patron; and Erastus Corning:

"An institution among public officials, who cannot be with us physically today, but who has been with me from the beginning of what appeared then to be an improbable pursuit, a man of strength, stature, and splendid style, the Mayor of the City of Albany."

Among those recorded as having listened to the Governor's words of gratitude were Mayor Koch; Dorothea Noonan, Corning's "unofficial representative," and Whalen, observed "in close conversation" with Lew Swyer.

On New Year's Eve, in fact, Swyer had been in Boston to call on Corning. The prolonged disability had developed into an on-going concern in the mind of Albany's prime dreamer-builder, whom the Mayor had once called "a true friend" although their relationship wasn't especially warm, especially in comparison with the Swyer-Whalen friendship. Swyer designed devices for both the City Hall office and the Glenmont dwelling to make existence more bearable and even relatively comfortable when and if Corning were able to resume life in the outside world.[3]

In mid-January, the time-frame for Corning to go home was changed to "within the next six weeks," meaning the end of February. A reporter, noting that Corning was said to have walked "as much as 250 feet in a single jaunt," quoted "aides" as intimating he "might not be able to wait six weeks." Rather, he would leave long before the end of February—perhaps even "walk out of there tomorrow . . . he's raring to go." Whalen and McArdle visited him for 45 minutes in January, all the time that was allowed.

At the very end of January, Jack McEneny was summoned for the first time. He hadn't seen the Mayor in more than four months. He was unprepared for the further deterioration in his mentor. Real shock came when he saw the desperation in Corning's face as he struggled to communicate his request. Over the two-dozen years in which downtown had been deteriorating, Corning had grasped every available opportunity presented by business failures to buy up properties for the city. The idea was to stockpile toward a significance they presumably could attain in an urban renewal program. (In addition to this land bank, he had reached out to acquire outlying areas of farmland and unproductive open space that would become a thousand-acre greenbelt for the city's southerly borders.)

It was the helter-skelter collection of properties within the city that, as he explained, he wanted McEneny to catalog, looking ahead to a concentrated renewal effort in a someday which his destiny was to deny him.[4]

But as he conveyed this mission to his loyal aide, the Mayor was interrupting his concentration on unofficial paperwork that lay spread about on the bed before him. These were the registration forms for a vehicle he had just purchased.

Corning—with brave and resolute stubbornness but in a totally unrealistic euphoria—at great expense had ordered a van equipped with custom-made controls so he could drive it. Envisioning his return to Albany, he was intent on carrying it out by himself. He would not be a patient in an ambulance; he would not be a passenger in a car. The first citizen of Albany would make a grand entrance to his city, behind the wheel while citizens lined the streets to cheer and wave and marvel.

Like the fabled toy soldier, the van stood and waited for its owner. Eventually, it was returned by his estate to the dealer who had decked it out with the special equipment for Erastus Corning's magnificent return home.

NOTES

[1] Thomas J. Pendergast, who controlled Kansas City for decades and greatly influenced Missouri's elections, once was quoted as follows: "I am the Boss. If I were a Republican they would call me a leader."

[2] In past years, the O'Connell-Corning Organization had elected these three as, respectively, the county's state senator, sheriff, and district attorney.

[3] In City Hall, Swyer's assessment of the possibilities for giving Corning an adequate supply of oxygen included the potential use of one of the four registers (grilles) in the office floor. Once upon a time, they had been part of the building's heating system. These opened directly into a storage room immediately below the Mayor's private office. The Swyer plan for venting oxygen from basement tanks up through a register never had a chance to come to fruition. The ancient registers, however, remained in place. Whalen was made aware of the folklore—apparently very well founded—

which insisted that even a low-pitched conversation in his office could be heard distinctly in the storage room. He never took action to close off the registers, but put his trust in a locked door that barred entry into the room. Only three keys were known to exist: The Mayor kept one, another was in the possession of a trusted staffer, and the third was in the hands of the building's superintendent. Presumably, the faith placed in this rather loose security system was justifiable.

[4] The Whalen administration, accepting a strong recommendation by the Strategic Planning Committee in 1985 and, subsequently, Budget Director Dan Klepak's negative view on the clutter of properties extraneous to current goals, adopted a policy of disposing of as much as possible of Corning's collection. Some of the buildings remained vacant and conspicuously on the market for years. Displaced tenants frequently were vocal in their displeasure about the inconveniences involved.

The Gang of Four

On 1983's first business day, with the Mayor insulated from reality 60 leagues nearer Mecca, and with the Aldermen poised for the rather novel task of asking bids on a small project, Whalen—fresh from the agreeable chore of presenting ceremonial keys to New York's newly arrived Governor—dropped his pinstripe suit jacket over a handy doorknob, loosened his six-button vest, and pulled up a chair around a table to resume a unique and unsought duty. With the help of three others of City Hall's principals, his task was pulling Albany back from the brink where it had been led.

Two days later he enumerated so relatively many planned and potential fiscal reforms that his comments—made to the Council of Albany Neighborhood Associations—warranted a banner headline:

Albany Undergoing a Fiscal Face-lift.

Some dubious Regulars undoubtedly saw the City Hall quartet as Albany's own "Gang of Four." Empowered only by urgent necessity, Whalen and his colleagues were acting upon a logic which drove home the need for a unity of purpose. They were now the only practical hope for confronting the mountain of minutiae required to successfully manipulate the municipal machinery and prevent the city's collapse.

Simultaneously, an unsettling question quietly took shape in Whalen's mind. "What have I gotten myself into?" he asked himself repeatedly, remembering the old Chinese curse:

"May you live in interesting times." A news article coincidentally provided a candid answer: "A mess" was the term it chose
for Albany's fiscal and physical state.

Who would bell this cat? The initiative for the meetings was Whalen's. He and his compatriots—the city's lawyer,
McArdle; the new comptroller, Chuck Hemingway, as of the
end of January; and his replacement as Deputy, Robert
Kukla—had worked together effectively while wrestling
valiantly with the 1983 budget's preparation in October and
November. The assignment of creating a credible document
from a mass of unrefined data had been daunting in itself. But
line-by-line revelation of the actual condition of Albany's fiscal
outlook—resulting from years of careless practices, compounded by months of neglect by the man at the top—convinced Whalen that a crisis was approaching. A damning
report by the state's Department of Audit & Control just as
they completed their work was the climactic blow—and he
had been unable to refute its sharp criticisms that constituted a
virtual ultimatum for reform of irresponsible and failed practices. Some effective though unobtrusive action was necessary
to save the city from ruin. In the late fall, after their budget had
passed muster in Corning's hospital room and then in the
Aldermen's chamber, he had quietly gathered the same small
ring of Albany's answerable officeholders. He and McArdle
had talked it over. The Corporation Counsel—who had trav-
eled to Corning's bedside twice following the budget's
approval—had informed the absent Mayor of the group's
preparations for restoring a degree of leadership and efficacy
to his government.

Nonetheless, Corning himself never voluntarily initiated a clear-cut mandate publicly delegating duties and responsibilities on an interim basis or otherwise. Nor did he designate Whalen (or anyone else) as the one person to whom others in the city's government would look for guidance, instructions, and decisions. Such delegation, even temporary and
subject to being rescinded, suggested a loss of influence that
Corning would not concede or of powers that he could not sur-

render. And, perhaps, indicated a personal weakness that he could not face.

If he had just once told the Loyalists and his city employees, "Tom will be in charge until I get back. I want you to follow his lead and do as he says," Whalen's ability to function with full effectiveness in the long interim would have been vastly improved. But Corning could not bring himself to speak those scant two-dozen words, and so both Whalen and the city paid the price. He hardly could have failed to comprehend the impact of the black hole his absence created.[1]

To forestall chaos by creating the appearance of able hands ready at the tiller, Whalen was assuming responsibility without an actual directive to act. It was risky, as he realized. In the background was a recognition that new ways could be construed as a break with Corning's. His role could prove to be as transient as the mischievous Prince Regent's when mad George III suddenly recovered his sanity in 1810.

In the early days of budget preparation, a headline placing McArdle "at the helm" introduced an article that said Corning was relying on him for day-to-day coordination of municipal affairs. Whalen, it was noted, "also has taken on some added responsibilities." But after three months had passed, it was Whalen who had sized up the imperative that the city's business must be given genuine momentum. He had, in effect, seized the moment—motivated, on the face of it, only by an impulse to assure that what was best for the city actually became an action agenda for its responsible officers. The fact that his grasping of leadership at this juncture eventually earned him credibility as *de facto* leader seems to have been only a byproduct of that agenda.

* * *

Meeting in McArdle's office, away from City Hall's distractions and onlookers, the self-appointed group began providing direction to a work force whose momentum had dissipated through lack of control and accountability.

If any doubts prevailed for Whalen about the tenuous-
ness of their labors, he was amply reminded by a realistically
cautionary note in a January *Times Union* commentary by Bob
McManus, the perceptive and often wise columnist:

"This is Albany, and any change, however minor, is
basically an implied criticism of the 41 years of Corning's
reign."

The collaborators' chosen path had many a potential
pitfall. They pressed on, with the warning in their ears.

The police and fire chiefs were asked in writing for
ideas on how to save money in buying equipment and uniforms. The chiefs were reminded that "there appears to be
some disparity" in the prices Albany was paying in comparison with nearby cities. Ever polite, the printed memorandum
sought "to solicit your thoughts," which—the chiefs were
told—"will be appreciated."

What the chiefs were not told was that their City Hall
questioners had just received comparative prices from a Police
Inspector who was looking for advice and support in a lonely
effort to make purchases at the lowest possible cost.

* * *

The degree of disarray in City Hall gained definition by
an effort of Whalen's to explain what he was up to. "I want to
find out if everybody is doing what they're supposed to be
doing. Or what they *think* they're supposed to be doing. It's
not a futile exercise to have people sit down and try to define
what their mission is."

History and the prevailing climate, in other words, discouraged the top brass and the squad leaders as well as the
pencil-pushers and even the layabouts from doing their job—
or, perhaps, actually understanding what it might be that they
could perform for the city. The Corning tradition, it appeared,
would not die easily. For the record, however, employees by
the hundreds did—in Whalen's words—"sit down and try" to
figure out how to describe a justification for their jobs. As the

unprecedented request implied, the point in it all was the exercise itself rather than much of a review from above.

The watchdogs' assignment immediately took significant shape, in effect putting the numerous commissioners on notice that now someone really was in charge, even though the "someone" was a committee.

City Hall had been on automatic pilot for the first months of Corning's absence. As Jack McEneny, the Commissioner of Human Resources, remarked, "Anything within your department, you just do," even though the Mayor's traditional guiding hand was not available. More complicated issues tended to become stalled, and in department after department the missing direction was harmful, because of either inaction or of overreaction in the form of profligate spending. Only "three or four" memos were being received from Corning each week—and they chiefly went to McArdle.

The Gang's earliest chores tended to focus on details similar to the busywork that characterized Corning's tenure: Removal of a couple of trees, sidewalk replacements, a heating-system failure at a theater (the Palace, which the city had taken over), job priorities for the new hires.

In the same vein, the economies that were instituted tended toward the seemingly trivial (deciding to borrow a high-rise truck from Traffic Engineering for work on city-owned trees, joining in a state purchasing contract when police equipment was to be bought, assigning Public Works to board up abandoned buildings rather than contracting for it).

But in the second week of the Gang's sessions the truly crucial issue of reforming Albany's government and distinguishing it from political control began to emerge. The discussion focused on how to improve purchasing practices. When the first tentative sentence on this question was uttered, the old way of doing business in City Hall was doomed. In exactly three months, this revolution was worthy of a page-one banner. Summarizing an interpretive article, it proclaimed:

**City officials are dismantling fiscal
practices long regarded as integral
cogs in [Corning's] political machine.**

* * *

As they labored together Whalen and his confreres
received an official visit from a pair of the Comptroller's cor-
porals. Matter-of-factly, without a trace of testiness, the gentleman callers laid out the law for Albany's survival in the
wilderness of Corning's finances. Their ultimatum warned
that unless Albany's makeshift squad adopted a string of four
measures, the state would install the dreaded financial control
board.

The mandated reforms included adhering to the bidding procedures that the state would dictate, halting the
issuance of bond and tax-anticipation notes, totally abandon-
ing the practice of paying operating expenditures with funds
obtained for capital-program purposes, and ending the roller-
coaster assessments of property for taxation.

"We were able to tell them we'd already started to commit the city to some of these reforms," Whalen related, "specifically, requiring bids and ending the favored-vendor practices."
In effect, with the city's business now obviously in different
hands—for at least the immediate future—and with these
players judged to be working in apparent sincerity, Whalen's
team had bought time to produce results. When the change in
personnel matched the new atmosphere and was seen as complete and permanent, the Comptroller himself would then
materialize on the scene.

* * *

"*To be completed at your earliest convenience*" was the
considerate but firm bottom line of a memorandum that shortly went out to all departmental heads enclosing a question-

naire requesting data "for the 1984 General and Capital Budgets."

A "capital budget"? Though "What's *that?*" may not have been a universal response, the newness of the concept rattled numerous commissioners as they absorbed another hint that the bar had just been raised.

"We were using the questionnaire as a device to let the department heads understand what the issues and problems were that we were going to focus on," Whalen explained. "It worked quite well in that respect, though there was a mixed degree of responsiveness. Our Public Works commissioner, Harry Maikels, consistently looked for advice from the most conservative group within the party before he could decide how far he could cooperate. There was a certain amount of foot-dragging." A test of wills was under way, to be resolved only later.

Simultaneously, the *Times Union* published a column-long editorial sharply critical of Commissioner Maikels for having "steadfastly refused to comply with the bidding laws." The editorial called the refusal "apparently obstinate" and cited "the State law that requires competitive bidding on all city contracts in excess of $5,000."

The inquiry quickly got down to business with questions that went to the heart of the matter: "*What is the primary function of your department?*" and "*How do you perform that function?*" For certain, few of Albany's commissioners had ever faced a demand to explain their existence.

The businesslike approach continued: "*How many employees do you have in your department—full-time and part-time?*" And, "*How many did you have in 1980-1981?*"

Then, a shadow of things to come: "*Does your department use outside contractors? Name them and indicate the services they perform.*" In view of the customary way Albany's government acquired services and materials, the next question was even more pointed.

"*Do you bid?*"

The key to virtually everything the Whalen administration would undertake and accomplish thus was reduced to three little words, eight little letters. Whalen had to gain for himself the credibility of visible policy and practice in this fundamental manner of committing the city's funds. Only this performance would underscore his untarnished integrity. Lacking it, he never could have attained the level of confidence he needed for a program of good works built on honest dealing. On the other hand, the policy simultaneously endangered him by igniting a smoldering, outraged enmity among many politicians and camp followers. For generations, they had prospered because of the persistent failure to simply buy goods and services at the lowest available price. Apart from any personal profiteering, the old way supported the party's operations, its successes, and its continuity. The new way, Whalen's way, inevitably was hurtful to the party's ability to function as before, and also hurtful to numerous people influential within the party.

The real and earnest outlook for those who had read the three-word key question was made evident in the next sentence: "*Explain your experience for the past two years and how you accomplish this.*" The straightforward request was a loaded one for most of the recipients. Their responses added very little in specifics to Whalen's knowledge, but much to his enlightenment.

* * *

The brisk memos that went out from the meetings week after week—while subtly signifying that "someone is in charge here, and don't forget it"—were tempered frequently by surprisingly deferential expressions: "If you would care to meet with us," "Your help with this will be appreciated," or reasoned explanations for requests: "Your help in this matter is necessary." Such modest references were a concession that, in truth, there was only one person who could *command* genuine performance—and therefore the little group in charge must merely ask or, perhaps, plead.

The tone often was impersonal, distant:

"It is understood that," "It is requested," "It is noted," "It is felt."

The velvet glove occasionally could contain iron. A memo to the City Engineer and City Purchasing Agent courteously began, "It is requested that, working together, you draw up bids for trash collection"—but the next words were underscored: *as rapidly as possible*." Within City Hall, however, the polite approach and its questionable authority were being tested again and again by some of the staff, including visible—and audible—men at the top of key departments.

In the first month, the Gang confronted problems in enforcing their new requirement that department heads work with Purchasing in developing specifications for goods or services and workable procedures for bidding with effective results.

Early in January, several days after the city took the plunge of hiring its first plumber and electrician, some of the nuts and bolts of a city's governing had almost literally emerged.[2] The new employees were experiencing difficulties in being able to get down to work because they were at a loss as to how to acquire a supply of light bulbs, wire nuts, faucets, washers, and other essentials of their crafts. An urgent memo from the Engineer to the Comptroller and Purchasing Agent demanded some simplified solution. Purchasing appealed, citing unspecified problems in making such items readily available. "We are working on establishing blanket orders with various suppliers," one alibi explained in response.

Then the baffled new employees were found, instead, busying themselves inventorying buildings. They had to be told that their priority should be tackling the big backlog of jobs requiring their attention. "It is requested," one more memo appealed, "that you make sure that they are out and working on the jobs that need to be done." This was nearly a month after they had been placed on the payroll. As the plumber and electrician continued to experience frustrating bureaucratic bumbles, Whalen grabbed the bit and instructed the Purchasing Agent that he must put emergency purchase orders into effect "*at once.*"

* * *

Albany suffered severe punishment for its ancient sins twice during the winter from the two major national agencies that establish credit ratings for municipalities making offerings in the bond market.

"Poor financial management, lack of fiscal controls, and imprudent use" of $9.9 million previously received for capital projects but used instead for day-to-day operations, were cited by Standard & Poor's in dropping Albany's rating three notches to the bottom of its 10-grade system. Comptroller Regan called this decline "precipitous," and predicted a 1% increase in the interest which the city would pay—as much as $1 million more expense for the taxpayers for each $15 million borrowed through future sales of bonds.

The second rating agency, Moody's Investors Service, soon followed, deploring "deteriorated financial operations" caused by the years of inaccurate budgeting, recurring deficits, and inappropriate diversion of capital-purpose funding to pay current expenses. Both agencies now placed Albany at the lowest investment grade.

But the true state of Albany's governmental emergency at that time—taking into account Corning's virtual eclipse—was worse than their experts could conceive. Even so, they were pictured as "all but turning their backs on Albany." Little wonder that Whalen was exclaiming, "What have I gotten myself into?"

NOTES

[1] For Whalen, the penalty of Corning's silence naturally was multiplied in the years following. An acknowledgement of Whalen's right to the office, and of his need to act on the responsi-bilities that were coming his way, would have prevented much of the stubborn, ill-tempered suspicion and resistance to his policies and management decisions.

[2] Their hiring, which instantly meant much less business for two major no-bid vendors and thus much less income for the party, had been lengthily deliberated in search of justification for such a radical break with previously unquestioned practice in keeping with O'Connellism's fundamental principles. The decision was an initial challenge to the old way—and, implicitly, to the Tories of the Old Guard. The move, prominently reported, was enthusiastically received at the taxpaying level, however.

Cosmetic Deceptions

Whalen and the Mayor were not in touch in the last half of January and until February 6. Then in mid-month, he and McArdle had 15 minutes with him. (Later, Whalen identified this brief opportunity as the last time Corning exercised any decision-making powers.) Soon thereafter Corning required major surgery that included removal of half of his colon to stop bleeding and remove a tumor. Now he was again on a respirator with a catheter in his chest to monitor his heart and lung function. Even so, McArdle contended that the surgery was performed at that time "because he's feeling so darned good." The ongoing strategy of employing such deceptive exaggeration had by now taken on a rather weird, counterproductive unreality.

Mercifully, the rehab program was abandoned at this point after about three months of futile efforts seeking to cause it to somehow become meaningful.

* * *

The caregivers' emphasis on protecting Corning in his prolonged absence was framed by their repeated insistence that he was sure to be back in Albany, at his desk, by a series of certain dates. But that date kept receding into the uncertain future—moving from the late fall to the Christmas season, to the year's end, to January, to February, to the end of February, when the predictions disappeared. And the lame explanations' theme and tone became, at times, outlandishly assertive. So much so that all the ideas, desires, and decisions attributed to him must now be considered of questionable authenticity.

The excruciatingly sensitive issue of not offending Corning came clear in Whalen's defense of the city's status and prospects during Audit & Control's critiques. He maintained that Corning had "indicated" he wanted his administration to adopt "a positive direction." And, he added, the Mayor would be asked to approve as-yet-nonexistent policies aimed at correcting causes of the fiscal problems that he himself had permitted to flourish throughout his long administration.

By being hospitalized, Whalen was suggesting, Corning was blessed with "the time to look at the overall city rather than putting out the brushfires." Hardly a persuasive argument, but it was merely one in a long series of straight-faced efforts to reassure the public and, more especially, the Mayor's partisans. They needed to be told that he was creatively aware and issuing instructions, approving proposed developments beforehand, endorsing what was good while holding in check any wrongheaded ideas from his subordinates. "Tentative in nature, essentially cosmetic in outcome," was Bob McManus's volunteered prescription for Whalen's activity.

Fundamentally, Whalen hoped to restore credibility to Corning, to avoid wounded feelings, and to assuage any suspicion that Corning was being subverted.

But it is easy to find a more positive justification. So long as Corning clung to his office, the viability of his government needed verification. Full realization of his inability to perform his sworn duties could be expected to result in sanctions by Audit & Control. And the rating agencies easily could have tipped toward decisive actions more extreme than those actually imposed during the charade. Such an estimate is quite apart from the anger imaginable from the electorate. Already, opinion polls and some public discussion were becoming weighted toward requiring the Mayor's resignation. And Albany's citizenry didn't even know the truth.

Representatives of the State Comptroller, reiterating earlier warnings, declared that if Albany's fiscal practices failed to show real improvement the State would be that much closer to imposing the threatened financial control board. One effect was to reinforce the Whalen group's resolve to increase the effort to tidy up some abuses while tightening expenditures. Their work in the early months was driven mainly by on-the-spot necessity. Almost entirely, the remedial moves were undertaken with Audit & Control's threat overhanging like Joe Bltfsk's black cloud.[1]

And meanwhile the hospital's spokesman was cautioning that "When one speaks of chronic illness, one does not usually speak in terms of 'cured.' Chronic means 'not curable generally.'"

"I had this problem," Whalen recalled, "both in the months before I actually took office and also after that:

"How could I persuade the public, especially the Corning loyalists, that I was not disrespectful to what he stood for?

"I resorted to the assurance that 'Mayor Corning knew that this was coming'—whatever particular change was being tried or questioned.

"'He is aware of the winds of change,' I said more than once. And I would point out that he certainly was savvy enough to realize that everything couldn't stay the same way forever."

In any reconsideration of the deceptions, Whalen's descriptions of Corning's participation in the city's governance are certainly open to review. His principal motivation presumably—and quite understandably—would be to avoid the dread prospect that hungry scoffers and sutlers within the Old Guard might paint him as a Plantagenet princeling plotting to dethrone the rightful ruler. Since that portrait would have been ill-fitting as well as ill-becoming, he was well advised to tilt—albeit awkwardly—toward absolute loyalty to Corning's personal interests even while he could see, only too well, these as harmful to the city's government. As portrayed graphically in *Times Union* cartoonist Hy Rosen's inspired ink—the one

with Whalen balancing perilously in a high-wire act—
Whalen's stance was made even more insubstantial by the
ever-present possibility that Corning might call down a miracle and reappear on Eagle Street, powers fully restored.
Whalen very logically scrutinized the turf ahead before each
foot went down in a next step, and his normally taciturn nature
served effectively in precluding embarrassing references. (This
last advantage held true in all but a single instance—in late
spring, when he slipped while speaking informally to a class of
William E. Rowley's students at the Albany State University
campus and indiscreetly doubted that Corning would be
returning.)

"An open secret that lines are forming" on just who
should turn out to be Corning's successor was reported by
McManus as the gravity of the Mayor's illness began to be
more widely understood despite the rosy reports from City
Hall.

"The enmity of Polly Noonan, who appears to have
ambitions that don't include Whalen" was particularly cited.
During this period, a report of her "regular" visits with Corning
was published. After noting that Whalen's own aspirations
were "not clear," McManus reported, however, that he and
McArdle were believed by committeemen to be "quietly cir-
cling the wagons in anticipation of a Noonan-backed challenge." He credited the beleaguered pair with more strength
than commonly believed at the time, and forecast that they
would prevail if a showdown came. It was a strong and accurate public indication of their teamwork throughout the long
period when little could be certain in Albany.

The commentary, however, may have confused
Corning's two jobs. Whalen and McArdle focused on managing the city government. But for those to whom power is all,
Whalen's existence as Mayor-presumptive seemed threatening
to their wholly political sphere.

* * *

Corning received a Whalen letter in late February that he may well never have read coherently because he was slipping into the slough which was to end only at his death.

"We both wonder sometimes if we are getting too far out front. A couple of our 'friends' are quoted as saying that all Whalen and McArdle are doing is trying to make the boss look bad. Remarks like that make a delicate situation even more difficult." (Was he hoping for a show of support? The hour was late.)

"But we are both getting into exciting areas of government and, for the most part, it's enjoyable to be in on the decision-making process."

Without question, there truly was excitement to be mined in arriving at decisions that flew in the face of tradition and expectation. And then employing the amazing, undiscovered weight of his puny office's negligible status to scattershot those decisions. Among the targets were the ranks of startled layabouts accustomed to recognizing power and to heeding instructions from one source only. Excitement, too, in witnessing those judgmental initiatives visibly create desperately needed remedies for civic sores.

And, surely, to innately recognize a basic truth in the long months of Corning's descent: If a Tom Whalen were not available (by grace of Corning's scepter), those fateful, timely decisions would have been fatally postponed, if indeed ever made. Here we are finding confirming evidence that Whalen was to be, for his own city-state, the man for his time as Horatius was for his.

McArdle, sharing some of the day-to-day responsibility and public semi-accountability, tended toward florid excess in his reporting of Corning's "directions" and in his ever-optimistic predictions. He and Whalen properly enough had to serve as sources of interpretive reporting on Corning's outlook (aside from the hospital's own, often obscure, statements). Comments by the two men on the day in mid-February when together they saw him for the last time were typical of their respective approaches. Whalen limited himself to remarking that Corning was being "missed." McArdle declared that he was "right on top of everything." Unhappily, it was on that same day that a hospital bulletin conceded that disappointing progress in improving his condition meant a further delay in his hope of going home. In an earlier interview, McArdle saw Whalen as a "logical successor" to Corning—but added that on the other hand Whalen (who then was 48) might be "too old when the Mayor (then aged 73) retires." Once again, the commendable loyalty was wearing thin to the edge of implausibility.

A question logically presents itself: Just where did Corning actually fit in these days of change?

Could it be that—realizing, against instinct and tradition, the old games were now passé—he had finally decided the time had come to passively accept a new-style budget? Such a concession to reality would have been fueled by unwilling recognition of the toll being taken by his illness and, too, by what must have become an appreciative awareness that his "new people" were well motivated and functioning effectively.

* * *

Whalen's progress in commanding change for his government's way of conducting its business appeared to generate a new atmosphere suggestive of that civics-class shibboleth, "participatory government." Thus, his administration was implicitly creating expectations of improved performance by the Common Council rather than its traditional drab and meek acquiescence.

For more than a half-century, the Council had been its own worst enemy. Compliant to the dictation of the party as voiced by O'Connell through Corning, the members had long since sacrificed their prerogative of initiative, ideas, ideals, and independence. Their style was capitulating in roll-over-and-play dead obeisance. "Don't rock the boat" was the motto and the goal was to avoid trouble that might erupt if the bosses were annoyed. Structured as a "weak" legislative body, the membership readily conformed to the assigned role.

Along with the expanding pressures of the mayoral responsibilities, Whalen was still the Common Council's presiding officer. In mid-stride, he noted that he was finding that long-inert body becoming, as he said, "more responsive to what comes before it." Members were asking more questions, he was pleased to report, "on even the most mundane matters."

"Most of them," he added, "are becoming more interested in the legislation before them." Although "most" can mean "not all," he did not dwell on identities. Pat Gorman, a discerning Council of Albany Neighborhood Associations activist, regarded Whalen as the impetus causing the Aldermen "to become more responsive to their constituents' needs and the city's" as they trod gingerly on untried sod.

Corning's long-standing lord-of-the-manor relation with the Council had been ritualistic. The Aldermen had accepted the position that if they found an agenda before them, "It's there because the Mayor wants it there. And if he wants it, it must be OK."

But no longer were there blind "Yes" responses from the chamber as many members became better informed, began to grapple with issues and to ask "Why?" when it appeared necessary.

NOTE

[1] The pessimist made famous by Al Capp in "Li'l Abner."

The Up-Front Guy

Over the many weeks, the conferees kept track of an astonishing array of housekeeping management chores—from specifications on uniforms for firefighters, to the Palace Theatre's faltering heat supply. In taking on such tasks as these of Corning's, the Gang of Four was functioning—as the cynically popular byword has it—"above their pay grades."

Early on, in a break with Albany's no-bid tradition, instructions were handed down to solicit bids for 80 gross (11,520) small American flags for graves on Memorial Day. The order heralded a year in which the bidding process was to be promulgated as routine under the new Mayor's forced draft; soon it obligated removal and replacement of the purchasing director in order to obtain adequate performance. Public confidence was growing that the city was now engaged in aboveboard dealings.

In February—many months earlier than Erastus Corning had ever started to think about his annual budgets—the Gang began to ask departmental commissioners for data that eventually would create the framework for a 1984 budget. The members were reluctant to go quietly into any future budgetary emergency such as the one they had survived in the preceding autumn's crisis. Late that month, McArdle was saying that "We are moving in the right direction toward fiscal stability."

Their memos were dispatched under all their names, but none of the quartet possessed a prerogative to initiate the city government's single most important document. Intuitively, they were acting out their acceptance of the inevitable—Corning's continuing incapacity and absence. The timing coincided almost precisely with his emergency surgery, as prospects grew slim that the Mayor could share significantly in budget drafting—or in any matter of substance. Anticipating budgetary realities was only a relatively low priority, however, for too many day-to-day issues and contemporary crises demanded attention and decisions.

Whalen, now recognized by many as certain to become the Mayor, gradually was assuming the leader's role. He did not shrink from it, beginning a course of action which—in those cloudy days—could be seen only very dimly and, if challenged, could be defended only with understandable difficulty.

Later, he used this initiative as an example of his personal missile-shield defense in case of an attack of second-guessing. For instance, if Corning were to return and question what he'd done, Whalen planned to say, "I used my best judgment"—a strong "want-to-make-something-of-it?" response that was more testy than merely explanatory.

But the most telling item in the incessant flow of memoranda was the February 18 reminder that "Capital Budget forms are due in the Comptroller's office no later than March 1."

"We want to keep this deadline!" the department heads were warned. The deadline was met.

Behind the flimsy authority of such an elbow in the ribs, however, were striking intimations of a huge event: The city's government was grimly but discernibly working its own revolution[1]—a mini-version of Ronald Reagan's "Morning in America" theme which was still resonating everywhere. The tumbrils were ready to roll for some of the inadequate or reluctant Loyalists in the employ of the city.

A capital budget! Albany never had taken a first bite of this fruit. Among the detail that Erastus Corning preserved in his Phi Beta Kappa brain cells were rumbles from the fault lines within Albany's infrastructure. But government was still stepping to the drums of ancient O'Connell summonses for the Mayor and the school board's president to come and confess to him about absolutely inescapable expenditures that they discerned on the horizon.

But budgeting, the seldom-mentioned joke of Corning's 40 years, was truly coming into vogue at City Hall now that he was absent. Whalen's handiwork was all over these new goalposts. Early in the winter, another tight-lipped reminder went out from the quartet, this one warning departments to "closely watch (their current, 1982-193) budgets" and "to continue the restraints therein."

Almost simultaneously, Whalen reported to Corning: "Vince and I have had Chuck produce three-month print-outs on current expenditures, by department. Then we can see who is overspending. We should be able to get a better handle on it with the controls we have put in through Purchasing."

McArdle, as ever, is meticulously included in a mutual-security "we" partnership. And Corning invariably is addressed in such missives as "Dear Mayor"—any suggestion of first-name familiarity or presumption is notably absent.

A fortnight later, the feedback from departments was promising: A review of computer printout on activity—chiefly, expenditures and commitments—turned up the agreeable conclusion that "for the most part, departments are on target." Still, a "closer review to detect problems is mandated, and monitoring continues." The advantages in Whalen's business-administration diploma and his two decades of law practice in the world of business, banking, and bankruptcy were all too evident at this stage.

And now a novel concept is heard in the land: a budget-maker other than the Mayor himself. Whalen had talked it up even while the *ad hoc* budget was being shaped in 1982. "Albany has a budget of a size which requires full attention for the full year by one individual with expertise in the budgeting process," he maintained. The Four took it upon themselves to initiate a few tentative steps, after word was passed that apparently no objection would be forthcoming from Corning. He did, in truth, contribute tangentially in advancing the idea of a budget director for the government that was still legally his. In mid-winter when he sent word that a budget specialist would be acceptable to him, the concession was linked to an assumption that this person would be subordinate to the Comptroller who (though himself an elected official) was controlled by the Mayor. Ultimately, after Corning's time, the outcome was diametrically different from what he had been envisioning.

* * *

Whalen's own vision of a solid and strong money manager for budgetary development and oversight, and his comprehension of a priority for segregating operating requirements from capital-expense commitments, could have resulted in some genuine initiatives to the credit of the Corning administration.

A budget director would be the first for Albany, a capital budget would be another first. And the administration, in its months of final agony, would have achieved two firsts after 40-plus years.

It didn't quite work out that way. Whalen, showing increasing willingness to accept the helm, knew the principles and was a daily witness to the needs. But summoning enough strength to successfully spur Albany's calcified system toward accomplishment on a short calendar was just too much, a Sisyphean task obligating both adequate time and political muscle. Even an "acting" Mayor would have lacked sufficiently credible powers, and Whalen didn't have that much status.

Although the Gang had begun work on gathering data for installing a spending plan on capital items, it was fated to go into effect only at a date five months after the old administration had come to an end. A director was hired, but likewise was on the job five months too late to be an achievement of Erastus Corning's; thus, his administration sacrificed a claim to these "firsts." Accordingly, they became early landmarks for Whalen's administration.

Would they have been realized had Corning survived what proved to be his terminal ailments? Considering his lack of energetic initiative to introduce these "reforms" over many, many years, its difficult indeed to conclude that at a very late date he'd become a willing convert to orderly, efficient municipal government.

"I came to believe that if Corning hadn't been ill he never would have come to grips with the need to become a proponent of some very important changes," Whalen speculated. "He had too many blind loyalties: to people he had to rely on, to contributors, to Dan O'Connell's friends.

"As for the fiscal reforms we initiated, he would have had none of it." In this, Whalen was solidly in agreement with Holt-Harris's "inside" views.

* * *

In session, the conferees agreed to ask the staff in the Comptroller's office to prepare a "list of responsibilities, etc. for a Budget Director or Clerk." The "etc." mirrored the uncertainty of some as to what a budget specialist could be expected to do. And the word "clerk," in all its trivializing import, again suggested strongly that expectations were low-level indeed. The Comptroller's people were advised to ask around in "other cities and counties" about how such a person might perform. And what he or she might produce other than a great deal of clucking. These timid steps were undertaken within the official assumption that the absent Budgeter-in-Chief, the Mayor, would soon materialize again in Albany and, as ever, would take charge of all fiscal judgments—leaving the "director" to wither in his shadow. Indeed, Corning's tepid okay on the proposed position was certain to support the idea that he didn't expect much. The staff responded accordingly.

And the Comptroller—as well as his dozen staffers— had to be aware that this individual they were helping to recruit might easily usurp some parts of their own turf. (How very true this turned out to be is quite another story, and not a happy one for Chuck Hemingway.) Comptroller-types had very small incentive to enlist a zealous budgeter, or even a competent one.

So it should have come as small surprise that the Comptroller's report to the Gang of Four, providing "basic information for a Budget Director/Analyst"—note that Hemingway had altered the title unilaterally—proposed a salary range "in the neighborhood of $21,000." Such a range was not unbelievably low in those days before a new Mayor put some facts of economic life into payroll practice, but the Comptroller's salary was over $30,000 and his two deputies were over $25,000. An incoming budgeter would have first-hand evidence of what his place in City Hall's hierarchy was to be.

* * *

Meanwhile, Whalen and his conferees targeted more alterations in the city's operations, all directed toward economies and, almost incidentally, efficiencies. Some of the cash-saving decisions and directives were tiny but usefully symbolic. Bills were to be paid twice a month instead of every week, so as to increase the funds that Treasurer Ray Joyce had on hand for investments which, one day, would bring in a few more dollars.

At the same time, the order went out to save postage costs by ending the old practice of mailing receipts for tax payments and sending notices to parking violators. A price was put on maps of the city, hitherto free. Records demanded through Freedom of Information Law requests were to be supplied with a charge attached. Fees for sewer inspections were raised.

More importantly, a contract with an outside contractor for work on the sewer system was cancelled. So were service contracts—and here the steps became bold indeed—with two

heavily favored vendors, Brownie's tree service and the exter-
mination services of Linindoll, the Thirteenth Ward leader
who'd had sacrosanct business linkage between party and city.
City employees could perform numerous services that chronically cost a pretty pence: Pest control, if largely removed from
private hands, could save $30,000 a year.

"Reforms" which in virtually any other city would have
been unnecessary were hurried into effect. One slow-moving
project—a central garage for the city's fleet, where fuel for fire
trucks and healing for bent fenders would be mutually available—made regular agenda appearances, a foretaste of problems in Public Works for many moons. Trees for the parks and
curbsides—23,000 of them owned by the city—were a costly
item to be revalued, with the outcome that householders were
to be charged for new plantings along the streets. Water rent
collections were lagging—what to do? The department's
deficit presented a potential 14% increase in rates. For sewer
project excavations, city personnel were now trainees preparing to operate backhoes so that the work need not be contracted out. A costly bulge in overtime for the animal control crew
was ordered to be eliminated. At once.

Purchasing and the City Engineer were told that—"as
rapidly as possible"—they must draw up specifications for
city-wide trash collections. (Only part of the city was being
covered by this sanitation essential; in other sections, homeowners and businesses had to deal individually with haulers—
from among whose ranks Corning had recruited the
Commissioner of Public Works.)

The agenda was truly broad. Department heads were
called in to receive instructions—politely, on the first telling—
or to offer explanations for malfunctions or nonfeasance:
Representatives of Public Works, Parks, Water, Purchasing,
Fire, the Engineer, the Planner—all made appearances. To the
new jobs assessors, it became clear that the responsibilities
were far above the abilities of many incumbents. Some of these
were further handicapped by their built-in assumption of
immunity from normal employment obligations—rewards of

political servitude with no results expected or required above absolute minimum.

*   *   *

The absent Mayor figured in it all sporadically and peripherally, with respect for his office and his prerogatives publicly maintained. In early winter, two salary increases of $1,000 in Public Works were to be reviewed in Boston. Corning was to hear, through Whalen and McArdle, of the City Engineer's wishes on the issue of tree planting and trimming. He was reported to have offered "instructions" on purchases for the Police and Fire departments—where, historically, suppliers were intimately tied to the Albany County Democratic Committee. But the city's government and its services had to be maintained, too, and most decisions could not wait for scribbled OK's or, alternatively, for an annoyed and negative comment to turn up.

A summary review in late spring provided encouraging data on the effects of the Gang of Four's efforts to hold down spending. For the first six months of the fiscal year, expenditures were $3 million less than for the same period of 1981-1982.[2] Part of their goal was to quickly impress the bond-rating agencies, in hope of obtaining a reversal of the recent downgradings. That desired result was not soon forthcoming, but at least the city could negotiate in a warmer climate.

In a sneak preview of a much more costly and disruptive Normans Kill landslide 17 years later, Whalen informed Corning that "We still have to resolve that $200,000+ landslide out in Delmar on the main water line coming in from the Alcove (Reservoir). NM Power (Niagara Mohawk) has agreed to some liability but not much. In the meantime we have contractors who haven't been paid." He anticipated meeting "with Mike Cahill, the new GM of NMP, to see what kind of solution we can reach." The "solution" clearly didn't confront the essence of the real problem, which could be deferred to a distant day. And the report elicited no response from a helpless Corning.

* * *

The Four concurred that Whalen and McArdle should draft an Annual Message for the Mayor to submit to the Common Council. In reality, the document, of exactly 300 words,[3] went to the Council before Corning ever saw it. Whalen wrote an apology for his carelessness (possibly willful), but by that time Corning's body and spirit, much less his intellectual will, were barely functioning. The message was one of the last official papers he would ever handle.

In Corning's name, the message indirectly delivered to Mario Cuomo a due bill for the Mayor's record of support in the recent primary and election. The actual message was clear enough. In response to the Governor's Executive Budget, proposing a round of State Aid cuts which in Albany's case would subtract $1 million from the anticipated aid package, Cuomo was assured that "Albanians have always prided themselves on their willingness to 'pitch in' during difficult times." But a plea was appended to the effect that "We should not, however, be called upon to bear more than our fair share." This appeal—which fell on ears no more compassionate than ever—pointed to Albany's "very small tax base" caused by "tax-exempt State-occupied real property."

"Some form of special aid should be given to Albany." This lay-it-on-the-line tone, which Corning might have chosen to withhold from a public document if he'd been given the chance, produced not even a "Sorry, pal" acknowledgement.

Otherwise, the message largely consisted of harmless data compiled to help reassure Corning's constituents that he really was doing his job in his old style. The maneuver apparently created that effect, for a news report was headlined "*Corning's aid plea a test of Cuomo's political debt.*"

The city was understandably slow to comprehend the true picture because of the distortions created by Corning's apologists, including Whalen.

Their confusing left-handed/right-handed stories erupted into bold type in the first days of April when Whalen was assuring reporters that the cabinet-style referrals by the Regency advisers merely formed "the basis for constructing recommendations" for Corning. A few days after Easter, he offered the explanation that "All we're really doing is updating some of the practices of the city and improving the economic climate." But simultaneously McManus's inside scoop was insistent that Corning hadn't been making any decisions for some time and "hasn't been consulted on governmental or political matters for at least two months," or approximately the date of the final Whalen-McArdle visit with him. Bill Keefe, the confidential messenger who for months had made repeated round trips to the Mayor's bedside, "hasn't been in to see him in a long, long time." Such information, now less than confidential, presumably would have derived only from Keefe.

In speaking to service clubs during the long spring, Whalen was surprisingly upbeat, given what he knew. Remarking that Corning was "still in charge"—which was true only in the narrow legal sense—he ran down a list of positive indicators: "Budget changes, including a capital budget," and administrative changes (the plumber and electrician, whose hiring was still providing popular mileage; a new central maintenance garage; revised policies on demolition of city-owned properties; a hiring freeze; and zoning ordinances). The recital was, he explained much later, "part of the ritual we followed to keep Corning in the arena."

"Keeping the Old Guard in the loop" was now his explanation for such repeated assurances as "Corning's directions are paramount because he is still the Mayor." He needed to head off discontent and dissension in the party's uncertain ranks, while maintaining a calming consistency in his message. It was his own version of "a touch of old Harry in the night," as one scribe has Henry the Fourth referring to his midnight rides among his troops awaiting battle orders.

But the burden of his talk straightforwardly clarified

the directions he wanted to move the city: Improvements in local government operations—"cost-effective measures and purchasing practices," with strong attention also to "downtown rebirth" and "quality of life." He and his Gang had accumulated a handy (and valid) set of what came to be termed, in the Linda Tripp era, "talking points."

Joining a delegation from the State Conference of Mayors, Whalen spoke up to remind New York's two most powerful legislators of the day, Senate Majority Leader Warren Anderson and Assembly Speaker Stanley Fink, that "The cities are up against the wall—today it's the cities that house the majority of the poor; have the unemployed to take care of; and, too, this new category, the homeless." (So, the problem of homelessness arrived on the public's conscience in the winter of 1982-1983?)

"If there ever was a time," he said, "when federal and state aid should be coming to the cities—it's now!"

In fact, however, producing a viable budget document—challenging enough in any circumstances—was being victimized by the impact of the Reagan fiscal follies. Following Congressman Jack Kemp's trickle-down theory, the administration in Washington continued to slash federal revenue-sharing, a severe blow. And the Cuomo administration was clamping down on aid to localities—in the midst of a year for which that income already had been budgeted.

Whalen's new responsibilities had broadened his perspective on layers of government and their respective functions. And his unofficial office had given him a snapshot of the "new category, the homeless," that was to be heard from in full volume everywhere. In its touching way, his comment—and certain of its language—represented an awakening. And Whalen's boldness in standing up as not only a newcomer but as merely a pinchhitter for an absent mayor was striking indeed among that closed-shop fellowship. At the moment, it was uncertain whether he'd ever join them again, but *by Jove!* he was heard! Albany was in the ranks, Corning or no.

* * *

The struggle to save the city was barely beginning. The dimensions of the task came more clearly into view with each adverse event. For the next months, the team would function usefully together. But as the days shortened and then began to lengthen again, the leadership was devolving onto one man.

A newspaper editorial had mentioned Whalen as "out front." Of himself, he saw "an up-front guy."

* * *

During the late winter and early spring, both Albany newspapers returned to mine a theme that carried plenty of paydirt: the city's long and continuing record of tricks and dodges that sold the taxpayers short. Among these, the most significant outlined the practice of keeping public funds in checking accounts that paid no interest, mostly as a favor to a single bank.

Such articles may possibly have proved to hasten the Whalen responses as he began—even before becoming Mayor—to change so many of the sneaky or slovenly habits that had characterized the Corning administration. The exposure of bad practice was an exemplary journalistic service deserving of commendation. But editorially the *Times Union* could not refrain from observing that "While Albany, under the leadership of Common Council President Thomas M. Whalen, III, has been moving swiftly to correct many abuses, it must be noted that none of this reformist zeal became apparent until after the *Times Union* and its sister paper, the *Knickerbocker News*, published numerous articles revealing wasteful and, in some cases, illegal fiscal practices."

The boast that the Whalen group's "reformist zeal" was brought about only by being shamed into it through the newspaper revelations seems an unnecessary putdown. Albany was in the throes of shedding many of the practices that had prospered in the departing administration. Whalen was feeling—and responding to—the pressures and ultimatums of the State Comptroller, apart from his own inclinations and conscientious judgments. The incoming managers—in their earliest weeks—could fairly be expected to tackle improprieties once they had the opportunity, without being impelled into action by news stories.[4]

NOTES

[1] Sudden and radical—even momentous—change was in the air. In November, the *Times Union* had hailed "a revolution of sorts" when Whalen's Gang of Four produced Albany's budget for 1983, and by the next summer, soon after Whalen became Mayor, the newspaper saw a "big revolution" in the city's governance. Similar expressions were appearing daily in many forums.

[2] A notable exception to the general acceptance of the mandate for fiscal prudence was being persistently encountered in Public Works, the umbrella department with multiple interests, a major one being as a receptacle for patronage jobs. One of its bureaus, Parks, was building toward a huge, uncontrolled—and apparently uncontrollable—deficit that later in the fiscal year would require major retrenchment, including much of the traditional unskilled work force.

[3] It is noteworthy that of the total of 300 words Whalen composed for Corning, 182, or 60%, were what might easily be termed "short and sweet"—words of one syllable containing one, two, three or four letters, none longer and averaging less than three characters per word. The result was a terse, punchy statement, a fine example of understandable English Composition. Coincidentally but serving to point up the uncertain status of Whalen and his colleagues in undertaking each new direction, an editorial that day in the *Times Union* noted that they had "responsibility but not the proper authority."

⁴ Whalen probably could have been more generous in acknowledging and lauding such examples of the papers' good work when it paralleled his own objectives and efforts. On the other hand, the newspapers obstinately seemed unable or unwilling, over the years, to recognize and report that their city, after generations of scandalous practices, now had a new man in charge whose standards and objectives deserved support. Whalen could have accomplished more in his time, and the press could have found gratification in the outcome, if a mutual myopia approaching a moral blindness, could have been eliminated. The failure to achieve that state was to be Albany's costly loss.

(When the essence of this proposition was expressed to Whalen, he concurred without reservation.)

"When I Get Back"

Through the fall and early winter, each forecast of Corning's early release had been followed by another postponement. But each was combined with assurances that Albany's Mayor was on top of his job, directing the city's governance and approving work of subordinates who were still described as merely carrying out his wishes.

Whalen was now more than ever in a thumb-in-the-dike situation: Without being able to know when relief would occur, he faced indefinite prolonging of major municipal ailments (ultimately, the delay was 100 additional days) while lacking authority to execute policies or to initiate whatever cures were advisable.

Promises to the State Comptroller and his auditing legions, reassurances to the bond-rating houses, action to satisfy a skeptical media—all had suffered from a distinctly hollow sound. They were issuing from an unproven second-fiddler who conceivably might be displaced by a vexed Erastus Corning. The absent Mayor's loyal partisans were still regularly renewing their optimistic predictions of a reinstated Corning. When his acquisition of a specially equipped van and his plan to drive it triumphantly back home became known in City Hall, the preposterous aspect of his dream was all but put aside by this seeming confirmation that he still possessed the will to return—and might even pull it off despite the huge obstacles. An overly zealous agenda could easily be not merely embarrassingly presumptuous but downright dangerous.

But the delicate and confused situation was about to enter a new phase.

* * *

A note of resigned realism—semi-disguised in a couple of lines of feeble humor—appeared in the final paragraph of a rambling dictated letter to Whalen, less than a week before the drastic abdominal surgery which marked the onset of his final decline.

"There is nothing I want more than to get back to work," he managed to indicate through Roberta Miller, one of his two secretaries. "But," he continued, "you and Vince are doing so well I may just hang around here a little while longer." (Whalen seized upon this somewhat obscure—"doing so well"—vote of confidence as a reason to thank Corning for the encouraging words.)

Corning's remark contains the telltale signs of a wry joke, left open for the recipient's interpretation. Implicitly, he assumed that Whalen would share an awareness he had no choice but to "hang around" the hospital, and that "a little while" didn't really mean several days or a few weeks. Rather, an indefinite period lay ahead which, by now, offered little expectation of escape from the series of setbacks punctuating the official forced optimism The letter to Whalen contained two other "When I get back" references likewise essentially modified by the "hang around" expression.

The message incorporated about 250 words, covering a dozen different areas of concern at City Hall and harking back to items Whalen had brought up in a letter of his own a week earlier.

The Mayor "would be glad if Chuck"—Hemingway, whom he had appointed as Comptroller to fill a vacancy only a month earlier—"would create a budget director."[1] That was bracketed in a sentence with the hope that "a good deputy" for the purchasing agent's office could be provided by the Democratic county committee. This constituted an acknowledgment—in response to difficulties Whalen had cited—that the purchasing department was not functioning effectively.[2]

The letter mentioned another city employee as "nearly useless," but wanted the man's firing to wait "till I get back." A pair of others "are just trying to do the best job they can," clearly an off-putting response to a Whalen complaint.[3] A further "when I get back" referred to efforts to enlist a prominent educator's help as a volunteer on a project that was of interest to him.

Strangely, the longest single reference undertook to explain that Albany County takes in 10 towns and three cities—a most elementary political fact learned in grade-school texts. He then repeated this statistic in a tangled suggestion that counties could be given "the right to distribute Medicare [he should have said Medicaid] on a number of different plans." This would "help," he said twice, but his references lacked any realistic connection to the problems his city administration was facing.

Another paragraph quite needlessly explained that New York City embraces several counties, somehow making it impossible—he said—for Mayor Koch to understand that Upstate's cities and town's are distinct entities.

The letter, dated February 17, was signed in his name by Bobbie Miller. It was the last communication from Corning that Whalen would receive.

* * *

Coincident with this final letter, just before the surgery, the *Times Union* devoted 400 editorial words urging tactfully but pointedly that he "declare himself officially absent" so a "temporary mayor" could be installed. The cost to the city inflicted by the absence of "hands-on leadership" and the handicapping lack of "the proper authority" to govern were sharply mentioned.

Gently, Corning was advised that he personally might be better off "if he (were) allowed to concentrate all his efforts

on his own recuperation" rather than having "the burden (of)
the more routine issues and problems of city government."

Considering his condition, it is wholly possible, of
course, that he never read or even heard of this editorial counseling. But it is at least equally plausible that a visitor would
have informed him of advice intended "for your own good,
Erastus," as well as for his city's.

However well meant, an editorial was certain to be the
most ineffective means of accomplishing a reasonable resolution of the city's dilemma.

Whether or not the Mayor knew of the gratuitous
advice, the idea of stepping aside most assuredly would
already have entered his mind—repeatedly—but been quickly
discarded. For him to acknowledge—to himself or to his public—that he was influenced by an editorial was unthinkable.

Erastus Corning did not need publishers to tell him
how to behave, or editors to write even a tentative *finis* to the
long chapter he had himself composed. The disdain—and the
language—in which he would dismiss the suggestion is readily imaginable.

No answer came from him, nor any action. He would
ride his horse to the finish line, blinders and all. As his intimate friend Doug Rutnik has analyzed Corning's psyche, he
always intended to die "with his boots on." His stubbornness,
of course, was satisfying to him—but it ignored the best interests of his city and defied the spirit of his oath of office.

* * *

No matter what the realities were for him, Corning
adamantly believed that he was going to return, Holt-Harris
was convinced. "But I knew he was dying. To see that wasn't
hard even without any specialized knowledge."

Whalen was struck by the eventual realization, somewhat belatedly reached, that even if Corning did come back to
Albany he was not going to be functional. The need to push
ahead with business-like measures—beyond the matter of

"reforms"—was spurred by that growing awareness. Against his will, he was being persuaded that full responsibility was hastening his way.

NOTES

[1] An odd way of referring to a history-making selection of a person who would head an office Corning had resisted for 40 years. Obviously, Corning saw such a person subordinate to an untried official who was, in turn, subject to control by the Mayor himself. To "create a budget director" was much more of an issue than Corning would allow himself to concede.

[2] A deputy purchasing agent, Charles Thorne, was recruited in early spring to help improve procedures, and eventually he was advanced to the top job. After a few years, he became the Mayor's executive secretary.

[3] Whalen disposed of two of the three persons mentioned in this paragraph promptly after he became Mayor. The third retired about a year later.

A Change of Tune

One positive event in Corning's first six months in Boston came about in mid-March. Governor Cuomo signed a bill bestowing his name on a towering (589-foot) office building. How responsive to this monumental tribute Corning could have been is problematic. Only then beginning to emerge from the effects of several hours of emergency surgery to stanch life-threatening bleeding from multiple abdominal ulcers, he was downgraded by his surgeons to "guarded" condition. He had little enough to cheer him. Having suffered a heart attack in addition to undergoing the surgery, he was alive thanks largely to a catheter aiding his heart's functioning. He could breathe only with the aid of a respirator, and was receiving nourishment intravenously. All of this further isolated him. That same day happened to begin the tenth of his 11 months of hospital confinement.

By this time, his mail was withheld. But at such a critical hour, Hemingway sent him a letter proposing appointment of another Deputy Comptroller. "No!" someone answered. For his caregivers' use in sharply limiting access to his room, Corning had identified 10 individuals he "would need to see" on occasion. Whether or not Whalen's name was included, he never saw Corning alive again. Considering Corning's condition, the surprise is that he would enumerate as many as 10, and doubt is inevitable that he ever saw them all. McArdle was allowed to visit him once, briefly, later in the spring. For months, that was the entire contact with official Albany.

Whalen and his three colleagues were moving ahead, obviously now without any genuine directions. Their unglamorous agenda required attention to such dreary issues as specifications for trash removal, fixing charges for haulers' dumping at the city's landfill, and moving against delinquencies in their payments. More in the reform mode, a decades-old no-bid deal which was costing the city $126,000 a year for the services of two electricians was severed at last in favor of a pair of $20,000 payroll slots.

Occasional glimpses of the old way of doing business flared repeatedly. Numerous commercial haulers (the worst offenders) were taking advantage of the landfill without paying the proper fees. These cumulatively totaled over $250,000. Two Parks employees were suspended for setting up a no-show job during the winter. Their scheme netted only several hundred dollars, suggesting that they weren't very efficient either on or off the payroll.

More significantly, Whalen and his little cell spent hours comparing departments' expenditures with the budgeted items. Never far below the surface was the ongoing need to root out foot-dragging among the unpersuaded in City Hall and it's outposts. Some of the unconverted had adopted schemes aimed at covertly handicapping any efforts to push forward on the new agenda.

Advice on threading his way through minefields of unwelcome surprises and past each newly turned stone was ample. Swyer, Drislane, and Holt-Harris were the principally reliable sources, though numerous other wise friends such as Alan Iselin and Steve Fischer were readily available. Much of the useful counsel was earnestly sought, some was volunteered. In the latter category, the most significant was offered by Francis Bergan, whose experience was rich in both Albany political lore and in apolitical judiciousness.

The mayoralty, past and future, was looming as Bergan insistently spoke to Whalen on the nuances of power within his imminent responsibility. The judge, long a witness to just such power, was acutely aware of its immense value. Power,

unprecedented and largely unimagined by Whalen, was waiting in the Mayor's office—to be *used*, Bergan reiterated often,
distinguishing the potential for political power from innate
governmental power. He cautioned the Mayor-to-be against
surrendering the political power or failing to exercise it effectively.

"Give it up," he warned, "and you will find someone
using it against you!"

The accuracy of his assessment was borne out soon
enough. From Whalen's first week in office, Albany's streets
were mobbed with ambitious souls eager to compete for a slice
of this prize that Erastus Corning had finally handed out. And
the recipient already was revealing indications that they
couldn't depend on him.

Before a service club, observing that "Cities cannot create jobs; what they can create is an environment where positive
and progressive things can take place affecting the quality of
life for everyone," Whalen offered a prelude to a theme he was
to pursue for the next several years.

* * *

The morning paper on March 15 carried a Page One
article anticipating a Whalen mayoralty. But in the obituary
page was news of Tom Whalen, Jr.'s death from a heart attack
just days before his seventy-sixth birthday. His health had
been consistently good and his sudden death came as a major
shock, intensifying the loss.

Vacationing in Florida at Pompano Beach, he had written a chatty letter to his son only a few days earlier, expressing
hope that "all this indecision isn't bothering you too much—I
can't understand Corning's thinking other than he's a very sick
man—so hang in there."

"I'm sure you have things under control," he added
reassuringly.

This was to be the abrupt end of the father's many years
of sagacious counsel, leavened as it was by his affectionate con-

fidence. The letter remained in the Mayor's desk drawer for the next 10 years.

If he had lived only several weeks longer, he would have seen Tom installed as Mayor—an especially heavy emotional loss for the son.

* * *

From the sidelines, Whalen could read Bob McManus's commentary that he was "up, looking down, an advantage appreciated by infantry officers and politicians," while a "scramble for power is clearly under way." In Albany, McManus wrote, "The old-fashioned Irish Catholic Democrat machine has become irrelevant to many, a vehicle for the advancement of very narrow and selfish special interests."

He quoted a committeeman, otherwise unidentified: "Whalen is unassailably in—he's gilt-edged." This observer was unassailably right; the wonder is that anyone in Albany that spring failed—or refused—to realize Corning was dying and his lawful successor was already doing much of the job.

But McManus also described Whalen's position as "very delicate, to put it mildly." He'd become "something of a target, both governmentally and politically." Whalen thought the targeting was by the media, with editors and writers "looking to me for signals on Corning, whether he'd be returning—and how far I was willing to go in reforming the government while he was still alive." (His indulging in the word *reform* about his actions is striking, in contrast to his earlier positions and affiliations.)

Whalen's answer to the "how far" question was, "Not very far, considering the whole picture.

"It would be foolhardy," he felt, "to go too far and unnecessarily raise the ire of the politicians. Over-aggressiveness would be seen as disrespectful. They (politicians) were hanging back, willing to wait and see, although only a very little wasn't a concern.

"And they had to first accept that I was there because

Erastus Corning had put me there—whether they liked it or not. Meanwhile, they weren't going to come after me. Rube (Gersowitz) probably was massaging the other ward leaders. So, politically, all their latent opposition didn't materialize at that time." Once he had taken office, his policies did indeed raise ire among the Tories.

* * *

Heartlessly, perhaps, 70% of the Mayor's fellow Albanians told a poll-taker in the early spring that he should resign or at least step aside. Promptly, the Common Council responded by fatuously agreeing to a resolution brought by Alderman Gerald Jennings complimenting the virtually coma-tose Corning on his "truly extraordinary job" under "such diffi-cult circumstances," and "unequivocally" dismissing "any con-sideration by the Mayor that he temporarily step aside." Unfortunately, the kind words could not alter the "difficult cir-cumstances" or make possible a better chance of success in administration of the city's affairs while its Mayor languished close to death.

Confusing the picture further, McArdle said that Corning was doing "better than 150% of what any municipali-ty could expect from its mayor." When, on a mid-April Friday, he had his 10-minute bedside visit, it was the only real contact by anyone from City Hall with the Mayor in the last three months of his life. Unable to speak, Corning "mouthed the words" and did not squander his waning energy to write out his end of the exchange. Nonetheless, his visitor emerged from the gloomy encounter reporting that he "just looked good—he had that gleam in his eye. He's ready to get back into the swing of things." Corning had exactly six weeks to live.

As was true of McArdle's numerous extravagant remarks on Corning's prospects, this was an attempt to main-tain relative calm among the worried politicians at home, but without meaning to influence official business at City Hall.

In the same tense period, Whalen, after having frequently insisted the Mayor was approving all their actions, changed his tune. He began admitting outright that actually he and McArdle jointly arrived at many decisions. He'd been referring to Albany's "government by committee since January," but with Corning continuously in intensive care, it seemed preposterous to continue the pretense that his efforts were at Corning's direction or, alternatively, at least in tune with his priorities. The protective terminology was showing signs of basic amendment: "Between us (McArdle and himself) we have a pretty good handle on his mental processes and the direction he would want us to take," was typical of Whalen's newest choice of language.

In his abruptly adopted new scenario, he now was particularly firm in asserting his own prerogatives (usually acknowledging also the participation of his "Gang of Four") in such precedent-setting functions as hiring the electrician and plumber or accepting bids on jobs customarily done without the nuisance of bidding; and on the other hand, the severing of several consultants to create economies worth some $35,000 annually. Such responsibilities, he explained pointedly, especially lay outside the focus of Holt-Harris's Regency, the other partners with whom he was engaged. They were "not running the city, by any means—we are!" That is, it was he—along with the Comptroller and Corporation Counsel—who was taking the advisable initiatives and necessary responsibility. He was persistent in emphasizing this point. McArdle joined in publicly recognizing that Corning had transferred to Whalen most of the routine functions of the mayoralty, including approval of ordinances and contracts.

These concessions were a bold change from previous practice. Designation of Whalen as Acting Mayor was not possible legally, and he stepped back from admitting that this really was his true role; here, it was clearly more politic to refrain from any such claim. "I don't consider myself Acting Mayor," he said, "but one of a number of key city officials who have agreed to act in concert in doing the day-to-day operational measures that need to be carried out."

* * *

His workday on the combined public and private jobs
started at 8 and—after frequently skipping lunch—he usually
worked through the evening to 7:30 or later. His city salary
was at the rate of $38 a day, far inferior to a lawyer's hourly
billing level.

Seeking to stabilize awareness of his City Hall presence—if not necessarily his status—he would borrow a desk in
the City Clerk's office adjacent to the Council Chamber.
Previous Council presidents had lacked enough stature to win
them respectable quarters. When the hour arrived for Whalen
and the 15 Democratic aldermen to caucus before their public
sessions, they could only crowd into that unprepossessing
office, lining up against a wall, perching on desks, or possibly
grabbing a handy chair.

Twice weekly, he'd been holding office hours in
Corning's office—with makeshift arrangements to avoid a
takeover appearance—but soon these sessions had to expand
into daily events to accommodate staff queries and respond to
constituents. The sense of an endpoint was inevitable.

* * *

Now that we seem to have the respite of a chapter without a footnote, perhaps we should be faithful to the author's
predilection by creating a pseudo-footnote. Just for fun:

Of the footnoting habit, John Barrymore said[1] "It's like
having to run downstairs to answer the doorbell during the
first night of the honeymoon."

NOTE

[1] As quoted by Gene Fowler in *Goodnight, Sweet Prince* (Viking, 1944).

The Two Missing Words

Erastus Corning was "revered" by Mario Cuomo, said the Governor's top-drawer assistant, Tim Russert, whom Cuomo, as Governor-elect, had quickly recruited from Senator Daniel P. Moynihan's staff, where his natural political instincts and savvy had won him respect and prominence. The Governor credited Russert with having gained him access to people and places otherwise inaccessible to him. Now, a month into the new State administration, Russert assured Albany that "anything the Mayor says is important to us."

But, he added, "The Governor will stand by his announced reductions in aid to localities," costing Albany about $1 million. Additionally, the state's takeover of local Medicaid costs was aimed at benefiting counties, rather than cities—and since New York City's huge population was organized into five counties, that's where the great bulk of this change brought more funding. Corning alluded to all this inaccurately and confusingly in his last letter to Whalen in February, as we have seen.

Despite the early optimism about patronage, Albany County never received any major appointee from Cuomo, who hardly could have been pleased by the repeated newspaper speculation about the anticipated payout rising from his "debt to Corning"—and to Albany's job-seekers. The shortfall was rationalized publicly as merely exemplifying O'Connell's great preference for many low-level jobs that would tie in the loyalties of large numbers of families rather than a single grandee.[1]

The rationale, however, ignored the hunger and thirst of a corps of lawyers, political appointees and officials at lower stages of government, and just plain Loyalist Democrats eager for name recognition and regular paychecks.

Success, even, in acquiring an unusual number of lesser favors from Cuomo and his patronage advisors, Fabian Palomino and Andrew Cuomo, is questionable. Polly Noonan, who had sponsored a $100-a-plate dinner for the ticket at the Polish Community Center just before the election, was given a title as a vice-chairman of the Democratic State Committee, clearly as a cost-free courtesy to Corning. One of her daughters received a good job (after she had been dropped by Whalen from the city payroll) placing 800 applicants in short-term work processing tax returns.

Altogether, Albany Democrats' patronage porridge was thin gruel in the Cuomo years, though as that uniquely placed observer, John Holt-Harris, said, "He was very, very grateful to Erastus."

During such developments over a period of more than three months before his death, Corning was all but incommunicado and virtually a complete non-participant in the governing of Albany. His physician-friend dating back nearly a half-century, Dick Beebe, who had admitted him to the hospital months earlier, had only despairingly gone along with the Mayor's decision to go to Boston for unrealistically envisioned rehabilitation. Visiting him there in mid-May, Dr. Beebe found him "very ill—he recognized me and smiled." Some others who visited Corning's room reported that he did not indicate any recognition.

A published report confirmed that he did not always know people who had been familiar to him over many years, that he slept much of every day, could not speak or write, and had grown even more gaunt, an indication of his weakening condition. "A very delicate situation," Whalen said, in effect echoing a remark made two months earlier about his own position. Another account employed the word "deteriorating" exactly a week before the end, contrasting it with "improving," the state which the long trail of optimistic reports had encouraged the public to imagine might be true.

The time had come for even the more loyal among the Loyalists to recognize that the end was near. A reporter discerned a "subtle change" in Albany's "political climate." Bill Keefe seemed to recognize this when he volunteered that Corning had "a lot of faith and trust in Tom Whalen."

Quite coincidentally, in the city where Erastus Corning lay helpless that city's mayor was at the end of his political life. On Friday, May 27, Kevin White finally announced that he would not, after all, seek reelection. His trial run had lasted almost precisely the length of Mayor Corning's ill-fated stay in Mayor White's troubled city. "The media got Kevin," wrote George V. Higgins, the novelist and critic.

* * *

With weirdly unfortunate timing, precisely as the last 48 hours of Corning's life ebbed, Albany's afternoon newspaper, the *Knickerbocker News*, topped its front page with a two-line banner in a bold type large enough to chronicle Grant taking Richmond:

**Albany work force
one of NY's largest**

The big "news" was that the number of municipal employees remained among the largest—and lowest paid—of the state's "major" cities (the 13 with 50,000 population). Albany, sixth most populous, hired more people (per capita) than any of the others except for New York City, as of both 1977 and 1981. But, save for Binghamton, those employees earned—or, at least, received—the lowest salaries, averaging $1,077 a month. Additional data showed, for example, Albany Parks payroll of 304 exactly equalling the *combined* comparable payrolls of Rochester and Schenectady. But Albany's 304 were paid only 40% as much as those two cities' 304.

These revelations' 1,100 words failed to include the two words "Erastus Corning." He was referred to once, only cryptically, as "the hospitalized mayor." The omission suggested the degree to which Corning's importance to his city had waned along with his vitality in his final months. The figures, and the underlying conditions which they exemplified, were essential portions of Corning's legacy after four decades at the helm.

The sole individual quoted was Whalen: "We have made substantial progress in cutting city spending," he observed without elaborating. Reduction was a trend already in effect. The city's 1981 payroll of 2,300 was now down to 1,820 as a complete transfer of responsibility loomed. The 20% drop in staff produced an actual saving of only 15% because the pruning surely began at the most expendable level. In that 1981-83 interim, Albany's fiscal outlook had darkened dismally as the severe national recession took hold, along with the trickle-down atmosphere inherent in the early Reagan administration. However much of the cut in jobs had occurred in 1983 under Whalen's sponsorship was not reported.

* * *

Readers of the *Knickerbocker News* would find no update on Corning's health on the day his long ordeal finally would come to a close.

But Friday's edition, 24 hours before the fatal heart attack, had reported that he "remains in stable condition," in two short paragraphs of 46 words, almost all of them simply retelling the discouraging year's familiar story.

Another page, however, held an extensive article which in effect poignantly profiled the government he had presided over. It was a City Hall announcement resulting from one of the fiscal reforms already begun under the forced draft of Tom Whalen's brisk approach:

Albany's cash had just begun to draw interest at KeyBank after decades of sitting there interest-free throughout

Corning's mayoralty. Initially, the deposits would now start
receiving interest at 7.98%.

No "last word" of Erastus Corning's was noted or
recorded. As for Tom Whalen's "last words" before he assumed
Corning's office, among them was this insightfully fatalistic
comment:

"I don't expect to be loved by everyone."

NOTE

[1] "I would rather have the charwomen and the janitors"
(than the white-collar bureaucrats), O'Connell has been quoted.
"They need the work and usually come from large families with a
lot of votes and a lot of friends." (It's entirely possible that he did
actually give voice to this bit of practical philosophy, although such
a clear-cut statement uttered within the hearing of someone who
could be expected to write it down, hardly is characteristic of his
what's-it-to-you attitude. Equally likely is the prospect that a person knowledgeable in the O'Connell policy on patronage took it
upon himself to express it.) Note that "they need the work" is more
than somewhat off the mark. What the O'Connell subjects truly
needed was income, not merely work as such. The Organization's
role was to distribute pathetically tiny bits of cash, and plenty of little jobs provided a practical way of spreading the money around.
(The Organization's theme of "Jobs, Jobs, Jobs" was a cynical version
of that three-centuries-old comment by Francis Bacon: "Money is
like muck, not good unless it be spread.") A dollar or two could
purchase dependence, gratitude, and votes, in that order.

January 1, 1970: Whalen, not quite 36 years old, is sworn in by
Erastus Corning as a judge of Albany's City Court. Oldest son
Tommy is by his side.
(Courtesy of the Whalen Family)

Many happy returns: A jubilant Erastus Corning and Whalen
exchange congratulations at a victory party in the county
committee's headquarters.
(Courtesy of the Whalen Family)

At a press conference on City Hall's steps heralding the
Tricentennial, Whalen bantered with the media. Enjoying a laugh
were Lew Swyer (far right), Dick Barrett (in hat and glasses), Chuck
Hemingway and Dusty Miller (both with hands raised), and
Charlie Cahill (far left).
(Courtesy of the Whalen Family)

Ed Koch didn't care much for Albany, but he didn't deign Whalen's
office as a setting for "Big Six" mayors' lobbying calls at the Capitol.
(Courtesy of the Whalen Family)

A Tricentennial highlight was a costumed reenactment at the
Capitol featuring Governor Mario Cuomo, Lewis A. Swyer,
and Whalen. Matilda Cuomo is in the center.
(Courtesy of the Whalen Family)

Few people would have adopted an unwelcome familiarity with
Tom Whalen, and when Alfonse D'Amato took that liberty, the
Mayor's tolerance was strained.
(Courtesy of the Whalen Family)

The man behind two Mayors, Bill Keefe. (See "The Placid Hudson" chapter.) He served Corning for 10 years, worked for Whalen for 30 months, and knew more voters than either.
(Courtesy of the Whalen Family)

Candid counsellor John E. Holt-Harris (center), a frequent visitor in the Mayor's office, and Alan Iselin, who managed Whalen's 1985 reelection campaign.
(Courtesy of the Whalen Family)

Assemblyman Dick Conners predicted Corning's legend would
overwhelm Whalen, but their relations always were cordial,
as (above) at the county committee's annual picnic.
(Courtesy of the Whalen Family)

The city's lawyer, Vinnie McArdle, a Corning protégé, advised
Whalen throughout his term. Lew Swyer, partially visible at right,
often was in camera range.
(Courtesy of the Whalen Family)

"The sunny smiles could blind you," wrote Bob McManus after comptroller Ned Regan's urgent visit in June 1983 ended in surprising amity.
(Courtesy of the Whalen Family)

A rare scene of joviality between the Mayor and Alderman Gerald D. Jennings, Whalen's antagonist and successor. State Senator Howard Nolan is at far right.
(Courtesy of the Whalen Family)

CORNING-WHALEN

★ ★ ★ ★ ★ ★

AKE

How about adding → *Vote the Democratic Team*

A Team For The Future

Whalen was new to "the Democratic team" in the spring of 1981
when he jotted a significant suggestion on the proof of a proposed
campaign poster. Mayor Corning then initialed his "OK."
(Courtesy of the Whalen Family)

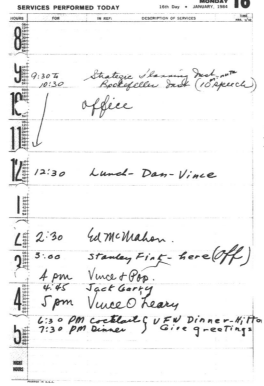

The Mayor's day had
been long and busy on
January 16, 1984, before
the late-afternoon call
came to inform him that
IBM was no longer inter-
ested in converting old
Union Station.
*(Courtesy of the Whalen
Family)*

On occasional summer days, the Mayor carried a brown-bag
lunch out to the Joseph Henry Memorial in Academy Park and
invited conversations with constituents.
(Courtesy of the Whalen Family)

The Special Olympics were special for Albany's Mayor, who worked
energetically to bring the event to the city for annual competitions.
(Courtesy of the Whalen Family)

The "First Night" celebrations on New Year's Eve were in their fifth
year (1990-1991) when Astro the Clown and Hardtimes Howie
caught up with the celebrant-in-chief.
(Courtesy of the Whalen Family)

Hy Rosen's pen (for the *Times Union*) depicted the spirit of two of
the highlights of Mayor Whalen's administration—the coming of
the 1986 Tricentennial celebration, following his 1985 election
certifying the "Whalen Era." Identifiable mates were Dan Klepak
(far left) and Vinnie McArdle (right).
(Courtesy of Hy Rosen)

The Mayor, recognizable despite the Superman regalia (phone booth and all), was the exhilarated champion who won "All America City" distinction for his hometown.
(Courtesy of Hy Rosen)

A tale of two cities' mayors—Watervliet and Albany.
J. Leo O'Brien was also the party's county chairman for Whalen's first seven years in office. Both died in 2002.
(Courtesy of the Whalen Family)

Whalen was over 50 when he took up sculling, described as "aquatic tightrope walking." He liked to row on the Hudson soon after dawn, then be at his desk before 8.
(Courtesy of the Whalen Family)

Winter hiking in the Adirondacks with Finn McCool, a companion for away-from-it-all weekends.
(Courtesy of the Whalen Family)

IV:
On the Ground
Running, *Running*

Introduction

Although that hackneyed expression, "Hit the ground running," with its imagery of paratroopers swooping down to free hostages, or Marines dashing ashore to overwhelm an enemy redoubt, is often applied figuratively, it can boast very few parallels to Tom Whalen's arrival in Room 102 just as venerable City Hall began its second century.

The demands that now were his to confront had offered valuable exposure. Within a limited scope, a variety of essential changes already had begun under his prodding. But overriding any opportunity to halt the city's downward slide was a lack of authority. On administrative issue after issue he'd not been able to act with true and decisive effectiveness. Legal authority remained in a man who, by hanging on to power while his health deteriorated to the edge of oblivion, was blocking normal channels of governing.

This, despite agonizing frustration, did etch with great clarity—and urgency—what needed to be tackled and accomplished. Albany's dilemma required a person who would indeed "hit the ground running." The city's good fortune had brought it such an individual who understood what he must try to achieve.

And, of equal importance, a man not hesitant about trying or timid about the possibility of failure, and unafraid of the challenge.

* * *

Those recent months had enabled him to see at first hand the extent of the city's troubles and learn what needed to be done, and done quickly. "Seeing" meant confronting those ills face-to-face and taking steps to remedy them now that he had received authority to do so. And even instituting long-range cures far beyond palliating the immediate crisis.

"It was a very valuable experience," as he afterward assessed it, "with benefit to me from both a political standpoint and the governmental one. It all helped me determine just who the political players were and the roots of their influence. And it enabled me to start with a real understanding of how the city worked—or didn't work. It was a gradual indoctrination into the Mayor's job. I also had the benefit of being seen in City Hall because people came to recognize a familiar face. They could connect it with someone and something actual, not just speculative.

"I knew enough about the city's finances to understand that there had to be radical surgery." This urgent fact had become more and more evident as the weeks had passed. "I didn't know a whole lot yet, but I recognized some of the political connections that were keeping the city from arriving at a 'good government' stage."

Bankers were better equipped than Whalen to deal with fiscal matters. Politicians' skins were much more sensitive to the electorate's wishes and whims. Career administrators were more adept in practicing mandated by-the-book management rules.

"But I had accumulated experience," was Whalen's rejoinder, "in a lot of ways and fields distinct from what their specialized areas could provide. A specialist is steeped in one discipline, but ordinarily lacks the desirable familiarity—much less, expertise—in useful additional areas of knowledge. I had done work that somehow was relevant to the daily demands on a city's chief executive. I'd had the opportunity to know at least a little bit about a lot of things. When I came to the Mayor's office, I came as unique in this particular respect. And this proved to be exceptionally useful to me."

One other ingredient from his past shared in his preparedness. Close-up observation while afoot for the party had fostered understanding of how misshapen politics had in turn warped the city's governance. This exposure, too, was significant in shaping the "map" he graphically reported as having guided his direction as he took over.

The Outsider Takes Over

Exactly a week before he became Mayor, Whalen seemingly had needed to be introduced to his prospective constituency. A newspaper story informed or reminded readers that he was a "49-year-old redheaded Irish Catholic born and raised in the Pine Hills section of Albany, a lawyer with five children." Actually, his identity had been prominent in the news almost daily for several months.

The concise last-hour guidepost to the nature of the about-to-be Mayor appeared in the first sentences of a City Hall reporter's summation of the tense political scene in Albany as Erastus Corning lay dying. The story also looked askance at the "virtual political unknown" who had held a relevant public office—the Common Council's presidency—for little more than a single year. It spared very little in forecasting a rough tenure for him.

As he took over, a public comment by the veteran legislator, Dick Conners, who'd served with Corning for 35 years in city government and for 15 years was first in line of succession, sounded a note that typified the uncertainty of most Albanians:

"I don't envy Tom Whalen in any way, shape, or manner. It's awfully tough to succeed a legend. He has really good abilities, but will always labor under comparison to Mayor Corning."

Focusing on the unsettled outlook, the *Times Union* account did offer a positive slant by acknowledging an apparent trend among most city employees toward finally accepting Whalen as their leader and the inevitability of his succession to the Mayor's office. But latent doubt already was being expressed as to how long he could hold on to leadership and office.

He would face "almost certain opposition in an election that may be held as early as November" (five months distant). "Opposition would likely emerge" from any of "several Democratic factions" aiming "to place (one of) their people in the Mayor's office" and "there are plenty of quarters from which opposition could arise to Whalen's candidacy if"—and this language surely intimated an opinion that he might back out—"he runs for his own term as Mayor." Five "possible opponents" were identified by name.   "Grumbling about Whalen already" by the party's "Old Guard" was mentioned, along with potentially "determined opposition from the Democratic machine." An outsider somehow had slipped in past all the lean and hungry Loyalists; he must be deposed. Volunteers for the role of Brutus were at hand.

It was not difficult to gain the impression through this preview, but also from other seers and their "sources," that as his mayoralty began it shouldn't be taken very seriously. One story actually referred to Albany's outlook in the hands of a "caretaker Mayor."

In fact, Whalen ruminated after his term ended, "I could have become a caretaker.

"That's what they"—the Democratic establishment— "expected, but I surprised them.

"On the other hand, I was seen by a lot of people as a traditionalist who would do everything in the way the party had always done them. After all, I had no track record. There was no cause for anyone to predict, 'This guy will turn things upside down.' But I saw what needed to be done.

"I felt that I had no choice but to do my best to accomplish it. What I did turned out to be largely a matter of conscience."[1]

He would be Mayor "for the time being, at least," a

Gazette reporter conceded in an article that speculated about various people who could be counted on to contest his right to the office. The story foresaw that Charles Touhey—who had lost elections for president of the Common Council in 1979 and Mayor in 1981—"can well be expected to dip into his family's fortune for another run," this one "against a less well-known opponent"; that is, Whalen. It mentioned that Nancy Burton, the independent-minded member of the Common Council, "may want to test her appeal in a citywide election." And Senator Howard C. Nolan was "also a force to be reckoned with."

* * *

Whalen quickly realized that some Loyalists seriously believed that while he held the office they would be able to indoctrinate him into Corning's way of running the city government—not only by autocratic micromanagement but with an understanding of their own privileges, prerogatives, and perquisites.

Their expectation clearly was that he should be a spiritual clone of one of the pre-Daley mayors of Chicago, of whom Mike Royko had written that his job was to "sit quietly in his office, cut ribbons, go to banquets, be a charming figurehead, and refrain from meddling" with the way the aldermen wanted to run City Hall.

The Old Guard, embracing a variety of departmental commissioners, vendors, and ward leaders, repeatedly applied pressures, subtle and overt according to the particular issue. Among the more troublesome of tactics was inaction itself, in Whalen's words: "Whatever it is he tells you to do, don't do it—because he's not going to be there very long." Harry Maikels, the trash collector turned Public Works Commissioner inherited from Corning, was open in advertising his disdain for change and his contempt for Whalen.[2]

Maikels and Charlie Cahill (distinctively pronounced as "Cal"), the Water Commissioner, endlessly enjoyed a private derogatory jab when they had to speak about Whalen: "Tommy-One-Two-Three-The-Boy-Mayor." (They were careful that Whalen never heard the sing-song slur and no one dared repeat it to him.) Both men's powerful party connections— Maikels was on his way to becoming the leader of the ever-muscular First Ward—and their reputation for bullying the County Legislature, where Cahill was the chairman until his retirement early in 1992, served to cement them in their city jobs for years regardless of performance and attitude.

They were bad news for Whalen, in the way that a loose screen on a summer night is bad news. Whether wisely or not, he persisted for years in trying to jolly them into compliance and cooperation—in effect, playing their own sport.

By Thanksgiving week of that first year—six months after taking over—the Mayor let himself be quoted as "disturbed" by resistance he was encountering within City Hall itself. "It makes the job more difficult." The "power plays" could be "distressing" to him. "For some reason, there seems to be a constant testing from within." He attributed this in part to the egging-on repeatedly felt by some lesser players (the Purchasing Department was a focal point). He considered that outsiders, among them Maikels, were the provocateurs. Yet he made no move against the commissioner, frequently allowing him into his own counsels and appearing with him in buddy-buddy mode publicly. He had chosen a tactic of dubious value in practice or of intrinsic worth.

Even some Aldermen were engaged in a similar "subtle testing of how serious I am, of how strong I am," Whalen remarked in the same week. He attributed the harassing to ward leaders' resentments reflected in their Council members' behavior.

Did he have political enemies, the Mayor was asked. He conceded that this was indeed true, but "I prefer to call them opponents." It appears likely that a recollection of Richard Nixon's "enemies" list had soured him on that kind of expression.

His all-out approach to his big new responsibility

apparently left neither time, energy, nor disposition to efficiently dispose of the scoffers and detractors in the political arena, many of whom were (or had been) answerable to him. This certainly was evident on the surface, but among those closest to him there was movement directed toward a Whalen triumph in the 1985 voting.

"No doubt, I was really alienating some people. I didn't have the luxury of saying, 'To hell with 'em.' But somehow I went ahead and did it anyway. I must have been reasonably confident that I could make my case . . . that sooner or later the voters would tell the politicians, 'We like what this guy is doing.' I can remember thinking: I have at least the self-confidence to tell myself—you're going down this road just once. Do what needs to be done.

"On the other hand, I *was* concerned about whom I was offending. I had to give due consideration to such a question as, 'How do I keep the malcontents from forming coalitions against me—but still get the job done?' In some cases, I was adversely affecting certain people personally. Financially, I mean.

"I wasn't uncomfortable with all the risks in undertaking a great deal of change. Part of my confidence derived from having a profession when—and if—they were able to get rid of me.

"And from the outset, the citizen feedback was good, very favorable. As I got around town, meeting with neighborhood groups, for instance, I would see that people did understand my policies. Even some political people—Leo O'Brien (the county chairman) and Ruby Gersowitz,[3] for example, and some of what I'll call the statesmen of the party, Judge Bergan, Holt-Harris—fully understood what was going on. They did their best to be supportive and to make that support known. This readiness to stand up, to be out front for me, meant a lot."

* * *

The expressive words of Parks Commissioner Dick Barrett—that Tom Whalen "wanted a victory every day," offer a suggestive portrait of an insatiable George Steinbrenner with an overlay of Joe Torre's dugout dignity.

"We had an integrated, communicating government. He set the targets. He would work with us, the department heads, and let us make our contribution. He gave us his gift of knowledge. We did a lot of writing, because that was his best way of reaching out to each of us—hearing back from us and satisfying himself that a great deal was always going on, being accomplished or at least being tried," Barrett recalled.

"In the Tricentennial, all events were his doing. He was the orchestrator of what he was determined would be a grand event. And he got his way.

"He was the leader in an incredibly wide range—collaborating with Charles Touhey to expand home ownership and with Mark Simmons in rehab housing, or bringing free Shakespeare to Washington Park along with the Park Playhouse."

* * *

Whalen's first official contact as Mayor with his administration's principal adversary-in-ambush was not long in coming. A fortnight after taking over, he brought into his office two men representative—in different ways—of concerns created by a new industry. The first of these visitors was an executive of Capital Cablevision, a company wiring the city's streets to carry its products into Albany's homes in an unheard-of fashion. The second was the Common Council's designee to help oversee this intriguing innovation—Alderman Gerald D. Jennings.[4]

NOTES

[1] The conscience may well have been Mary Broderick Whalen's. "My mother was a small woman but very outgoing and forceful. Like many Irish mothers, she was very religious, too," her older son related with respectful pride. "Whatever sense of justice and fair play I have acquired, I can only attribute to the upbringing my brother and sisters and I received from our mother. She was a remarkable woman. She instilled in us a determination to get things done, an 'Irish determination,' it seems to me. But she was also a New England Yankee with Yankee self-discipline. She was the kind of parent who makes sure that the child conforms to what she feels is appropriate. A caring role-maker. In our family, she was the disciplinarian."

[2] Maikels, who had owned a trash-hauling operation, became Public Works Commissioner in 1974, when Corning dismissed his predecessor. His position, which was associated with the party's historic solution for its policies on patronage, came to an end in January 1987, in the month of a snowstorm's disastrous impact on the city's transportation. Mayor Whalen had retained him as the department's head for nearly four years, even though Maikels appeared to question many of his policies. (See "The Gang of Four" chapter.) In the First Ward (which had included Daniel O'Connell's home) he was a committeeman for many years as the Organization regularly turned out legendary 4-to-1 majorities. When Robert Bender died in 1985, Maikels became the ward leader, a position he gave up in 1994, when he also resigned from the County Legislature. For many Albanians, he represented admirable exercise of partisan power, and for others that power exemplified a conflict between partisan zeal and governmental effectiveness.

[3] Gersowitz, the Old Guard leader in the Fourteenth Ward, and a politically savvy Loyalist from the O'Connell era, was one of the first to volunteer help to the new administration. Beyond his own opinions on what the city needed or would accept, Rube brought excellent intuition as to when policy could be "adjusted."

"Dan would be adjusting," he advised the Mayor on frequent occasions. No hardline functionary, Rube considered that everything should always be on the table for re-examination. With his flexibility, he served effectively—backed by Whalen's complete trust—as a link to the party organization. Their close friendly association dated from Whalen's first political candidacy in 1969.

"As long as I had Rube sitting down at the table, they couldn't completely trash me as having destroyed the party," Whalen remarked about the potential for trouble from Rube's Old Guard associates. "And if I was forgetting something that ought to be done for better relationships, Rube would remind me."

Rube became an active solicitor for the Friends of Tom Whalen, organized later to receive contributions to the Mayor's campaigns. He was its treasurer from the outset. Whalen's confidence in him never flagged, although the ever-sensitive aspects of double loyalties hardly could be avoided. But "There weren't very many Rubes," Whalen commented, putting it mildly. (He was also manager of the city-owned Wellington Hotel, by appointment by Corning in 1975. For years it was a substantial drain on the city's finances and was justified in theory as preferable to having such a large abandoned building on Albany's principal street.)

4 Although he had never been closely identified with the Old Guard, throughout Whalen's mayoralty Jennings mounted by far the most persistent assaults on his policies and programs. His verbal cannonade (very faithfully recorded in the Albany newspapers) created an impression of a maverick—and credibility for his eventual citywide candidacy. Whalen soon prodded the Council into designating Alderman Harold Greenstein as its cable specialist, though Jennings continued his salvos, choosing seniors' discounts as his issue against Whalen. Greenstein held a series of public information hearings throughout the city. Because the cable channels granted Cablevision interim moments for its promotion spots, Whalen seized the opportunity to use some of this free time to promote events such as Albany's first Columbus Day parade and Washington Park's "Alive at Five" performances. To keep Cablevision current on events his administration was projecting, the Mayor invited Anthony S. Esposito, Cablevision's regional manger (later, president), to attend staff meetings so he could anticipate City Hall's causes and celebrations and thus be better able to plug them on the available channels. Tom Whalen and Tony Esposito established a warm bipartisan friendship—though the Mayor never became a cable viewer, much to the amusement of his friend, who was able to appreciate the irony.

Turning the Corner

Tough sledding was only a few wakeful nights distant from Whalen's Day One. State Comptroller Edward V. Regan had called for a must-see appointment in the old Corning den. They would meet on the fifth business day of the new Mayor's term. This crisis had to be a priority for Whalen, among all the items claiming his instant attention. He needed to provide satisfactory answers for the Comptroller. Any of several potential missteps could trigger a quickly adverse reaction.

Whalen could read in his morning paper of the dismal report, newly issued by the state's auditors under Regan's direction, warning again that Albany could be forced to accept fiscal controls imposed by the state, a real possibility that had been dangling, sword-like, over Albany for a half-year.

What distressed the auditors most was the diversion to improper uses of $9 million in the bond anticipation notes which, floated for specific purposes, then were spent otherwise and elsewhere in each successive fiscal crunch. Corning's history of "routine borrowing to pay operating expenses—which is illegal" was blamed, complicated by "unrealistic budgeting," a term employed repeatedly in the State Comptroller's reports. Albany's total debt, by now exceeding its revenues by $25 million, was $12 million greater than its limit as defined by a formula in New York's Constitution.

"The financial condition of the city is of paramount importance right now," Whalen told an interviewer as he prepared for Regan's crucial visitation. "I want to understand it and I want to make sure we have a handle on it." He of course already understood the sorry condition of Albany's finances only too well, and the priority was inescapable. Even so, he feared that worse might lie ahead. The significance in Regan's own mind was made obvious by his decision to interject himself so very personally in the affairs of one of New York's almost literally countless governmental entities to which his department related. The tide was ebbing rapidly; Whalen realized that he must act or be carried out by it, a victim of events beyond his control. Now or never.

The outcome of the meeting was momentous for the Mayor, establishing a bold pattern of action and independence from Corning. He assured Regan that he was hiring a budget director and, more important, he was already committed to asking the Legislature for special legislation to change Albany's fiscal year to coincide with the calendar year. He could thus avoid the costly annual borrowing needed to tide the city's treasury through income-deprived fall months. Regan, happy to be taken by surprise, offered a comment that served as a hotfoot. Move up your schedule on this, he advised; do it now!

The Comptroller's support, becoming confident rather than wishful, was essential. From the threshold, prepared to take over as Albany's overlord if necessary, he now conceded that "For the first time, perhaps in decades, city government in Albany is starting to turn the corner in the way it handles financial practices."

"I believe that our proposals for prompt action are what persuaded him to give us more time," Whalen said later, his relief evident as the pressure diminished. "The sunny smiles could blind you," commented Bob McManus. Supported by the Comptroller's strong urging, Whalen expedited a request to the Legislature on June 20 and the shift's approval was completed within summer's first few days. (Corning's public position always had been that the effort would be too discouragingly difficult. Holt-Harris testified from personal knowledge that although he had been very concerned for a long time about the fiscal year, and the debt it invariably produced, this concern never motivated him to do anything.) The legislative request also asked an extra $12 million in loans to cover obligations during an entire 14-month "year."

Midway through the month, Regan dropped another hint as broad as a Groucho wink. "We might have had a different opinion two or three years ago," he remarked pointedly. "But there is reform and fiscal responsibility in the air."

The Comptroller's language easily could have been even more severe, for his department's management experts were well aware that Corning had never employed a businesslike approach to governing (after O'Connell's death, as before) but, rather, was committed to one in which political gain ruled all considerations. Political decisions in Albany, they understood, regularly were superimposed on top of concepts basic to governing effectively and efficiently. And as for Whalen, it was evident to him that he had fallen heir to what he called "the epitome of old-style city government."

* * *

In the long term, Whalen could lead from a fistful of aces: He was far from a stranger to the intricacies of investment, borrowing, and public finance. More than two decades practicing law in a firm intimately connected with a prominent commercial bank and also with a major savings bank had led him into close acquaintance with many useful aspects of finance and business. He had, after all, even arrived in this world of commerce with a degree in business administration.

An onlooker caustically familiar with the complex arithmetic lesson Whalen was meeting head-on that summer maintained that he'd been able to persevere because of three related factors: "He can count. He can read a budget. He can understand and respond to economic forces."

As Cervantes philosophized for his Don Quixote, if you're well prepared, you've "already half-fought the battle."[1] And throughout Whalen's adult life he'd had the prized advantage of learning from his father, an expert in municipal finance, with more than four decades' experience in cities' tight spots. It seems highly credible indeed that this latter ingredient would have been a plus-factor in the attitudes of Regan and his deputies, who greatly respected the elder Whalen's acumen and principles.

* * *

While the economies to be realized through fresh administrative standards and practices were considerable, the administration's actual commitment to them was even more significant, for it signaled a desire to follow lawful procedures. This revelation thrilled Audit & Control, but the impact on Albany's citizens (and on other observers of Albany's way of "doing business with friends") was far greater. A hands-on-the-table policy was being seen as a first sizable, high-profile step in the city's newfound way of conducting its business, commendable progress toward the "pride" which the Whalen administration came to adopt as its hallmark, the rallying cry for residents.

Albanians began to sense the advent of the new way, to smell the difference as burning leaves once heralded arrival of a new season.

* * *

Before taking office, Whalen had become increasingly aware of a costly practice involving the banking of large amounts of the city's money. He had scrutinized newspaper references to deposits that did not earn interest. Without power in his quasi-mayoralty, he learned as much as he could about such a wretched practice, and wrote "*Must Do*" notations toward rectifying it when he was able to act.

For many years, he found, Corning had a clearly self-serving interest in each aspect of his administration's relationship with National Commercial Bank & Trust Company and its successor, KeyBank.[2] As one of its shareholders, he was a direct beneficiary of any condition that improved its profitable operation. By encouraging policies and practices carried out by his own government to the bank's advantage, he was rewarded regularly by its dividends.

- He endorsed and maintained the bank's undue privilege of holding very large sums of public funds which it then could invest for its own benefit but without paying a dollar of interest to its depositor, the Mayor's treasury.
- He permitted and encouraged another practice detrimental to his government's fiscal well being and to its taxpayers. Repeatedly, Albany disadvantageously obtained loans at rates higher than the lowest available. This at-best-negligent policy was compounded when National Commercial/KeyBank simply renewed notes as they came due—thus solidifying its unadvertised grasp on Albany's credit business. Additionally, and at least as importantly, this reinforced the city's avoidance of its obligation to seek preferable interest rates elsewhere.
- As chief executive, Corning was also playing a conflicted role in continuation of these practices. While he was a member of the bank's board of directors, a policy-setting committee, he was ethically responsible for keeping its membership on notice that their profit-and-loss position was enhanced by his nonfeasance in certain duties for which he was responsible as an elected official. Then, as a major depositor and customer, he authorized practices contrary to that responsibility. Throughout the decades, his conduct,

reflecting divided loyalties between his sworn duty and his personal interests, should have been subject to critical review. It is noteworthy that, soon after his death, the bank acted to negate the favored position he had conferred on it.

* * *

Exactly four weeks from the day he took over, Whalen annulled this 40-year marriage of convenience.

Corning's practices were thus quickly ended. His personal interest in their perpetuation had ceased also. He was beyond accountability—a particular advantage of having been "mayor for life." But the implications of the cozy arrangement that had profited him for so long were not as effectively erased as were the practices that were changed as soon as he was gone.

* * *

Published analyses in the earliest days of the Whalen administration underscored the extent of the handicap put on the new Mayor's efforts by the poor credit rating that burdened the city. He was, in effect, challenged to find ways to offset this crippling legacy.

One major way—nullifying the city government's costly and prolonged special relationship with a bank—carried a significantly larger meaning. Tradition demanded that all decisions were made by a single elected individual. Sensitively aware of "implied criticism" of Corning, Whalen nonetheless went ahead, intent on gaining the best deal for the troubled city he now headed. In doing so, he also was implicitly taking advantage of Albany's history of edicts unilaterally handed down from above. (It was this same unquestioned practice, however, that he later did much to repudiate.)

In two decrees, quietly executed, he ensured that Albany would henceforth make money, or save it, in the management of funds. Unguarded, these public funds had been flowing solely to the one bank.

Of the policy changes the one especially notable—because it involved the more public action—was Whalen's unprecedented call for bids seeking to obtain favorable low interest rates on borrowing. "We need to be competitive in the marketplace." he declared.

In the first test of the newly mandated practice, KeyBank promptly lost out. Two other banks—Chemical and Union National—were the low bidders on interest charges the city would pay on four notes, totaling $13.6 million, that had been held by KeyBank. Interest on these, when automatically renewed, had gone as high as 11.25%.

The new loans from Chemical and Union National[3] required less than 6%. These loans were for only four months because the debts were to be incorporated within a $41 million long-term bond issue that the city then was to sell in consolidating its large indebtedness,

* * *

Albany's revenue sources—primarily local taxation, State assistance, and federal grants—yielded $70 million a year at that time and most of the income had been placed in accounts at Corning's bank, which did not pay interest on the large deposits. Sometimes amounting to $1 million on any given day, the deposits had accrued to the bank's benefit at the city's expense. Now they were placed, by the new Mayor's order, in accounts that would net about $100 for the municipal treasury on such a day. The practice maintained in Corning's time was saving the bank interest payments of $35,000 to $40,000 every year on this account alone. Over 40 years. . . .

"You can't really blame the bank," Bob McManus observed, "if the city preferred to deposit most of its money in non-interest-bearing accounts all those years—but from the taxpayer's point of view that's like burying it in a box near the Moses statue in Washington Park."[4]

* * *

The potential for conflicts of interest in the old relationships were recognized by the bank in the immediate post-Corning era.

In a barn-door burst of propriety, bank officers were quoted by the city's lawyer, Vincent McArdle, as cautioning that Albany's banking business should be open for bidding "so everything is right—and everything looks right."

This pointed concern about rightful practice and appearance was expressed only after Erastus Corning's death. But if it now became advisable that "everything is right," should this not have been equally a concern throughout those many previous years?

* * *

Where was the watchman during the long night?

Corning had contended, in a conversation with Jack McEneny, one of his principal staff members, that favors of this kind for a bank represented insurance for the city's fiscal stability under certain circumstances. By keeping bankers on the pad, so to speak, he was hedging against the eventual day when Albany might be unable to meet payroll (or some other critical exigency) and would need a touch of compassion from someone—such as a bank officer—who could overlook just a few trespasses (perhaps some debts, as well) and provide the rainy-day cash. Because the bank had accumulated obligations to Corning and his government (interest-free deposits, etc.), the Mayor theorized, he would be protected by some friendly assistant vice-president if the city treasury had the shorts on payday. In constructing his theory, he was ignoring the exceedingly strong personal influence he surely had in the bank anyway.

Whether the beauty of this theory had been put to the test (and how often) was not included in Corning's rationale for his running game of footsie with those banking professionals within their wickets.

"Bankers' only currency is cash," he complained with a degree of indignation which underscored his preference for back-scratching with shared dividends.

In reality, such a trade-off might be conceived only in a Corning-style government, where other outlandish fiscal practices could keep a city in perpetual hazard of insolvency.

When discussing the Corning explanation much later, Whalen pointed out that during his tenure—after ending the unorthodox arrangement that had prevailed—Albany's municipal government never experienced a problem that would call for special treatment by a bank.

NOTES

[1] "Chance favors only the prepared mind," Louis Pasteur.

[2] Corning, a director and shareholder, also had a business relation with the bank, which was one of his better customers for the insurance coverage he sold.

[3] Both banks' identities have changed: Chemical merged with Chase Manhattan, and after a series of purchases, Union National ended up in Manufacturers and Traders Trust Company in 1998.

[4] In his administration's first five years, interest earnings increased by about 500%, Whalen reported in an article published in *Governing* magazine in 1989.

Signs of Change

Coincident with the administrative turnover, a sharp controversy was creating a great deal of public attention and annoyance. This bur took the form of an outsized sign that KeyBank had erected atop its ten-story 60 State Street building. The sign itself was four stories tall. Blatantly, and arrogantly, it implied that the bank was bigger—bolder, brasher—than the city. And it sat there as though pretending that Albany was lacking in genuine issues and problems.

Corning's bureaucracy had, in fact, thoughtlessly issued a permit for placement of the sign, whose exposure on three sides totaled more than 2,800 square feet—about the area of many building lots on the city streets. That such an issue would become a big deal when Albany's fiscal roof was falling in seems difficult to comprehend, especially in latter days of huge, jarring advertising displays.

Indignant over the environmental blotch, though without having had real power, Whalen mirrored the public's mood. He obtained and displayed photos of the skyline in some high-profile, high-repute major-league cities—Toronto, Boston, San Francisco, Chicago: No huge signs visible there. The impact of his graphic display was rivaled by two hard-hitting blows at the bank by a pair of Hy Rosen's cartoons in the *Times Union*, unusually and strongly critical of a local institution.

In now challenging the sign, Whalen was also taking on a proud and powerful opponent, and someone at Key sniped back. Whalen was anonymously alleged to be merely a tool of Lew Swyer, whose view from an upper floor of his shiny new building at State and Pearl would be threatened. Gossip could be heard alleging the sign to be an updated version of the old "Spite Building" nearby whose only purpose had been to ruin the view for the Hotel Hampton's roof garden patrons, generations earlier. In this current account, the bank's sign was regarded as an insulting way to visually assault occupants— including Swyer himself—in his office tower rising just to the west.

"I just felt the sign was inappropriate for Albany," Whalen explained. "There were no such objects in the landscape of the city." (Not very many years before—and for many previous decades—a very large illuminated sign had topped the former Ten Eyck Hotel, itself a dozen stories tall and situated more visibly up the State Street hill at the town's most prominent crossroads.)

KeyBank, long responsive to Corning influence, was now recognized as Victor Riley's. In the mid-1970s, Corning— like Swyer—had resigned as a director after his old-line management faction within the directorate was toppled by an inside coup successfully engineered by Riley, who had emerged from the ranks to persuade large shareholders that he had the stuff to transform the demure old lady into a Miss America. Now he was well on his way to accomplishing just that.

And Victor Riley himself came to call. Promptly on the heels of the Regan showdown, he phoned to invite himself for a visit. Less than an hour later, in he walked, determination in his stride. The drive and decisions required by his rise to the presidency of the bank had made him unaccustomed to losing. His influence was formidable. As untitled interim mayor, Whalen hadn't held any face cards for a showdown. What would he draw now that he had moved over to the Mayor's chair? The outcome could influence his credibility and effectiveness. Did he have the right stuff? Another Minuteman performance? Over his shoulder, his city was watching, quietly kibitzing hopefully.

The meeting, like the one with Regan, was brief and cordial. Victor Riley's capitulation on the sign was forthright and total. "Tom," he said immediately, "you have made a decision as *Mayor*. The city has been drifting without a leader. Now we have a leader. No one in authority was making decisions on this matter previously. I respect your decision now. Let's put the matter behind us. The sign will come down." Without rancor, he was conceding a $160,000 mistake.[1]

Another issue between Whalen and Riley's bank never entered their conversation even though it had much greater importance. The Whalen administration was initiating practices in the use of the city's money that would be costly to Key both promptly and in the long term. It was only sound business, replacing shoddy arrangements, and Victor Riley surely understood that a protest would be futile. And clearly he perceived in this younger man the personification for potential change in a city mired in its stick-in-the-mud traditions.[2]

* * *

This initial spark ignited a long, warm, and productive friendship. Both KeyBank and its chairman became convinced supporters of Whalen's administration. Dramatically, they demonstrated their backing by accepting a fundamental share of responsibility for downtown's renaissance. The Mayor could count on KeyBank as a major investor in virtually every aspect of the never-ceasing celebratory and cultural endeavors. And this commitment was endowed with the reality of concrete contributions to a resurging Albany structurally and economically—most importantly, two new office towers that rose on South Pearl Street and a smaller, older building reconstructed nearby on lower State Street. They were significant statements of belief. And he spread his gospel as the godfather of a Center for Economic Growth, aimed at developing the Capital Region.

Victor Riley, who at the time occupied a townhouse in a Lancaster Street row within the rejuvenated Center Square area on the fringe of downtown, sat down with the Mayor frequently. They regularly scheduled conversations at serial breakfasts throughout the several years before he moved on to Cleveland just before Whalen's term expired.[3]

"The Mayor's ability to manage is very apparent—and has been appreciated by the business community, particularly because of the minimal tax increase and the budget balancing," Riley said in parting.

One of Riley's addresses at his traditional year-end review sessions, arranged for scores of the region's commercial, financial, and municipal CEOs, gained an afterlife. It served as the inspiration for a spurt of curiosity about intergovernmental coordination across arbitrary jurisdictional boundaries. The positive promise teasing the skeptics won an earnest advocate. Whalen, at first likewise skeptical of the concept's feasibility, soon became not only a convert but an evangelist for integrating many local government functions and services at every level. He was an effective missionary on behalf of expediting this slow-motion icecap, building on his own ideas to complement Riley's. After leaving office, he chaired a study of the concept under the auspices of the Rockefeller Institute of Government, where for months he pondered and plotted and exhorted with high dedication in the Institute's academic cloister on upper State Street. The outcome of such effort is yet to be posted on the scoreboard.

* * *

But, as we step back through the years to prehistory when Tom Whalen was experiencing a bold encounter with dragons named Doubt, Disbelief, and Denial, we can see how his administration strode mightily forward on the strength of his unyielding subscription to ancestor John Parker's flat-footed declaration two centuries before, "Stand your ground! Let it begin here!"

He had stood his ground, had emerged with more than he might have hoped—and with his own authority intact and respected.

NOTES

[1] Less than three weeks later, the sign was down. Volunteer crews were recruited from the union ranks of the Bridge, Structural and Ornamental Workers and in short order they dexterously dismantled the six tons of aluminum.

[2] He was an iconoclast in numerous avenues, including phrasemaking. He was responsible for drastically changing the identity of the icon he now bossed and, unimpressed by another Albany icon, he was known to refer to "the Fort Lemon Club."

[3] In the view of some well-informed banking associates of Victor Riley, the elements which caused him to give up his Albany base included three items of not-unreasonable disappointment: The stalemate prolonging the disreputable condition at the Albany County Airport, the perceived negative tone of the Albany newspaper, and a personal slight, namely the failure of Mario Cuomo to reach out with a signal that he recognized the importance of Riley's accomplishments in the Capital Region and elsewhere.

Upon word of the unhappy event in October 1993, Whalen wrote to former Judge Sol Wachtler that it was "the most disturbing news in a long time. . . . It is a blow to the prestige of the city in that we can no longer say that we are the home of this Fortune 500 company."

A "Must" Victory

Even while still lacking the Mayor's powers, Whalen had seized the lead in terminating the unethical cozy relationships between vendors and city officials, who ordinarily also were, themselves, party functionaries. Businesses having a large volume of sales to City Hall were obligated to return a slice of their income to the Democratic party—or, alternatively, to siphon it to the elite who stood high in the party's favor. As we have seen, strong hints of Whalen's initiative had been rife in his leadership while Corning still lived.

Departments now received instructions on proper procedures for purchasing and contracting through competitive bids. Across the rotunda from the Mayor's office, the comptroller had orders to no longer pay on "confirming" vouchers, but instead shoot these back to any department still submitting them. Whalen's directives required that Hemingway, the comptroller, and Dewey Hensel, the purchasing agent, were to pre-approve all purchases of services or goods—and that competitive bids were to be obtained whenever and wherever possible. His demand was backed up by Audit & Control's repeated complaints that violations of proper practice continued as important factors in Albany's fiscal ailments.

"If he (Whalen) insists on this competitive bidding, he'll take a tremendous amount of grief from 'insiders,'" was a common expectation. "And if he follows through and does it anyway, we'll know it's serious."

Most undiplomatically, for an officeholder speaking of

his own party, Whalen denounced "some city contracts in the past that built in extra profit—not only for the Organization but extra profit for themselves" (meaning, city employees in collaboration with vendors supplying commodities, materials, or services). He repeatedly mentioned "20%" as what had prevailed as the anticipated markup for political or personal gain from the city's purchases. Of individuals receiving such illicit money, he added: "What they did with it, who knows?" As for the Organization, the markup financed its operations because the money was to be remitted—in cash—to party headquarters.

* * *

The mere principle of competitive bidding, when carried out faithfully, was serious indeed. It immediately ended favoritism and nullified the 20% markup for kickbacks. This promptly shut down the flow of cash dollars to the county committee and therefore terminated the easy availability of money for normal campaign expenditures and also for any under-the-table handouts either directly or indirectly connected with winning elections. Benefits to the party's elite and, occasionally, some favored friend were similarly halted abruptly. The party's *modus operandi* was forced to change; operating funds now tended to come from staged events such as the annual picnic that had been initiated by Harold Joyce and Paul O'Brien, county legislators and ward leaders. Individuals were hurt, as well as the Organization and the friends with whom Corning liked to do business (as he proclaimed happily). No wonder the level of anger rose, and hatred, and vituperation, and character assassination. And no wonder that few could stomach the irony when the man responsible for causing all this trouble also began to raise his own campaign funds, violating O'Connell's rules and succeeding so overwhelmingly that any conceivable opposition was stifled.[1]

All because of one, previously unspeakable, three-letter word: B-i-d!

* * *

Much of the current dilemma had been previewed and certified exactly a decade earlier. Passage of time meant only a need to revisit the problem issue. The 1973 report of the State Commission of Investigation (known familiarly as the SIC) elaborated on an inquiry it had conducted in the previous year into Albany's purchasing practices. (In turn, *that* investigation was a follow-up to one in Albany County in the 1960s.)

The 1973 SIC report concluded that "the continuous yearly practice of underestimating appropriations and overestimating revenues" caused "actual expenditures to constantly exceed actual revenues received," a process which, in turn, created the "recurring problem" of operating deficits. So, in 1983, the same problem—now additionally familiar—was indeed "recurring." The earlier reports and whatever attention they'd received had changed essentially nothing. The issue was in Whalen's hands to resolve.

In the four years preceding 1973, the SIC report continued, Albany's tax rate had increased by 100%. "Subterfuges" . . . which "clearly evaded legal requirements . . . negated the purpose of the Purchasing Department" while "the benefits and economies of competitive public bidding . . . were voided and thwarted."

Bluntly, the SIC continued: To improve the state of purchasing practices and procedures in Albany, it "is absolutely essential" to insist on "honesty, integrity, sincerity, and competence in the public officers and employees who administer purchasing affairs . . ." in place of the "extensive deficiencies, incompetence, and poor administration. . . ."

Erastus Corning testified twice during the investigation, and the SIC found that his testimony had been "to some extent characterized by indefinite and evasive answers and at times was contradictory. . . ." It appeared to indicate "personal lack of knowledge of City operations."

Now Corning's successor—who surely had read the 1973 report more than once—at least had the benefit of seeing

the basic issues sketched out before him in strong and unfor-
gettable language. The SIC's repeated emphasis on purchasing
and bidding was a flashing red light. The "absolutely essential" remedies demanded a decade ago could wait no longer.
He must take action promptly or be marked for failure almost
as quickly. He'd not be able—or willing—to plead "personal
lack of knowledge" even though new to the executive chair.
Historians as well as contemporary observers would judge the
degree to which he insisted on "honesty, integrity, sincerity,
and competence."

For months, Whalen experienced subversive difficulty
in obtaining performance by a few of the departments where
commissioners retained a stronger loyalty to the profitable old
ways and could enforce their will on the offices that should
have throttled the practice: the comptroller and the purchasing
agent.

The awarding of purchase and service contracts had
revolved around those "confirming orders." A commissioner
who matched political contacts and influence with constant
need for material and labor could arrange for goods or work
and only later submit to Comptroller Hemingway the vendor's
unilaterally prepared bill, with instructions, "Pay it!" Such
truculent demands found an easy mark in "Hem-and-Haw,"
who readily caved in, perhaps swallowing hard but nevertheless ignoring the new requirements.[2] He was aware—and
apprehensive—of the Organization's influence.

Effectively putting an end to this was an obvious necessity for Whalen, if for no reason other than that the squandered
costs destroyed any overall spending plan.

But enforcement was a further challenge. Recalcitrance
by some commissioners was bad enough, but support for
Whalen by Purchasing was sorely lacking. That department's
head, a key man, was useless, in Whalen's estimation.

The Purchasing Agent, in bald fact, didn't purchase
anything. What he did was to approve the bills submitted by
the commissioners who had bought what (a) they needed, or
(b) wanted, or (c) would provide sales revenue for vendors

who then could renew the flow of cash to the party. In effect, the Purchasing Department was just as "negated" as the SIC had determined all those years before.

A colorful example of (c) in practice came to light early in the Whalen administration when a new commissioner noticed a sagging ceiling in a city-owned building within his jurisdiction. Examination revealed that the roof (shielded from view by the walls' extension above it) was overburdened by a massive collection of unneeded supplies hidden there. Over years, they'd been bought from an approved vendor even though there was no use for them. Piled two feet deep, they were rotting and rusting away while the roof gradually succumbed. Meanwhile, the bills for their acquisition had bolstered the balance in the county committee's treasury.

Months after Whalen's takeover, some bills were still being paid without formal authentication. These soon became an issue in the fall campaign for City Comptroller, vigorously pursued by the Republicans' candidate. Whalen was publicly placed in the posture of a general who couldn't persuade his troops to march forward.

By this time, he was questioning whether he should pay more heed to the grandfatherly advice handed down by the venerable judge, Francis Bergan, even before he took office. Bergan had repeatedly cautioned him against failing to use all the influence he could muster to buttress his strength as an ambitious executive. (Bergan, for such a softspoken intellectual almost shy in manner, was "a tiger, very forceful," Whalen found, if confronted by a situation that offended or nettled him.)

"I'm not sure that I used the political power of the office to the extent that I could have," Whalen once somewhat ruefully second-guessed. "If I had adopted a very hard-line approach to the politicians in the beginning, would I have saved a lot of anguish and concern later in dealing over and over with the same people? I doubt if they ever would have given up."

In his view, reluctance to wield political power "was at

least consistent with my feeling that the political aspect was only incidental to getting the job done for the sake of the city itself."

(Is the defiant line, "Can't afford to be a politician!" pertinent here?[3])

* * *

After five months of frustration and now suffering embarrassment by appearing not to be in charge, Whalen was outraged by the growing evidence his rules were being ignored. He cracked down with a shape-up ultimatum bearing the unheard-of, or-else penalty of "consider other employment." *"Angry Mayor Says Heads May Roll,"* a headline shouted.

Hensel (the Purchasing Agent) "didn't do me any favors," said the Mayor. "He put me on the spot, because if he'd told me this was still going on, I could have been prepared.

"Why has this been allowed to happen? I intend to find out," he thundered. "Apparently, some people did not take me seriously when I issued those directives. The time has come to impress upon them just how serious I am.

"I was exasperated," he later explained, "that they were not paying attention. By going public in my criticism, I was giving notice to whoever was behind those actions. I felt sure that breaking the law in this way was not something my department heads would ever think of doing on their own.

"They'd been asked by somebody. Continuing to get money unlawfully was the goal. I had some weak individuals who would collapse under pressure, and some who just were not up to the assigned task. They were victims of pressure from within the old school, people who considered me an interloper who wouldn't last long, so the tactic was to just stall until I was gone." He made his point successfully, for the devious skullduggery quickly tapered off. "Within weeks, confirming vouchers were a thing of the past and we were operating in line with the requirements and with state law on competitive bidding."

Honest bidding—which was to become a highly visible ingredient of the Whalen administration's policies—was a "must" in any reform mechanism, as made obvious in the State Comptroller's reports.

Whalen described the old practice of non-bid awards and their accompanying dividends as "part of the games that were played in Albany." This game's final innings included a percentage (varying, depending on circumstances and personalities) of the vendor's gross, which was to be remitted to party headquarters.

The traditional and accepted practice of avoiding normal (legal) processes in acquiring goods and services meant paying escalated prices to the vendors. Its disappearance represented a sea change for Albany. The change was not merely in the direction of the impartial, the legal, and the economical. It became a signal, received by the business sector, that City Hall would now deal fairly, so they need not assume a stacked deck against them. "It was also, in a large way, symbolic to people who loved Albany," in Whalen's view.

"This was far from a smooth road," he summed up. "We were stepping on toes and had to contend with the political fallout." With several advisors, he talked over the politics of this issue he had created. Rube Gersowitz, still a trusted ward leader, conveyed the positions of the Regulars; Steve Fischer of the Urbach accounting firm was consulted for his wide scope among the business community; Holt-Harris offered counsel based in his breadth of experience in both fields; Dan Klepak (who had taken over as Budget Director; see "Juice Worth the Squeeze" chapter) described administrative quandaries which the Whalen innovations invariably produced. But on the political front no advice ever brought about a real resolution. The Regulars remained angry, suspicious, and adamant. *"What is this man trying to do to us?"*

As to his insistence at the outset on competitive bidding, he firmly believed that he didn't act blindly—"I wasn't naive." He cited his "mindset from the beginning." Beyond all other considerations was the matter of legality.

Arriving at an understanding of "the way it should be done" required years of observing, acquiring a knowledge of what was going on and of the public's latent disgust with the time-honored practices benefiting the insiders. As for his own earlier status within the Organization that perpetuated those practices, he insisted that—despite having been a committee-man, having run for office as the Organization's candidate, having chaired the Albany Housing Authority with its range of involvement in many aspects of Albany life including its parti-san political potentials, and despite his having collaborated with insiders to aid Corning's renomination in 1977—"I was still not an insider." He considered that when the *Times Union* named him in 1979 as one of 10 possible successors to Corning as Mayor and county chairman, he didn't truly belong in that group.

"I never was really one of them. But, I can't overstate the importance to me, when the time came, of the years of watching and learning, meanwhile listening also to people out-side the Organization, their thoughts and their frustrations. For me, it was a most significant experience, gained bit by bit over a lot of years.

"I was in a unique position, though: a foot in each camp, certainly not entrenched in the Organization, but I had the advantage of seeing the way it worked and knowing the people."

Could a known "reformer" have become Mayor and taken the route he did? "I don't see how such a person could have acquired the knowledge, made the 'soundings' that helped me so much."

* * *

When Whalen sat down much later to count out his administration's accomplishments, he could quickly enumer-ate three dozen items which ranged from those *correcting* long-standing fallacies and abuses, to others *initiating* socially desirable practices, and also some *looking forward* toward future challenges. Well down in mid-list stood "ending of no-bid contracts."

This seemingly is an odd contradiction. How could it be that he would undervalue the principled policy he'd adopted from every text on management and had initiated in Albany for the sake of simple good practice, aside from the matter of honorable dealing as opposed to several criminal concepts?

The answers appear to be in his innate emphasis on results. The three-dozen items were actual, they were achievements as real as a remade golf course or "First Night" celebrations. They had produced the pride, the recaptured spirit which he was so fond of preening. Competitive bidding was but a mechanic, only a tool, even if it did make possible the accomplishing of a "real thing." Theater in the park or sculling on the river could have been depicted in hieroglyphic sketches on the cave wall like the trophy of the hunt or the invention of the wheel. A concept such as honesty was much more difficult to display and celebrate.

But from a more objective viewpoint, this new policy deserved to lead all the other advances. If Whalen as the good government Mayor had not been able to control the built-in extra costs of his commissioners' at-will spreading of public funds, his budgeting practices would have come to nil. He would have been as perennially broke as Corning was. At least as unfortunate—perhaps worse—his own subordinates, having had their way with these differences about the city's resources, would see an open road to do as they pleased with any of his other programs. The Whalen administration—an abbreviated one—would have been as effective as Jimmy Carter's and as credible as Richard Nixon's. And of ultimate far-reaching importance, the Albany citizenry would have shrugged off any idea that honest dealing had been installed in their City Hall. Fear would have continued to dominate the local government's (and the party's) relationships with the people it professed to service.

Because none of this came to pass, however, Whalen and his staff were able to carry through on the rest of their agenda, either corrective or creative in nature as each circumstance required.

NOTES

[1] Having met with a curt rebuff from Whalen as soon as he heard a request that political contributions be included (as usual) in city employees' pay envelopes, the County Democratic Committee never tried this tactic again. Beginning in 1983, each job in Albany's government no longer meant a sure source of money for the party.

[2] Hemingway, forced to seek election in an off-year because he was in office only as an appointee of Corning's, won an overwhelming majority in November despite numerous negatives including an aggressive opponent, poor press notices, and heavy editorial disdain. But his victory would "severely complicate Tom Whalen's life," in the trenchant view of Bob McManus, who saw the vote as, superficially, an enthusiastic endorsement of "the shabby way the city has done business over the years." He added that, unfortunately, "Hemingway's mandate will not be lost on the other dinosaurs in municipal government, who now have even less reason to take seriously Whalen's apparent efforts to restore the city's shattered fiscal reputation." Later developments proved this to be an apt prediction.

[3] From Frank Loesser's stirring "Praise the Lord and Pass the Ammunition" of 1942.

"The Ten" Stouthearts

"Give me some men who are stouthearted men/Who will fight for the right they adore; Start me with ten who are stouthearted men/And I'll soon give you ten thousand more!"[1]

The outsider who moved alone into City Hall was standing in need of prayerful support from just a few good citizens ready to go the last mile with him in an effort to save the city and advance its decrepit fortunes.

Tom Whalen had his ten to start.

They were a mixed bag, clad in a variety of uniforms and carrying differing colors and emblems—somewhat akin, perhaps, to Washington's army at Cambridge in the summer of 1775. Some of these patriots possibly came with varying motivation, but rare indeed were those who might even be suspected of personal designs and ambitions, or of any intent other than to help a friend—and their city—succeed and prosper. Almost half were lawyers; all were men of attainment and discernment. All certainly were Albanians, chiefly of native stripe though a couple were aliens. Only one already had a direct connection with the city's governance, though at least half possessed very strong ties to the party which for so long had controlled that government. In their fashion, they quite likely could be said to "adore the right." And they were *there*, a tremendous personal resource.

All that Mayor Whalen needed to do at any hour was

to "lift the phone" and the counsel or company of each of them was readily at hand.

A desk diary begun by Bill Keefe in the earliest weeks of Whalen's term showed that in this critical period every one of The Ten had made appointments to come to his office, some of them for several visits. Their appointments cumulatively totaled at least 40. (The diary, of course, gives no indication of the purpose of these meetings with the Mayor.[2])

Because of the antagonisms and enmity that his policies aroused, he relied heavily on such support as these friends afforded. Among them he was likely to find welcome encouragement and reassurance or a useful suggestion. It was a substantive plus.

And they were men whose fundamental loyalty was to him as Mayor, perhaps in part to do honor to Corning's selection of him. Not more than possibly one sunshine soldier could be found among them. They were Loyalists of a different breed—though from one limited vantage they might be branded as quasi-subversives abetting a revolutionary.

* * *

Whalen's closest friends were Lew Swyer and Jimmy Drislane, mentors who two decades earlier had found promise in him and helped with coaching and counsel, both informal and formal, to steer him along his way, years before he had even a dream of public life.

Amid the discouragements of the early months—both before taking office and later—"I had terrific resources," and he named "Lew and Jim, who were always there, willing to help me get through the most difficult parts."

An important colleague of Whalen's in the Regency had overnight become a *de facto* member of the new administration and a principal (and principled) arm of it: Corporation Counsel Vinnie McArdle, a sagacious advisor, was the only department head who went on to serve every one of the 3,870 days of the Whalen term. A faithful counselor and advocate, he also maintained great respect and loyalty to Corning. He was one of few among The Ten who were younger than Whalen.[3]

Another younger man was Steve Fischer, a partner in the aggressively successful, Albany-based accounting firm of Urbach Kahn and Werlin. A lawyer as well as an accountant, he was a New Yorker recruited as a comer who could help build the local firm into one with national and even international connections and reputation. Impressive with his acute instincts in politics or business, he had become, over a decade, Tom Whalen's friend and sometime colleague in certain cases that required his particular expertise.

Alan Iselin, an Albanian with important connections and varied business interests, was a long-time law client with additional links to the Mayor: Chairman of the Albany University Foundation, and of the University Council, positions Whalen himself had held; and advisor to Bankers Trust, the successor to First Trust, with which the Cooper Erving law firm had long maintained a close relationship.

For Jack Pennock, whose friendship dated back nearly 20 years, Whalen had performed two significant good turns at times when he was embattled and his judicial career imperiled. Ray Kinley, very close to the late Mayor for whom he was accustomed to taking on a variety of unofficial assignments that Corning could not do for himself, was involved in almost every benevolent enterprise to which he might convey the good offices of State Bank of Albany (by 1983, Norstar). He was extraordinarily intimate with the party's Old Guard, but for now was devoted to Tom Whalen's interests too. Kinley had befriended Whalen as a young lawyer and made him the attorney for the Sales and Marketing Executives Association. His wide circle of friends included both Jim Drislane and Tom Whalen, Jr. A North Albany native, he had owned a plumbing supply business before State Bank decided that his intimate contacts within the party and in City Hall would make him a good public relations man. He ended up as the bank's senior vice president for business development. The range of his influence—not always readily visible—is suggested by the position he had acquired of treasurer of the Democratic State Committee.

As the Whalen administration began to make its own record, Kinley heard complaints from within the Organization that the Mayor's policies were ruining the party. He developed "serious misgivings about what I was doing," Whalen recalled. "Ray was a conservative of the 'old school.' He went along only very reluctantly with some of the changes I was trying to make. If the ward leaders weren't happy, he was certain there had to be a legitimate cause for them to be upset. But I needed him to sell important portions of my program to the sort of people he was always in contact with. An edge developed in our relationship, and that didn't help." But Ray Kinley's was the name on the second "good citizen" memorial marker placed in Academy Park by Whalen's own decision.[4]

As described earlier, Ruben Gersowitz, a ward leader and businessman, retained close connections to other insiders. But his dedication to Whalen personally was, in the long run, the stronger as he discreetly carried out missions on the Mayor's behalf. As an O'Connell loyalist, he brought a particular perspective now that was sensitively understood by all hands.

These men were either native Albanians or, as in the case of Lew Swyer, had arrived so long ago he was accepted as Old Albany. More recently a part of the Albany scene were Vince O'Leary, president of Albany's State University, who had many interests in common with Whalen; and John Krueger, perhaps the least well-known of the group but nonetheless the kindred outdoorsman with whom Whalen could share many relaxed hours (as on the fateful canoeing weekend) and whose personal support and counsel were never to be doubted.

Those were the stouthearts, Whalen's stalwarts.[5] They never met together as a coherent group. Though their identities and reputations certainly were evident to one another, none had reason to consider himself as part of such a team as is arbitrarily assembled here. With slight exception, the relationship of each with Whalen was singular.

The "ten thousand more" came in good time, attested by the good-hearted Albanians who turned out to take part in the city's prideful revival and who subsequently gave him an all-but-unanimous vote in two elections.

"The Ten" and those who later also became advisors were hardly innocent of political awareness—of how the great game of politics is played in American culture—but their essentially overriding reason for involvement was to help bolster their city's government and, in so doing, to help their friend.

NOTES

[1] *Stouthearted Men*, words by Oscar Hammerstein II, music by Sigmund Romberg; copyright 1928. From the operetta, *The New Moon*.

[2] The diary includes more than two dozen additional names of prominent Albany "players" in this same period. Mario Cuomo descended from the Capitol once, and his chief of General Services, John Egan, with on-going liaison responsibility assigned by the Governor, was a regular caller. Old friends and advisers—from Holt-Harris to Art Mitchell—showed up with a notable constancy. Erastus Corning III was in twice. Republicans such as Peter Kermani and Matt Mataraso came in, but so did Democrats Bob Bender, Rube Gersowitz, Jim Coyne, and County Chairman Leo O'Brien, whose 10 visits were the greatest number by any individual. Two Court of Appeals judges were neighborly visitors from next door.

And among the most potentially potent of all was a brother of the Governor of Massachusetts. Arthur Dukakis, regional director for the U.S. Census, was brought in by the county's population authority, Jack McEneny, just before he handed in his resignation from his City Hall position. The 1990 census was years distant, but this early contact with Dukakis and the resulting warm association

Whalen established with him were to be significant for Albany.

³ Whalen was seven months away from his fiftieth birthday when he took office; he left office a week before his sixtieth. He had spent the entire decade of his 50s as Mayor of Albany.

⁴ Kinley's disillusion before his death in 1987 points up the early existence and extent of the Old Guard's frustrated descent into anger and enmity. These Loyalists were people with whom Whalen had fraternized in Democratic party ranks, whose help he had sought and used as a candidate, and to a considerable degree they were those with whom he had grown up, gone to school, done business. They had seen him photographed with O'Connell, running with Corning, chummy with mainstays of their lives from Charlie Ryan to Gene Devine. Now, by his condemned policies, he was being seen as the Organization's ruination.

⁵ Four of the ten passed from the scene long before his term in office was up (Pennock in 1985 and Kinley in 1987, Drislane and Swyer in 1988). Their loss was grievous. Other friends—the staffers, Dick Barrett, Bill Keefe, Dan Klepak, John Dale—would become trusted helpers and advisers, but as of the earliest days when everything was new, these were the ten whose stoutly loyal efforts he could count on. The roster must include certain other bench and bullpen members, if not in the starting lineup: Bill Hennessy, John Egan, Dick Nathan, Lou Vaccaro, Matt Mataraso, Jim Patrick. Among the group were even some Republicans.

A Precious Hundred Days . . .

The quaint imported phrase *coup de théâtre*
sums up, in its three words, how Tom Whalen
burst into Albany political legend:
"An unexpected and dramatic event,
(it testifies in translation) especially one
that overturns an existing situation."
Can there be a better definition of
the opening of the Whalen Decade?

Ever since Franklin D. Roosevelt lifted the country back
on its feet in the spring of 1933, "The first 100 days" have been
demarked as an arbitrary period for judging relative accomplishment of chief executives—presidents, governors, mayors.

In one perspective, the hundred days is as unfair as it is
arbitrary. But three months-plus really is a reasonable period
of time for the new officeholder to indicate imagination, or
pedestrian thinking; determination, or a tendency to fold;
boldness, or caution; character, or profile; goals, or just more of
the same. Will he be an overachiever or will he be revealed as
an inept dreamer, or a hopeless bumbler, or a well-meaning
procrastinator with his feet on the desk? Perhaps a smiling
prevaricator?

Much more than a gimmick, the 100-day performance
review holds greater import than merely as a contemporary
yardstick. The review actually is measuring depth, not linear
width. As David Gergen has described it,[1] the first hundred
are "the most precious" of a government official's days, a gold-

en opportunity "to define who he is and what he is seeking to achieve through his leadership."

Though he was remarking specifically on the presidency (having observed three U.S. presidents at very close range), Gergen's comments are equally applicable to a mayor's response to his (her) new challenge: "More than at any other time . . . he (she) sets the stage for an entire stewardship."

By the time his hundred days are ended, the chief executive's "story . . . takes shape in the public mind and it tends to remain in that same shape for a long time thereafter."

* * *

If ever there was a crucial show-and-tell occasion for such an official, Whalen's running start exemplifies it handsomely.

His hundred days conveniently fit into three summer months between Memorial Day and Labor Day. He was sworn in the day before the first of these holidays and 100 days were up precisely on the holiday marking the end of summer. On the face of it, the period hardly seemed auspicious for action and accomplishment during the traditional lazy-hazy days of vacations. An added distraction vying with productivity and progress was in the uncertainty of Whalen's term before he would face the voters in an election.

A fortnight of Whalen's hundred days still remained when Bob McManus's editorial-page column noted in mid-August that:

> *"Things are more than a little different in Albany. A whole lot of tradition has been turned on its head—and it appears that (the city) is never going to be the same again."*

Achievement on such a scale may be in the eye of the beholder, but the undeniably concrete facts are fast in the record. Several glimpses tell the story; in combination, they are impressive—or, as the language of the time would have it—"awesome."

VI's old number 12 had to take charge from behind the goal line:

His first moves necessarily needed to contend with reality limiting time or energies for even thinking of longer-term outcomes, and surely not in search of applause, votes, or wide recognition. Nonetheless, those first moves were intrinsically linked to the policy successes, reforms, and popular acclaim that eventually came to characterize the Whalen administration during its hundred-day run 40 times over, 1983-1993.

If October in the preceding year, as Whalen assessed it, had been a watershed month in his public career, June of 1983—his first full month in the Mayor's office—deserves consideration as the critical point in his entire mayoralty.

On the second day of June (his fifth in office) he'd been recognized as "the single voice" that now would speak for Albany's beleaguered government. Yet within the next ten days he'd made evident a new "share the duties style," a clear-cut change from his predecessor's secretive decision-making. It accurately foretold the Whalen approach to his later emphasis on finding capable departmental leaders and holding them accountable for quality and integrity of performance.

* * *

Already he was trying to unload the old Wellington Hotel, a large white elephant on the State Street hill that a bank had passed along to the city. Looking for budgetary reforms and controls, he hired a likely-looking candidate (but then saw the recruit disappear before he even got on the job.) He quickly killed, very decisively, stalled plans for an $18 million garage for parking 1,700 cars downtown, but soon was developing plans for a viable alternative. He ventured before a newspaper's editorial board's quizzical members to explain where he aimed to go. He held his own in crucial and major negotiations with the State Comptroller, who had arrived with a poor-performance checklist plus mandates for improvement and reform.[2]

In quick succession, he won the state's permission for new borrowing so he could prudently reschedule his fiscal year, then successfully petitioned the Legislature to okay the calendar change. This was accomplished in little more than three weeks of his assuming office. At his request, the Common Council petitioned the Legislature to allow the city to change the fiscal year, and this authorization was granted within days. These two initiatives alone were major triumphs for the city which could stand as a whole year's worth of substantial progress. Corning had resisted these strategies as formidable if not impossible, whatever his motivation had been. Intent only on doing what was vital for Albany, Whalen unintentionally had drawn a deep contrast with his predecessor.

Quietly, he put a new proposal before IBM for effectively using old Union Station (a pumpkin which seven months later magically turned into a royal coach for a prince with a handsome glass slipper).

Garbage haulers' highhanded behavior at the city's dump created an expensive and illegal shellacking for his treasury, so the Mayor toughened the controls and barred some of the haulers. He lucked into an amicable and effective pact with a bank's wizard-of-the-hour on a controversial environmental issue—while depriving the bank of some sloppy and costly deals Mayor Corning had maintained with it. (As is true of many of these items, more detailed telling lurks in another chapter.)

He ordered sharp cuts in the swollen payroll of that patronage wallow, the Bureau of Parks (which had just acquired a new acting superintendent by his appointment). The reductions were to be sizable enough to bring its budget into balance—virtually a first-time-ever feat.

For the only time in more than 40 years (covering Corning's entire term), Albany's government asked banks to submit quotations for the interest they would charge in order to compete for the city's business. One outcome was to remove $13.6 million in short-term notes from the one bank which, minus competition, had held this business for decades.

The consultant hired by Whalen's Gang of Four in the spring to stabilize the tax rolls reported an assessment schedule for commercial properties which was aimed at eliminating the roller-coaster inflating of assessments that would be lowered following appeals by the aggrieved taxpayers (often to the advantage of lawyers favored by the Organization).

Whalen recognized the imperative of impressing municipal employees to begin making effective use of forgotten and rusted initiatives, including ways to reduce expenditures. To make his point with due effectiveness, he summoned a large staff meeting so they could hear the word in person. And in another move to emphasize the new broom's sweep, he launched a housekeeping effort to make old City Hall—just starting its second century—more presentable and self-respecting. A reporter unearthed an old-time denizen's complaint that the clean-up had removed "some of the warmth and friendliness." The effect was an early indication of the "pride" campaign that would become a keystone of his term. "It won't be the same without that old rug in there (the Mayor's personal office)—but that's the point, isn't it?" was an acute McManus observation.

All this in one busy month of days invariably ending with bulging briefcase toted home for late-night work to catch up, keep up, stay on top, even find stray hours for creative thoughts. As June came to a close, an audit showed that the interim government piloted so largely by Whalen had reduced the long-term debt, solved some of the short-term deficit problems, and halted the illegal practice of covering current expenses with money borrowed for capital projects.

This was more than enough to sound a cheery note as the Whalen family flew off to Ireland for a two-week holiday, planned long ago and carried out through the Mayor's insistence that his duties mustn't crimp family opportunities together.

As Harold Rubin observed, "During his first month he's taken the initiative toward resolving many of the problems which built up during the past decade. . . . He's systematically doing those things that have to be done."

But there was a sour note, too. With an odd untimeliness, an editorial complaint was published in only his third week. In a severe criticism of a recently expressed reluctance to "go into the unknown" of self-insuring the city's workers' compensation coverage, the editors suggested that "either Mr. Whalen scares easily or he is unaware of how other government self-insurance programs are run." Unawareness—or, more bluntly, ignorance—did appear to be a very plausible possibility reflecting the new Mayor's probable level of useful information on such a complex, specialized topic at that point. The editorial's stick-in-the-eye approach seems unduly harsh and unforgiving in view of all the circumstances. Whalen commented, much later, "I probably didn't understand the subject and had no reason to commit myself on a matter I knew very little about." He also came to understand that the occasion had offered a tip-off as to the editors' readiness to second-guess superciliously, uncaring of how his motivation contrasted with what had been going on before his arrival. He'd learn even more before long. (In due time, his government reached a decision in favor of self-insurance for workers' compensation.)

* * *

July's major event was the creation of a new Department of Parks and Recreation (broken off from Public Works, where it had been a bureau) and selection of its first commissioner. But like a distance runner, Whalen picked up the pace as summer wore on. The Mayor caused the demise of one more stagnant holdover, the Downtown Albany Development Corporation, a private enterprise funded by businesses, and two weeks later he established a new Advisory Committee on the Future of Downtown Albany, involving the State University's chancellor, Clifton R. Wharton, in its genesis.

His firm decision that no-bid purchases and contracts must be ended was receiving heavy emphasis. For starters, bids were to be required on purchases of police uniforms, another step away from "friends" favoritism—and another blow to the Organization's finances. Bids now were sought for planting trees, previously a sinkhole of uncontrolled expense.

At the same time, one of the city's insurance carriers—Fuller and O'Brien, which had provided property and liability coverage for 20 years—announced that it would reduce its premiums to the tune of $95,000 a year.

Area banks were asked to compete for the reissuance of short-term notes, for only the second time in more than 40 years. And Whalen was now able to predict that he'd have a budget surplus for the fiscal year.

Scrap metal stockpiled at the landfill was sold, producing an income that would become a steady source. The 30,000 tons of scrap on "Mount Canmore" were beginning to melt away advantageously.

In a move that carried significance insufficiently recognized at the time, the Mayor reached an understanding with a new "first" budget director who would officially begin work at the first of November. But this 66-year-old recruit, Daniel Klepak, started immediate consultations in City Hall, where his giant impact and imprint would be felt unmistakably for more than a dozen years. He would shortly be Whalen's own 800-pound gorilla. If only coincidentally, Klepak had been in office less than a week before a new order went out to all departments: *Reduce your budget by an additional 5%!*

August's progressive developments in reduction of insurance costs, bidding on street reconstruction, slashes in spending, requesting bids on bond issues, and other innovations were almost overshadowed by contrasting incidents. For weeks, Whalen was assailed sharply and insistently in the press for an arrangement he made for the loan of an automobile from a dealer-friend.

On the other hand, Corning's final opponent, Charles Touhey, who some had deemed likely to take on the "weak" successor, announced that he wouldn't think of contesting Whalen because he was in sympathy with so much of the new Mayor's effort.   Altogether, it was an encouraging way to measure the gains of this critical period.

* * *

Moved along effectively during the 100-day summer, though completed only after Labor Day, were numerous other projects, such as establishing the new office of employee relations (a "first" that soon would publish recognized standards of performance); merging two related departments, traffic safety and traffic engineering; and, always to be ranked as the most important of all, carrying out the intense examination and modification of bidding and purchasing procedures that had begun in the spring. This area, so ripe for reform, was a minefield always treacherous. Change was not to be accomplished by good intentions or by fiat alone. Wishing would not make it so. The last-ditchers among the Old Guard hung on to their trouble-making ways so long as there remained some ill-gained dollars to be wrung out through their flagrant insubordination.

And within the hard-bitten fiscal policy, the 14-month $88.2 million budget (covering 1984 as well as the last two months of 1983) was produced and adopted—without raising property taxes—while a crucial testing of the bond market with a $37.4 million offering was successfully completed after Whalen led a team to Manhattan to argue for holding the line on the city's ratings which had been sharply downgraded early in the year. He couldn't afford to go into the market with virtually unsalable bonds.

Albany was paying "substantial attention to fiscal prudence, an essential criterion in a time of national recession," as Mario Cuomo noted somewhat later.

One other fiscal item, which had been percolating during the honeymoon, boiled over in November in a showdown from which Whalen emerged as the winner but which created a dark stain suggestive of struggles to come. Its essence was the city's share (in common with other municipalities) of the county's sales tax revenue. The division of this money had been well established as 60% for the county government's needs and 40% for the cities, towns, and villages. The County Legislature's finance committee—chaired by Harold Joyce, representing Albany's Twelfth Ward legislatively—brought forward a proposal to increase the county's share to 61%. The impact of the absent 1%, though seemingly minor, was significant enough for local governments—especially Albany's—to create a resistance movement. A lion's share of the movement was in one man's hands.

In a tense Saturday session held—significantly—in Whalen's office, Joyce was successfully urged to recognize the position of the city. As a very important ward leader in Albany, he was arguing on behalf of the county. In this oddity, Whalen saw the hand of a putative rival, County Executive Coyne.

"There were two major aspects," Whalen pointed out later. "First, the prospective loss of revenue. That would have been hurtful. The other issue was political with long-range implications I couldn't overlook or permit: Was I going to let them take me on, in a matter that not only was damaging to my governmental responsibilities but that could be considered a test of how strong a Mayor I was going to be? Could I afford to be seen as a pushover if I couldn't—or wouldn't—protect my turf and my interests? No, I could not."

So Albany, which had the most to lose, and the other localities were able instead to continue to share their 40%. It was a timely victory for Whalen. But Joyce's move was suggestive of an appetite for influence and position within a political sphere to which he was deeply committed.

Tectonic plates were shifting, ever so slowly, under Whalen's feet. Eventually, attention must be paid.

* * *

In a remote corner of his search for opportunities to prod Albany's self-image, Whalen began to build on references recalled from history books: in less than three years the city should be making suitable note of its three-hundredth year. Celebrations could do much in raising spirits, and though he was unable yet to actively plan for a "tricentennial" as he identified the occasion in his mind, Whalen made a point of noting the kinds of events that ought to mark what he instinctively envisioned as a year-long observance.

The anniversary in 1986 would mark the granting of a charter to the tiny, fragile, but stalwart community of Albany by the English governor of the New York colony, Thomas Dongan. (*See accompanying article, Albany's Limerick Charter.*) Eventually, the Mayor's fondest dreams for a year combining respectful attention to history with parties and fireworks were wholly realized in a blowout that was an acclaimed success.

Meanwhile, Albany would prepare for the grand celebration with a preview in the early fall of 1984. In the "Kennedy Weekend," a sentimental outpouring of tribute to the author William Kennedy suffused the whole area in pleased and prideful acknowledgement of the honors he'd recently received. In April he had been awarded the Pulitzer Prize in fiction for his latest novel *Ironweed*. Months earlier, he had won one of the fabled MacArthur awards which recognizes extraordinary talent and potential achievement.[3] The coincidence of Bill Kennedy's attainment and his reflected glory fitted very neatly into the city's aura of surprised pleasure. A relaxed air of confidence had descended on the populace along with the new-broom Whalen administration. And in the area of coincidence, the Pulitzer award, bringing Albany a touch of fame, was announced only a few days after the happy news of Union Station's revival-to-be. The author's new international fame, appreciation of his fond elevation of his hometown, and celebration of his high good fortune was observed in "A city-wide celebration of Albany and William Kennedy." With prolonged fanfare over four days, the festival embraced a dozen events, alternately lively and thoughtful, including reconsideration of

Albany politics, present and past. Among the parties was a huge one thrown by the city at the Lakehouse in Washington Park. "Albany had never done anything like this, but this was perfect for the time," Whalen recalled happily. "It captivated people, and reminded them of the good things about Albany. And it underlined for me the continuous desirability of looking for such reminders, and the need to celebrate them." This hardly could have been foreseen in the summer of 1983, but spontaneously it became a prime force in Whalen's hope of igniting Albany's own sense of destiny in a way that would have gratified a W. J. Bryan.

* * *

In June's first days, Whalen had sat down with Holt-Harris to talk about the issue of tenure. Did charter and law make explicit a rule clarifying how soon he must expect an election? *1983 or 1985*, that was the question, a big one. Already, he and Vinnie McArdle had begun researches on the applicable statutes and precedents. For months, rather witless speculations had occupied columns of newsprint, arguing stray possibility against hapless prospect as to what clause might ultimately be invoked to determine the length of term for Corning's successor.

Some of this guessing was linked with the supposition that hungrily eager opportunists were ready to mount a challenge, whatever the date. The succession itself was a non-issue, for both State law and the municipal charter were clear that the Common Council's president was first in line to fill a vacancy. As a principal holder of one of four city-wide elected offices he clearly out-ranked either of the other offices filled in the same manner, the Comptroller's and the Treasurer's.

Twice during Corning's own political career, in fact, filling a mayoral vacancy had been routinely handled by elevating a Council president. An interim Mayor was needed when a vacancy occurred a year before his first election to the office, and an Acting Mayor took over for him while he was on Army duty, serving for a year and a half until Corning's return.

Now, in 1983, like it or not, Albany's irreconcilables had to reconcile themselves to the unavoidable—Erastus Corning really wasn't going to return this time. And he had already determined the "who" of his successor.

All that remained was the question of "for how long?"

Having faced the need to make a choice quickly and establish a position publicly, Whalen already had firmly decided that he wanted to hold the office through 1985. He had taken into account some—but not all—of the complications implicit in this commitment to a much more political life. Professional career and family obligations were major priorities to be granted serious consideration as he sought political office that would encumber other factors for at least seven years. Fundamental to all his thoughts was his strong desire to have enough time to make his mark in office.

"I'm just going to bite the bullet," the Mayor told Holt-Harris. "We'll see if we can't get this settled right away. I don't want to wait for events to overtake us, very possibly to our disadvantage."

We, our, us? His use of the plural pronouns was inadvertent, for any disadvantage would be his alone to sustain, however much friends might commiserate over any ruling contrary to his interests. Now that he had responsibility and accountability, he was intent on trying to make certain of a fair shot at having enough time to do the job right. A decision requiring a special election only five months into the Whalen term would be more than a distraction for his pressing duties. Despite the odds favoring incumbency, the timing of such an election conceivably could turn out of office an unproven Mayor, whose job—as Whalen construed it—was sure to mean upsetting more apple carts and further distressing numerous significant psyches.

Holt-Harris's response to Whalen's declaration of intent was a lawyer's cautionary "Are you sure you want to do this?" To force the issue, as Whalen proposed, might produce an undesirable ruling in the courts. But without perceptible hesitation, the Mayor's answer came: "Yes!"

Though his goal was to attain what he saw as the advantage of a longer interim term—29 months until November of 1985—his illusionary move was precisely the opposite. He would argue for the short term, pressing for a speedy ruling—highly desirable—apparently ready to be tested and tried in the few months ahead, rather than be seen as unwilling to go before the voters simply as the lucky incumbent. Publicly, his posture was "Let's have an immediate decision on the term's length so I can defend my right to the office promptly." His avenue to success in this disarming maneuver was a legal device very familiar to all lawyers though in its very simplicity often bewildering to the lay public. It was a gamble with high stakes, but with the traditional three lemons if all went well.

At this stage, Whalen's credibility was reminiscent of a scenario played out a few years earlier in a much larger theater when Gerald R. Ford became the nation's Vice President and President without ever having been chosen for either office in a popular election. Richard M. Nixon had picked Ford to be Vice President, subject only to the Senate's approval. Erastus Corning had selected Whalen as a running mate, presumably subject to ratification by voters in 1981. But in reality Whalen got a free pass and arrived at the Council's presidency without opposition on the ballot. As in the instance of the vice-presidency the citizenry had never actually voted in a contested election to put the individual into office. It was not the most stable of perches, at least until performance could paper over the question-mark created by the public's uncertainty. Lofty credentials and innate decency were good for no more than once around the carousel.[4]

* * *

But strong legal argument, much less a winning one, never coalesced behind a quick vote. Nor was it ever clear-cut that such opposition would be more effective by November rather than in 1985. The knife cut both ways:

Whalen presumably could benefit by tenure—acquiring nearly two and a half years of experience and accomplishment before facing the voters. But the added time could produce damaging stumbles, too, while an opponent might gather friends, funds, and favors for an all-out attack in a Democratic primary. Some published accounts added specific potential opponents to the early speculation about who could be counted on to contest Whalen for the mayoralty—"the sooner the better," in the view of the displaced Loyalists. Or even produce a plausible Republican offensive in 1985: The toothless Albany Republicans were prompt to make mewling noises about demanding a prompt election, suggesting that Whalen was some kind of usurper.

But though the opposition forces in his party might somehow quickly be able to demolish Whalen in a short, brutal assault by early fall 1983, the even larger question remained: Who had the money to make the idea more than fantasy? Even the rumored candidacy of Erastus Corning III seemed exceedingly problematic (as it was). Interestingly, though the late Mayor's son might seem young because of the generational lapse, he actually was several months older than Whalen.

The suspense for nearly three months, the uncertainties and corresponding concerns, the apprehension and the resultant devious strategies all were tied to a transient issue of a personal nature rather than governmental. It was more than a small diversion for the Mayor from the major decision-making that necessarily occupied his thoughts. But its vexations were unavoidable if the proper outcome was to be achieved. To have left to others' hands, or to a haphazard fate, his positioning at each stage of the question's settlement would have unduly tempted that fate. Whalen, Holt-Harris, and—more directly on the firing line—McArdle correctly saw the deep significance of the legal skirmishing. If Whalen were denied the opportunity he was fighting for, the culmination of the reforms he already was seeking would be aborted—and the issues yet to be fought were certain to be stillborn.

Every hour that Whalen and McArdle devoted to shaping their arguments was worthwhile, directly related to the future of the administration's capacity to attain the aims that the new Mayor was establishing for his government and the city.

By the first day of September, less than 10 weeks before what conceivably might have been an election date, the Court of Appeals rendered all the questions moot. Mercifully prompt and unmistakably decisive, the court ruled that the election should take place in 1985. Whalen had attained his breathing space, presenting him with the clear opportunity to make his own record. For the next 26 months he was home free. Dissenters might plot and carpers could connive, but he held the office as securely as though he were chained to the desk, elected by acclamation.

And the beautiful irony of it all was that, in gaining the legal system's authentication, his reverse strategy, arguing that an election should take place in November 1983, had succeeded. Technically, he had lost the argument—and the case—but by losing the battle he had won the war. Somewhere, MacArthur was once more wading ashore.

NOTES

[1] *Eyewitness to Power: The Essence of Leadership,* Simon & Schuster; copyright 2000 by David Gergen.

[2] He closed out his first week as Mayor by returning to the Common Council's chamber offering amiable recollections and ceremonially handing over its official gavel to his successor. The Council's new president, Steve McArdle, had been the Thirteenth Ward's Alderman, but, as the president pro tem, now was elevated

by law to the city-wide office. He read a list of six "worthwhile accomplishments" put into effect in the 17 months of Whalen's presidency. One was, in fact, Whalen's record of "never having picked up the gavel." Other achievements, as recited were: 1) Alterations in committee structure now gave more responsibility to Aldermen. This was indeed a break with tradition. One important new requirement obliged committees to hold public hearings. 2) The format of the hearings was greatly modified so that any citizen would be permitted to speak up; and proponents of whatever matter was being considered were to be heard first instead of as an afterthought. 3) The calendar had been so improved that it now was "the envy of other cities," in McArdle's perhaps slightly exaggerated opinion. 4) A streamlined agenda was now prepared on Whalen's initiative. This printed document was made available a week before each scheduled Monday meeting. 5) And even reporters were said to get a break because their table was moved so they "could receive a better sense of the proceedings." The stirrings toward independent thought and action that developed in succeeding years may be traceable to members' increased sense of their rights.

[3] His "urban tapestry," *O Albany!*, was published late in 1983, shortly after *Ironweed*. In its subtitling, it celebrated an "Improbable city of political wizards, fearless ethnics, spectacular aristocrats, splendid nobodies, and underrated scoundrels." Not surprisingly in fearlessly ethnic Albany, published references to the book frequently came out as *O'Albany*.

[4] Five years after Whalen left office, a clause incorporated within a new, updated version of the charter changed the language—at the new Mayor's insistence—so that in certain circumstances a Mayor of Albany could unilaterally designate an interim appointee to act in his place if he were unable to carry out his sworn responsibilities. Whalen publicly opposed the changes, publishing a letter enumerating his reasons.

Albany's "Limerick Charter"

The "Dongan Charter," though in effect in Albany for nearly 200 years, probably would have enjoyed an even more celebrated era if only the lifespan of Governor Thomas Dongan's elder brother had been shorter. Had it been known as the "Limerick Charter," it would have gained greater respectful attention in the tricentennial observance fostered so vigorously by Tom Whalen in 1986.[1]

Governor Dongan became second Earl of Limerick by inheritance through his brother, but this came about only several years after he had left New York and returned to England as a broken refugee.

His six-year administration in New York was inextricably mixed with the vicissitudes of English royalty late in the seventeenth century. Born in Ireland in 1634 (just 300 years before Whalen), he embarked on a military career. Late in the tumult that marked the reign of Charles II (whose father had been beheaded), he was appointed to be Governor of New York in 1682 by the Duke of York, the king's brother. Dongan granted Albany its charter (one was provided also to the town that became New York City) a few months after the death of Charles and the duke's ascension as James II on an even more controversial throne.

Contemporaneously, the Governor convened a New York Assembly, which proceeded to draw up a "Charter of Liberties" that served as the basis for a constitution when New York attained statehood a century later. But this charter never went into effect because although King James signed it he failed to return it to the colony, presumably because of its "extreme liberalism." Dongan's other pioneering efforts were remarkable and laudable—he helped fix New York's boundaries through treaties and agreements; and his policies in dealing with Indians set an example for the English colonial governors thereafter.

But when James was forced from the throne in 1688, Dongan was relieved of his governorship and had to flee to New England for refuge from the persecution of Roman Catholics known to be sympathetic to the king. Dongan finally reached England in 1691 (later succeeding his brother in the Limerick earldom, but by then all its lands had been seized and he never recovered them.) He lived through the Protestant reigns of two of James's daughters, Queens Mary II (with her husband William III) and Anne I, but as an effort to gain the throne for their Catholic half-brother was flickering out, Dongan died in poverty in London in December 1715. His great gift to Albany thrived on and on until late in the nineteenth century.

Albany has streets named James and Dongan, and a fabled area in the north end styled "Limerick" but no official recognition of what might have been.

NOTE

[1] The source of much of the detail is from the *Encyclopedia Britannica*, 1953 edition.

Tom, Dick—and Harry

Fifty-four days into Whalen's tenure, an articulate 36-year-old student of theoretical physics and modern British history took over Albany's troubled network of 40-odd parks, together with a motley assortment of other recreation areas, many of them decrepit and untended. At the same time, he became the first commissioner of a new city department, for Whalen was chopping Parks off from all the rest of the bulging Public Works empire where, as only a bureau, it had languished for decades as a highly prized patronage gully.

Public Works had grown into a huge conglomerate, where largely unrelated functions were jammed under an umbrella department: Streets, Sewers, Engineering, Planning—Parks and Recreation. It had been glued together in the Great Depression to foster made-work for the 1930s' unemployed. Its dimensions meant that its Commissioner could boast a range of influence second only to the Mayor's. Now Whalen's move chipped a sizeable shoulder off the block.

With the removal of Parks, 260 jobs moved, too—significant patronage opportunities that now came into the Mayor's control, no longer under the thumb of an Old Guardian, Harry Maikels. "The rookie Mayor has clearly demonstrated that he knows how to play politics," Bob McManus remarked, an observation that many other players accepted without quibble.

On this day, July 21, the new commissioner, Richard J. Barrett—a native of Albany's West End and a committeeman in the Joyce Twelfth Ward who'd been notably underemployed as superintendent of Bleecker Stadium—was moved ahead by Whalen's hand like a bishop overtaking a pawn in a studied coup that deserved the self-congratulatory chuckle it earned. Barrett's designation effectively overrode a political mare's nest, the stalemate between two party stalwarts, deputies in the bureau, both of whom had seemed to stand in line for a promotion. Whalen's preemptive move was a brilliant stroke administratively as well as politically.

Beyond the merit of his personal choice, his show of decisive independence, and the I'm-boss-now reminder in his timing, Parks and Recreation is deserving of particular attention. In significant part, it is an example of the sweep of Whalen's vision, his readiness to defy Organization expectations, and the fundamental changes he'd make throughout the sprawling governmental arena into which he had been dropped. True, he was exceedingly fortunate in his selection of Barrett, but Parks stands out for its textbook view of Tom Whalen, CEO, and the outcome of his Fiorello-like involvements.

The unlikely Barrett appointment[1] was accurately hailed by Whalen as a "most significant administrative change" and interpreted elsewhere as an indication that he expected to shape Albany's government in his own image. In truth, Barrett's spectacular elevation was indeed an exceedingly meaningful move, although the full degree of what the Mayor had achieved became evident only over the next several years. Barrett's administration of the parks turned out to be a huge success for the patrons and a major plus for Whalen himself.

As for shaping the government, that surely was Whalen's prerogative, especially in view of the floundering enterprise he'd just inherited. Seizing control of the parks system—including its payroll's dimensions and political impact— did not necessarily appear to him as high policy at the time, just as the mason setting a rock into a cathedral's foundation probably isn't contemplating the spire that ultimately will rise above it.

And over the next 10 years, apart from the benefits accruing to citizens and city from a healthy parks system, Whalen's move was rewarded by development of an exceptionally creative and industrious administrator and a consummate political operative. Throughout, Barrett made himself indispensable to the Mayor, not least for his unquestioned personal loyalty.

Explaining the surprising repositioning that first summer, Whalen reassured doubters that he believed "in the patronage system, and jobs—but," he added, "we have to step back and see what the city can afford." What Albany certainly could not afford was the current 14% cost overrun in the bureau's operations, amounting to $411,000, with 15 weeks remaining in the fiscal year. Nor could it afford many of the 260 employees (swollen in the summer by some 400 old men and teenagers) that were moved over from Public Works. Dick Barrett's first assignment would be damming this disastrous leakage, probably beginning with the two ancient "public baths" (actually swimming pools). He found a muddy swamp, 18 inches deep, below one pool. However outmoded in the late twentieth century, the pools still claimed an ardent if dwindling bevy of bathers and retained a sensitive mystique politically.

That was "a summer from hell—a desperate time" for Barrett. Faced with preparing a new budget for the coming fiscal year, he first had to burrow through the chaos to determine where his new department's previous managers had left everything. One thing was certain: They'd been badly over-spending; cost overruns were rampant. Immediately he confronted the complication of preparing for a 14-month year rather than following any precedent. But precedent for Parks was useless anyway. Its year-round schedule was like no other department's. A single budget plan would not work. Activity and spending could not follow a flat line across the calendar. They were uniquely seasonal. And within the seasonal aspect each individual service to the public had its own season which had to be considered separately and spending for it gauged accordingly.   Realistically, he had eleven distinct budgets to prepare.

Barrett had already been required to cut back on the swollen staffing.   Payroll reductions could trim $345,000, reducing to $66,000 an overrun that had been projected at more than six times that amount. For the first time ever, Parks was being forced to live within a budget, even the unrealistic one he was inheriting. The previous bureau, buried as it was within Public Works along with numerous others—streets, sewers, engineering, planning, buildings—in the massive conglomerate, had grown fat as a tick on its chronic deficits.

* * *

In effect, a wholly new philosophy was being introduced, upgrading the place of the parks in the city's life through enhanced recreational opportunities and even its arboreal attractiveness.   But before the improvements were possible, reforms were essential.

A basic innovation was in Barrett's insistence that for every dollar spent a dollar's worth of goods or services were received. Albany had been getting very little in return for its heavy expenditures. Money had to be redirected to assure that the limited funds would be able to produce a result as envisioned and planned. The procedures to achieve this assurance were, in fact, a radical departure. Vendors had to learn—frequently, the hard way—that full deliveries were expected and would be checked to make certain that, for specific instance, if 100,000 tulip bulbs were ordered, 100,000 would be planted. Purchase of a dozen trees meant that 12 would arrive. Many purchases had been at double the market rate, or higher—and the ultimate outcome was a state of decay.

The mercenary army of rakers was now sent home like so many Confederate soldiers after Appomattox. The victories won for the public were as actual in their way as Grant's victory over Lee. And then there was the early matter of filtering from the city's payroll those "employees" who never showed up for work. Time sheets were introduced for the parks workers who remained. Trimming of "people on the edge" from the bloated payroll was necessary in those revolutionary days of realistic budgeting accountability, if the parks were to be made respectable enough and safe enough for public use. Barrett, who considered that he'd been hired to make the park system "the best," was relieved to know that he didn't have to please the county committee with his hires. Even the summer youth corps, part of the "Albany Plan" for providing paid employment for anyone who applied, was required to be productive; the Mayor himself came and satisfied himself about the worth of their projects.

The facilities posed another issue. In playgrounds, the equipment—if it could be found in the overgrowth—often was only a rusted hazard. A major renovation of the Lincoln Park pool was a vital portion of a million-dollar upgrading of all pools. Their filtration and chloration systems demanded and received overhauling.

The old policy of slight attention to maintenance and replacement of the city's infrastructure included a universal practice among departments using mobile equipment, such as Public Works, Fire, and Parks. As outdated and timeworn machinery gave out, similar items were simply cannibalized. Now Parks bought new mowing equipment as well as modern machines that could do the rakers' job, just as major firefighting equipment meant added effectiveness and Public Works at last could operate its own snow-removal apparatus instead of renting from private operators in expensive times of emergency.

New sites were added: a fishing dock, a boat dock, and a boathouse on the banks of the Hudson. Three new parks were opened; the Corning Preserve received necessary rehabilitation upkeep. The municipal golf course, a relic of WPA construction of the 1930s, with a "back nine" that many regarded as unplayable and with a squalid clubhouse, received a $3 million rebuilding.

The Mayor "made time for Parks and Recreation every

day," Barrett recalled. "He was resurrecting a corpse. And he was big on beautification of all kinds. All this was true apart from insisting on policies and practices that meant square dealing in all phases of our operations.

"The parks blossomed because he wanted it to be so. I received support from him for improving the tulip beds, for the swans on the lake, for the paddleboats . . . all were his ideas.

"But his greatest contribution was his invention of the Park Playhouse. It began with the concept of free, outdoor, live theater for Albany and it was initiated as 'Live at the Lakehouse.' But it became more. For the summer-long revivals of classic musicals, he was the prime mover. In order for them to be presented in circumstances that would attract audiences a setting had to be devised."

The result was a reconfiguration of an area of Washington Park facing the lake. A bowl was created by regrading the site, and equipped with appropriate lighting and other technical requirements for successful stage presentation.

"It was his masterpiece and it deserves permanent recognition as such," in Barrett's opinion. "It's an important part of the way he refocused the Capital District's attention on Albany. He shared much of himself through the festivals, the regattas, Cityski and other recreational diversions, and also on his aggressive ideas and efforts for making a beautiful city."

* * *

Of the new parks Whalen and Barrett created, one seemed to have nearly as many side-issues as the 384 special plants it held within its vest-pocket setting.

A few weeks after Erastus Corning became the 37th Albany Mayor interred in Albany Rural Cemetery, a strong undercurrent of public sentiment for creating a memorial to him became unmistakably evident within City Hall.

Whalen decided that a committee could provide some options for ways to appropriately honor his predecessor. Its members included the late Mayor's widow, the Episcopal cathedral dean, David S. Ball, Norman Rice, Lewis Swyer, and Jack McEneny. From among them, one or another tenable idea would emerge—with "taste and meaning," as Whalen emphasized. But even with the benefit of a scope brought by prominent people extremely friendly to Corning's memory, suitable ideas were limited by precedents as well as by funds.

During the last weeks of Corning's illness, Governor Cuomo had announced his intention of creating a tribute in some suitably monumental form. He ended up giving Corning's name to an existing structure—the tallest among the forest of stone and concrete in Nelson Rockefeller's governmental plaza. Such a designation would be hard for the city to rival.

Just a few years earlier, another Governor had granted a similar designation for State property that would honor Corning during his lifetime. A narrow stretch of land along the Hudson's western shoreline was identified as Corning Riverfront Park (or, as it came to be called, Corning Preserve). Just as Mario Cuomo owed Corning for his early support in 1982, Hugh Carey had owed him for early support in a primary contest he had to win before the 1978 election. The "preserve," incidentally, continues as state-owned land that is leased to the city.

Albany also had the Edwin Corning Homes, a housing project in the city's north end that had been named for the Mayor's father (slated for demolition in 1999), and the Louise Corning Senior Center, named for his mother.

Thus substantially circumscribed as to potential areas for honoring him, the committee agreed upon a park as a memorial. The intent was clear enough—a site specifically honoring Erastus Corning and therefore bearing his name. An appropriate locale was immediately obvious: the unoccupied plot directly behind City Hall and offering access from both Maiden Lane[2] and Pine Street. On it, a jail had stood, many years earlier.

Corning's little corner of the world would become

Corning's memorial: Corning Park. But something unexpectedly got in the way of this smooth transition. In his excitement
about the Tricentennial and in his desire to tie as many span-
gles as possible to that celebration, Whalen became temporarily blinded to the basic rationale for the new park and declared
that it would be titled "Tricentennial Park." Samson-like, he
also was blind to the shock and distress at what promptly
became perceived as a slight.[3]

The clamor of objections was immediate, loud, and
sharp. It could have been prolonged save for Whalen's quick
recognition that he had committed a political error comparable
to a LaGuardian "beaut."[4] Within days, he retracted his ill-
starred suggestion, and the desired identity was restored to
Corning Park—which, of course, didn't exist as yet anyway.

Corning Park's cost approached $500,000, and depend-
ing on whether certain items are included, it may be considered substantially greater. The city was still scratching for
funds after the park was dedicated. The initial bond to finance
it provided $240,000, reflecting an overly optimistic view of the
work that needed to be accomplished there. Additional bond
authorizations increased these expenditures by $165,000, and
more public funds later had to supplement these amounts.

A city employee having personal contacts with the
Cornings had received the impression that a $50,000 gift would
be forthcoming from the family to cover the cost of a fountain.
Accordingly, this sum was budgeted into the early cost projections. But a $24,561 check from a Corning account at the
Norstar bank in November 1986 completed the entire contribution, and this seeming shortfall compounded the city's problems in reconciling its accounts and paying the bills. (As the
billings became a matter of very public awareness, a headline
applied the word "jinx" to the financing fiasco.)

Compared with the $240,000 total financing proposed
at the outset, $222,000 eventually was paid out merely for pur-
chase of adjoining property and for its demolition, a handsome
gesture by Whalen intended to suggest Corning's stature by
enlarging the park's dimensions and enhancing the ambiance.

Some $20,000 was paid for designs, $158,000 for construction (the fountain's price was $52,500), and many thousands more for the 60 trees and 324 shrubs planted in every one of the plot's crevices and crannies. All this occupied many months of planning, designing, rethinking, construction, and fiscal scrambling. At almost the last hour before the 1987 dedication, Betty Corning thought of a memorial plaque.

Corning Park is an attractive corner of downtown in a rather lush though unobtrusive way. As "Tricentennial Park," it undoubtedly would have been somewhat less extensive and, in a materialistic sense, somewhat less expensive. It stands as a desirable improvement over the jail that, long ago, occupied the space sloping eastward down Maiden Lane/Corning Place some 50 yards to the stern west wall of the Masonic Temple which since 1896 casts a long shadow at the garden's edge.

NOTES

[1] A rather similar Whalen appointment was that of his Buildings Commissioner, Michael J. Haydock. Holding degrees in history and political science, Haydock was an authority on numerous aspects of military history. Whalen recruited him in 1985 in a striking instance of shunning the patronage mill (after having given notice to the county committee of a vacancy in the position). It was an unusual selection for a responsibility that is demandingly technical with review of plans and specifications for commercial construction permits and oversight on compliance with codes and with federal standards on sites. After leaving office, Haydock published a book, *City Under Siege*, a scholarly analysis of the 1948-1949 Berlin blockade and airlift. Altogether, his appointment—which turned out to be very successful—was ideal for a mayor who responded to untapped human potential, succeeding in matching it effectively with responsibility.

² The most westerly portion of cobblestoned Maiden Lane, which had become reduced to a single block when the Hilton Hotel was constructed, was renamed for Corning when the park was dedicated. Not long afterward, a *Times Union* staffer's error identified Corning Place as "O'Connell Place."

³ He was neglecting the sage admonition of Frederick Scott Oliver, who wrote in 1930: "A wise politician will never begrudge a genuflection or a rapture if it is expected of him by prevalent opinion." Whalen later ranked this mistake as one of the most hurtful of his political career.

⁴ Not long before he was elected in 1941 to his third and last term as New York's Mayor (an election that coincided with Erastus Corning's first as Mayor of Albany) LaGuardia was offering testimony to the Foreign Relations Committee of the United States Senate on foreign aid policy when a question was raised about a controversial appointment he had made. LaGuardia answered: "Senator, I have made excellent appointments. I think I am good at it. But when I make a mistake, it's a beaut!" The latter expression quickly became a byword in political folklore.

Juice Worth the Squeeze

"He'll try to run things if you get him in here!" Albany's new Mayor was cautioned by Holt-Harris in the early summer as he scouted the countryside for the city's first budget director and began to give serious consideration to Daniel Klepak as a candidate. "He has the ability to aggravate, and I don't know if you want or need that."

In his first days, Whalen had filled the newly authorized position, only to have his appointee, a ward committeeman put forward by Harold Joyce, back out within a fortnight.

In starting afresh in his search, he was hearing strong advice to follow where his own instinct was tugging him— installation of a wholly qualified individual with knowledge and authority to establish a genuine fiscal plan. With an acute awareness, he recognized how much he needed a system replacing Erastus Corning's—promptly, for he never could forget or ignore Comptroller Regan's warning, "I can give you six months to clean it up. Or we'll have to come in." Whalen's own reputation, as well as the city's, was on the line daily.

In recruiting a budget director, the issue was not so much putting out Corning's fiscal conflagration. Its flames had to be battled and managed immediately, a process that Whalen was diligently tackling. The longer-term requirement was starting to be able to develop fiscal plans and controls that would demonstrably establish a solidly professional and functional base for day-to-day operations with adequate oversight.

Whalen solicited suggestions from three well-placed

executives—two bank presidents and an entrepreneurial CPA—and from one of them, Richard F. Lindstrom of Bankers Trust, he heard Klepak's name proposed as a strong prospect. He already had good reason to have well-informed opinions about him, for they had been close collaborators in the 1960s as key volunteers at a downtown settlement-house agency.

Interviewed, Klepak was amenable to the idea and, in fact, eager for what he had no difficulty in seeing as an irresistible challenge. As a comfortable retiree from high-level State managerial positions, he maintained a confident personality that assured him a piece of cake was being placed in front of him. The invitation was made more attractive by the vision of routing the opposing political forces. They would fight his instinctive solutions and his hard-nosed supervision of the city's income and its dispersal. He could anticipate sharing in the policy decisions behind it all and beyond the balance sheets.

Discussion of how to seal the deal offered little real problem. Klepak had already retired from a series of top-level "exempt" jobs in a variety of New York State departments,[1] and he arrived with a very agreeable pension. He settled for a salary that was, as of that time, slightly higher than the Mayor's $33,000 (the latter soon to be corrected). But he had one decisive request: assignment of a city-owned vehicle for his use, a matter of domestic convenience. So, despite the misgivings voiced by Holt-Harris, agreement was reached whereby the City of Albany would compensate him for liberal use of his talents.

For budgetary considerations, the appointment was not officially effective until November 1, but by late summer Dan Klepak was very much on hand, sitting in effectively at Whalen's sessions with his commissioners checking their fiscal performance against the current year's limitation—and then shaping up their needs for the looming 14-month fiscal year that had been authorized by the Legislature. Altogether, it was a highly demanding subset in Albany's money crisis, and Klepak's informal arrival was just in time.

Though timely steps to address financial problems had been taken in Whalen's first months—notably in purchasing practices and action to amend the odd and costly fiscal year—by the time Klepak reached his desk he confronted a situation desperately needing further reforms.

Promptly, he and the Mayor began an action plan that would last for a decade. Opening with a mandated cutback in expenditures across the board, it featured tightened budget controls and a wide-ranging attack on critical issues: Insistence on lawful bidding practices, ending the roller-coaster assessment policy, sharply reducing the payroll, improving services, financing numerous innovations, establishing a capital budget, developing a realistic work-week for employees, rebuilding the municipal infrastructure, and disposing of city-owned properties that lacked an actual function.

Their impressive results would include regaining a prized "A" rating from the bond agencies, and achieving a fund balance that rose to more than $30 million before its logical service as a budgeting cushion when revenues fell during the nation's economic difficulties in the first Bush presidency. Concurrently, despite higher operating and capital expenditures, they held property taxes 9% below their 1983 level up until the final Whalen years. Then, gradual tax rises brought the tax rate back to where it stood at the beginning of the administration. Compared with taxation everywhere, this accomplishment was little short of astonishing. But all this was to be in the future, after years of sustained effort.

* * *

Along with his own rules and expectations, Klepak imported experience and expertise, and he conveyed confidence that some called overbearing. He had a take-no-prisoners outlook. His conversation habitually was in doomsday terminology for its shock effect, but Whalen learned to discount most of the warnings. Somehow, the two of them, essentially very different persons and personalities, meshed. And each gained his own claque of detractors. Klepak was frequently the butt of tirades against "that damned Republican from Guilderland." (His residence outside the city was deemed almost as bad as his party enrollment.)

One line of gossip, predictable under the circumstances, alleged that he was performing his budgetary legerdemain as a "co-mayor," presuming beyond his defined duties, and usurping statutory responsibilities of the elected Comptroller. Whalen, after leaving office, could identify no issue that had festered between them as to who was the Mayor. The impression, however, could easily germinate and flourish. The budget director's high degree of competence and daring initiative promised not merely action but positive consequence. He could empathetically comprehend what financing the Mayor would need for his program. Whalen could afford to be tolerant, even to encourage bold and brash behavior. He saw Klepak as a "good front man," meaning that, being conspicuous on unpopular budgetary strictures, he would take some of the resulting heat.

The man known as "Hawk" during his days in decisive state positions had found a new home where his rare background chanced to fit precisely.

"Is there money to get this done?" was Whalen's frequent query. And almost always Klepak could find a way to finance such large-scale projects as community policing, construction of an amphitheater in Washington Park, and development of Albany golfers' New Course. This was especially true when intuition assured Klepak that the proposal represented a desirable means to a worthy end. Then, the money was likely to appear as if by a waving wand. "*Is the juice worth the squeeze?*" was a favored Klepak testy inquiry—his own version of "Is the result going to warrant the effort and cost?"

At times, Klepak's wand was slow in responding, and then a bit of a prod was required to produce results. The two disagreed on policy rather often over the years, the standoff possibly ending with an occasional abrupt, "Dan, just go *do* it!" They differed most notably early in the final term, when

Klepak wanted to raise taxes but was rebuffed. After it was all over, however, Whalen conceded that "I should have raised taxes by perhaps 5% in 1991 and the two following years."

Their differences barely seemed to ruffle their working relationship or, for that matter, the more personal aspects of the closeness in their day-to-day connection. Eventually, a direct phone line linked their desks.

* * *

"We were both pregnant with ideas," said Whalen.

He was recalling the days when he and Klepak sat around bouncing off each other their late-night and early-morning dreams, sudden inspirations, and far-out ideas. This was particularly true in the earliest years—1984 and 1985.

A Whalen ploy would be, frequently, "I've been thinking about this kind of program," identifying another off-the-wall prospect for housing or street-cleaning or perhaps just another celebration of some kind. Then putting it directly to the money man: "Is that something that we"—meaning, Klepak—"can find money for?" Or, alternatively, "that we could use Community Development money for?"[2]

Klepak would scowl quizzically, proposing in little more than his habitual mumble, "Think about this . . ." and speak some previously unmentionable item of municipal lore.

Strongly interested personally in the seven lively arts, he was likely to offer enthusiastic support for any Whalen project that would advance a song and a dance, a good drama or a startling mural. A not inconsiderable part of the Mayor's sustained record of encouraging cultural events was attributable to the Klepak skill in locating support in the city's treasury or in identifying ready money in private pockets. The result was a reputation earned for the administration of placing unusual emphasis on the arts, of which popular examples were Shakespeare in the Park, the Park Playhouse, and First Night entertainments.

* * *

Klepak was indeed a major player in the Whalen administration. He designed his role and then filled it to overflowing. Neither rules nor customs and expectations had preceded him into his chair in the diminutive hideaway on City Hall's second floor.

After three decades of making things happen in a much larger bureaucracy, he exercised a very large influence on Albany's government. "I basically generated the policy ideas," the Mayor analyzed in retrospect, "but Dan would dig in to make things happen—and not just fiscally.

"I had to be a lot softer than Dan was. I had to expend a lot of energy on damage control—but, believe me, it was worth it."

In a variety of ways, Klepak "made up for his abruptness," Whalen had said, employing a term that has been applied to his own manner on occasion.

"I realize that he damaged some staff relationships—between Vinnie McArdle and me, as one important instance—but his contribution was greater than the negatives," was Whalen's view. In his opinion, Klepak and some of his most vocal detractors "got along very well" in spite of the underlying points of friction.[3]

* * *

Could Dan Klepak's epitaph have been of his own composing?

A highly laudatory editorial, "The hawk who saved Albany," appeared in the *Times Union* a week following his retirement in 1996. Later, he told many friends and former associates that he had written the editorial and successfully submitted it for publication. (When asked to verify this rather outlandish contention, a *Times Union* editor replied: "The *Times Union*'s staff does its own work," with the strong implication that this policy would have applied to the editorial.)

Whoever its author may have been, he credited the budget director with "administrative talent . . . no-nonsense style of management . . . foresight . . . skills and integrity" and having "succeeded brilliantly" in establishing an "astonishing turnaround" that "rescued Albany from certain fiscal disaster."

Some details were supplied by a writer who assuredly could claim intimate and expert knowledge of Albany's fiscal operations. It was Klepak who was able to "stave off insolvency," "insist on competitive bidding and strict internal controls,"[4] "amass a $34 million surplus" and "prudently resist" critics who wanted larger tax cuts. If he had "given in to the critics," Albany would have been in bad shape.

The Mayor's function in all this? Because he "had a keen eye for administrative talent," he had recruited Klepak and then gave him "strong support."

The editorial noted that the budget director had "bruised more than a few egos." Dan Klepak's apparently remained healthy and intact.[5]

NOTES

[1] On state payrolls for 38 years, he had risen from mailroom clerk with Civil Service rank to become a budget examiner, Deputy Commissioner of the State Health Department, Deputy State Comptroller, Administrative Director of the Office of General Services (OGS), and director of two powerful but controversial semi-autonomous agencies, the Office of Education Performance and Review and the Welfare Task Force, before, ending his state career in 1979 as Commissioner of the Office of Drug Abuse Services. Meanwhile, in night classes he had earned a degree in business administration (like Whalen) and a master's in public administration. He nonetheless defined himself as "anti-bureaucrat."

2 When one of the Whalen commissioners wrote to thank the budget director for having made funds available for purchase of some desired equipment, he received this note in reply: "Actually, you should know that the credit goes to the Mayor. I just try to develop funds to help him carry out his policies." It was not a common admission from a man who took pride in his (conferred) status and (derived) power.

3 Whalen's and Klepak's own generally cordial ways were strained in the Mayor's last month (and thereafter). See "When the Party's Over" chapter.

4 Actually, policies to accomplish these two goals had been put in place in the months before Klepak joined the Whalen administration.

5 A year later, the *Times Union* published a rehash as a memorial tribute.

The Placid Hudson

Very few early-morning minutes elapsed between the departure of City Hall's overnight cleaning crews and the moment when William L. Keefe switched on the lights in the Mayor's office. From his arrival, ordinarily no later than 7:30, he was attentively, accommodatingly, and efficiently part of the scene until Erastus Corning or Tom Whalen was ready to call it a day. In style, manner, and even appearance, he was a perfect "Hudson," the Upstairs/Downstairs majordomo for a titled lord.

Bill Keefe, not quite 60 when Corning promoted him from anonymity in an antechamber to become his executive assistant, looked after the interests of his two Mayors for somewhat over 13 years. He was the front-office manager, ushering or intercepting visitors and would-be visitors—recognizing, greeting and, often, chatting up those callers. Recognition, the art of summoning up knowledge of connections, awareness of faces and egos, calling on the memory bank, served him as an extraordinarily useful asset. By earned reputation, he was said to know more Albanians than did either of his Mayors.

Anyone calling on the Mayor had to pass through Bill's scrutiny, and leave it feeling properly welcome and important. For this, he was compensated at well below the minimum-wage scale—about $3.50 an hour for Corning, approximately half as much again for Whalen.

* * *

Corning and Keefe—only about a year apart in age—had been "more than friendly," said Holt-Harris, attributing their extraordinarily close relations, which began rather late in the careers of both, to a "base in good humor." The bond was sealed by the Mayor's recognition of the unique asset he had in Keefe's storehouse of arcane political detail which somehow had eluded his own radar.

Exaggerating a bit, Holt-Harris declared Keefe "knew everybody in the city, the State Legislature, and the administration of whatever governor was on hand." He did repeatedly demonstrate an unexpected talent for cultivating connections with the policy-makers in the Capitol just up the avenue from his window in City Hall. On a birthday, Governor Cuomo called with regards. Here he was several leagues removed from his committeeman's routes in an uptown ward, or from the military/industrial stronghold upriver where he'd had a prior 20-year career pleasing a series of colonels[1] as their knowledgeable Man Friday in civvies. He was ideal for the kind of job that has come to be known as "customer relations."

"Bill knew more people that even Erastus did, and the Mayor regularly asked for his advice," said Holt-Harris, who had a close-up view. "He sought Bill out for his insightful commentaries."

No ordinary chief of staff, Keefe's loyalty to whomever he served magnified his potential value. Psychologically, he was prepared to retire in 1983 (he was 72). Responding to Whalen's question in his earliest days in the Mayor's office: "What should I do first?" his answer was "Replace me!" But, open to persuasion, he and Whalen reached an understanding that he'd stay on for the terms remaining 30 months. The continuity brought by such a Sancho Panza amounted to a plus—Keefe's insights and skills aside—for Whalen when he first faced his multiple windmills.

The continuity was especially valuable, for only Bill Keefe—figuratively—knew the combination to the safe. He was truly "the staff." In those days, and historically, there was no need seen for a big-city style Deputy Mayor with actual authority to carry out administrative responsibilities in the Mayor's name when the elected official was absent or preoccupied. (The office of Deputy Mayor was created in 1995.)

* * *

Keefe, who referred to himself as "the Mayor's top gun," particularly relished two aspects of Whalen's approach to their relationship, even though overall this was somewhat more impersonal than were his relaxed exchanges with Corning. He liked the occasional assignments from Whalen to be out front as the city's official representative. When Jesse Jackson came looking for support in his 1984 presidential effort, Bill introduced him to his audience. Jimmy Carter, he thought after close-up contact, "should have been a preacher." Ed Koch was "a fun guy" (who liked Corning despite the Mayor's strong support for Cuomo, his opponent).

Sometimes Bill lunched with Whalen (never with Corning) and occasionally he went along to official events. Together in the "A" car's back seat, with Dusty Miller discreetly up front, they took advantage of the opportunity to converse with casual informality. This was rewarding recognition for Bill, and he apparently seized the occasion to venture bits of advice to the Mayor, such as one he remembered about decorum when meeting with groups: "Arrive with dignity and self-assurance—but never be pompous, unlike some we know."

"Keep in mind that you are a star," he volunteered at another time. "Keep your head high. And be sure you shake the right hands—it's easy to be blocked in a crowd." The need Keefe perceived for such gratuitous counsel never was clear.

"I like to think we had good relations. I enjoyed every moment. Sometimes we would discuss some ideas, mine as well as his. If I didn't agree with him, I felt free to say so, as I did with Mayor Corning. I was there to help. It was a nice relationship. A lot of fun. Laughs really help."

Of Whalen's mayoralty, he summed up: "He had a good ten years. He accomplished a lot. It's a tough job to hold. A mayor can't run and hide. It's the nature of being a mayor. Tom liked the job—that means a lot. He raised the entire pay scale for city employees—not easy to do." (When Whalen came in, Keefe's salary was $10,400. Before he retired after two years, his pay had gone up by more than 50% to $16,000.)

When the Corning-Whalen term ended at the close of 1985, he left, as amicably agreed originally—but not without a sense of disappointment as he faded from public life. (He then worked for four years for the Democratic State Committee.)

Could Bill Keefe, continuing longer in the Mayor's outer office with Whalen's full confidence, have provided greater help and success in fence-mending, ego-stroking, and bridging the occasional troubled water? His reputation for diplomatic tact mixed with straight talk—to his employer, to the media, and to the Organization—could have been a plus for Whalen, in the opinion of some friends of both.

Would his continuing counsel and his credibility have forestalled some problems marring that new term? At times, following his departure, the public-relations picture hardly could have been more distressing. (Mayor Whalen's own view of the potential advantages suggested here was dim.)

"Whalen did a real good job. Corning would have been pleased," was Bill Keefe's response when pressed for a final estimate.

*　*　*

His glibly sketched picture of the Whalen-Keefe office glossed over the large gully that lay between them—a cleft based not wholly on personality but on beliefs as to a principal duty in their respective roles. As one acute observer graphically expressed their quiet but fundamental differences, "Bill was playing baseball but Tom—with Dan Klepak's loud support—was playing football." Philosophically, in other words, they were not attuned. Their issue: What is a main function of a municipal government?

The Keefe point of view—sourced in his boyhood in

Sheridan Hollow, one of the ravines on the edge of downtown; fostered in the Depression; ratified in WPA-type social solutions; and still thriving in the O'Connell-Corning context—put the onus on government to be steadfast as "the employer of the last resort." This essentially humanitarian approach held out the promise that someone (an Erastus Corning, Leo Quinn, or Bob Bender) would find something (a job requiring little but paying just enough to get through the month) somewhere under the municipal umbrella (Public Works, Parks, maintenance) when emergency disaster or chronic need brought a right-thinking citizen (check the enrollment books) to City Hall or county committee headquarters. If private enterprise had failed or personal qualities were in short supply, the public payroll could be available. Corning himself relished this task and the do-good crown it conferred on him. As a rationale, support of human dignity was often cited as a substantial advantage for the city's role as employer of last resort: Work, not relief; a job, not a handout. More pragmatically, this system inevitably proved out over many years as a political bonus. Job-holders' families could be counted on to turn out as grateful voters.

Keefe was a thoroughly ingrained believer in this O'Connell-Corning philosophy. Whalen was not a believer at all. Keefe had served efficiently as a liaison between Corning and the county committee, first with Donald Lynch, then with Jimmy Ryan, and finally with Bob Bender, and this was a fulfilling portion of his position. He and Corning hewed closely to the unspoken understanding that they would be hiring their own generation, mostly white males with relatively few skills or none but able and willing to take on the demands of a day laborer. And, too, Keefe was willing enough to compile and submit dossiers (often with very personal information) on those seeking jobs or promotions. For each, the significant question ultimately was "Is he on the team?"

Whalen, determined that his administration would not be chained to the old philosophy (and made a victim of its costs), truncated Keefe's position in a most significant way. A major result was a smoldering conflict—a real sore point made more abrasive for Keefe because he correctly recognized Klepak's hand in the mix.

Even without Klepak, Whalen was innately tilted away from the attitude that Keefe represented. His own philosophy was transplanted from the world of business. He would not stand for Corning's low-wage army with their rakes and shovels. He would hire and pay equipment operators, rather than laborers. The rakes would be displaced by leaf-blowers and a vacuum system. The payroll would have fewer job slots—drastically fewer, in this particular category—but the occupants would receive better wages, be relatively well paid in return for a job well done, virtually a professionalized corps. To fill higher-level, decision-making, policy-executing positions, Whalen instinctively considered himself a free agent. Without a by-your-leave, he made his selections and appointments independent of party custom and preference (save for an occasional gesture acknowledging the presumed interest of the county committee in any potential source of patronage). His intuitive choices—sometimes seeming to border on the whimsical—were to be the keystone of his administration, for he felt and displayed confidence in his dispersal of management responsibility while relying on the managers' counsel as well as operating judgment—but regularly letting everyone know where the ultimate authority resided.

Tom Whalen, all business whenever there was work to be done—his own or others—got his way. Big Lincoln Park, for generations the scene of scores of men with rakes and a scattering of other rudimentary hand tools, eventually was staffed with two permanent employees, expanding by another eight or nine in the busy summertime. This tight-ship picture was replicated in department after department. To the observing public, the change testified to responsible management, and thus to lower taxes.

The Whalen strategy reached right to the chairs in his own offices.

The combined chronology of Keefe and the three other

men whom Whalen found sitting in his vestibule approached three full centuries. They were the front line in processing of licenses for the barbers who wanted to give "the usual" legally, for food vendors who aspired to dispense their moussakas on the law's right side, for junk dealers who aspired to ever-higher aspects of their calling, and for a pleasing mishmash of numerous other small tradesmen. The old-timers answered the phone, opened the mail, intercepted walk-ins, heard out their complaints and queries. And they had permitted a few to pass through to beard Erastus Corning himself.

Whalen observed and assessed these activities for four weeks, then persuaded the aldermen to amend the ordinances so that the City Clerk could take over the licensing chores. That accomplished, the receptionists clearly were less necessary in his office. They were promptly dispersed elsewhere, to the City Clerk, to a new information desk in the rotunda—leaving Keefe as the only intermediary between Mayor and Constituent. Correspondingly, the volume of demands on Room 102 dropped dramatically. Requests handled by the veterans in the Mayor's name were redirected. The action was akin to the scrubbing of the grimy walls that Whalen had ordered in the public spaces, and the ripping out of the grubby carpet, but its meaning was deeper. Corning's reputation of extreme availability actually was structured behind a forbidding wall of old male bodies. Whalen abhorred the ambience that all this created, the evidence of payroll-padding, and responded accordingly. Purpose and function, not patronage, were to be the decisive elements. Such efficiency and economy were accomplished at the cost of an underlying friction which inevitably meant that the easy Mayor/Assistant relationship of Corning and Keefe would not come close to realization in Whalen's office.

Bill Keefe revered Corning, extending his loyalty in a very public way. Ten years after Corning's death, the late Mayor was memorialized at a mass, arranged by his old assistant, at St. Mary's Church, a block from City Hall. The timing coincided—presumably by a whim of Keefe's—with Whalen's own last month on the job. The Mayor, whose attendance was both a courtesy and an unofficial obligation, arrived tardily, evoking a comment—a snide one—in the *Times Union*'s report. Whalen left office shortly thereafter, in a somewhat less-than-happy ending to this particular chapter of his mayoralty.

NOTE

[1] Author's note: Keefe had come to the Mayor's office after a career as a civilian employee at the Watervliet Arsenal where he ultimately bcame a public relations man for the commanding officer. I had known and benefited from his expert assistance when I contacted or visited the Arsenal in connection with my duties as a U.S. Representative. Bill, a Democratic committeeman in Albany, couldn't have been more solicitous and helpful to the Republican Congressman.

Doctor, Lawyer, Merchant, Mayor

Mayor Jacob C. Ten Eyck, in the long ago when Albany's Mayors were appointed by Governors, was known as "a man of wealth," presumably implying no need for the bother of a sustained occupation. But the 73 others in the three-century line of succession earned their way—the 30 merchants and traders, the bankers and entrepreneurs, the pharmacist, the grocer, the machinist, the pair of physicians, the trio of brewers, the two publishers, the tobacconist, the accountant—and the 17 lawyers.

If Albany's Mayors have been tireless toilers leading double lives their dual roles were essential. They have responded to the challenging worlds of enterprise and livelihood as well as to their city's summons for temporary duty. Mayoral salaries were notably modest, especially in comparison to the eminently respectable facade that the city's First Citizen might feel called upon to exhibit. In return for quite nominal pay, any obligation that Mayors be full-time executives was waived with the shoulder-shrugging consent of the governed.

Albany's residents expected, too, that these second careers would require their Mayors to absent themselves from official duties as the particular occasion might necessitate. A benign, gentlemanly accommodation was assumed—and this sentiment prevailed all through the years up to the very late twentieth century.[1]

Such was the tradition that Tom Whalen inherited

along with the key to the Mayor's office. Accordingly, he had good reason to feel that these new duties would mesh well with his law partnership. Coming to the mayoralty from his elected position as Common Council president, he hardly could be faulted for assuming he was within his rights in anticipating that he could sustain his family's needs by combining a mayor's duties with a diminished law practice, receiving relatively modest salary from his public office and reduced income from the partnership. But it was destined not to work out so conveniently, and eventually a highly unofficial arbiter—a newspaper's editorial column—clamorously declared that a law practice is irreconcilable with a mayor's responsibilities. Though this extreme position never was directly contested, it did prove decisive in determining Whalen's own choice—even though this was contrary to long-established tradition.

During the first three centuries, the most unusual combining of mayoral responsibilities with another, income-producing occupation occurred in 1881-1883. Mayor Michael Nicholas Nolan, a son of County Carlow who had been a California gold rush prospector before returning to Albany to open a brewery business, was a popular businessman who took office in 1878. He was still Mayor when, in November 1880, he was elected to the United States House of Representatives. Rather than quit City Hall,[2] Mayor Nolan served concurrently in Albany and Washington throughout the Forty-seventh Congress. Holding down a seat in the House obviously demanded his presence away from Albany for extended periods of time . But if a public complaint was heard about his absence, or an outcry about diversion from attention to his duties as Mayor, or outrage about the double-dipping into two public payrolls, research fails to disclose any controversy about Mayor/Congressman Nolan's presumptuous behavior. After all, pretty much the same electorate approved him for both offices. Nolan also continued to operate his brewery throughout his term.

In more recent times—that is, during the three-quarters of a century in which six Democrats have served an unbroken string of 21 terms in office—those Mayors' practical need for outside earned income continued to prevail until unsought circumstances brought about a change at last.

* * *

When the O'Connell and Corning brothers scored their breakthrough to establish Democratic control of the city in 1921, they chose as their candidate for City Hall an unlikely politician, William Stormont Hackett, a 55-year-old Scotsman who—like the O'Connells—had emerged from Albany's South End. It was, however, his business acquaintance with Edwin Corning that won him their favor. In what seemed to surprised observers "a whirlwind campaign," Hackett was elected with a 7,100 majority over the Republican candidate, William Van Rensselaer Erving, (who subsequently became a principal partner in Cooper Erving & Savage, eventually Albany's leading "Democratic firm" of lawyers).

After just two years of schooling at Albany High,[3] Hackett had become a bookkeeper, the traditional Horatio Alger model who would work his way up in a bank and finally be appointed as its president. Hackett, in fact, did just that. He was a bachelor, one who escorted his mother to morning service every Sunday at one of the two Protestant churches where he sang in the choir.

The Mayor's bank was City Savings (through various combinations a forerunner to Home and City Savings Bank of the late 1900s). His presidency there had begun long before his election, and it continued throughout his four years and two months in office. During his career as the bank's head, the imposing structure at 100 State Street was built, incorporating several floors of lawyers' offices above the bank.

Oversight of the mortgages, safe deposits, or builders' loans, and his sober attention to customers' special pleadings continued to require his presence after his election. His daily schedule brought him to 100 State at 9 o'clock sharp, but he arranged to hurry up the hill by 10 o'clock to the new office;

then, it was said, "back to the bank, back to City Hall, and in the meantime all over the city, inspecting everything with his own eyes."

Easily reelected in 1923, he more than doubled his majority, to 15,000. (Mayoral terms were for two years at that time). Overwhelmingly elected again in 1925 for what was to be a four-year term, Mayor Hackett's fate determined otherwise. Barely six weeks after his inaugural for a third term, the Mayor was severely injured while vacationing in Cuba. He died on March 4, 1926; he was 59 years of age, and the solemn bell in City Hall tower tolled 59 times.

One published tribute—"The greatest friend of man the city of Albany ever produced"—suggests that an extraordinary individual occupied City Hall's corner office. Even so, a memorial statement acknowledged that he was "not known to the man in the street and certainly not to the ward workers of his party." And, as noted, he also was capable of carrying on a full-scale and demanding occupation while holding the mayoralty.

So did his successor, a lawyer elected City Treasurer in 1921 and then moved up by Ed O'Connell and Edwin Corning to become president of the Common Council just before Hackett's death. John Boyd Thacher II formed a law partnership at virtually the same time he took office, and this firm— also located at 100 State Street, incidentally—continued throughout his 15 years in office. The importance of his private practice was underscored when he resigned the mayoralty in 1940 to assume another office that was predicated upon a practicing attorney's career. His firm, Thacher, Casey, and Honikel, offered a bulwark at a time when the mayor's job was deemed worth a very small salary.

He was a phenomenal vote-getter, even by the standards set by the Albany Democrats. In his last election as Mayor, he received 61,257 votes, a total greater than Corning ever obtained and, actually, well over twice Corning's vote in his last campaigns (or Whalen's) and four times greater than the votes needed to win the mayoralty in the next century's first election. In 1940, as a candidate for the Children's Court (forerunner of the Family Court) he led the head of the ticket, President Franklin D. Roosevelt, by 9,000 votes in the city.[4]

When he resigned as Mayor, Thacher had held the office for almost 15 years, and was at the peak of his prestige and influence. Throughout those years, he pursued other occupations as well: After graduation in 1906 from Albany Law School, he went into business with his father, a banker and a "car-wheel manufacturer."

* * *

Erastus Corning had just passed 30 when Mayor Thacher resigned. With the regular quadrennial election a year away, Dan O'Connell (brother Ed had died a year earlier) opted to have the office filled temporarily while young Erastus matured a bit more before being put forward in November 1941. Meanwhile, Albany would have the magisterial services in City Hall of Herman F. Hoogkamp, a 52-year-old printer employed by the *Knickerbocker News*, which then was published by the Gannett chain as one of its several upstate dailies. Inasmuch as the "Knick" was an afternoon paper, the mechanical work had to be done early each weekday, and this freed the Mayor to leave the dingy composing room in a rickety firetrap on Beaver Street just off Broadway and make his way up the hill to the relatively palatial quarters he could occupy for the rest of the day. He continued on the Gannett payroll throughout 1941, his mayoral term.

A revealing aspect of the Hoogkamp interlude in the Mayor's office is how he got there. The Common Council (sometimes referred to in those days as "the Common Scoundrels") had a president who was a real estate salesman, Frank Salisbury Harris.[5] By provision of the City Charter, he should have become Mayor when Thacher resigned. Instead, he fled from the responsibility, and in his place Alderman Hoogkamp of the Fifteenth Ward was designated by his mates

as the Council's new president; from that eminence he graduated quickly to status as Albany's seventy-first Mayor.[6]

* * *

Corning, like his predecessors, came to the Mayor's
office already established in another occupation, partnership in
an insurance business. "Albany Associates" became a name to
reckon with for the next half-century. And the name became
synonymous with Erastus Corning's. If his long tenure in public office was remarkable, his proprietorship of a politically
related business throughout that term was equally remarkable
although, in fact, almost totally unremarked.

Estimates, presumably reliable, placed the worth to
Albany Associates of merely the Albany County account at
$1.5 million in premiums in the year just before the Mayor's
death. For such an attractive source of revenue—plus the very
considerable volume of policies bought by businessmen who
thought it advantageous to be favorably known—he obviously had to devote many hours' attention to Albany Associates'
affairs. Corning was known, in fact, to meet with insurance
customers in his City Hall office. The practice was a gross violation of propriety and ethical conduct, but nothing ever was
made of it. Thus encouraged to claim it as something of a *droit
de seigneur,* he continued to write policies and accept premiums
at his official desk to the end of his tenure there. In short,
Erastus Corning's outside professional interests inevitably represented a substantial demand on his available hours in a business day, wherever he chose to work on his private commercial
business. This proposition, however, never became an issue in
his 13 campaigns between 1941 and 1981 (including a primary
and a statewide election). Nor was there discussion about it in
the media.

* * *

This absence of controversy about the private enterprises of Albany's Mayors over many years was, in effect, a land mine ambushing Corning's successor when he took second place on the ticket in 1981. There seemed little reason to expect that complications lay beneath the placid surface.

As president of the Common Council, Whalen had anticipated a degree of public exposure, a modest stipend of some $13,000, a minimum of accountability, and a rather minor investment of attention.

Scarcely five months into that term, however, the unexpected turned quickly into reality: Corning's illness and increasing inaccessibility mandated more duties and responsibility but no real authority. He found far less time for his law practice. None of this had been foreseen, though a thoroughly realistic preview might have suggested it because of Corning's age and ailments.

The problem inevitably hardened in June 1983. As Mayor, he was able to devote substantially less time to the firm's clientele or even to those with whom he had long-standing relationships. This was particularly true of his first several months in the office, when he was regularly carrying home a briefcase full of "must read" papers. He needed to feel confidently informed and on top of the struggling city's problems and issues. If the common folk of Albany happened to "wonder what the king is doing tonight," they would have found him at his desk until the late hours.

Asked by a reporter about implications of his continuance at the law firm, he replied, "We don't do business with the city—we're conscious of that." That is, his partners would decline to represent client interests if these would impinge on matters before a city agency or officer. His comment, however, related to only one aspect of the question of limited attention. Relying in part on precedent and custom, he did not touch on the matter of his availability in a workday or the possible perception of divided interests as well as attention, whether or not such questions were justified.

His decision was pragmatic: In order to hold his elect-

ed position he needed income beyond its salary and so he'd
rely on a logical pre-existing source, while making necessary
adjustments in allocation of hours.

What he failed to anticipate was the prospect that
someone was ready to make a presumption about his suscepti-
bility to corrupting influences—largely because of the mere
fact of his profession. It was a costly oversight.

He continued to meet occasionally with clients at the
law office and, having retained his partnership, he took part in
the firm's management decisions. When the partners agreed in
1986 to merge with a younger firm, Nolan and Heller, which
brought a somewhat different clientele and welcome energy,
Whalen took on the widely coveted prestige of "name partner."
The new firm's letterhead read: "Cooper Erving Savage
Whalen Nolan and Heller." (The first three names did not sig-
nify living individuals, nor had they for many years.)

The steadily enlarging demands of running the city's
business, however, eventually proved the determinant in his
priorities. Without publicly commenting on his changed perspective, he was responding with more and more attention—
and time—to official duties. A sharp contrast is easily notice-
able between his confident tone about balancing two jobs after
his 1985 election, and a 1987 interview in which he considerably distanced himself from the burden of the law office. Then,
after nearly four years in office, Whalen described the status of
his practice.   "Working at this job (the mayoralty) 60 hours a
week—sometimes as much as 70 hours—doesn't leave much
time for many other things, including the practice of law. My
hands-on practice is very limited. I am the executor and
trustee, and hold the power of attorney, for some clients that I
have represented for years, and these instances relate not necessarily so much to legal work as financial . . . making sure
their money is properly invested, making sure I pay their bills,
making sure their needs are taken care of. I do not get into
forming corporations or closing loans, unless it's a very unusual personal case, for someone I may have represented for 20
years, such as the sale of an old friend's home, which has hap-

pened. Then someone else (in the law firm) does the paper-work, and it will take me an hour to go to the closing. I may agree to draft or amend somebody's will if he or she has been a long-time client. I don't get into litigation, or bankruptcy, or corporate work as I did when I was a full-time lawyer, heavily involved in business and commercial law."

Could he find a conflict with his official position? "Absolutely not! I have not used this office to further the gain of the firm. The record will stand up to any kind of inquiry."

Within a year, however, he had withdrawn from the law practice. He resigned from Cooper Erving in the winter of 1988, slightly less than five years after taking office. He was not quite halfway into what turned out to be his total tenure as Mayor. Through experience, he had decided that his two positions—one private, one public—were irreconcilable, not because of conflicting obligations but because of the pressures of available time. He almost certainly was influenced by the steady blast of criticism about his maintaining ties to Cooper Erving which persisted in the *Times Union*'s editorial page.

". . . His ongoing partnership in a busy and popular Albany law firm invites the frequent appearance of a conflict of interest—if not an actual conflict," a 1987 editorial, "Our Busy Mayor," asserted. While extreme, its comments sum up the newspaper's persistent argument against Whalen's professional connection.

"How could it be otherwise?" the editorial asked rhetorically. "A person who acts as both mayor of the city and a member of a law firm, many of whose clients do business with the city, is inviting controversy, not to mention questions of propriety." In so many words, this is a declaration that a lawyer cannot serve as a mayor (anywhere) without inappropriately creating issues of propriety and controversy (and, in a parallel context) of conflicts of interest.

Beyond the essential matter of the issue's questionable pertinence, this editorial's clever selection of language—"busy and popular law firm," "invites the appearance," "if not an actual conflict," "inviting controversy," "questions of propriety"—danced around an actual allegation with intimations and insinuations. The most unsuitable portion lay within the nine words "many of whose clients do business with the city." While lacking a direct accusation, this seemed to slyly imply that clients, lawyers, and Mayor all were selectively corrupt.

Such commentaries created a problem—at least, a mental hazard—which ultimately was solved only by the Mayor's withdrawal from the firm and from the highly restricted practice to which he had retreated

It is impossible to know how his limited practice during 1983-88 might compare with John Boyd Thacher's career as a name-partner in his own firm for more than a dozen years while Mayor. But parallels can be seen as well as distinctions. Each had established an enviable reputation as a lawyer before reaching the Mayor's office because of a predecessor's death. Each had special issues to confront—the Depression's impact, for Thacher; and for Whalen, the city's overdue need for fiscal stringencies and reforms. The size of the city and, in many respects, the demand for services on limited budgets, were roughly comparable for the two administrations. Their available hours for the city's business might be regarded as approximately equal.

On the other hand, Mayor Thacher maintained his practice to the end of his long term, and whether it was restricted as Whalen's cannot be measured. Standards either truly changed during the intervening 40 to 50 years, or some circumstance made it easier for outsiders—projecting a seeming objectivity—to simply impute improper ethical standards and potential opportunity for misconduct.

Albany's neighboring cities can scarcely be seen as offering comparable examples of full-time attention to mayoral duties. It is true, too, that instances abound in which lawyers have served as mayors without questions being raised (George Pataki, a lawyer in a New York City firm, was Peekskill's mayor). Dentists, osteopaths, and professionals in a wide variety of other occupations, have occupied city halls in many cities in New York State and elsewhere. And in countless instances "full-time" mayors, on the other hand, are merely scavengers for whom public office is actually their only career or livelihood.

The issue—if indeed it merits status as such—resolves into a pair of aspects in which opinions can differ but for which there is no genuine rule.

- Does a city (such as Albany) necessarily require the services of a mayor who is devoid of any other occupation or sideline interests? and
- Does association with a law firm while serving as mayor inevitably, and of itself, constitute a conflict of interest to be avoided at the risk of creating a cloud of suspicion involving those familiar standards of the mystery yarn, "motive and opportunity"?

By the 1980s, in any event, Mayor Whalen was repeatedly declared by an editor to be a suspect who should be obligated to hew to a purported standard of ethical conduct which, in fact, has had no place in any canon for either lawyers or municipal officials.

At the time he took office as Mayor, his choices—according to this new standard—would have been to resign promptly from the office or to abruptly quit his law practice.

With the city in crisis, he understandably felt no alternative but to stay and do his best to keep it afloat. On the other hand, at the existing salary for the office, he could not meet his enduring obligations, especially with five children in or ready for college. He made the feasible choice: Stay in office, limit the law practice and its demands (and income), but meanwhile instill some reality in the official salary level. The rack on which the Mayor was editorially pinioned finally took its toll with his retirement from his law firm.

NOTES

¹ An interesting clue is to be found in a 1994 book, *Henry and Clara*, by the novelist and political observer Thomas Mallon (published by Ticknor and Fields) which contains a reference to Albany's Mayor Jared Rathbone (1839-1841). In a factual aside, the book notes that he "was a merchant even when he was Mayor." And that was, after all, the period when another of Albany's Mayors (1834-1837) was the original Erastus Corning, whose prime business interest was building the New York Central.

² Mayor Nolan was in office when the City Hall burned in February 1880, and it was he who ultimately was responsible for retaining the distinguished architect Henry H. Richardson to design a replacement. The new (and present) City Hall was completed in May 1883, as Nolan left office, and precisely a century before the Mayor's office passed from Erastus Corning to Thomas Whalen.

The Forty-seventh Congress did not meet for more than a year following the 1880 election. Its two sessions (December 5, 1881 to August 8, 1882, and December 4, 1882 to March 3, 1883) covered nearly 350 calendar days. It's reasonable to assume that somewhat more than half represented days when the House was actually in session and Congressman Nolan's presence was desired at the Capitol, trumping City Hall's claim on his attentions. He was one of 36 representatives from New York (by far the largest delegation), and the other 37 states filled out the House membership. Mr. Nolan's colleagues included a future President (William McKinley), a future Vice President (Levi P. Morton of New York City), two future iron-fisted Speakers of the House (Thomas B. Reed and Joseph G. Cannon), a former Vice President of the Confederacy (Alexander H. Stephens), and a grandfather of Nelson A. Rockefeller (Nelson W. Aldrich). Another New Yorker, Chester A. Arthur, had assumed the Presidency upon the death of James A. Garfield in September 1881.

Mr. Stephens had written a two-volume history of the Confederacy, a copy of which Daniel P. O'Connell had on hand for possible reference in one of his countless "read-to-me evenings."

3 Hackett, recognizing a need for a bridge between the sixth-grade schooling common to most Albany youngsters and the psychologically remote high school, dedicated much effort to a campaign for a junior high school that would encourage more advanced studies. He succeeded in establishing the large Delaware Avenue structure—now a "middle school"—which was given his name by his successor as Mayor. Hackett himself had experienced the difficult transition from grammar school to high school. But for thousands of others, particularly in the South End and other areas where arriving immigrant families settled, sixth-grade graduation ended their formal education, even well into the twentieth century. Daniel O'Connell's abbreviated schooling is a prime example of the shortcoming in Albany's system which prevailed before Hackett's enterprise.

4 He served one term, then sought election to the State Supreme Court in 1946, but that was not a good year for Democrats in New York and he was defeated by a sitting judge, Isadore Bookstein, in the seven-county judicial district. He died in 1956 at age 74.

5 For 17 months late in World War II, when Erastus Corning was in the Army, Mr. Harris, an Episcopalian bachelor who was 75 years of age when he entered the office, served as acting Mayor. What he had avoided in 1941 fell to his lot eventually.

6 At the time, he was designated the sixty-eighth Mayor of Albany, but 50 years later a previous miscount was discovered, and everyone moved ahead three places.

Memories of Finn
by Thomas M. Whalen, III

Finn was a favorite of the City Hall staff—Jo-Ann Trim, Thelma Dooley, and Pat Storm. They would vie to see at which desk Finn would choose to curl up.

But mostly it was Finn as "Deputy Mayor," greeting all callers, young and old, whether official, foreign visitors, or outsized local politicians.

My best memories in City Hall are of Finn-the-Conciliator, who would quickly defuse a confrontational meeting just by walking into the room. At times, people would arrive in the Mayor's office, usually a group of four or so, disturbed by something the City had done which was adverse to their interests or, just as importantly, upset that the City had failed to act in accordance with their wishes. The leader of the group, escorting the others into the office, would see Finn coming in the door from the left. Finn, cool as in "Finn McCool," would walk slowly, head down, and tail swishing right to left. Invariably, they would meet near the sofa, where the leader would say something like "Good fellow," then sit down to pet Finn. And then we'd start our conversation—by talking about animals. The atmosphere was completely altered from one of confrontation to one of conciliation.

It may be only my imagination but I even remember Finn once leading the group out of the office after he had accomplished his mission!

Gone with the Whirlwind

Symbolic of the municipal housecleaning's momentum as it gathered throughout 1983—and as an apparent heritage of the Whalen whirlwind—the Common Council's final session expunged a variety of ordinances that once had seemed significant but had been outpaced by 20th century life. Many would be precisely a century old by 1984, so their removal seemed particularly timely. They dealt with such concerns as "horse-drawn vehicles"; sleighbells, sleds, snowballs, and sliding; ice delivery; loose cobblestones; ballplaying and the "game of skinny"; and circumstances appropriate for removal of hats. More soberly, the regulations for burying contagious-disease victims were now determined to have outlived their purpose.

Other moss-covered laws were relics of issues from early in the century: The "hitching of animals to trees"; fastening of horses to porches; junk dealers' citizenship and licensing (a hint here of ethnic discrimination?); use of bicycle lights;and concerns about streetcars' operators and their passengers. And echoing "The Music Man" with his warning about "Trouble in River City," Albany once had been regulating the hours and days when pool might be played—and even mandated a required number of windows in pool halls.

Breakthrough on Broadway!

"You may be indecisive in personal matters but
you know where you're going career-wise.
Expect a very productive day."
 —Astrologer's horoscope reading for
 Peter D. Kiernan on January 17, 1984.

The morning paper's big news that wintry Tuesday
detailed a 10% jump in the state's $35.4 billion budget pro-
posed by Governor Cuomo. Readers who reached the editorial page were confronted by an elaborate Hy Rosen cartoon featuring a blowzy blond matron exclaiming "The days of wine
and roses are back—right, Mario baby!" A partying Governor
was on hand, brandishing a Champagne bottle labeled "Ronnie
Reagan Recovery." (See accompanying article, "An Artful
Storyteller.")

The page also included a brief letter signed by Albany's
Mayor explaining why two parking spaces had been newly
reserved for the press on Hawk Street, a long block from City
Hall but nevertheless considered more convenient for
reporters' use.

In the news pages, subscribers could read of County
Executive Coyne's scheduling of a hearing on two more plans
for a "civic center" in suburban Colonie that would cost only
$11 million.

And they might also find a report quoting a particularly disappointing message just received by Mayor Whalen.

Within days of taking office seven months earlier, he

had acted promptly on an inspiration to turn away from the various schemes floated and promoted in the previous dozen years for salvaging the abandoned and derelict Union Station, long a hub of northeast rail traffic. The varied range of these had included a shopping center, a visitors' information center, a convention hall. Some had linked it with dreams of an adjacent office tower or hotel.

Instead, he envisioned the possibilities that the depot's fortress-like construction might offer for heavy-duty electronic equipment of the computer age. He carried the idea to a friend, Patrick Brady, the area's man-in-charge for IBM, and Brady started his suggestion up the corporate chain of command.

The corporate response during the Mayor's months-long courtship indicated that IBM was very favorably inclined to come to closure on Whalen's proposal that the old depot be converted into a data processing center. IBM had sunk $100,000 in a feasibility study. As recently as Christmas Eve, the prospects were being cheerily talked up, with the corporation stating that it would be investing $10 million in the conversion if agreement could be reached on a purchase price from the State.

Unfortunately, one fragment of corporate lore that ultimately spelled the idea's doom was known only at the topmost echelon.

It involved a member of the IBM board of directors, William W. Scranton, the former Republican governor of Pennsylvania. In his hometown—where else but Scranton?—a railroad depot also sat abandoned and deteriorating. Governor Scranton likewise had a bright idea: Induce IBM—where his suggestions were sure to receive a very respectful hearing—to convert the abandoned station in Scranton (where five rail lines converged) to some use that IBM's thinkers would come up with. But try as they might, the corporation's own idea-men couldn't find a way to justify the investment there.

And by the time the proposal on Albany's Union

Station reached IBM's top-drawer executives, someone recalled the Scranton precedent: If IBM couldn't accommodate a wishful proposal from a member of its own board of directors, then certainly Albany's rail station was destined to be turned down. Soon after the New Year's holidays, the word was started back down the ladder. Tom Whalen's desk was its final stop.

A call from Brady told Whalen that the affair was over: "We concluded that, in the long run," explained a so-sorry letter he read to his friend the Mayor just before public announcement of the change of heart, "Union Station does not represent a viable alternative for our unique business needs. It is no longer a consideration."

The rejection was a bitter blow to Whalen, who had just cheerfully celebrated his fiftieth birthday, optimistically looking forward. *Spurned again!* as a *Times Union* editorial observed. Now, more than seven months into his term, he had lost out in attaining what he hoped could be one big break generating confidence in downtown Albany's commercial future. During the frustrating spring while he was a Mayor-in-waiting, he had gone on record as calling Union Station the missing link in that future. Once he gained the office of authority, he'd placed a tall stack of chips on the square marked "Big Blue."

* * *

The old building had been in a long downward spiral since 1968, when rail service ceased in Albany in favor of a dumpy little station-stop across the river. The elements, vandals, and scavengers had all but completed the Albany depot's destruction while, as Thomas Finnegan expressed it,[1] the city looked on, chagrined but helpless.

A "Union Station advisory group," whose members included Whalen, was designated by Governor Hugh Carey in the late 1970s to consider a number of development possibilities. One of these, put forward by Whalen, proposed a tourist and information center serving all of upstate New York and focusing primarily on economic development. Altogether, at least 10 best-laid schemes had, in effect, "gang agley," including an aquarium, various kinds of museums, a theater, even a heliport.

Lew Swyer had joked privately that the structure should be made into an "instant ruin," much like the Acropolis, its roof gone, the columns standing free. But in 1981 he came forward with a plan for a $50 million office-retail development, in which the state would become a major tenant. The prospects were regarded as promising, and one of Erastus Corning's last acts before his final hospitalization in late spring 1982 was a flying visit to Washington in support of a $7 million federal grant. Soon after that, Governor Carey's office shot down the whole concept. The projected cost to the state for leasing space in such a structure was finally deemed excessive. Accordingly, any plausibility for its public financing disappeared.

With Corning removed from the picture, efforts for the station's revival necessarily were on hold until a new Mayor became empowered, on his own authority, to offer a credible answer. And for more than seven months, IBM held that Mayor's hopeful solution.

* * *

If the Mayor, that morning, consulted his own horoscope, he would have found it affirmed his gloomy outlook that a January drizzle was damping down:

"*Difficult to concentrate on work. Guard against escapism.*" But one final bit of advice: "*Enjoy the company of friends.*"

Several miles distant, catching the 6 o'clock TV news in an English Tudor dwelling out in suburban country-club territory, one of Whalen's friends, Peter D. Kiernan, an aggressive insurance executive turned banking entrepreneur, listened thoughtfully as he learned of IBM's pullout. He pondered whether the news should represent an opportunity for his gung-ho enterprises, which were heavily engaged in data pro-

cessing. What would be the benefits to Norstar, the new identity he'd given to the bank enterprises he headed? What might
the cost be? What hurdles and obstacles?

That evening, the next early morning, and throughout
the day, he turned the questions over and over in his mind.
Then, impulsively, he reached a decision as to a first step. At
the close of the business day, he headed for City Hall and
pulled into an empty parking spot.

The Mayor's outer office was quiet when he looked in
on Whalen, preoccupied behind his desk. The formalities were
brief. In his buoyant enthusiasm, the visitor couldn't wait to
take off his greatcoat, but dropped to the edge of a couch
between the front windows which disclosed the gloom of the
wintry nightfall.[2] He perched there, hat actually in hand, as he
started to outline his adventurous thoughts.

As so many others had been, he was struck by the
romance in Union Station's possibilities. Not by the particular
site, not the location as such, though these were significant factors—but by the colossal 85-year-old building itself, to be
reconstructed, modernized, perfected just as he would like it to
be and, incidentally, to house Norstar's intricate and swelling
innards. If, that is, engineering and architectural delvings
found the derelict susceptible of salvage.

And, he added deferentially, "if it would be all right
with you"—in other words, if the desperate City of Albany
would have no objection! He acknowledged that his dream
was less grand than some of the projects previously contemplated and promoted—and discarded.

The Mayor of Albany smiled at the polite tentativeness
in the words protective of the audacity in the best workable
idea to hit his city in many years. But he swallowed the glee
behind the smile.

"I'm sure there will be no objection, Peter," he reassured
the man who—he suddenly felt confident—was the doer who
really would make it happen.

Now Whalen's smile was three feet deep. Aloud, he
involuntarily exclaimed—in words recapturing sentiment

recalled from some of the happiest days of his life—"Merry Christmas, Tommy!"

* * *

Fortunately, Kiernan had a long and cordial acquaintance with Whalen, and had approvingly watched him perform in his earliest days as the Mayor. In 1983, he'd been recruited, along with Eli Werlin and Dick Lindstrom, to advise Whalen on identifying and recruiting a Budget Director. Soon after, he shared in the successful effort to return competitive rowing to Albany which Whalen made a project of the city. Accordingly, he felt comfortable dropping in on him—two vigorous athletes envisioning the payoff on a far-out brainstorm.

Thereby, the whole turn of events which capitalized so broadly on the old depot's potential, owed its creative spark and its irresistible momentum to the trusting alliance between two forceful individuals.

In retrospect, Whalen assessed Peter's view of him as a younger brother whom he was interested in finding ways to help. But what if Peter Kiernan had lacked positive vibes and a confident expectation that a kindred soul would give him a receptive ear? What if—when he happened to hear the TV news report—Erastus Corning had still occupied the Mayor's office . . . Erastus 2nd, a joke in Albany's business community for his habit of calmly hearing a visitor's "good idea" but then doing absolutely nothing? The Mayor of whom it could be safely said in the media that "Things for which Corning lacked enthusiasm had a way of staying undone" and "a sheaf of proposals, commissioned at taxpayer expense, gathers dust at City Hall"? Then would direct-action Kiernan have bothered? Would Union Station have been saved, lacking a lucky string of coincidences? As Paul Newman has summed up:

> *"Luck plays a big part in everything—right place, right time, left turn rather than right turn, avoidance of illness, the right genes—all luck!"*

Was it only Kiernan's estimate of Whalen's do-it attitude that made the fortunate difference?

* * *

Whalen's excitement, as accurately explained by Tom Finnegan in *Saving Union Station*, "must be viewed in the context of Albany's ongoing struggle to overcome a despairing downtown situation." Norstar's general counsel and corporate officer Harry P. Meislahn is quoted there, as well: "The city's eagerness to promote the project," he said, should be seen "in perspective of the winter of 1983-1984 (when) there was *nothing* going on."

Finnegan cites the renovation's benefits to Albany, whether the city is considered as a pulsing community, a governmental unit, or a commercial entity. "The catalytic effect of this major downtown rehabilitation was valuable beyond dollar calculation, but there were immediate and tangible benefits, too, such as the return of the property to the city's limited tax rolls. It was sure to induce more response from the business community than would yet another government-facility adaptation of an existing building. Here, at long last, the city had a reliable private developer with an attractive plan for public-private collaboration and a viable financing arrangement."

Small wonder, then, at Whalen's quick assurance, on the spot, to the Aladdin who had appeared, unbidden, in his office doorway: *No, the city government would not stand in his way!*

* * *

If Peter Kiernan, a man of his word, could thread his way through the thicket of obstacles—those fiscal, physical, and legal—he was certain to encounter, then the Union Station incubus was off a Mayor's back. The offer was like a dream come true, except that it was so far out its precise likeness had hardly been dreamt. (In fact, of course, Norstar and its successor made extensive use of the structural assets for electronic equipment akin to what IBM would have installed.) Restored, the station could be expected to spark renewal in other areas of the desolate downtown landscape. Hope for fulfillment of Whalen's semi-formed scheme for Albany's future had arrived with Peter Kiernan and his vision.

On the wings of that vision, 1984 was off to a flying start for Albany. It would be a good year, a watershed year for Tom Whalen's administration. Numerous other rewarding events—largely unsuspected in days occupied with plotting, devising, fretting—would reveal themselves later—along with occasional frustrated outcries from the unconverted.

And, simultaneous with the positive and promising news, an ominously discordant threat loomed. Just as Whalen was rejoicing that the savior had been found for downtown's prospects, the first stores at Crossgates, a new super mall, began to open—outside the city limits—and pull more and more shoppers from within the city. This disheartening development hardly was unexpected, of course, for work on the mall had begun in the summer of 1983 within days of Whalen's assertively going on record intending to restore downtown's vitality. Crossgates cut directly across the grain of his declared design for rebuilding the once-thriving mecca represented not so long ago by such bedrock names as Keeler's, Whitney's, Myers', Van Heusen Charles, the Ten Eyck, Farnham's, Cottrell and Leonard, even the Elks clubrooms and the Waldorf cafeteria.

Excitedly, the Mayor summoned talented and incisive John Egan, New York's Commissioner of General Services who held the building's fate within his control. The call anticipated a critical session with Kiernan at 8:15 the next morning, a rapid response in keeping with the promise which the moment held.

The excitement was contagious. Under Pieter Schuyler's monitoring gaze, the atmosphere rivalled, say, an ecstatic moment in a California barn after Seabiscuit had sired another colt.

Within minutes, the deal was struck; Kiernan never even removed his coat or took a seat as he bargained the asking price down to $450,000, a 10% reduction though it also was 50% more than he'd hoped to pay for the treasure.

* * *

After those gleeful mid-January handshakes in the Mayor's office, discreet silence prevailed for more than two months while endless innovations were explored (and often discarded), numerous ramifications were weighed, and ideas were assembled and problems deconstructed like so many Tinker Toys. But architects (the Einhorn Yaffee Prescott partnership of Albany) were enlisted to find answers on how to double the square footage while maintaining the exterior's integrity, plus reconstructing the interior's shambles. And, perhaps most sensitively of all, multiple fiscal concerns were rolled out of computers for analysis on table after executive table to determine the best routes for financing what was then being called an $8 million project.

Kiernan was ready in two months—on March 21—to take his dream formally to Norstar's board for approval. A few days later, the *Times Union* had learned enough of the proposal's essentials to publish them a full fortnight before the planned official disclosure. The fragility of the daring enterprise was pointed up by a comment from the Governor's office suggesting that the plan "could fall into place—or fall apart soon."

Kiernan's and Whalen's secret was finally confirmed on April 11 at a ceremonial news conference on Broadway in front of the depot—where Tom had swung aboard the Empire State Limited for Grand Central Terminal en route to Manhattan College, and like Peter, had later jauntily embarked for an Army training camp.

The Governor himself came with a message emphasizing the big picture of renewal broader even than rescuing of an architectural treasure or the improvement of a downtown business area. John Egan, recognized as the indefatigable doer who had been instrumental in pushing the right switches to transfer the property smoothly from the state to the bankers, was less conspicuous but nevertheless a key man to be thanked and thanked. Aggie Kiernan joined hands with her husband on his great day, and the speaker's platform was jammed with officialdom eager to be seen as spear-carriers in this bit of history-in-the-making. Peter Kiernan had brought a great lift for Albany that early April day,[3] and all the 200 merrymakers were endlessly happy to play their walk-on roles in the drama. Sentimental history received its due, briefly, when Mayor Whalen burst out with a sudden exclamation: "Erastus, we did it!" while lauding the Norstar decision as representative of old and new blending to strengthen the future of Albany.

* * *

Eleven days after that formal public announcement, Norstar paid the agreed-upon $450,000 to the Urban Development Corporation, which had just acquired it from General Services (an arrangement concocted by Egan, who repeatedly helped sustain the deal's momentum). The roundabout transfer made it possible for the State to avoid an otherwise obligatory auction for the depot's sale.

Within a month, a Norstar plane carried Whalen and Kiernan to Washington in successful pursuit of an Urban Development Action (UDAG) grant, calling into action an influential ally, Senator Alfonse D'Amato, who, as a member of the Senate's Banking Committee, effectively put them in touch with the head of the UDAG program at the Reagan Administration's Department of Housing and Urban Development. The grant yielded $2.8 million toward Norstar's rehab costs. It was made to the city, which then loaned the funds to the bank corporation. Together with $7.2 million obtained through Industrial Revenue bonds issued by the Albany Industrial Development Agency, it made feasible the ultimate realization of Norstar Plaza. The city reached a negotiated arrangement with Norstar for a "Pilot" (payment in lieu of taxes) which almost, but not quite, equated to what a fair assessment would have produced in property taxes. Additionally, by scrupulously qualifying for federal tax credits granted for hewing to the exacting historic preservation requirements, Norstar was able to deduct 25% of its total renovation costs. To qualify, as Kiernan later related, Norstar had to withstand the demanding scrutiny of 42 regulatory agencies. These requirements included meeting various standards for sufficient hiring of ethnic minorities by all the contractors. Norstar surpassed the state's demands on these numbers, and approached the city's expectations—which are even higher; the Whalen administration had established a formula related to each minority's actual percentage of the city's total population as found in the national census.

A key portion of Whalen's role in encouraging the entire enterprise was his eager readiness to provide the garage needed for Norstar's staff as well as for improving the public's access to off-street parking. The solution offered 800 spaces on two levels directly east of the building itself, edging the superhighway (U.S. 787) that had destroyed the rail station's viability. Norstar built the garage for $4.6 million and sold it to the city's Parking Authority which became its manager. Bulldozers were on the site within six months, long before work could begin on the depot's reconstruction.

* * *

Whalen led the cheering section when Norstar announced its goal of beginning to occupy its spectacularly renovated headquarters by the spring of 1986, barely a year after work crews were on the job. But change-orders originating in expanded ideas for making the interior ever more splendid, as well as unwelcome surprises such as a new roof, created delay upon delay—and sent the total cost soaring. The original estimate of $8 million shot through that roof and reached $18.5 million worth of grants, loans, and Norstar's cash investment.

Kiernan's January dream became certified reality in a joyously gaudy ceremony 32 months after the naked concept began to take shape. And it did occur within the Tricentennial year, as both Whalen and Kiernan ardently hoped.

The September dedication was a celebration indeed: Bands, choral dramatics, light displays, speeches, flags, fireworks, crowds. A "time capsule" was buried, to be opened a century hence. Simultaneously, Albany's newest park (for which Whalen gladly had allocated $378,000) gained official status—aptly named to memorialize the Tricentennial. Fronting the Norstar building, it featured a six-foot, three-dimensional representation of the city seal. Commissioned by Norstar, it was sculpted by Hy Rosen.[4]

Whalen hailed Norstar Plaza as "the jewel in Albany's renaissance." He refrained from claiming or assigning credit for the city's revival but voices offstage served effectively to link the occasion in a quite glorious perspective: Lew Swyer, who had entertained more than a few ideas for the Union Station's renewal, praised Norstar's successful effort as a notable part of Albany's reach for greatness—"Each day brings us closer to becoming a modern-day Camelot!" It seemed a fitting hyperbole from a man who himself had been figuratively cast as a Merlin, the enigmatic enchanter, for Albany.

His estimate was topped only by Bill Kennedy's. "A city on the rise in every way you can imagine," was his compliment to his hometown, formerly best known for its "Gut" of speakeasies and whorehouses and for the synergy of political machinations that abetted them. In contrast, "You have to outdo yourself with superlatives when you talk about Albany these days."

"I don't know of any better place to live," declared the author whose successes and acclaim had already carried him to virtually every port in the great world except Stockholm.

Tom Whalen had what might be called an official last word:

"As the inspiration for what has come to pass in downtown Albany," he said a few years later, surveying his changed city, "Peter Kiernan's Norstar Plaza is unparalleled."[5]

In its significance to Whalen himself, it likewise can be seen as unparalleled, for its emergence—from inspiration to completion—was indeed a breakthrough, a very visible and tangible beacon of hope.

* * *

Wistfully hopeful expectations had for years reassured Albany that "*If only Union Station* had" . . . a savior, an angel, it could turn overnight from decaying pumpkin to royal coach, the entire downtown landscape would be restructured, modernized, beautified—and the city's business climate would magically revive.

The most important early impact of Norstar Plaza, however, was just around the corner—45 seconds from Broadway, as a songwriter might describe it. At two office buildings on lower State Street extensive adaptations were carried out for Keycorp, Norstar's rival, by a developer from New York City, Richard Zipes, who owned more property in downtown Albany than anyone else.

But Victor Riley's ambitious response to Peter Kiernan's coup was even more impressive a couple of blocks away on South Pearl Street. Having suffered tongue-in-cheek teasing by Albany's Mayor for allowing the competition to seize such a visible advantage in local prestige, the Keycorp boss contracted with Zipes to build not one but two major office towers which were leased to the bank. As had been the case in the Whalen administration's collaboration with Norstar, construction of a large parking garage was an integral part of the encouragement that Keycorp logically requested and received. It added places for 600 cars off the streets where, not long before, Albany's well-known phenomenon of endless double-parking had seemed to be the only solution.

NOTES

[1] An excellent review of the Union Station project is to be found in a book sponsored by Norstar, *Saving Union Station*, by Mr. Finnegan. The book was published by Washington Park Press, Ltd. Copyright 1988 by Thomas Finnegan.

[2] Thomas Finnegan places the timing of this encounter quite differently: in the morning of January 17. But the Mayor's recollection of the hour and the circumstances of his meeting with Kiernan is firm.

[3] In the *Times Union*, though, the next morning's front-page play of the big story had to take second place to seemingly more significant news: raises given to seven senior members of Comptroller Ned Regan's staff.

[4] Later, a bust of Peter Kiernan was executed by Mr. Rosen for the interior great hall of what had been renamed "Kiernan Plaza" to honor the enterprising financier. Mayor Whalen, with the Common Council's assent, named an adjoining street "Kiernan Way" during a memorial ceremony in 1989.

[5] The success story of Union Station's transformation dwindled to a sadly anti-climactic denouement. Almost precisely two years after Peter Kiernan's celebration opening his Norstar Plaza, he died of a stroke at the age of 65.

Earlier that year, 1988, he had merged Norstar with the larger, more complex, and more aggressive Fleet banking enterprise that had hungrily pushed out of Rhode Island. Before long Norstar was becoming less and less visible. Norstar Plaza became Kiernan Plaza one year after its founder's death. A justified tribute, but it also effectively removed the old identity. Ten years later, three dozen Fleet retail locations dotted the area plus an active beehive of other customer services. Norstar had vanished.

An Artful Storyteller

During the Whalen years in City Hall, Hy Rosen, the *Times Union*'s poet of the drawing board for four decades, depicted the Mayor in more than 30 different guises.

Some offered several variations on a series of themes, such as snow removal, the Mayor's ties to his law firm, and the fate of Erastus Corning's official papers. But for the most part, the broad range of ideas—from Millet's "The Gleaners" to an FTD delivery of a bouquet—was little short of inspired.

Only two characterizations even came close to duplicating one another. They were separated by six years. Each showed Whalen as Superman, once boasting a $10 million surplus in the city's treasury, and later bringing home the All-America City designation.

Three times, the Mayor was shown in royal raiment, though the detail was quite different in each. But at other times, he was a woodcutter, a park-bench occupant eating a sandwich, and a barfly asking the piano player (the Democratic county chairman) to "Play it again."

From time to time over the years—once every three to four months on average—Albany's Mayor became another person: a mother reading fairy tales to the press, a steamroller operator, Dorothy in Oz-land, a dancer bursting out of a Tricentennial cake, a kibitzer around a computer, and, during Corning's illness, a tight-rope walker.

Once he was shown riding on a big snail (the city's public works commissioner). He was also a clergyman remonstrating with a parishioner (the County Executive) whose hand was in the sales tax collection plate; a magician; a drum major leading the band for a parade of community events; a gunman holding off the police (who were negotiating for a contract), and then an angel after a contract was signed. He appeared as both a baby and as a little boy with Santa Claus; a prince and a king; and as George Washington in a rowboat—as well as a tree stump with roots 300 years deep.

A Rosen cartoon published October, 1991, in the *Times Union* noted the awarding of the All-America City distinction to Albany in recognition of the Whalen administration's achievements in an anti-drug abuse program, affordable housing, and cultural initiatives.

The extremely recognizable likenesses and creative depictions which were a Hy Rosen specialty endured popularity as a *Times Union* feature several times a week from the late 1940s until his retirement as an editorial artist in 1989. His skillful execution of detail based in incisively pointed ideas and commentary was additionally memorable because of the contrast with the *Knickerbocker News* cartoonist of past years, Jerry Costello, and particularly with the slapdash style of the *Times Union*'s cartoonists who followed Rosen on the editorial pages.

"This Is the Enemy"

Five-hundred angry words published at the top of the *Times Union*'s editorial column on Friday, October 12, 1984, marked the end of whatever romance had existed between the newspaper and the Whalen administration. It was titled "The Corning Tradition," but it was concerned with very current events.

In the very highest tradition of editorial writers, "The Corning Tradition" mingled sarcasm, irony, hyperbole, sly denunciation, disappointment, righteous indignation, and implication of serious wrongdoing. In style, it mocked Claude Rains's immortal "Casablanca" line, "I am shocked! Shocked!"

"Whalen has chosen," the editorialist wrote, "to continue the tried and true practice of government secrecy and closed-door decision-making."

In lieu of an appeal or effort to find a compromise solution which might save face all around, the editorial launched what became essentially an era of hard feelings. The occasion was Whalen's attempt to recoup from a false step onto a rotting stair tread. He had opened up for inspection the countless boxes of papers that had amassed during Erastus Corning's 13,000 work days in City Hall. The first folders proved to contain a few minor embarrassments for some scenery-designers in Governor Mario Cuomo's school of dramatic arts—and also touched on certain topics peculiarly sensitive for the zealous keepers of the Corning tradition's flame. Rather than open himself to their attack as willfully conspiring to subvert that tradition, Whalen reversed himself—"awkwardly slammed the file drawer shut," the editorial said—and withdrew access to what the writer termed "the so-called Corning papers," as if their actual existence was uncertain.[1]

"The *Times Union* was among those who thought Mr. Whalen was about to introduce Albany to open government," the writer mourned. "It appears we were wrong." Whalen's stumble had dropped him into an ambush.

The editorial's bitter language, a calculated response to the Mayor's move, was teamed with a Hy Rosen cartoon depicting a padlocked filing cabinet and, beside it, a reporter on the lap of a bonneted, befrilled Mayor who was reading from a "Sanitized Version of the Corning Papers."

The whole effect of that editorial page seemed to denounce Whalen rather than to gain access to the Corning papers. As a tactic, it hardened the lines of burgeoning controversy, which then entered month after month of court-tested argumentation.

Nearly three years later, the ultimate judicial ruling favored the newspaper. And then, not a bang but a whimper. Very little of the files' actual contents ever was reported and published. The matter was quickly dropped, with an absolute minimum of embarrassments revealed. The net outcome was of a squabble created and prolonged as an annoying point of vulnerability for Whalen. Whether or not this was the true motivation, the molehill effect seemed evident indeed.

* * *

October 12, 1984, was a date worthy of marking in Albany's political almanac, for it was the day the newspapers really turned on Tom Whalen, 16 months—501 daily issues—into his administration. From his vantage point, the timing was especially unfortunate, for it came just as his political enemies were trying to rally strength enough to take him on in the next year's election calendar. Though as a declaration of war it related only to a single difference of opinion, the tone of comment—and coverage—in the *Times Union* (and, at the time, its then-sister paper) had changed forever.[2]

The Mayor composed a letter objecting that the editorial "seriously misinterprets my position and the city's policy on the issue of open government." He argued that "the editorial creates a wrong impression on how the executive files are being physically handled," and explained that "the files are being reviewed and parallel files are being set up to store documents whose confidentiality is protected by the Freedom of Information law. . . . Both sets of files will be maintained under strict security in the City's archives."

After stating that "All aspects of life require a certain amount of privacy and government is no different," the Mayor went on to contend that: "Elected officials and government employees must be free to exchange information, ideas, and criticism without the fear that their every word will be subject to public scrutiny and, very often, ridicule. . . . If we open all of the doors and windows of government to public view we will stifle the creative, and we will silence the outspoken."[3] When the letter was published nine days later, his 588 words were answered by an explosion on the same page. In 650 words, a new editorial sharply rejected his explanation and argument. And on that same day a *Times Union* column on the same page called Whalen a "gruff Irishman" with "shortcomings as a political personality" and a "blunt and temperamental side" (while conceding the likelihood of his reelection a year later).

Whalen was in the process of learning the old adage—as Hendrick Hertzberg quotes it—"about the unwisdom of picking fights with people who buy ink by the barrel." (On the Corning Papers alone, six editorials critical of him were published in the final weeks of 1984.) He'd already made a mistake by letting it become apparent that second-guessing nettled him. Like toughs bullying the teacher's pet at recess, reporters now seemed to look for new ways to get under his skin. "I dug my heels in after a couple of bad articles," Whalen recalls. "My instinctive attitude was, 'This is the enemy.'" (Remember that he maintained that he didn't have enemies—but perhaps this applied only to opponents among the politicians.)

In the preceding 16 months of the Whalen term in office, the newspapers' reception of the new Mayor had been generally upbeat and supportive. Two instances of quick-draw harsh criticism, however, had already occurred within less than three months of his taking office.

In his administration's first few days, he was confronted by an editorial rebuke for not being prepared to peremptorily change Albany's protection for workers' compensation coverage to a self-insuring arrangement. Weeks later, he was severely chastised for having privately worked out an arrangement with a personal friend, Walter Otto, an automobile dealer, who executed a lease to provide a new Oldsmobile sedan for the Mayor's use, with Whalen and the city sharing costs. (His company did no business with the City of Albany.) Apart from the long-standing friendship, Mr. Otto undoubtedly was aware of the value of an Olds bearing the mayoral "A" license plate visible around Albany.[4] To editorial writers, this seemed less than a good idea, a point they drove home repeatedly. (The issue appeared to be more a simple case of heckling than was true in their later denunciation of Whalen's presumed motives in the Corning Papers episode.) "Chill settling over City Hall?" a headline asked soon after. The text below amplified the intimation with a sentence that "some quarters" (namely, the reporters) considered his irritation "just one symptom of a creeping case of thin skin which"—in a prime example of self-fulfilling prophecy—"could cause him problems in the future." In other words, those same reportorial "quarters" were promising to rub it in whenever their scrutiny found a sore spot. (They made good on the promise.)

The same article contrasted what the writer saw as an instance of Whalen temperament with a positive description of his earlier disposition: affable, approachable, accessible, candid, willing to be quoted on controversial issues instead of ducking (as the working press considered it now often found his inclination). To the extent that he strayed from that open stance, he unquestionably was victimizing himself.

It was after October 1984 that editorial treatment—and, more importantly, attention in the news columns—adopted a tone that Whalen saw as generally ranging from skeptical to unfriendly. A more revealing indication of the newspapers' attitude soon began to appear. Like picking at a scab, criticisms of Whalen's law firm partnership while he held office as Mayor[5] dotted their pages. It resembled guerrilla warfare, with ink for ammunition.

Much of the coverage and commentary eventually seemed to reveal a hostility to him personally. Not atypical was a 1989 editorial bearing the caustic headline, "The Mayor's Raw Nerves." It was based on a sarcastic remark made by McArdle, the Corporation Counsel, whose "distemper" was termed "typical of city figures who are growing more irritable." The Mayor thereupon was said to have become "also testy," the only reference even barely supportive of the headline's denigration. "One of the joys of being Mayor," Whalen observed to his staff, "is getting blamed for what someone else says."

* * *

Year after year, an essentially negative tone could be perceived, ranging from the trivial (how the Mayor parted his hair) to sustained rigor. An even slightly less personal approach to Mayor Whalen over the years almost certainly would have produced a healthier climate for the reforms and governmental effectiveness that his programs sought. The Mayor felt that through the attitude (made evident in their published words) of a small number of reporters and some members of the editorial staff, the newspaper gave aid and comfort needlessly to opponents of his policies and detractors of his principles and motivation. It was the printed record that gave birth to his own "This is the enemy" outlook.

Just before he left office, Whalen sent a handwritten letter to the newspaper's publisher, saying in part that "I will always be saddened by the fact that our local newspaper could not get itself to 'build community' when there were ideal projects for it to refer to." In response, the publisher, Timothy O. White, wrote: "Your comments are helpful. As I continue to make changes at the *Times Union*, we will seek to provide a more balanced view, recognizing the good while we continue to ferret out the bad."[6]

NOTES

[1] A column "On Language" by William Safire stated that "In American English, 'so-called' is falling into disuse; it has the flavor of usage by speakers whose English is a second language." (New York *Times Magazine*, 2001).

[2] There were, indeed, islands of favorable comment subsequently, including an editorial endorsement for Whalen's reelection in 1985. For a variety of factors, the chemistry between the Mayor and reporters rarely was a healthy one, and their stories very often reflected this.

[3] The sensitivity of his problem in seeking to avoid distressing the Corning family or irritating ardent adherents of the Corning reputation, is suggested by the way the Mayor made certain that Elizabeth Corning, the late Mayor's wife, received a copy of the letter. "I think it gives an indication of the dilemma that I face," he told Holt-Harris who was to make the special delivery. "He's in a Catch-22 situation," was the messenger's view.

[4] The unique "A" license had decorated and identified Albany Mayors' autos for many years, a low-budget courtesy created in the distant past by Motor Vehicles commissioners from their exceedingly limited supply of single-letter plates. (A comparable compliment is the "H" license which was given to Patrick Cardinal Hayes in the 1920s and which still is assigned to the Archbishop of New York.) Mayor Whalen accepted his "A" happily as one of the untaxable perks of his office. After he left office, the "A" was retired without explanation.

[5] See chapter "Doctor, Lawyer, Merchant, Mayor."

⁶ Change began at a high level within the next few months. Nevertheless, in the newspaper's attitude toward Whalen, little modification ever became evident, a mindset blatantly obvious in the repeated speculative and callous reporting on circumstances of the accident that caused his death in March 2002.

Plotting Priorities and Perspective

His administration had been barely old enough to sustain life when Whalen—summoning impulses nourished at Manhattan, the Law School, his commercial law practice, and even his military career—boldly ventured the first steps toward long-range goals still distant from the daily grind of bids and bonds, cash and trash, Old Guard and new revenue. Who might identify the hour when the word "planning" merged in his head with the concept of strategies, horizons of oncoming responsibility which would be his, and his abiding confidence in the potential for unleashed good-citizenship?

As such elements began to coalesce, a call went out in early 1984 to that eminently available solid citizen, advisor, man of distinction—who but Jack Holt-Harris?—bidding him to take on one more chore: lending his authority and his capacity to another extended assignment. He was destined to chair a huge committee—eventually its members numbered more than 40—that would labor and bring forth a "strategic planning report." The shade of Daniel P. O'Connell and that of Erastus Corning 2nd—they who always knew best for Albany—were convulsed.

What dream prompted Whalen to move toward making an actuality of an easily postponable goal? He stood squarely at a stage where the hourly demands were daunting enough and even his short-term hold on his office was subject to doubt. Worry enough, without peering ahead to the long term which might never come. "He wanted people to recognize what was being done, and to be moved—inspired—by the changes and achievements," as Holt-Harris interpreted a portion of the Mayor's motivation.

Certainly, his schooling provided the foundation for this inspiration (which turned out to be timely indeed, and wise). From years of problem-solving—analysis plus action—he was capable of envisioning forward thinking—"strategic planning"—or, in his own words, "a conscious effort to rise above mundane concerns."

By gaining a perspective on prospective developments, the Mayor could make use of it in setting goals for his administration, establishing priorities, plotting strategies. With a plan on the table—even a flexible one—he and his people presumably could adapt more readily to take advantage of changing circumstances, initiating action if opportunity opened. But if trends appeared portentous, the administration could "reverse, block, or at least soften the impact," he suggested.

Even though most of the committee's recommendations were useful, even valuable, on a practical level, additional worth evolved simply in how citizens' ideas were plumbed, wholly new for Albany. The group effort was symbolic, Whalen pointed out, over and over, "because for decades the Democratic Organization had aggressively discouraged citizen participation in decision-making and policy formation.

"But Albany people now had a forum in which to express their ideas. They could be confident that they would be listened to. When we followed through, the citizens themselves owned a sense of accomplishment."

The fact of the process itself, the Mayor's willingness to delegate a wide-ranging responsibility instead of assigning it to city employees, dovetailed with the clearly serious and diligent efforts that occupied those who served, the candid language occasionally employed in the resulting documentation. All these elements, and others, were at least equally important to Albany as were the recommendations and eventual evaluation.

Up to an early point, the committee and its prospective

product were Whalen's own. He not only had instigated the means of acquiring a plan but selected the people who would do the work. It was both representative and also considerably reflective of the range of his own experience. Within limits, the nature of the representation offers interesting and perhaps significant light on Whalen's view of Albany at that point. For starters, at least four of those he selected were among his own closest advisors, and several others were good friends.

Government was disproportionately represented with a half-dozen elected officials and four appointive officeholders, one of whom was Dan Klepak, the only City Hall employee. Somewhat more appropriately numerous were professional administrators, including three college presidents among a total of five campus delegates. Organized labor had three representatives, starring Harold Joyce. Practicing lawyers, including Holt-Harris, also numbered three, as did the members from the banking profession. Two downtown merchants were outnumbered by five local-area representatives of businesses with national scope.[1] The Jewish Federation had a seat in the committee, and so did the two bishops of area dioceses. The Right Reverend David S. Ball, newly elected as bishop of the Episcopal Church, was selected—as he subsequently was again and again by the Mayor. The Most Reverend Howard J. Hubbard of the Roman Catholic Diocese of Albany accepted this membership but never again served the Whalen administration in a similar office.

Just five of the 42 were female. And minorities also were noticeably underrepresented, barely there at all when compared to their numerical standing in the population. (This belatedly resulted in an exhortation by the reconstituted committee in its follow-up evaluation three years later.)

The 42nd member, selected after an indignant protest over lack of representation of the city's neighborhoods, arrived just in time for the first meeting. He was Peter Rumora, of the Council of Albany Neighborhood Associations. The omission was an anomaly, for Whalen had from the outset worked closely and cordially with the association and its member-groups, even at the cost of further alienating the Organization's most vocal Tories.

Organized into four "task forces" (Business Opportunities and Employment, Downtown Albany, Government Finance and Services, Housing and Community Development), the members worked away at their assigned tasks most of 1984 and into the election year of 1985.[2]

Their published report presented 32 recommendations in reasonably general terms, without specific means for attaining them. The range, obviously, was broad—from planning, zoning, and parking for example, to Albany's port, student housing, and opportunities for women and minorities. Receiving first and most dynamic attention was the concept of public-private partnerships "to address the major problems and opportunities in the years ahead."

Simultaneously, an "implementation schedule" for moving ahead with the proposals was prepared and published, based on advice sought from Holt-Harris and his "task force" leaders, and then supplemented by ideas and opinions garnered in public hearings.

A second extensive document, this one from the reconstituted committee—Holt-Harris still commanding—assayed the administration's liveliness in following up on the initial recommendations, and found the record quite satisfactory, although not without sufficient room for some mild chiding. Within this area, the most vexing point cited for urgently needed improvement was—again—adequate representation of minorities' and women's issues.

However, "The creation of the Strategic Planning Committee is indicative of the openness with which the city approaches its relationship with the community," the 1989 review remarked. . . . "In fact, this review is being conducted at the request of the Mayor—a departure from the days when the city's business was considered 'private.' Historically, Albany has not been a city that invited participation in decision-making from outside city government."

In sum, the Strategic Plan's initiative, involvement, and

ideation constituted a major positive focus of the Whalen years.

* * *

Without acknowledging that their final words closely paralleled the Mayor's own roseate contentions, the committee closed the initial report on an upbeat note:

"There is a new spirit of confidence in Albany. Albanians are beginning to realize that they have something special. . . . Everywhere there is a sense that Albany is moving ahead."

NOTES

[1] One of these, John J. Grace, managing partner of Coopers & Lybrand, the accounting firm, had just cast a vote of confidence in Albany's future by taking on the annual audit of the city government for a five-year charge of $147,500, a minimal figure compared with the $375,000 the service could have cost if the previous year's unbid charge were extended, or the $282,000 bid that same firm—a Corning favorite—entered for the five-year period. Five firms had responded to the unprecedented bid request (not required by law). Grace said his firm's low bid was a "civic responsibility" prompted by the Whalen government's "honest attempt to clean things up."

[2] Perhaps by coincidence, the committee's follow-up evaluation of progress in implementing the 1985 document also was reported early in the year of a municipal election.

Humor on Wry, Hold the Mayo(r)

Did an actual "Corning in Exile" conspiratorial cell during the Whalen years, as widely supposed, seek restoration of the pseudo-Stuarts and perhaps the accession of Bonnie Prince Jack? The term appears to imply as much.

Though his name is indelibly included in mention of an early anti-Whalen grouping, Albany's tenacious Assemblyman, John J. McEneny, smilingly decries any idea that "CGE" (for "Corning Government in Exile") ever existed.

"The term was a joke—probably the best one I ever was associated with," is his disclaimer. "'Corning in Exile' had only humor value. The few of us"—he mentions Jane McNally and Pat Devane—"tried to make sure someone in City Hall could overhear our remarks about 'CGE' as we called it and our elaborate references to 'dues notices' and 'a larger hall' for our meetings. But there were no meetings and no such organization. We hoped for a laughable over-reaction to our joke, and we got it. We used to drive one of Whalen's people crazy." His reference apparently was to Parks Commissioner Dick Barrett, who was inclined to regard all of politics very seriously.

Humor aside, however, the jokesters and many others were indeed afflicted by the drastic change from Corning's comfortable governing style to an abrupt Whalen style and personality. Their humor was wry, understandably so. Needing new employment, they tended to find shelter in the rival government of Albany County under its executive, James J. Coyne, who had his own agenda amid the uncertainties that followed Corning's departure. Coyne and Whalen were maintaining official relationships that were mutually civil but chilly.

Corning as benevolent employer, Corning as a role model of a smooth operator and successful politician, Corning as caring friend or father figure, Corning as wise mentor and patron, the cool civic hero whose legend easily painted over reality, Corning who seemingly went on forever and reassuringly always came out on top—the ache of his absence from all these roles was as hurtful as an amputee's virtual limb.

Plainspoken Tom Whalen offered them little in the way of solace or substitute for the qualities they missed. His clock and calendar provided neither time nor patience when he perceived someone's failure to produce as expected. Nor was he interested in holding hands or giving a hug when a toe was stubbed, much less a kiss to make it well. Had he possessed those capabilities, he could have saved himself a certain amount of grief.

Whalen viewed the dissidents as Old Guard Loyalists who "looked for opportunities to take potshots" at him and his programs. He considered that they had "disconnected" themselves from his administration. Regardless of respective attitudes and motivations, the ongoing clamor was a distraction from pursuit of the city's business and inescapably a negative for the new Mayor. Unintentionally, the dissenters surely made a point.

The Lord Mayor's Show

Whalen's ambitions and goals for Albany were as spectacularly discernible as a Roman candle in a backyard fireworks display. They would flare in bright, glaring bursts for all of the Whalen Decade. These bursts, reflecting quantities of his quick enthusiasms, expanded as his confident mastery of the city's business became notably firmer. He exemplified a description once conferred on another mayor: "A cheerleader who perfected the rhetoric of optimism and boosterism as he articulated the good news about the city."

"The New Albany—Fun City—With Somethin' Cookin' All the Time!" was Hy Rosen's caption for his editorial cartoon that celebrated one in the annual "Cityski" series. Each winter, a 550-foot run was created down State Street's formidable slope, beginning at a 20-foot-high ramp at the Eagle Street crossing. Requiring 700 tons of man-made snow, a base of at least two feet was provided for skiers of all descriptions—including the Mayor.

Cityski had received Whalen's enthusiastic endorsement. He saw it as one more occasion to enliven Albany's self-image. But, he reasoned, if he was to be a sponsor of some outrageous fun on his city's main street, he'd better be prepared to join in. Before the first of the Cityski winters he planned ahead by showing up at an early morning hour like the little pig outwitting the wolf. Predictably, no one was on hand to watch him cautiously hone his downhill skills. Reassured by the results in his practice session, he boldly and gleefully showed them off later in the day for the curious but receptive spectators.

Cityski's offbeat, upbeat excitement seemed to redeem all the skeptics' sneers and all the problems visited on downtown, including traffic rerouting (to say nothing of eventually carting off all that somewhat-used snow). To draw upon a line from the old song, "The King's Horses," it was successfully putting "a little pep into the Lord Mayor's show."

Skiing was the focus of another winter competition, this one in Washington Park, where it was carried on for several years—the "Beat the Mayor" 5-kilometer race. In cross-country gear, Whalen set the pace, daring all comers to beat his recorded time. (His best was 17 minutes, 28 seconds.) Several competitors did improve on his time each year and everyone who entered won a certificate. This event had a specific purpose along with the fun, for the modest entrance fees were contributed to the Association for Retarded Children.

* * *

Typical of his zestful readiness to participate in his city's doings, the Mayor with three companions (Denie, and Dick and Lee Lindstrom) ended up across the Hudson one summer's night in a Rensselaer County apple tree.

During the Tricentennial's many celebrations, Dick Lindstrom, as head of First American Bank's branch at State and Broadway (where it figures in more than one incident to be found in these accounts), had arranged for his fellow bankers (Clark Clifford et al.) in Washington's First American headquarters to dispatch its distinctive red, white, and blue hot-air balloon to Albany.

Early in the evening of what developed into perfect starlit night, the two couples and their pilot lifted off and floated away from its Albany mooring. As dark fell, after well over an hour's jaunt, they were able to discern nothing in the near distance except forest. Following a unanimous vote for discretion, the decision to descend was prompt. In short order, they found themselves in a leafy nest, at risk of being tipped to the sacred soil of East Greenbush. The owner of the soil and the tree wasn't really amused as they cautiously clambered down. But Albany's Mayor had notched one more exploit to his record of "being there."

Crossing the Delaware

Bill Keefe called Whalen's 1985 campaign the most boring he'd ever experienced in his 40 years inside Albany's politicking. On the heels of the clamor and glamour of Reagan's stunning reelection, Whalen's wish for a four-year term of his own was, on the face of it, modest. But the "boring" aspect had other roots.

The prolonged process of eventually ratifying his administration's record on November 5 was indeed a tedious, predictable exercise—and it was drawn out over 10 months.

Its really significant segment began—and effectively ended—in January. The outcome, however, could have been drastically different.

The 1984 presidential referendum had buttressed the Mayor's beleaguered stature as a genuine Democrat by providing campaigning appearances with the top of the ticket— Walter Mondale and Geraldine Ferraro as well as Joan Mondale and Ms. Ferraro's daughter Donna. Previously he'd never taken an active interest in a national campaign, much less worked for one. It was a rare opportunity for him to demonstrate lively concerns for his party's outcome in the big picture. The public exposure and the excitement primed him for the all-out effort that he must mount in the year ahead. He was now psychologically ready for action.

Having said publicly that although only 10% of his time was required by political matters, he realized that politics nonetheless seemed high among the most stressful and compelling of all his concerns.

Newspapers' specialists in coverage of politics are fond of writing that one candidate or another is "fighting for his political life." Whalen, basically a non-politician who'd ventured into a political morass, could discern the dangers that might afflict his career in government service. And thereupon he turned temporarily into a political strategist—and, for this make-or-break occasion—a superb one.

Even earlier, he had reached a decision to demonstrate that he could play the game hard. He arrived at this judgment together with his advisors (principally Jim Drislane, Alan Iselin, Rube Gersowitz, and Steve Fischer). He'd stage a series of one-on-one sessions with the 15 uncertain ward leaders, telling each that, committed to be a candidate in 1985, he was seeking their support and their public approval of his policies. It was definitely a nod in the direction of Judge Bergan with his insistence on a show of power.

The First Ward's Bob Bender was a particularly sensitive button to push, so he was scheduled for the first interview in the Mayor's office. Not only was he surprisingly friendly in spite of the plaintive cries from many of the Regulars, but Bender—an O'Connell favorite—had broad influential discretion in leading the troops as the day-to-day operative for the party at 75 State Street headquarters. His formidable clout there was now especially timely because the well-intentioned new chairman, Leo O'Brien, was no O'Connell or Corning.

"Take on (Harry) Linindoll and (John) Martin pretty much last because they are upset," Ray Kinley advised, contemplating the potential for explosion when Whalen asked for help from the men who'd suffered most from his policies. Linindoll, previously the city's exterminator, and Martin, the displaced plumber, had been receiving an average of about $400,000 a year between them through the largesse of no-bid contracts extending over many years. Each was a powerful ward leader potentially critical to Whalen's survival.

Ultimately, the outcome of the wooing was inconclusive. Months later, an unofficial rollcall of the wards turned up more than half (including Bender) who were unready to endorse their party's Mayor. In the 1985 election count it was difficult to track any enthusiastic effort by the Organization's troops who would have been following their leaders' vigorous prodding—or lack of it.

By Thanksgiving week, hard upon the Mondale disaster, Whalen was busily planning an aggressive declaration of his goal and drafting the vigorous steps to achieve it. But contrary to every expectation of normal political jousting, he was not preparing to take on an opponent from a rival party. His strategy would be directed against fellow Democrats. For many months, he had understood the true nature of his not-so-loyal opposition.

Whalen's own judgment—confirmed in agreement from his trusted counselors—had warned him to open the election year on a strong note. He would do this by firing an unmistakably offensive salvo proclaiming his intention to defend his turf—a critical decision. But it was just one-half of the strategy he mapped with a small handful of co-conspirators at his downtown law office during five queasy weeks in November and December. Abetted by news reporting that fostered skepticism, doubters seemed to be sprouting within the party. Committeemen were listening to the malcontents whose private interests were being damaged by Whalen's policies. Discouraging indications could be heard emerging from clubs and bars throughout the last half of that year.

The accomplishments of his barely 18 months as Mayor obviously were to be written off by the Old Guard as insignificant. As his administration headed toward the close of a fiscal year with a $10 million surplus and a budget in full balance submitted for the oncoming year, other triumphant achievement such as Norstar/Union Station would be repudiated, the spirit of the recent Kennedy celebratory weekend ignored; the party came first. Accordingly, it was on his record of saving the city—placing it above the party—that he would have to build a campaign. But in this night of long knives he would need weaponry surpassing laudable intent and good deeds. The chosen riposte to fierce antagonism would comprise two elements for which the Loyalists never would be ready: The strategy of surprise and the tactic of early, all-out aggression. For a charger intent on tackling the Organization, it was again 1966 (when a surprise attack on it had notably succeeded). Or, for that matter, 1066. Standpattism again could lose!

In late-evening sessions, Whalen's conspirators knit together a skein of moves designed to ensure his success in holding City Hall. As they quickly determined, he would first seize the advantage by an unexpected offensive—figuratively crossing the Delaware as the enemy slept. In real-world terms, he would shut down opposition before it could take effective form. In a sense the campaign dated from 1983, for soon after taking office he had decided with single-minded determination that he wanted the vindication—and opportunity—a full term would mean. And now the satisfactions to be realized in outsmarting the Old Guard became a trophy virtually as rewarding as ultimate victory itself.

The strategy selected was worthy of the most brutally efficient machine: a smart, decisive response to a potentially dangerous vulnerability. Published reports alleged that he was still "considered by some as Acting Mayor." In that light, he was very susceptible to challenge.

"The opposition of some old-line Democrats," as a *Times Union* analytical article referred to a Democratic faction, had a virulent rationale. Promptly after taking office, Whalen recognized that his biggest hurdle was destined to be found in his own party's leaders, too many of whom were assuring themselves and their followers that as Mayor he was not to be taken seriously.

(A 1997 editorial in the *New York Times* perceptively observed, "Sometimes a politician's achievements are best defined by the enemies he makes in his own camp.")

The opposition was soon enough dismayed by the implacable man they had badly underestimated. The Mayor's problem centered on his alienation of those hard-liners because of a major alteration in policy and process. A second-generation Loyalist in one of the city's prominent political families complained in indiscreet—though private—anger that "He's beginning to really hurt us now!" An interpretive article stated that Whalen had, "in many ways, gutted a long-standing patronage system of little jobs and big contracts. . . ."

Such a comment, picked up from the sour gossip of the Old Guard, was inaccurate as to destruction of the patronage system, for jobs (though not so numerous, for other policy purposes) continued to be cleared through party headquarters to verify Democrats' credentials. Whalen himself was quoted as affirming that "The patronage system is a very integral part of the political process, and as long as you have qualified people it's the American way." To this frank though unduly effusive endorsement, he added that the system would endure in Albany because it was an effective way to dispense jobs to loyal Democrats. Boss O'Connell hardly could have put it more directly, but Whalen also gave himself important wriggle room: "When we're not able to find qualified people, we have gone outside the patronage system—and that's with the knowledge and full consent of the (county committee) chairman."

Credentials, both professional and implicitly political, consistently were underscored in this touchy relationship. When he wrote to O'Brien announcing a staff vacancy, he included not only a job description for an "important" administrative position but also the requirements (a degree and "two or three years' experience on a professional level") for a $23,000 salary. "I would appreciate your recommendations," he told the chairman, specifying that he needed "qualified" candidates, with the "recommendations" clearly subject to his own approval. It was hardly the spoils system in action, but Whalen had gone out of his way to honor the party's interests and the chairman's ancient prerogatives of involvement—however much watered down—in placing loyal and deserving (qualified, degree-holding) Democrats. It all did rather resemble "the American way."

* * *

Contracts were indeed another matter, for as purchases of goods and services were put out to bid in keeping with state law, many vendors and the party's treasury paid a heavy penalty.

"Sweeping changes from the way Corning did business" were mentioned in another article which cited Whalen's having "alienated many old-line Democrats with reforms that deprive several political insiders of profitable contracts with the city." And, he had "made enemies in City Hall by bringing in a hard-nosed budget director to streamline operations and slash spending." This truth can hardly be overstated. Furthermore, it was said, Whalen "lacks Corning's aristocratic charm." Yes indeed, Erastus had seemed (as the *Times Union*'s farewell editorial put it) "a classy ambassador"—but for a crumbling principality. Charm had become a quite expendable quality.

All this coincided with the *Times Union*'s blistering critique of Whalen's reconsidering his initial policy of providing access for the press to the mountain of paperwork left behind when Corning departed. Repeatedly throughout the fall, sarcastic commentaries had kept alive this adventure, rehashing the purported transgression.

Whalen could do little to satisfy those who wanted charm—aristocratic or otherwise—but he could add to the frustration of alienated old-timers and City Hall laggards by his end-runs around them. By "promptly solidifying his base," he had "created his own political organization," in the view of an outsider who happened to be well educated in comparative status—the Republican county chairman. He considered that the Democratic County Committee had acquired a partner, an (actually non-existent) Albany city organization within the party.

"Whalen owns that organization," declared the Republican, George Scaringe. "He can do what he wants." From the mouse's hole, the cat looms very large. The chairman's exaggeration is understandable. An echo from Dan O'Connell's overstuffed parlor, voiced by Whalen's old friend

Charlie Ryan, alleged that he "could get away with murder" as he abused the entire committee concept by enlisting volunteers to staff some municipal enterprises. "That's no way to run an Organization!"

Discontent truly was fed from within City Hall where some underlings were chronically outraged because of new expectations that they would actually perform full-time duties well.

Whalen Opponents Likely, a *Times Union* page-one story was headlined, forecasting a development that never came off despite the assurance given to reporters' ready ears by individuals described as "insiders." Dorothea "Polly" Noonan confirmed to a reporter that "Several have been mentioned as interesting possibilities." She was alluding to Democrats who would take on Whalen in a primary. In speaking out, she took on the hoary old stepmother's role for the "Corning in Exile" contingent in this drama. She now had an ally in John Clyne, a vocal Whalen detractor. He was represented as believing that the Mayor was "selling out" the Organization. As close as anyone to the O'Connell mold, he was not at all in favor of Whalen's democratic ways, and he mirrored Polly's dislike of him. The stern former County Judge, previously a very influential and effective operative as County Attorney for O'Connell and Corning, had left the court, presumably to fight O'Brien's leadership of the county committee as too modernly flexible.[1] Polly's hopeful semi-prediction of active opposition to Whalen was given some life by Jack McEneny, the first Corning commissioner to leave the Whalen administration. He reported having discussed a challenge to Whalen. "There seems to be a considerable amount of interest in the subject— and I never refuse to talk to anyone who has approached me," he reported. "No one has been advising me not to run, and an awful lot of people have expressed interest and support." Exhibiting the energetic optimism that continued to characterize his career, McEneny predicted that a Whalen opponent was likely.

A shadowy favorite among many Regulars was jocular

Tom Keegan. An ambitious lawyer, Keegan—always seen by many in the party as a natural rival for Whalen, though he was several years younger—was the focus of a great deal of wishful speculation. His admirers were intent on suiting him up as the "real Democrat who could replace Whalen and bring back the good old days." Having followed the well-blazed trail through the Christian Brothers' military school (CBA), Manhattan College, and Albany Law, he then distinguished his career from Whalen's and numerous other sobersided lawyers by his breezy hail-fellow demeanor that colored even his loose manner on the Police Court bench where his patron—none other than Dan O'Connell—had placed him. His crushing loss as the O'Connell choice to run for District Attorney more than a dozen years earlier was now excused as only an impersonal happenstance in the transient aberrations of Republican virility, 1966-1974. A substantial bloc among Albany's police union became prime Keegan supporters, sharply divorcing themselves from their civilian chief, the Mayor, whom they picketed openly and harassed covertly. Keegan's classmate, Doug Rutnik, in spite of possibly having been the original Whalen booster three years earlier, talked about him as a suitable 1985 candidate. In the Tom-Tom competition, Whalen was to pay the price for dereliction of duty to the party.

The newspaper's survey of ward leaders 12 months before the election found no more than one-third of them ready to give unqualified endorsements of Whalen. An equal number simply answered that they would support the election of whatever candidate the county committee might select in May. One limited his response to offering the opinion that the Mayor was "doing a very good job" (though he really was active in stubborn opposition). Another declared only that he would await Whalen's actual declaration of candidacy before disclosing his intentions. Of the two leaders who had personally and directly been most damaged by Whalen and his policies, one refused to give any answer and the other hedged. And these were the very men who, following a tradition of more than 60 years, were expected to deliver the votes for him in ample quantity. The *Times Union* published a rhetorical question put by an anonymous "high-ranking Democrat": "Are the rank-and-file willing to go out and work for him?" And County Chairman O'Brien uttered an uncharacteristic public gripe, suggesting that Whalen was naïve to announce a committee of volunteers: "The only thing I can think of is that his campaign chairman doesn't understand politics. Maybe he doesn't realize it's the committeemen who will get out the vote on election day."

When the newspaper covered the Mayor's strong announcement of candidacy as the year began, its reportage focused almost equally on future opponents, as the editors deemed them to be. Once more the names of Jack McEneny and Tom Keegan were listed, along with an unidentifiable thin-air "candidate sponsored by the city's black community." In what properly was, journalistically speaking, Tom Whalen's story, more than a dozen paragraphs reiterated the prediction that one of these Democrats would force him into a primary. Repeated frequently enough, such a possibility came to appear to many Albanians as prophetic.

"Obviously," the Mayor observed when asked for his thoughts on all the negative chatter, "there are people out there who are unhappy." Subsequently, he considered much of the talk about an opponent to have been "generated by the *Times Union.*"

* * *

Whalen's need to squelch the gossip—and any threat—mandated an early rebuttal. He could almost taste the essentials of the need. But before the mechanics must come the suitable mechanic: A sage counselor but one with lively contacts and an uncluttered imagination—someone free of complicating dues payable to the Organization, discreet, with quiet "people skills" and flexibility of imagination, potentially attuned to the commitment he required—and loyal. Capable of exercising loyalty, to him personally and to his administration's goals and record, without conflicting obligations elsewhere. A key man somewhat like himself, who could further fracture the mold that Albany still expected in its political activists and leadership.

Fanning through his mental Rolodex of bank corporations' friendly and influential directorates, business executives, community do-gooders, and clients of the law practice, he put in a call to one of the latter, a man who already was a campaign counselor and whose advice had been accessible and useful intermittently ever since Corning's illness began. Within 48 hours he and his guest sat in the dining room at the Tom Sawyer[2] Motor Inn on the western fringe of the city.

Before their lunch had ended, he had signed up as his chief fundraiser and campaign chairman, Alan Iselin, an investor and investment counselor. If the decision was unexpected, the result was prompt. The campaign's nucleus left town for a working session 30 miles northward, at the Gideon Putnam in Saratoga Springs. Whalen introduced Iselin, saying "he represents the business segment of the city." It was immediately evident that he already was taking a prominent role.

"All of a sudden, there was Alan Iselin. We weren't prepared for the way he came in and took over," Holt-Harris recalled years later, still showing a degree of not entirely pleased astonishment at Whalen's choice of his chairman. He had deliberately turned far away from the Organization.

* * *

Among other principal plotters were Ruben Gersowitz (from among the very few Old Guard who ever signed on for the campaign); Jim Drislane (entitled to a campaign ribbon for his key role in the 1969 engagement); and Steve Fischer of Urbach Kahn & Werlin, who had found real commitment as he watched the administration's business-oriented progress. And inevitably on hand then and for those late-night sessions, was the Robespierre of City Hall, Daniel Klepak. Though never overtly a partisan politician during his long career in bureaucracy, Klepak was so steeped in behind-the-scenes plotting and scheming—plus a canniness in the intricacies of finding money to make things happen—that he was a natural in designing ways to frustrate the politicians whom he despised.

By default, among these *capitans*, the Mayor stood forward as the *generalissimo*, listening, learning, accepting, rejecting, deciding, and commanding the *"Charge!"* His stature and posture were that of the chief whose "Aye" constituted a majority even after all advisers voted "Nay," as a Lincoln legend has it.

* * *

In the very first days of the election year he declared himself a candidate for a full term in office. He made certain the official announcement would be a major display of biceps. Instead of standing on City Hall steps to announce as Corning invariably had done, he hired a ballroom at a downtown hotel and attracted at least 250 faithful to come in from the cold for morning coffee and pastry. The timing was months earlier than Corning's various candidacies were revealed.

Among the party's power structure who showed up there were the county chairman, Leo O'Brien, the County Executive, Jim Coyne, the county's State Senator, Howard Nolan, the party's local Assemblymen, Dick Conners and Mike McNulty, the District Attorney, Sol Greenberg, and an array of elder statesmen including Judge Bergan, Holt-Harris, Kinley, and Lew Swyer. Altogether, it was an impressive turnout bringing together a broad spectrum of politics and personality. The Noonan faction blackballed the event. Two Common Council members were not invited: Nancy Burton's stubborn independence on basic items such as the budgets proved to rule out this semblance of amicable collegiality, and Gerald Jennings had failed to respond to an inquiry about support for the 1985 ticket.

To his own management of the city's affairs, Whalen credited having—within barely a year and a half—brought

sound fiscal policies, revitalized its downtown area, rehabilitated much of its housing, and "developed an administration
genuinely responsive to the needs of our citizens."

He described his capacity to move Albany forward in
terms of "leadership, creativity, dedication and drive" that
would "guide the community . . . to the highest level of physical, spiritual, and cultural aspects for the quality of life." This
insistence on the unreachable star as a luminous goal would
eventually become his administration's most distinguishing
characteristic, just as his "efforts to turn around the city's
finances" in the first years had been described as its hallmark
in those difficult days.

"Even more than the development of a caring government," he told his audience, "I am confident you share my
vision of a new spirit which is alive in Albany." His emphasis
on "spirit" was the earliest note of a trumpeting summons to
Albanians to be aware of the pride evoked by the era of change
he had fostered. "These are exciting times in the City of
Albany. You can almost feel the electricity and momentum."
The spirit, he contended, "permeates not only city officials but
also leaders of the private sector and the public generally."

With Denie and all five children on hand to hear, the
Mayor intimated that his family would agree that he found "little time for anything" other than his job. "She (Denie) is still
supportive," he said, "because she shares my dream that
Albany will yet become the greatest city in the Northeast in
which to live, work, and enjoy the highest quality of life."

"The growing pride and revitalization of the city"
would, he predicted, "reach its height in the tricentennial year."
In this, he was peering far ahead, for even the first huzzahs of
that celebration were still a year distant. His forecast, however, proved to be gratifyingly accurate.

His job was far from an easy one, the Mayor conceded.
But, he told his listeners, he did find it challenging and—that
other overworked expression—"exciting." So, he added, he
would like to keep this line of work for some time yet.

The first move following this sturdy declaration of candidacy took shape in announcements of a Whalen fund-raising party—more than 4,000 invitations, or about one for every 10 enrolled Democrats in the city. To the incredulous old-line Democrats, this seemed a brazen act, for ironclad tradition decreed that only the county committee, rather than individual candidates, could collect campaign money and spend it. This declared policy survived from the earliest days of the O'Connells and the Cornings, enforced over the decades by the Quinns and Lynches and Ryans at party headquarters, and now upheld by latter-day Regulars, prominent among them being Raymond Joyce's younger brother Harold, distinguished for his hat trick of holding three powerful positions simultaneously. With energetic ambition but with a deceptively tortoise-like pace, he was effectively carrying forward the uncompromising Democratic ethos of his father, a senior Ray, who had been one of Dan O'Connell's buddies and the Twelfth Ward's leader for many years.

Schooled in the catechism of "Jobs-Jobs-Jobs" as the party's *raison d'etre*, Harold had succeeded his father at the top of the committee within the ward, then had climbed through the majority's ranks in the County Legislature on his way to becoming its chairman. And for always fighting the good union fight, Albany's electricians had rewarded him with the job of managing their business affairs.

For the blue-collar base remaining in the party, Harold Joyce was the man to see, the man to watch. On Whalen— product of the same party but of a very different ward, the same church but another parish, much the same national heritage but with differing qualities that took them in distinctly separate livelihoods and expectations, the same playing fields but idiosyncratic forms of scrappiness—his position was ambiguous for the record, but essentially far from admiring of the Mayor's deviation from accepted doctrine. At the big fund-raising event, he said with scornful candor, "I am not in favor of this type of fund-raiser and I never have been."

(Harold's quiet aspirations were to lead him to a louder voice in the party and outside. Meanwhile, he would exer-

cise growing influence—and impact—on the Whalen administration and the Mayor's chosen course. Over the next few
years, their basic differences grew more inelastic and unac-
commodating. In 1989, facing reelection and realizing Joyce's
closeness to much of the Old Guard who despised him,
Whalen managed nevertheless to persuade Joyce to become his
campaign manager. But, unopposed in the election, the Mayor
had no campaign to manage and Joyce drifted off to help handle relatively minor candidates who eventually created an
image problem and some political quicksand for the Mayor
when the candidates whom he did support turned into a
whole series of disasters. This was a bad habit that persisted
for the next three years, virtually to the eve of his decision
against seeking reelection in 1993. Meanwhile, Joyce's activities within the party—he became its chairman in 1991—were
little short of declared hostility to his mayor. And he was
repeatedly successful. Whalen's 1985 magic as a political
strategist was being eaten away as Judge Bergan had warned.
Joyce's rather lonely and wistful ambition eventually would
climax and crash in the Whalen administration's last months,
in principal part because the two men could never move their
poles into cordial juxtaposition. But all this was far ahead of
the challenging days of early 1985.)

* * *

Bluntly ignoring one more ancient rule, Whalen and his
conferees settled on January 31 for their rally. The timing, nar-
rowed down to days when Mario Cuomo could be available,
found the 31st to be his schedulers' preference. Whalen's readiness to yield to the Governor's priorities soon brought enormous returns.

Invitations to the rally formidably bristled with identi-
fication of heavy hitters in an honorary committee totaling
more than 70 members, including three women, six African-
Americans, and one Republican. Bill Kennedy had signed on,
as had eight physicians and a dentist. Such an independent

committee was, in itself, a violation of the Albany Democrats' basic precepts, for candidates were supposed to perform only as word came down from on high. Confident symbols— including those of defiance—were floating anew regularly from the Whalen campfires like Mohawks' smoke signals heralding attack.

* * *

A reporter on hand at the fund-raiser crankily observed that "It felt like a high-toned charity ball"—in other words, highfalutin and pompous—"in stark contrast to the proletarian touch."

Instead of the "proletarian" standard at the party's get-togethers[3]—he found guests "nibbling on quiche and little meatballs." In an era of shifting cultural and social expectations when a popular book could be titled *Real Men Don't Eat Quiche*, the new menu could have been construed either as a welcome mat for the newcomers or an abrupt dismissal of the old-line crowd that merely got out the vote. Albany Democrats' appetites were tasting more sophisticated political finger-foods. Harold Joyce made his own quiche policy clear: "I don't eat it."

As one of the party's younger politicians, Paul Collins, a lawyer and Albany County legislator, defined it, "The Mayor has expanded the appeal (to voters) beyond the traditional party supporters." Holt-Harris agreed that an "expanded base of support is needed" for otherwise "the party might not yet come into the twentieth century."

And certainly the guests represented a far different cross-section of the populace than was true of the early-January candidacy announcement, when career politicians dominated the attendance.

"A new local constituency for the Democratic party— it's happening," Whalen himself proclaimed.

"We're doing it for a reason," he explained. "Young people today don't have the same loyalties as (your) father and grandfather."   This undoubtedly was in at least partial response to a "party stalwart" who had been quoted querulously: "I don't know why he's doing all this. The only one who says he's got any opposition is the newspapers." Syntax aside, this stalwart in his nearsightedness had nonetheless caught up with the temper of the time, for the various tantalizing temptations to challenge Whalen in a primary had bloomed early but already were wilting. And the stalwart was also astute in determining that their shredded and frustrated remnants were kept alive only in the media.

Elevated expectations of Whalen's performance and their accompaniment—rising satisfaction—were significant in themselves. But other, more substantial, results were needed for this campaign: namely, instant effectiveness and material gain. Products of visibly creative—and, above all, decisive—action.

* * *

The Governor of New York—living symbol of power that all Albany must respectfully kneel before—came to the party. He understood what the situation required, and he wrote his own lines to deal with it. With a wolfish smile, he glared down from the podium and announced in his vibrant baritone that left no room for doubt:

"Tom Whalen *is* my Mayor. I want him *to be* my Mayor. I hope nobody is silly enough to even think about a primary. But if they are I'll work hard as a citizen of Albany to get that out of the way!" He was ready, he declared, to go door-to-door for his Mayor, if necessary.

With those point-blank words, Albany's mayoral election campaign was over. If any question had remained, every Albany Democrat became instantly persuaded that no primary would occur in 1985. Jack McEneny, for one, was present this time, saying: "I'm supporting Mayor Whalen, and one reason I'm here is to solidify that position."[4]

Cuomo's oratory rolled on:

"With Tom Whalen as Mayor, Albany is beginning to soar . . . and that is something you have to attribute to Tom Whalen's leadership. He's exactly right for the City of Albany. He fits it perfectly."

No one among the Whalen strategists had dared dream of such brass-knuckled language as they heard in the Governor's menacing endorsement. The warnings, no one in his audience could possibly forget, came from the national Democratic party's newest star. His acclaimed address to its national convention was only a few months in the past; the 1984 Mondale ticket had been repudiated even more recently. Mario Cuomo was their party's No. 1 voice now. Albany's Democrats, no matter what reservations some might hold, would listen respectfully to his tough talk. The game was forfeit: Whalen 9, Doubters 0.

Cuomo, known for his declarations of indebtedness to Corning, had produced little enough in patronage plums for post-Corning Albany, but he had come through magnificently now for Corning's heir. Any dangling issue of his owing something to Albany or its political dukes had been permanently interred.

"End of case," was Whalen's tersely gratified comment.

Although his demoralized opposition was shrewd enough to recognize they were beaten, in some rancor would fester. Whalen was heard to say on the record, later, "I don't have enemies." He seemed to be describing his own outlook at the moment, for—as he knew—baleful detractors would continue the rearguard sniping throughout his term. And beyond.

* * *

The second Whalen master stroke was to set a goal of raising an overwhelming amount—more than ever known before in a local campaign.

The *Times Union*'s City Hall reporter had predicted that he could expect no better than a 10% response to the 4,000 invitations and also that the inflated price of $100 a head—instead of $15 or $25—would bring in only $40,000.

Those invitations, in fact, received 1,400 acceptances—an unheard-of 35% return. And all 1,400 turned out, or sent their missionaries, producing a gross of $140,000.[5] Whalen's reputation as unbossed, vigorous, and incorruptible was proving to be exceedingly attractive among the citizenry and his growing credibility and popularity could be credited for much of the unprecedented result. The reporter's 250% error in underestimating his high regard among the people demonstrated that old expectations—altogether, the old-time way of political life in Albany—no longer were valid. At one time, Whalen's name was reported as recognizable to 99.3% of voters questioned in a poll, an almost unbelievable level of awareness. Even allowing for a substantial degree of error in that figure, the city by now undeniably bore his stamp.

The fund-raiser coincided with the climax of sharp and public recriminations between Whalen's negotiators and the police union on terms of a new contract and pay raises.

Uniformed demonstrators were in the cold outside the hotel where Whalen's supporters were rallying around hot hors d'oeuvres just as the negotiations wound up with an agreement satisfactory to both sides. The state's Governor, among others, had riskily defied the marchers whose loud procession could have been viewed as a forbidding picket line.

The unusual contrast could be construed in either of two ways, depending on what paper you read:

A *Daily Gazette* headline was:

1,000 Honor Whalen's 'Success, Achievement'

In the *Times Union*:

Police Settle as Whalen Parties

* * *

When the last of the party-goers had straggled out of the ballroom, Whalen and Alan Iselin sank onto two of the hotel's banquet chairs for a review.

Iselin, well on the road to becoming a mainstay as the Mayor's chairman and premier counselor though he brought very little prior experience in political affairs, smiled in satisfaction.

His arm executed an encompassing gesture like a poker player sweeping in the pot he has just captured. "We accomplished three things," he said, counting out on his right hand the 1985 goals, a whole year's prizes, already won in the first month.

"*We won the primary.*" This certainly was accurate in the sense that the concept of having to fight and win a primary election had been banished for good.

"*We won the general election.*" It was only a matter of time before this truth would be proven out.

His choice of the plural pronoun was interesting testimonial to the depth of his emotional involvement in Whalen's campaign success and future welfare. Now he reverted to a more impersonal comment.

"*And, third, the party now must recognize you as a major player, on your own!*"

How Tom Whalen would employ this last benefit was yet to be demonstrated.

* * *

In that same month, Albany's prized writer-in-residence, William Kennedy, whose prose authenticates the old city's raucous past, was heard to exult that "It's a different town now. The people are different. The party is different."

But Whalen's invoking of "vision," "spirit," "creativity," "dedication," "dreams"? Could these qualities really be alive and well in this city that only yesterday was Dan O'Connell's fearsome fiefdom?

* * *

Later in the season, Whalen's campaigning was heavy on vigorous activity and role-playing exposure, earning a newspaper's supercilious reference to his "public antics." From early in the year when, knickers-clad, he skied down State Street, to the summer and fall when he rowed in a double scull on the Hudson, rode in a bike race around the Capitol then toured with professional cyclists in pouring rain, he was exceedingly visible. His tactic probably climaxed in his hanging a "Welcome" banner in Washington Park, a feat accomplished from a "cherry picker" crane. "As long as I've got the physical capacity, I'm more than happy to try it myself," he said of the various occasions he seized to be a participant rather than simply a spectator or merely an official sponsor. (*See accompanying page, "The Lord Mayor's Show."*)

To an editorial's dismayed commentary about "Republican disarray" because of that party's difficulty in finding a credible opponent for Whalen, Iselin retorted that a blank line on the ballot would reflect the fact that Whalen's record in office "has taken away virtually every single campaign issue" that an opposing candidate could usefully employ. This proposition seemed fully validated by the supportive statements Whalen had received from Corning's vigorous opponents in past elections, Carl and Charles Touhey.

Iselin enumerated a half-dozen claims of Whalen administration achievements: The annual operating surpluses; ending of the "roller-coaster real property tax assessment" policies; the "advent of competitive bidding" on contracts, plus the "updating of purchasing practices"; a "general streamlining" of the city's governmental structure and operations; a "surge" in economic development; and "creation of a climate in which arts and culture play a dominant role."

The Republicans' ritual of quadrennially furnishing a live body to run against Corning eventually turned up an opponent for Whalen but this prospect soon foundered when the presumed human sacrifice, Louis Russo, became seen by his party's touchy leadership as too quirky or uncontrollable. (He had previously run as the Republicans' candidate for a variety of offices, including the State Senate and Albany County Comptroller.) He thereby sacrificed the party's even nominal backing. But he bravely ran anyway, mounting a minimal one-man campaign, spending about $400 from his own pocket, winning a primary on 28 write-in votes, and staging a forlorn series of press conferences. In these, he criticized Whalen for "chatteling off parcels of this precious area, the Pine Bush, for commercial development," and for "balancing the budget on the backs of the handicapped" by declining a lease extension beyond three additional years for a do-good tenant of a city-owned building that was on the market.

Russo offered a positive issue or two as well. To achieve a lower property tax and to create public works employment for the elderly and handicapped persons, he advocated a 1% tax to be levied by the city on all non-residents entering Albany for work. Whalen was able to avoid responding to this unlikely idea; in defense of his Pine Bush policies he pointed to a moratorium he'd placed on construction there while an advisory committee was overseeing preparation of a generic impact study on the area's future.

* * *

Both Albany newspapers published editorials anticipating the voters' foregone support of Whalen but their endorsements overlooked a highly significant reason for returning him to office. Nowhere to be found was any recognition of the altered atmosphere in Albany—residents' expectations of what their city government would do *for* them or *to* them. The palpable improvements in their outlook in response to the vastly different attitude in City Hall were ignored.

This strange omission was destined to persist in Albany's print media throughout the Whalen term. His overriding achievement—made very evident and magnified by its unexpectedness and one the Mayor repeatedly emphasized— was the "new spirit which is alive in Albany." This was impossible to overlook other than by conscious intent in assessing the state of the city after two years. As Kennedy said, Albany was *different*. Editorially, the papers seemed to reflect unfamiliarity with a basic condition of the city's past. Appreciation of monumental change was absent.

Only passing reference, too, was directed to the city's future. As it happened, the Mayor just then was deeply involved in plotting precisely where his administration would take the city during the next four years.

Surprisingly, the name "Corning" appeared only three times in the extensive editorial commentary. In 1983, though, one big question-mark had been: *Could Tom Whalen measure up?* He was to be measured by the record of Erastus Corning, whose 42 years had seemed to be accepted as a standard by which future Mayors should be judged. Now, the absence of comparative allusions—particularly, unfavorable ones— seemed to strongly suggest that this Mayor had soared beyond the level of expectations.

Also missing were the newspapers' contentious conflicts with Whalen on two matters that the editors had chosen to make into big issues (his retaining some of his law practice and his effort to withhold some of Corning's file). It's reasonable that these didn't fit properly into a fair review of the Whalen administration's achievements but, such issues having been raised persistently, silence at this stock-taking point seemed out of character.

The editorials again focused much lukewarm comment on the lack of genuine opposition by Republicans, reflecting the weakness of "the American two-party system" in the city. (After the voting, Whalen remarked, "The two-party system is up to the Republicans.")

"Fortunately for Albany residents, Mr. Whalen has shown himself to be an able chief executive and even something of a reform politician," the *Times Union* said.

"Mr. Whalen has overhauled some of the old organization. Many contracts for goods and services have been put out to bid. Some patronage positions have been eliminated, the city debt recognized as a serious problem requiring immediate attention, and growth and rehabilitation of the downtown area encouraged.

"In addition, Mr. Whalen has managed to end the city's fiscal year with budget surpluses for two years running, breaking the city's tradition of ending in red ink."

The *Knickerbocker News* referred to an "impressive" fiscal record, comparing it with a city "on the verge of fiscal collapse."

"Since then, there have been two city surpluses, ending a string of deficit years, numerous improvements in city purchasing and budget practices, new restrictions on special assessments for property owners, and an aggressive program to recoup payments from homeowners who have benefited from past city improvement projects."

All this was true enough—but emphasis on the fiscal record meant overlooking the truly significant dimensions of the Whalen record.

In some 1,200 words of analysis, the two editorials devoted relatively few to faint praise. Chief among these was the *Times Union*'s view that "While the operation of the city government is more open to public view than it was under Mr. Whalen's predecessor, much of government is still a closed-door affair" and that "Mr. Whalen's record and manner in which the city government operates is far from ready to be held up as a model for other communities to emulate." Straining to substantiate such a contention, however, the newspaper offered, as its only example of "closed-door government," a private meeting held by the Common Council on the preliminary budget. (This was also the other paper's principal gripe.) The complaint, of course, hardly belonged in an assessment of the Mayor's own record.

* * *

A responsive electorate was the essential goal of the Whalen campaign, and in considerable degree it worked out that way, for a remarkable relaxed amiability had overcome the populace, like a city on Valium. And on the first Tuesday of November he outpolled Russo by better than 10-to-1.

The county chairman, in deploring the campaign organizers' reliance on volunteer workers, had grumped that "It's the committeemen who will get out the vote." Their efforts and effectiveness were difficult to gauge. About 60% of enrolled Democrats voted for Whalen, compared with considerably higher percentages for Corning in his last few elections. The portion of this drop-off attributable to disenchanted committeemen rather than to the low-pressure contest itself is impossible to assess accurately, but undoubtedly it was a factor, made moot by the overwhelming support he garnered across the voting spectrum.

As to his further intentions, the Mayor came close to violating his own customary tendency to play down his political independence from the party. He would continue to run the city "*in my own way*." He would guide "a progressive government operating within its means financially."

But in another statement he made a point of speaking kindly of his party. In addition to "providing good government," he aspired to "keep the Democratic organization strong and healthy."

He would leave to others the satisfied smirks directed toward the Old Guard. In that same week of delicious victory, a reporter, sensing the sweetest smell of triumph, recalled for the benefit of the hard-liners that for many moons they had sneeringly proclaimed Whalen to be "only a stand-in until the right man came along."

Having successfully undertaken to follow Washington in a crossing of the Delaware, he now found himself with Caesar on the far side of the Rubicon. He could afford magnanimity.

"Tom, you have succeeded beyond my highest expectations," Holt-Harris wrote days later. "You have imprinted your own style and your own way of going on the office and on the city—and for the better of both.

"The future is virtually unlimited and you are in the

right place at the right time, a rare opportunity. I know you will make the most of it." He signed the note "Jack," but Whalen's spare reply was to "Judge."

* * *

Restoring themselves from November's chill and a morning's labor, regulars around tables in Jack's and other favored downtown bistros were trading varying versions of a theory (presented as imminent fact) on what Albany's Mayor now was up to, nearly a month on from the election success. He was alleged to be intent on mugging the Albany County Democratic Committee and making it his own property. O'Connell bossism?—make that Whalen bossism! "News" articles confirming this were inching into newspaper columns like so many impatient householders unwilling to await the Christmas season before stringing up the blinking lights. He would seek to replicate Corning's stunt of dominating both city and county governments and bring forth a newborn Whalen party.

But nothing even resembling a coup apparently was lurking anywhere in Tom Whalen's cranial passages. These were occupied with a quite different agenda.

What did truly concern the Mayor in those first weeks after his 1985 election? How he might capitalize politically? True enough, he had just outshone, in several respects, the most sweeping of Corning's electoral triumphs. But the troublesome question in his mind was almost academic in nature: taking on the mantle of effective chief executive throughout the four-year term to which he'd just been authenticated.

The record of his prior 30 months constituted a handsome trophy indeed. But in the "What have you done for me tomorrow?" tradition, now was the time to stow away the trophy and build on the record. Point the way and cause others to follow. Here's where his mind had moved, his imagination, also his worries and his impatience. Political gamesmanship claimed only a sequestered back alley in his mind and was noted only for its potential in helping him push onward in cementing his city's comeback to greatness.

So, on precisely a day when speculative articles were lending apparent credence to rumors of Whalen power grabs the Mayor was exhorting his two-dozen department heads to spell out "goals and objectives" for becoming more effective and productive. He challenged them with 14 items—both broad-gauged and minutely specific—that "have been brought to our attention thus far," implying that his ear had matched his restless mind in the "oughta" business. This is the man who "wanted a daily victory."

The 14 were to be only the starting point for progressive "planning and priorities" over the next four years. His proposals ranged from his dream of giving the Police Department a mounted troop, and making a daunting effort to somehow increase Albany's population before the 1990 Census, all the way to the monumental task of "modernizing all city departments and services."

Just four weeks, then, after ending his successful campaign to succeed himself as Mayor he was ready to set his train of thought in motion. Very typically, he wrote a memorandum summoning his administrators to tell him where they planned to win those daily victories.

"Successful Tricentennial"—its opening gun barely weeks in the offing—stood far up on the Mayor's own list. Indeed, his energized days and restless nights focused alternatively on warm anticipation or fretful midwifery. Execution of theme and spectaculars alike had been assigned to Lew Swyer's commission, but he remained the idea man, the dreamer as well as the spark plug. He it was who would costume Swyer, Mario Cuomo, and himself in outlandish regalia on the year's hottest day. The festival's patron saint for once couldn't keep his hands off detail regardless of what had been delegated as others' responsibilities.

NOTES

[1] Clyne had been among those a reporter "mentioned" in May 1983 as potential foes for Whalen when he was the incoming Mayor. Others were Howard Nolan, Leonard Weiss, Lawrence Kahn, and Charles Touhey. The writer conceded that it would be "foolhardy" for any of them "to show their hands until the time comes actually to mount opposition to Whalen." If such a time indeed ever appeared to come, they prudently passed it up.

[2] An Albany institution that disappeared about the time the Whalen administration came to a close.

[3] Tubs of pretzels and chips, 5,000 white-bread sandwiches with a choice of ham or bologna and cheese, 65 barrels of beer, and plenty of fried dough had constituted the menu for the party's pre-election rally in the preceding year. It was described as "good solid Democratic fare."

[4] Over the next few years, Whalen opposed McEneny in two elections by giving support to County Committee candidates. McEneny successfully ran for the Albany County Legislature, winning as a write-in candidate after a tie vote in a primary (1991). In the next year, he defeated a large field of aspirants for nomination to the New York State Assembly and then won overwhelmingly in the general election. Subsequently, he and Whalen often found common cause in political and personal issues.

[5] After six months, the total received from several hundred contributors amounted to more than $160,000. Although campaign expenditures were substantial, including $33,000 for the big party, the campaign treasury managed by Rube Gersowitz showed a $101,000 balance midway in the election year. More than two-thirds ($104,000) of the total was contributed by individuals; $41,000 by corporations (among which Norstar Bancorp's $2,5000 stood out); and only $4,800 (3.2%) from lobbying organizations that had taken on the mantle of "political action committees." Overall, the proportions were healthy.

An "Unfailing Loyalist"

In mid-January of 1985, the party's Old Guard sustained a new setback. Failing health forced Robert M. Bender, the county committee's 75-year-old executive secretary for the eight years since Dan O'Connell's death, to step aside though he tried to help out for the next several months. He'd been near the forefront of the party's apparatus for more than 35 years, and was regarded as the last O'Connell protégé. A triumvirate took over the patronage clearinghouse he'd run almost singlehandedly.

Tolerant of Whalen, despite being steeped in the O'Connell tradition, he had worked along with the Mayor on their parallel interests for a crucial year and a half. His loss from the sensitive hot spot was to be felt in City Hall. This was true even though late in 1984 he had declined to endorse Whalen outright in response to a newspaper survey among ward leaders. ("Whosoever the Democratic Party support, I support.")

He was three days younger than Erastus Corning, but as a lifelong South Ender he was on a very different track. When the future Mayor left for Yale in 1928, Bob Bender went to work for the D&H Railroad. There he stayed for 30 years, until becoming a full-time politician. He was fortunate in another coincidental link to the party chieftains: He was born in the downstairs flat of a humble dwelling where a young woman, Leta Burnside, lived one flight up. Leta became Mrs. Daniel O'Connell. The Boss eventually made him leader in the First Ward, certified him to serve as an alderman in the early Corning years, installed him as the Housing Authority's administrative head, and OK'd his semi-official helping hand for Jimmy Ryan at headquarters for a few years before he took over the secretary's job with all its discretionary powers.

One significant aspect of such powers became evident to Whalen in September immediately after Bender's death. The Mayor described a call from Chairman O'Brien (who had picked Bender in 1983 as his first vice-chairman) promptly upon receiving the news. The purpose was to recruit him as company for a call on Mrs. Bender, but the real reason turned out to be an effort to locate and retrieve a box believed to contain considerably more than $100,000 in cash.

Bender had confided to O'Brien that he'd taken it home from headquarters—for safekeeping, Whalen was informed. Such a box and contents never were found—at least by persons qualified to receive it. The incident, though unpublicized, shone a fresh light on the large amounts of money at headquarters. It even paralleled the well-remembered frustrating search for Leo Quinn's bonanza 20 years earlier. And, obviously, it raised questions for any inquiring mind about the source of this ready flow of funds. The questions, for some, had clear-enough answers but these were internalized, including the issue of a need for an official report.

* * *

Known for "unfailing loyalty" to the Organization and to the men who shaped what might be called its philosophy and exercised mandates, Bob Bender steadfastly adhered to that philosophy. But he was unfailingly true as well to a more mundane characteristic. Like O'Connell, like Quinn, Bender—a large-framed, obese man—earned the apt description conferred on others at or near the top: "very gruff." *Don't tread on me*, was the message. *Don't question. Don't deviate.*

In keeping with county committee tradition Bender, as the clearinghouse for all job applications, was the key man for party patronage in city, county, and state governments and the city school district. And, said Bill Keefe, he was "probably the most unselfish politician I have ever met."

"A Time Unparalleled"

It was New Year's Day of 1986, and for months Mayor Whalen had dusted and polished, swept and scrubbed, sanded and smoothed with all the fervor of an evangelical Mary Poppins to make the old city ready to gleam in its year-long anniversary party to come. Now the hour was right for savoring his new certification as Albany's elected Mayor rather than merely a legatee—and also for basking in the reflected sunlight of the shining recovery his own policies had fostered. The Governor had come with paragraphs of generous words, bishops and other dominics had conferred their blessings, the judge who delighted in him as a protégé had accomplished the swearing-in, and the big hall (itself an innovation in mayoral inaugurals locally) was packed with well-wishers among whom—as he said—were Whalen relatives "occupying the first nineteen rows." It was indeed a moment of pardonable pride—for the city and for this protagonist who now strode its stage.

It was his party, but he requisitioned less than five minutes in the spotlight at the podium. And in that terse message, no more than 40 words were devoted to enumerating material gains achieved in the first two and one-half years of the Whalen administration—the "fiscal house" at last put in order, the professionalization of the work force, the upgraded recreational, cultural, and entertainment assets, the private-sector partnerships formed.

Otherwise, the emphasis was wholly on invisible intangibles, which he confidently hailed as verifiable revelations. Much of his enthusiasm echoed his words of exactly a year earlier, when in proclaiming his candidacy he introduced the theme of a reawakening of spirit and of pride.[1]

"What makes me most proud," the Mayor now reiterated, moments after taking the oath of office for the second time, his face flushed with sentiment, "is the spirit and pride of the people in the city."

"This historic city is alive again!" he declared, and few skeptics were on hand to doubt. He recalled "those dark days" when Albany's residents, along with its industry and commerce, fled the scene. He lauded "the enthusiasm of our people" as inspiring—"Every aspect of our lives is bullish; you can feel the excitement in the air and see it on people's faces."

Even when he claimed to find Albany "literally jumping with activity and purpose," he turned such activity about by adding that it was, in fact, "designed to improve the economy and give meaning to our lives."

Tom Whalen spoke of "resurgence, renaissance, and revitalization throughout the city" and found parallels for these qualities in the citizenry's spirit and pride.

For that horizon of time—at least, for that midday—Albany had become, for him, endowed with virtually magical status and aspiration.

"*The year which began today may be the most exciting period in the history of our splendid city.*"

"*Other cities do not have*" Albany's intangible of pride and spirit, "*an intangible that may very well be peculiar to Albany.*"

"*We may be living at a time unparalleled in our history.*"

To be the Mayor during the chartered city's three-hundredth year—the Tricentennial, or Tercentenary as adherence to precedent would have named it—was for Tom Whalen a unique honor and privilege, one no other person ever could have. Into an exhortation for everyone to participate in the observance he added his own promise to accept every responsibility and challenge incumbent on him, the one individual fortunate enough to preside over it.

"I can think of no other reward, no finer remuneration, no greater pleasure than to be Mayor of the City of Albany today—and I thank God for my good fortune," he concluded in a summation of his personal pride and joy.[2]

* * *

Later that afternoon, in a program at the Common Council's chamber, Whalen swore its members into their new terms, and presided at the ceremonial opening of the year's celebration, with Governor Cuomo again a participant.

"Here's a man who got 92% of the vote—I want to listen to what he has to say," the Governor quipped, recognizing that the new year meant a reelection campaign for himself. He was awarded a tricentennial lapel pin, hailed later as "an unofficial symbol of the city's boosterism."

The Dongan Charter of 1686 was given its first outing in a hundred years, displayed in City Hall's rotunda for the benefit of visitors estimated at several hundreds. The Governor, Mayor, and Lew Swyer, the tricentennial's chairman, were protected by an honor guard consisting of two state employees attired as militiamen of the early Dutch period and armed with 10-foot pikes.

"A grand beginning for a glorious year," Albany's Mayor assessed this day when no panoply could have been excessive, no prospect displeasing.

During that year, writing in the magazine *New York Alive*, Duane LaFleche remarked that the city was "no longer dirty and no longer being stigmatized as corrupt," and he added that Whalen "appears to be succeeding in raising the city's spirits." Albany, he said, seems to be "a little amazed" at its newly won status.

* * *

Whalen eventually was to learn that although he and Cuomo could develop a "fine personal relationship there was not a pot of gold at the end of the rainbow for the city," a circumstance partially attributable to the country's sagging economy but also to an apparent lack of responsiveness at critical points in the Cuomo administration.

"I felt that Cuomo was quick to embrace me as the new Mayor despite his loss of the man he so greatly admired," Whalen said. "It was a genuinely strong allegiance to Albany that started when Corning stepped forward as the first Democrat with a statewide reputation who came out for him.

"The Governor was very supportive of me in many ways other than through direct financial aid.

"He made sure that his commissioners would work with us on joint projects, helping to resolve problems we might have with respect to over-regulation by the state, particularly in environmental matters." (On the other hand, Whalen's early move to abolish the huge, high-rise billboards along the city's entryways was voided by the Cuomo administration without notice or consultation.)

"I was careful not to knock on his door too often, and I think this was useful in our relationship. Some (people) can make the argument that I wasn't tough enough in putting across what we needed. But I believe that often—as in this case—there's a finesse that's important. So our relationship was low-key.

"The Governor knew that if I called, it would be on something important. I took that position out of respect for the demands on his time and his need to allocate it wisely. He appreciated that."

Mario Cuomo was generous with his verbal support and ceremonial appearances. But his staff, which often was seen in an adversarial attitude toward the state's cities, particularly the "Big 6" which included Albany, was repeatedly negative on downtown development projects which Whalen was zealous in advocating. John Egan's key collaboration, in expediting transfer of Union Station to make Peter Kiernan's big idea a reality, was a noteworthy exception.

Plans for a tower to house Audit & Control on South Pearl Street, behind and adjacent to one of the huge new KeyCorp buildings, died in an advanced planning stage in 1992 because of lack of interest by Cuomo's people. It would have been financed by the State Retirement System, as worked out for Comptroller Regan by Don Dunn, one of his top staffers. The only cost to the State government would have been office rental charges. But approval of a tenable lease for the Comptroller's occupancy was—at least for the record—the sticking point in the Executive Chamber. Richard Zipes's Omni Development Corporation, behind the proposal, brought in architects' renderings which included an apartment complex on top and a public atrium at ground level. Victor Riley, a hardshelled enthusiast for private development, had a hand in pushing this project. It seemed to make sense as a viable answer to the accepted proposition that Audit & Control soon would be forced out of its 60-year occupancy of the Alfred E. Smith tower, which had suffered the years' poundings. After the proposed structure was turned down, several years passed before another office building was put up for the Comptroller on another site.

In the same period, the Picotte Companies made a major presentation for construction of an office building to be leased and occupied by a state agency such as Environmental Conservation on available Broadway property north of Union Station/Kiernan Plaza. Again, private investment was the crucial element. The scenario turned out to be very similar to the one that had prevailed in the killing of the Omni project on South Pearl. The Cuomo administration turned a cold shoulder on the leasing terms (as the Carey administration had in 1982 on the Swyer proposal to rehabilitate old Union Station).

Somewhat earlier, developer William Bantz had his turn at frustration. He proposed a major office project off South Pearl in the vicinity of the intercity bus terminals. State Department of Transportation funding and occupancy were contemplated. It eventually couldn't be pieced together because of lack of interest once more by Cuomo's powerful staff.

Thus, virtually all the boosts that downtown Albany received in the Whalen years were the result of private enterprise, with the state government, the city's principal industry unfortunately adopting a posture aloof from concern or, certainly, responsive to a leader's will. (Ironically, it was Cuomo's successor, George E. Pataki, a Republican, who developed a strong interest in downtown Albany's redevelopment and who pushed through construction of three major office buildings for State departments on State Street and on Broadway. Two of the three housed the departments for which approval had been withheld earlier.)

NOTES

[1] His words were echoed in a comment he made after leaving office: "Call it what you will, we succeeded in instilling pride, a spirit, a sense of place. We brought about some intangibles that lifted up the heart of the city. It caused people to feel good about themselves—and where they lived."

In fact, the emphasis on pride was far from a phenomenon born of the immediate past. In the 1981 campaign, "pride" was a key slogan of the Corning/Whalen ticket. But as political memories go, that was now long ago. Probably, Whalen just forgot the words he had spoken in support of Corning's appeal for four more years and the Mayor's own use of "pride" and "proud" in his last election bid. Or, perhaps Whalen in 1985 was hearing a familiar but distant echo that he couldn't quite place.

Because in 1985 Whalen really could offer genuine evidence of circumstances and conditions deserving of citizens' pride, a freshness lingered in this reintroduction of the expression. The 1981 campaign's comments, on the other hand, were just the product of a clever ad man writing hollow words to be read aloud.

     [2] "No election or appointment conferred upon me ever gave me so much pleasure."—John Quincy Adams, upon being elected to the United States House of Representatives, 1830, after having served as President, 1825-1829; from his diary, as quoted by David McCullough in *Brave Companions: Portraits in History* (Simon & Schuster: A Touchstone Book; Copyright 1992 by David McCullough.)

Infectious Energies

After only a couple of years while he became increasingly restive about some of his top staff people who seemed locked into office chairs, Whalen challenged them to push away from their desks and find out what everyday Albanians were up to.

"We can pick up exciting ideas about what people expect of their government," he urged his commissioners. "And get us additional perspectives on the city. Learn what their problems are." He was asking for an hour a week—on the way from home or on their return; evenings; while at lunch. And quietly requesting "to hear from you (on the experience) every so often," he hinted that he might be seeing them "on my own rounds."

Whalen's energetic and visible style in office mimics (and anticipates) an illuminating essay on leadership[1] by Frank H. T. Rhodes, Cornell's president for 18 years (1977-1995). Energy, enthusiasm, and confidence, he argued, are "highly infectious qualities" for a leader's use to "achieve results through others." Though his comments were for the academic world, they happen to describe Whalen's own pattern of executive behavior.

"Effective leadership means not only framing the agenda but driving it to a conclusion," Rhodes wrote. "It means being accountable—but also being bold." This is a close delineation of Whalen's premise.

Rhodes's advice (which Whalen already put into practice) urged chief executives "to dream (their institutions) into something new." Each element had just been effectively employed in Albany's City Hall: Challenging its people to greatness, elevating their hopes and extending their reach, energizing them to new levels of success, and galvanizing them toward higher achievement. Whalen might well have composed the formula that Rhodes was enunciating.

So, too, with the leader's task. This would include establishing meaningful goals, recruiting the talent to serve the cause effectively, building a consensus, creating the climate, and providing resources to attain the goals. It also meant establishing a desirable relationship with staff. Responding to their "manager, coach or cheerleader" (Whalen, personified), top employees' example for the rank and file would foster single-minded dedication, unswerving loyalty, and what Rhodes called an unambiguity in their readiness to serve the group's purposes.

In turn, they should expect a close working relationship and frequent contact with the executive and an opportunity for regular meetings, as was the Whalen mode. A byproduct can be anticipated in the form of "a particular energy" (re-emphasizing the "infectious quality" of shared energies, along with implicit joint efforts and resultant high morale).

Whalen scored well in each of Rhodes's categories. Compared with a typical campus, however, his City Hall had much further to go in developing goals and defining all the other "tasks" within a leader's area of responsibility. He was at his inspired best in "dreaming . . . something new" and in asserting a "bold" role for himself while demonstrating the infectious "energy, enthusiasm, and confidence." Both in executing his office's duties and in awakening the people's latent spirit, he provided the impetus (and support system) for the talent he recruited to reach the new goals he and they established.

Among that new staff, performance was generally as high as expected. The total record, however, admittedly was blemished by the occasional reluctance or ineptness—or betrayal—of some employees whose services he'd inherited. Willingness to serve with "unswerving loyalty" was distinctly in doubt. In evaluating this unproductive and harassing problem, it seems evident that Whalen was victimized by a truculent and dissident fragmented minority who saw their interests and loyalties focused elsewhere.

On the other hand, certain of his own characteristics probably did contribute to an ineffectual bevel on the cutting edge of his administration's essentially productive structure. What might these be? From within one could hear reference to a certitude bordering on rigidity, an impatience tending toward an impolitic abruptness, an insistence on performance that could be disconcerting, a staff alliance where one employee's work methods were regularly alienating others. To the degree that these perceived shortcomings were actually operative, Whalen as Mayor must be associated with some personal and institutional disappointments.

Mike Royko, whose syndicated column was published in the *Times Union* in this period, had written of his hometown mayor, "In some ways he was this town at its best—strong, hard-driving, working feverishly, pushing, building, driven by ambitions so big they seemed Texas-boastful."[2] Though Tom Whalen hardly competed with that mayor in power, influence, and renown (as well as in certain other qualities), this description of Richard J. Daley offers striking similarities to his all-out style in Albany.

Successful officeholders, in Whalen's view after his decade of experience, must be (1) ready to invest enough time to look ahead and plan (even beyond their own elected term) but be able meanwhile (2) to make timely decisions (regardless of their quality), then (3) to collaborate effectively with other potential leadership (sharing credit as well as power and responsibility), and (4) to see the job as first priority despite any hurtful criticism, though (5) candidly admitting mistakes when this is called for.

These characteristics are high among his "elements needed in order to govern." More particularly:

"You'll need to be willing to make decisions, whether they are the right ones or the wrong ones—though it really is better to be right!

"People want to believe their leader is moving the agenda forward. If you can't make decisions, you thereby let events govern your actions. If a decision turns out to be wrong, then you've got a mistake to explain.

"It's natural to try to justify one's actions and to stonewall any admission that a mistake has been made. A good leader can quickly admit the mistake, put the matter firmly in the past, and promptly move on. But perhaps, as it seems, this must always be learned the hard way.

"Not only are mistakes inevitable, so is criticism. Especially if it's unwarranted, criticism hurts—and hurts a lot if it's conducted in the media—no matter who you are. I suspect that no one ever really becomes used to it, but good leaders try to rise above it. You must try to avoid being deterred by mean-spirited attacks—rather, set your mind to whatever the task is.

"Then, as difficult as it is to move beyond the crisis of the moment—snow removal, tax increases, combating crime— you have to set aside time to plan for the (city's) future. This usually requires thinking about policy beyond a four-year term—and that isn't very palatable to a lot of public officials.

"A good leader will cultivate partnerships. This obligates a willingness to share some of the power and responsibility with the 'private sector'—that is, the not-for-profit do-good area as well as the whole structure of business enterprise. Bringing other people to become involved in the policy-making process has obvious benefits for that process. It's also good politics.

"In working one's way through all this, the leader must commit a substantial amount of time if the job is to be done well. Including all the obligatory public appearances, the leader can expect regular 60-hour weeks, and frequently 70 or 80. And be resolute as well as tireless, for these are hours at the expense of a private life and that of the family."

* * *

Whalen had assumed that O'Connell's meetings with "his judges" probably focused on developing political strategies with the benefit of the scope of their pre-judicial experience and the presumed wisdom they'd derived. Later, he realized that in a way very similar to O'Connell's alliances, he himself had developed a habit of drawing on the counsel of judges, sitting or retired: Bergan, formerly of the Court of Appeals and earlier in various lower jurisdictions; Gabrielli and Bellacosa, also of the Court of Appeals; Foley, on senior status in the federal District bench; Pennock, of State Supreme Court; and Holt-Harris, of Albany's busy Recorder's and Traffic Courts. Chief Judge Wachtler was among his friends.

Whalen told an interviewer that "I bent over backward, in some ways, to avoid political influences. Such influence had been a major part of Albany's government—and a lot of it had gone wrong.

"My instinct was even to overreact in some cases, so there would not be a suggestion of undue influence on my judgment.

"But," he added, "I did recognize that a major ingredient of any elected official's life is a power base. For politics, I substituted a different kind of power base, depending on community leadership and the neighborhood associations rather than the ward leaders.

"And this immediately got me in trouble with the Democratic organization, from which I heard bitter complaints."

Upon taking office, he explained, "It didn't take me long to realize that I couldn't do it myself—I needed help. Having lived in Albany all my life (except for five years in college and the Army) and having practiced law here for many years, I knew that people were looking for opportunities to contribute to their city. It was exceedingly easy for me to reach out to friends and associates and ask them for help. In a variety of ways they have come through splendidly. I could count on the fingers of one hand the number I've asked but who couldn't serve as requested.

"What I did would have been tough for what I'll call a 'purebred politician' to do; that is, share the power. I had no misgivings about power-sharing. If I were able to get good people on board, I felt confident they would make the right decisions. There was and always is plenty of credit to go around.

"It was easier for me to have such an attitude because I had a profession to fall back on if things started to unravel."

* * *

His instinct to turn to others for collaboration and support had a natural background—a history of being an active participant in team sports: In football (as quarterback, running the show), in baseball, in competitive rowing. On the river in a shell he preferred to have a partner.

Teamwork obligations extended to staff responsibilities, for in Whalen's City Hall the departments were expected to come together to consult and develop workable attacks on problems having common implications.

One clearest indication of commitment to involving the community-at-large is found in the scope of the city's governance. This was in the membership of official commissions and boards to which the Mayor made appointments, especially in 14 quasi-municipal bodies such as the Parking Authority, District Port Commission, Industrial Development Agency, or the Local Development Corporation. "When I became Mayor, 100% of the representation on those bodies came from within City Hall. They had been structured that way for one purpose—to keep control of them right in the Office of the Mayor. Ten years later when I left office, 98% of the representation on those bodies was from the private sector."

With the exception of a few agencies where membership is *ex officio*, such as the Highway Safety Committee, the same changeover was very largely true. A check of the names and identities of the personnel indicates that well over 200 citizens unaffiliated with the government were appointed.[3]

Summing up, he observed during his last weeks in office that "If I have a legacy to leave Albany, to be remembered after 10 years of public service, it's that we worked together, that we established a public-private partnership—and made the city work."

NOTES

[1] "The Art of the Presidency," by Frank H. T. Rhodes, in *The Presidency* magazine, a publication of the American Council on Education, Spring 1998.

[2] *One More Time* by Mike Royko. Copyright 1999 by the University of Chicago. Published by the University of Chicago Press.

[3] Affirmation of such involvement as an operating principle, though in another category, appears in the 1989 report of the Strategic Planning Committee.

Regaining the "A"

Interviewed for a magazine article,[1] Whalen once mentioned a rather novel reward for officeholders such as himself: "psychic income." Purportedly, this non-negotiable intangible could make a tough job (specifically his own) seem worthwhile despite whatever drudgery and brickbats.

The concept is a clever one, and depending on how much the incumbent values achievement for its own sake, sufficient satisfaction may lie within it.

Occasionally other benefit does come the way of the plow horse, trophies that the show horse probably will never win. For Whalen, one of these appeared in a most timely way during a difficult year.

In 1989, an election year when his leadership would be tested at the polls, while his detractors were having a field day in the press, Whalen's compeers in the United States Conference of Mayors were singling him out. He was selected to receive the highest national award for fiscal management, for "rescuing Albany from economic doldrums and restoring it to financial prosperity."

The "Mayors' Financial Leadership Award" is reserved for "the mayor whose administration has demonstrated the highest standards of sound and innovative financial management, accountability, and adherence to highest levels of professional practice." It offered gratifying testimony as to consistently effective performance.[2]

He had earned it. With a neat coincidence, this was

also the year that Albany residents' property tax rate was reduced for the third consecutive time, a cumulative total reduction of more than 16%.[3] (In contrast, 75% of local governments—and all school districts—in New York State raised taxes in each of the two prior years). And Moody's Investors Service—which had joined Standard & Poor's in early 1983 in dropping the city's bond rating to the lowest possible level—now joined in raising it sharply to "A." Budget Director Klepak summed up: "The changes Mayor Whalen brought about normally would take decades, when one considers the enormous problems thrust upon him in May 1983."

* * *

Tracking various elements of the Whalen fiscal plan has an impressive payoff. We have seen how union contracts affected the budget and pay scale for the police and fire departments. For the city's non-union employees, a raise was provided every year, exceeding the annual increases registered in the Consumer Price Index in all but two years (once, the raise equaled the CPI gain, and in one difficult year the minimal raise lagged behind). Altogether, this payroll group received raises of approximately 50%.

They were part of total budgeted expenditures that began from a base of about $68 million in Corning's budget for 1982 and was at $90 million or more for Whalen's last five budgets. His cumulative spending was $147 million above the level of Corning's budget, averaging $12.25 million higher annually.

In the dozen revolutionary fiscal years between Corning's final funding allocation for the city's operations (in his budget for FY 1982) and Whalen's proposal for his own successor's first-year expenditures (the 1994 budget), money allocated to help ensure that the Common Council's deliberations would reflect the members' wisdom more than doubled.

In fact, however, if you compare this funding with all other functions of Whalen's government, it's hardly spectacular. At exactly 106% (from $252,000 to $521,000), the increase was only fifteenth largest in 20 categories of expense.

Whalen's ambitions and goals were demonstrated dramatically by several extreme shifts in funding. Beyond this personal priority, operations directly concerning or affecting the public were given the most impressive increases overall. Keeping Albany cleaned up was costly. The cost of waste collection multiplied (203%) but then disposing of all of it went up by 280%. Streets were less bumpy, better maintained, as the amount spent on them soared (294%). The parks system revived with 155% more money. Police officers' pay raises plus the expenditures on their department's effectiveness improved by 164%—to a level where at $23 million it claimed a very major share of the city's resources. Spending for the Fire Department (later including emergency medical services) rose even faster—by 187% to a total of $20.4 million. (Both uniformed departments experienced major capital programs producing new or renovated quarters, frequently in new locations.)

Commitment to the category labeled Economic Assistance was most evident among all the changes in the budgetary profile. In 1982, the $39,000 appropriation was directed entirely to programs for the aging, at least in part a recognition of the interest in such services by Mayor Corning's mother. By 1994, this category had been expanded to embrace three new departments of government: Housing and Community Development, Economic Development, and an Office of Municipal Policy and Communications. At $1,623,964 the budgeted costs for this varied activity were 41 times as much as the 1982 line.

Another department had won Whalen's special favor: Planning. Held on a very short $37,000 leash by Corning— who evidently was confident he could design whatever plans Albany might need—by 1994, Planning was riding high at $305,000, up 724%.

Another big increase (214%) went to the Purchasing Department. Even though invisible to the public eye, here was the most sensitive office actually performing a cornerstone responsibility supporting everyone's newfound expectations of honest dealings in the city government's operations, establishing credibility and respect for them.

In only five of the 20 categories did Whalen's funding end up less than doubled. The smallest increase (43%) was for Traffic Engineering, and even its actual dollars jumped to $699,000 from $487,000. On one item the increases surprisingly were restrained. Snow removal—always involving risky assumptions—was enlarged but by only 70% ($273,000). Snowfalls—foreseeable yet precisely unpredictable—impacted everyone in the city (and their tempers). Conservatism in guessing what the winter would bring and then allocating enough to cover a large margin of error was a dangerous game. Whalen and Klepak felt justified in hedging on this flashpoint by shifting away from huge outlays for intermittent rental of private operators' plows and trucks. Their answer lay in substituting city employees as crews for the fleet of equipment that was newly bought, paid for, and waiting. The strategy generally worked.

Two notable footnotes mark this performance. On the positive side, Albany governmental operations ran surpluses every year until the last few, and the fund balance—before it became advisable to start spending it down—grew to over $33.9 million by 1991. Year after year in the later 1980s, second-guessers loudly demanded that the surpluses be diverted to current budget needs, chiefly to provide additional tax relief beyond the remarkable record that was regularly being compiled. Adamantly—and with prudential foresight—the fund balance was preserved until the final three years, when it was gradually dismantled to keep the succeeding years' accounts in balance.

Very much less positive was Albany's experience with income from New York's State Aid formula for municipalities. It provided almost exactly $10 million annually as Whalen took office and over the next five fiscal years (1986-1990) it averaged $12.1 million. Over that period, the result was a cumulative $10.5 million bulge beyond the earlier base. But with the onset of the economic downturn that was marked by the Bush broken vow on taxes, the state's assistance for Albany promptly plunged by more than 30%, creating a $3.79 million hole in a Whalen budget planned without anticipation of such drastic surgery. In its best four years, the aid amounted to $49 million—followed by four years when the total was $32.5 million. Other cities' portion of aid were declining as well, but Cuomo and his people were remarkable in their readiness to brush off Albany's traditional appeal on the small tax-base issue, quite apart from the Cuomo "debt" to Corning's city.

The fallout immediately necessitated a $5.79 increase per thousand of assessed value in the 1991 property tax rate, a 7% jump. It was the first rise in six years, and followed three consecutive years of 5 and 6% decreases. The tax rate had fallen by $16.09 since 1985 (from $99.91 to $83.82 per thousand), an especially remarkable achievement because, year after year, Albany's budgetary decisions were still being impacted by all the minuses that were inherited in 1983.

* * *

One noteworthy budget area reported on expenditures for "culture" and "recreation," grouped together as though they were twinned interests in need of a common funding stream.

One of Whalen's most frequently cited concerns—and Klepak's, too—was in the sophisticated forms of diversion and entertainment. On a parallel track, support for the recreational interests was a strong point of the Mayor's for he shared many of the public's activities and enthusiasms. He revived and added parks and play areas, even rebuilding a golf course.

Corning's last budget (for 1982) allocated $4.8 million in this area. The "Gang of Four," patching together an emergency spending plan in his absence, managed a 7.4% increase, but this was only the beginning of a truly major improvement. Whalen's first budget allocated $7.3 million, a 51% increase.

In approximately 10 years, Whalen and Klepak put

$110 million into these activities, an annual average of over $10 million (including a three-year span when the average rose to $11.5 million). It's less than fair to assume that Corning if Mayor in this same period would have continued budgeting at less than $5 million, but without question in the Whalen years commitment was firm to those interests—rising further in virtually every budget and peaking at $12.3 million.

"Never have I met a public official whose *real* commitment to the arts is stronger. . . . He has translated his own interest and fondness for the arts to the city, a remarkable achievement. The arts are alive and ever-present in Albany," wrote the president of the board for the Albany Symphony Orchestra at the time, Peter R. Kermani, in advocating an award for Mayor Whalen.

* * *

After Corning had tardily announced his 1981-1982 budget (the last of his own contriving) in the late fall, Harold Rubin's neighborhood association—expressing exasperation within a positive framework—offered four major recommendations. The first signs of these reforms became visible even in the 1982-1983 document delegated by the ailing Corning to Whalen and McArdle.

And as the new administration's guidelines—authenticated by Whalen and whipped into being by Klepak—began to take hold in late 1983, three of the four points were achieved: Releasing budgets substantially before the beginning of each new fiscal year, explaining significant items in an accompanying narrative, and providing a formal hearing with revisions anticipated prior to the Common Council's budget debate and vote. The fourth proposal—for a series of hearings throughout the city to explain how and why the budget had been shaped— was modified to include public hearings held in City Hall and also an open briefing for the Council's finance committee.

In the long 1984 budget year, Albany's first capital budget was established and in the remainder of the Whalen

term more than $105 million was dedicated to an exceedingly
lengthy infrastructure makeover for dozens of purposes.[4]
Again, the national economic picture was responsible for the
limited expenditures on construction and rehabilitation. In
1989, the capital budget was $26.7 million. Two years later it
had been reduced by 80%, to $5.5 million. To minimize the
long-term effects of borrowing, one-third of all the spending on
capital projects was derived from current revenues.

The plan for 1985 demonstrated a budget in transition.
It incorporated the Mayor's message defining, describing, and
explaining the circumstances that went into the document's
formulation. It established a capital budget firmly and inno-
vated a five-year capital plan which created flexible priorities
for major projects to be undertaken later. And, of basic value,
it produced an orderly framework and schedules for development of the budget itself. The combined heads and hands of
Whalen and Klepak were very evident.

Separately, the budget made note of a highly significant
move that was underway. Steps had been taken for a water
and sewer "enterprise fund" that would operate those fundamental services like a public utility. The initial efforts were
limited to inventorying and appraising all the assets of those
departments, but the eventual result would have a great
import for management of the city's financial resources.

The numerous new practices introduced in these early
budgets, based in fundamental principles of budgeting, financial management, and accounting plus accountability, in the
long run proved to have established a productive pattern for
the years ahead. Straightforward dealings were faithfully
reported for accessibility to public scrutiny and evaluation.

* * *

Whalen's long-range hopes for real and continuing success, he decided, lay in attracting and keeping top-drawer staff.
And this inevitably would hinge in large part on how much he
could offer in their paychecks. He urgently needed to raise the

level of compensation from its chronic depression. Unless he could prevail on this issue, his government was doomed to perpetuation of second-class obscurity and worse.

Hoping to anchor the always-sensitive question of pay raises to a non-controversial base, he recruited three of Albany's business and fiscal elite and declared them a commission that objectively would judge the city's salary scale. The commissioners—who all had reason enough to be unintimidated by the concept of decent pay—were Robert W. Bouchard, who had emerged from a state payroll with Audit & Control to become Victor Riley's top assistant as president and CEO of Key Bancshares of New York; Carl E. Touhey,[5] driving force in the success of Orange Motors' big Ford dealership; and J. Richard Gaintner, a physician turned manager who had recently arrived to become the president and CEO of the Albany Medical Center and draftsman of its ambitious growth plans. They agreed on a thorough study of competitive salary levels within the region's private sector and in comparable municipal governments. From these data, they would draw conclusions and propose remedies. They were lending themselves amiably to an assignment which, in part, was designed to deny newspapers an opportunity to slap the Mayor for haste and over-reaching. This prospect was an active apprehension within the Whalen councils. Giving the raises "cover" through the commissioners' unassailable credibility made the maneuvering worth the trouble.

The city labored under an innate problem that had become acute. Historically, pay for city workers in Albany was minimal. At the lower levels, depressed pay was an intrinsic part of the old policy of hiring too many people—especially for unskilled, part-time jobs—and giving them slightly better pay than they would receive from "relief" or, later, "welfare" scales. Theoretically, this also provided the dignity of real work and earned incomes. The humanitarian concept was, of course, also fundamentally linked to political and voting loyalties. It had served that ancillary purpose with unmatched effectiveness over the decades.

From Whalen's viewpoint, one major problem was that the whole scheme reached all the way to the top. Not only laborers and clerks and supervisors, but department heads—and the Mayor—were affected. As Corning started his last year in office, his salary was $33,000, but it had only then been raised from $25,000. For a Mayor commanding an independent income, as he had, this was endurable, but it truly was far from appropriate to compensate for the job's responsibility. Nor could it be considered adequate for the scale of living expected from a person in that eminently visible position.

Tom Whalen came to office with personal responsibilities and commitments far exceeding what the city would be paying him, even though his law partnership, now greatly reduced, could somewhat augment the salary. Within months of his taking office, the Whalen-Klepak budget for the coming year succeeded in finding some spare change and a few bills in the mattress, enough for selectively moderate raises to several underpaid commissioners and the Mayor himself. Subsequent budgets over the next two years improved the mayoral income by half, to $50,562. This was his annual salary when the new commission went to work.

Over six months, from March to September 1986, the three commissioners analyzed masses of data and studied the job descriptions for a pool of high-category city employees. Eventually, they came out with a proposal for Albany's first broad salary upgrade in many, many years. They concluded that the city was underpaying its Mayor and the chief administrators—and that this, in turn, unfairly limited what other department heads could receive. Raises for 17 positions were recommended, including the top three elected executive and administrative officers—Whalen, Comptroller Hemingway, and Treasurer Joyce—plus the two top aides the Mayor relied on most heavily, Budget Director Klepak and Corporation Counsel McArdle.

When the proposal was to be made public, Whalen made certain that he had a statement ready. The purpose of the raises, he explained, was to attract "highly qualified, highly motivated people" into service.

The added cost, more than $100,000, could be readily absorbed by the treasury, and the citizenry seemed to take it in stride—except for a single vocal alderman.   Gerald D. Jennings, whose sniping at the Whalen administration already seemed endless, complained that the new pay levels were excessive.[6]

* * *

The long-overdue effort to improve salaries to a point where they would be sufficiently competitive to attract and hold qualified staff actually had begun soon after he took office. Even earlier, a substantial raise had been put through for "the irreplaceable man," Vincent McArdle, whose far-ranging workload and acceptance of responsibility during Corning's hospitalization was, like Whalen's, notable.

The Mayor's $33,000 salary in June of 1983 was about 20% of the income that successful lawyers in Albany could bank on. Whalen could not abandon his law practice and its income, but clearly a conflict in time and compensation immediately arose between his two demanding occupations. The eventual solution was complex and somewhat Solomon-like.

He accepted Albany's paychecks, as had Corning with his insurance business and its obligations. But in Whalen's case his salary as Mayor was deducted from the amount he would receive as a partner at Cooper Erving. Thus, as the level of pay for city employees—including the Mayor—went steadily upward toward reality, Whalen's total income remained relatively only stable. With each raise in the city's payroll, his share of the law firm's revenues decreased. And, in fact, as his available hours for practicing law diminished along with the permissible scope of his services, that income necessarily was even further reduced.

A series of raises in the Mayor's official salary thus was non-existent as genuine additional income. The salary-reduction arrangement which denied him the benefit of the rising pay scale despite the seeming sharp improvement in his salary never was disclosed publicly, then or since.

When he finally severed his connection with the firm after five years in office, his official salary—now to become available in full—had been increased to $73,000. His income thereafter, while in office, was far less than in pre-mayoral days.

NOTES

[1] "Thomas Whalen, III: Rich in Psychic Income," by D. Michael Ross, in Albany Law School alumni magazine, 1994. (The term originated with Elliot Richardson.)

[2] The Conference of Mayors awarded two other citations in recognition of Albany's performance in certain areas: "Partnerships for Our Children" and "Partnerships with and for the Elderly." A conference-related distinction for Whalen brought the mayors of nearly two-dozen capital cities (Boston, Austin, Sacramento, etc.) to Albany for sessions on the issues which they held in common such as their respective states' fiscal policies. Whalen was serving as chairman for the Capital Cities Task Force at the time.

[3] The award, and the attention it received, were timely in another respect, as well. In 1989, a temporary "ethics commission" appointed by Governor Cuomo went haywire. Its members had been asked to look into whether ethical practices in local governments statewide might be improved. Instead, they developed a runaway prosecutorial mode, seemingly seeking glory in the idea of "bringing down" a public official. Fed the residue of a discredited federal inquiry of 1987, the commission's staff went after Whalen's neck. This clearly pleased the *Times Union*'s reporters and editors, who gave it huge attention. Despite the bad ink, the commission's staff director finally conceded that he believed Whalen had done "the best he could" under existing regulatory conditions. The commission's ultimate recommendations to Cuomo were ignored and

no legislation aimed at changing ethical standards in the state resulted. But because of the very evident hostility of the commission's staff and at least some of the members, plus the newspaper's receptivity to their insinuations, it constituted an annoyance and embarrassment for Whalen. Such an occurrence as the Conference of Mayors' award was particularly welcome as testimony to his "adherence to the highest levels of professional practice."

[4] This roster includes 3 firehouses built or rehabilitated (plus a major updating of equipment), 3 police stations, snow-removal and street-cleaning equipment, storm sewer restoration, emergency communication equipment, landfill closing and constructions, solid waste facilities, Public Works garage, recreational facilities (including new parks), affordable housing, public-building rehabilitation and construction, traffic-control signals, bath house rehabilitation, reconstruction of the public golf course, and parking facilities.

[5] Carl Touhey, who in 1973 had come closest to defeating Erastus Corning, had quickly become a Whalen supporter. The Mayor quoted him with encouraging words: "Keep trying—you're 99.4% on target." Whalen commented, "Carl was always openly supportive. I was doing a lot of the things he'd have tried if he'd become Mayor."

[6] When he took office as Mayor eight years later, Jennings accepted the salary to which the Mayor's pay had risen by that time—about 50% greater than the 1986 figure he complained about.

Away from It All

"To hear nothing but the crack of tree limbs in the cold air"—far from ringing telephones in his office—that was the ideal escape from pressures of the mayoralty that delighted and relaxed Tom Whalen. His little paean even recalls Thoreau's line about "tramping ten miles through the deepest snow to keep an appointment with a beech tree or a yellow birch or an old acquaintance among the pines." Wilderness cross-country skiing in the Adirondacks was for years one of the activities that the Whalens could best share. Together, they relished hiking and climbing, using as a base their chalet near Wells in very rural Hamilton County.

Shunning cross-country trails, they would take off on all-day wilderness skiing trips, leaving behind the beaten path and instead following old logging roads and hiking trails cut by State Park Conservationists in the back country.

"I've spent thousands of hours in the Adirondacks, either alone or with Denie and sometimes also others, and I only wish I'd discovered the area 20 years earlier, " Tom once wistfully testified.

"I could start thinking on Thursday evening or Friday morning about a weekend discovering the wealth of opportunities in the hills, mountains, rivers, streams, and peaks. . . . A mysterious draw constantly beckons, weekend after weekend." He wrote of his sentiments in an "Adirondack Life" essay in 1989.

"Fall and winter are favorite seasons for exploring.

During the fall foliage season, no part of the Adirondacks can quite equal the Blue Mountain Lake area." It is interesting and probably significant that he employed the expression "a testing way" in reference to spending "a few days in the wilderness" as he described a canoe trip from the boat livery at Blue Mountain Lake up to Raquette Lake by way of the Marion River, which flows between the two lakes and the Fulton chain of lakes.

In the Siamese Ponds Wilderness Area east of Indian Lake off Route 8, he added, "I've hiked with my daughter Laura from Route 8 to 13th Lake and camped on Elizabeth Point on that lake in North River. And I've skied the same route in the dead of winter.

"But nothing can compare to a wilderness ski into Cod Pond or Cod Pond Flow (off Route 8 on the way to Wevertown). Many times, I had the company of our golden retriever, Finn McCool.

"Finn was naturally at home in the Adirondacks. Because he loved the wilderness he became a fine trail dog.

"In one heavy Sunday morning snowfall, we skied in to the bridge at Cod Pond Flow and found ourselves smack in the middle of a herd of deer.

"All I could do was watch in amazement as 15 or 20 took off in just as many directions—while an absolutely confused dog sat on his haunches and let his head turn in a complete circle."

"Over a four-year period, Finn and I had many weekends to ourselves as Denie, pursuing her interrupted career, studied for an advanced degree in occupational therapy at Dominican College in Rockland County. Her classes were every third weekend, from September through April. For Finn and for me, these were special occasions for bonding.

"We would head north to our place in Hamilton County on a Friday night or early Saturday morning. (On occasion, my good friends Jon McCloskey and John Krueger would be with us.)

"The most memorable times were in winter. In good snow, Finn would bound ahead of my cross-country skis a few hundred yards, stop, and come back to me. Only rarely would he leave the trail itself. He would then settle into a steady trot and we would proceed in tandem. We'd do eight miles or so, then relax someplace and have a bite to eat. There I'd change my inner shirt and we'd head back the same eight miles to the car.

"Back at the cabin, it was pasta for me and a nutrient-rich meal for Finn. And then quiet time by the fire before bed.

"Finn was equally adept at climbing some of the 'High Peaks' off of Keene Valley, very rewarding for both of us, especially in the fall when the foliage was aflame. During trout season in the spring, he'd sit quietly on the banks of the river while I cast for those most elusive of all creatures."

Taking Aim on Achilles

A harsh and bitter campaign was unleashed against Albany's Mayor and his administration late in 1986, the year of celebration. Aimed directly at Whalen's tenure, his credibility, and his reputation, it earns a detailed place in a review of his administration only because it attempted so much damage (and, in some ways, succeeded).

In the outset, it focused on a one-page note of 56 words, insignificant in themselves but susceptible of a veiled and vengeful reading. History could be changed by bringing down an acclaimed Achilles whose openness might have exposed his vulnerable heel. He fought back but at great personal and professional cost.

Throughout his career, behind a lawyer's desk or a Mayor's, Tom Whalen indulged a predilection for expressing his thoughts in writing, for putting ink onto paper. Some of his department heads exchanged memos with him almost daily. In a staff meeting, one burst out with a pained request that telephone calls often should suffice.

Whalen's firm, round script had been a kind of trademark ever since it won a nun's smiling approval in the fourth grade at St. Vincent's. Instantly distinguishable, it came to increasingly indicate a writer's decisive mind, a person in control of himself, one in command.

Whether his messages to associates were communicated in his original longhand or were transcribed into typewritten form, the Whalen Method was well known indeed to all who had contact with him. He shunned the verbal. "Put it in writing" was what he wanted, and by exercising his preference, he virtually obligated a written response.

And it was this quirk, this habit, that provided the ammunition for certain of his enemies in 1986, 1987, 1988, and into 1989, a year when he had to stand for reelection. The 56 words could have been spoken in seconds on an interoffice telephone. Instead, they had to go onto an official Office of the Mayor memo form and travel two floors up in City Hall.

When asked, years later, which of his acts as Mayor he most regretted, Whalen promptly identified having needlessly written that memorandum. His words, which he had considered clear, straightforward, and proper, were marginally capable of being twisted. He paid dearly for every one of them.

* * *

In the last few days of May 1985, on the second anniversary of his having taken office, and as his election effort was heating up, Mayor Whalen accepted a call from a law firm partner, Freling H. Smith, who had received an inquiry on property assessments from a new client, First American Bank.

Smith might have directly called the city's Assessor, Bruce McDonald, and thereby averted certain later complications—but he didn't.

First American was interested in learning (as Smith told Whalen) whether—because of its late 1984 acquisition of Bankers Trust Company's Albany-area branches—the assessments on the physical properties involved would be increased or would be stable. The old-style "rollercoaster" assessment policy would have brought about a certain and prompt increase, an example of the Organization's too-familiar "Welcome, stranger" practice following real property transactions.

Whalen might have told Smith to call the Assessor—but he didn't.

After an intervening weekend, Smith's call resulted, on

June's first business day, Monday the 3rd, in the Mayor's writing a longhand note that summarized the bank's inquiry. Then the note went upstairs to McDonald.

In response the next day, McDonald enumerated the individual assessments on four properties in Albany now owned by First American, including even their parking areas.[1]

He offered his opinion:

> "Taking into consideration the merger work-out, I would think that the $823,000 total (existing) assessment would be right in the ballpark." His reply ended, "I would appreciate your advice on the above."

On Wednesday morning, when Whalen riffled through the mail, he came across McDonald's response. Reading his opinion and request for advice, the Mayor again picked up his gold Cross pen and wrote a reply to the reply. On this occasion rather than sending McDonald a longhand note, he asked Thelma Dooley in the outer office to transcribe it.

The note was one long sentence:

> "In view of the fact that the sales price for the First American transfers only related to a merger transaction between Bankers Trust Company into First American Bank,[2] I believe we should leave the matter alone until such time as we conduct an entire review of the assessments on banking properties."

Albany's notorious reputation for the "rollercoaster" trickery logically would have prompted such a query as First American's, but now the Mayor's policy had invalidated the old practice. Real estate purchasers—for homes or for commercial property—no longer were victimized by the traditional and intentionally expensive conspiracy between the city and certain favored lawyers. This change was implicit in the

McDonald-Whalen exchanges. A probability appears that the fact of this proud reform would have captured a corner of Whalen's mind as he reflected on the bank's inquiry.

Re-reading his words in the typed draft, he politely added a line, "Thanks for your interest," and signed a re-done version with his initials.

The note then went back upstairs. The matter logically seemed to be handily resolved and, he could assume, was now concluded pending the "entire review" on which the ultimate outcome was predicated.

Not quite so. In addition to the original copy to the Assessor's office and one dropped into the Mayor's files, a third copy was dispatched to the Cooper Erving office atop First American's main building, whose rounded facade dominated the corner of State and Broadway. As it turned out this figuratively was also the intersection of Whalen and Achilles.

The copy, reviewed by Freling Smith, routinely entered the firm's filing system. That single sheet with its 56 laconic words rested in a gray filing cabinet for several months.

Then one night it was removed from the file and copied—it's easy to envision the out-of-hours maneuver. The next person to read it was an agent of the Federal Bureau of Investigation. The sly intimation was of wrongdoing within the 56 words. As a substantially detached observer, Holt-Harris saw Whalen's writing such a memorandum as "ill-advised" even though the contents were "innocuous."

* * *

A reasoned reading gives an impression of Whalen's low-key agreement with the Assessor's view that the existing assessment was supportable.

To interpret the Mayor's language more harshly—namely that his words were inappropriately directing an action in the bank's favor—seems contrived, especially so because the Assessor had already volunteered a similar opinion.

But, having leaped to such a tortured and troubling interpretation, a reader motivated toward suspicion then could jump further. Such a person might assume that Whalen's connection with the bank's lawyers would motivate him to improperly use his influence in the bank's behalf.

This biased assumption, in fact, was implicit in the act of stealing the memorandum from the lawyers' files and delivering it to an FBI agent. Whenever such an allegation of wrongdoing by any government officer reaches the hands of a federal agency, the United States Attorney is required by law to inquire into the matter.

* * *

The U.S. Attorney's first request for certain records arrived at City Hall in late November 1986. (Later published references insisted that the inquiry had begun in August or even earlier; clearly, such information—if true—came from within the investigation itself.)

Whalen consulted with McArdle and the two senior advisers, Holt-Harris and Bergan. The elderly judge saw it all as a political plot—an effort to "get a Democrat," one of high standing in the county Organization. (This was prior to the very real legal troubles that beset County Executive Coyne in the 1990s.)

"Make sure you fight this," Bergan exhorted. "Don't treat this lightly. Go after it as strongly as you can."

Whalen, however, was unpersuaded that the motivation was political. He attributed it to one FBI agent gone out of control, dominated by aspiration for a career mark and public attention. He did, however, accept the advice of another retired jurist, U.S. District Judge James T. Foley, to consult with Brian F. Mumford, a former Assistant United States Attorney, who later was retained to represent the city and, incidentally, the Mayor.

It was January 1987 before the first startling publication of what quickly became labeled an "FBI investigation of the Mayor."

Within the next six weeks, more than a dozen articles were published in the Albany newspapers, as well as three editorials. If all these are read consecutively, some striking angles appear:

• Mayor Whalen's June 5 note to Assessor McDonald (as insinuatingly leaked to reporters by U.S. Government employees) was only the starting point for the newspapers' attention to the federal inquiry, and became the rationale for numerous articles unrelated to the memo's substance.

• The identity of several law firm clients and the nature of their business activities suddenly also became "news." The information that formed the genesis of these articles obviously had been removed from the firm's files by someone with access to confidential material.

• Cooper Erving Savage, which in 1985 had seven partners, including a managing partner, became "Whalen's firm" in reiterated references. The implication was that he controlled it and managed its affairs, though his role steadily diminished in the previous five years.

• Although the June 5 memo was cited and paraphrased repeatedly, quite evidently its actual text had not been seen by reporters but, rather, described to them incompletely and inaccurately. His words, "I believe we should let it rest" were transformed in paraphrase:

> The words affirming the position already offered byMcDonald, "*I believe we should . . .*" became "*recommended*" repeatedly in newspaper accounts. But a variety of other suggestively active verbs appeared as well: "*urged*," "*requested*," "*advised*," "*suggested*," "*asked*" (not to raise the assessment); "*opposed*" (an assessment increase); "*reportedly argued*" and "*argued against*" an increase. Important subtleties of meaning were ignored, as were the concepts of accuracy and fairness.

Typically, a reference would be, ". . . a memo Whalen wrote *opposing any increase* in assessments for one of his law firms clients," or, ". . . a memo asking *the city Assessor not to raise* property tax assessments on buildings owned by a client of the Mayor's law firm." Scrupulous editing—even nominal editing, objectively approached—should have caught up with the reporters' misleading inexactness.　Meanwhile, apparently, those in authority who knew the facts failed to offer correct versions.

　• "Questions *have been raised*" became reporters' favored rationale for rehashing the articles.　One went this way: "Questions have arisen concerning *possible conflicts of* interest," but two days later the language was subtly though significantly altered: "Questions have arisen in the last few weeks about *the* conflict between Whalen's roles. . . ."　(The italicizing has been added for this account.)　No indication was offered as to where the questions originated.

　　The reach of the inaccurate reporting was exemplified by an article published in Schenectady by the *Gazette*, which reported that Whalen "had sent a memorandum to the city Assessor suggesting that the assessment . . . had been boosted too much."　This particular mistake was repeated later, quoted in a magazine article.

　　Requests for files made by the U.S. Attorney to the Mayor's office and city departments became "Federal authorities seized" . . . such documents.

　　For years after Richard Nixon's resignation in disgrace, young people—drawn to journalism by the ideal of replicating a Woodward/Bernstein feat—searched relentlessly for other instances of malfeasance.　In their zeal, excesses occasionally occurred when facts of fairness got in the way of a good story.

　　"There are too many journalists who are gunslingers," said Carl Bernstein, the 1970s reporting partner of Bob Woodward, in responding to Tim Russert's "Meet the Press" question about the belief they were responsible for having created "a whole generation of gunslinger journalists who just want to bring down government officials."　He mentioned "a feeling of sadness that . . . it has followed what happened in Watergate."

* * *

So with Whalen and his 56 words: Despite what was published repeatedly, he did not remotely refer to the assessments as having been "boosted"; he did not "request" or "urge" or "argue." He agreed with the Assessor's own judgment and offered a reason to "leave the matter alone" until all banks' real-property holdings were reviewed (and clearly assumed this review would take place).

But none of this would have come about except for others' acts: first, removal by an unidentified person of the memorandum from the file (to which he had access) and delivering it to a government agent, obviously for a trouble-making purpose. And then, at least equally important, misbehavior within the FBI in permitting one agent to excessively pursue the resulting inquiry in a declared effort to "get" Whalen.

For months, there was no official indication of any activity by the United States Attorney, who would have had to present the matter to a grand jury if it had been deemed sufficient to warrant indictment. Whalen was irate, however, about reports the agent in question was publicly predicting prosecution.[3] (Ten years later, *Vanity Fair* magazine published an article reporting that the agent had been transferred from Albany "for lack of effectiveness" and that this agent was disciplined in Atlanta because of Bureau misbehavior in investigating the 1996 Olympics bomb episode.)

After a full year, in December 1987, a brief letter from the government informed the Mayor that the case had been closed for lack of merit.

NOTES

¹ These properties included a main office downtown and three branches on the city's main arteries: Central, Washington, and Delaware avenues.

At that time, Albany had 14 commercial and savings banks, plus more than a dozen branches. The dominant banks were Norstar (formerly State Bank of Albany and subsequently a temporary part of the Fleet banks of Rhode Island) and Key Bank (an outgrowth of National Commercial Bank).

² The Bankers Trust branches in Albany (and elsewhere in the Capital Region) had been acquired from the First Trust Company, a long-established bank of considerable prominence and influence which had long ago grown from another bank known as the Albany Trust. Both First American and Bankers Trust were represented by the same law firm, Cooper Erving Savage, which for many years maintained a very close relationship with First Trust. The firm's senior partner, Edward S. Rooney, had been the bank's president before his death in 1970, same year that First Trust was absorbed by Bankers Trust. The law firm, occupying a full floor, was the only tenant in the bank's six-story building. Author's note: I believe that this text of the memo has not been published previously.

³ After leaving office, Whalen responded to an inquiry about the source of the bitter enmity he had experienced throughout his mayoralty, and how he had handled it personally.

"I guess I figured that there were certain things one had to go through to accomplish a major task like reforming a city," he wrote, "and I was willing to put up with it all."

Seeking to find a reason behind some of his political opposition, he suggested that "I think (they) saw me as 'lace curtain Irish,' and therefore undeserving of trust or support." He identified two of his persistent critics as having "spread vicious rumors about me for years (drinking, womanizing, car accidents, cash deals, etc.)."

"I didn't try to cultivate anyone in (that) camp, and maybe in retrospect that was a mistake, although I wonder, if I had, what it would have done to me as a person. Same with the T-U."

"Should I have been more compliant?" (to the Old Guard's wishes). "There is not a doubt that I was headstrong on a lot of things—and this probably caused me trouble that would have been avoided if I had behaved as they wanted."

Priorities, Dreams—and
Action, *Action*

When Tom Whalen expected his staff to act quickly, he let the commissioners know the urgency he felt. His tactic was unmistakable and distinctive.

Mayoral "Green Streakers" became renowned though hardly popular among his two-dozen departmental chiefs. *Green means this memo requires either immediate action or an immediate response* was the legend imprinted over a green border on memorandums dealing with matters which Whalen regarded as high-priority (a small portion of the many dozens that he dispatched daily). These notes were generally understood by recipients as meaning that they had precisely one day to perform as requested or directed.

Most of the memos—many of them handwritten—were issued in a milder climate. But his ingrained principle of regular two-way communication prevailed for the entire decade. "He wrote to us and we wrote to him," was one commissioner's summary of the experience.

With his radio tuned to classical music programming and a pile of correspondence and some notations of his own on the desk, the Mayor methodically reviewed their contents for their potential role in his communiqués to his troops. Dusty Miller, the office's handyman, distributed them to City Hall offices. Departments located in the field, however, tended to dispatch couriers to the Mayor's office—sometimes twice a day—to be certain they were fully up to date: "It was important to keep in touch!"

The secretarial staff originated some memos, such as those informing all commissioners of the time and location of a forthcoming Whalen press conference, for the Mayor liked to have a show of support then. Too, he wanted his principal aides to learn and be aware of his policies and his thinking. "There wasn't a day when we didn't individually have contact with the Mayor, and we grew intellectually as he progressed," another staff member recalled. All department heads reported directly to him (and he eventually regarded this as an administrative weakness he never made time to rectify).

A distinction between his managerial style and Corning's was actual even though the concept of the chief who expects to be in on everything appears common to each. In Corning's era, a department head was kept unaware of what others were doing although all were reporting to the Mayor. There was little interaction, if any. Whalen's contacts, on the other hand, tended to bring people together through practices ranging from distributing "cc" copies widely, to employing *ad hoc* task forces in which several departmental heads would work together. The entire supervisory group came together for an hour once a month in a session with the advantage of a firm agenda. And the Mayor regularly escorted them out of town for "retreats" to enhance opportunity for personal interchanges and comfort in the team concept, as well as for promoting ideation and advancing new programs.

And then there was the inspired occasion when Whalen invited all the commissioners to join him for a production of "Fiorello" at The Egg. (Seeing LaGuardia in action might make them more appreciative of the Whalen style, Green Streakers and all?)

* * *

The span of the Mayor's attention was broad but also precise. To his Parks commissioner, he wrote (on a day that happened to be his fourth anniversary in office): "Academy Park is looking a little seedy and needs some work." Part of the sprucing up meant adding "a few more concrete benches." "Keep up the good work," the commissioner was advised.

In his volunteered supervisory chores, he worked to maintain a positive tone, but the mandate for results could not be missed. "I'm sure you have on your list of things the maintenance of the new trail around Buckingham Pond. I walked it last nite and it needs some work," he remarked at another time. The "crew to do it" was given a few specifics for attention. "You probably will need a couple of loads of stone," his handwritten note suggested.

At least six city employees, including three lawyers, a commissioner, and a commissioner's deputy, became involved in trying to find a just solution to a knotty question: Should the county historical society be allowed to graze a small flock of sheep on the Ten Broeck Mansion property as a low-budget way to mow three acres of grass? At one stage the exchange of memos included a reminder of a cautionary note to be found in Matthew 7:15, as well as a City Code citation. Copies of the wordy exchange eventually landed on the mayoral desk. Matthew 7:15 puzzled him but even before he could consult his Bible the lawyers had supplied the significance of the reference (the wolf, etc.). His sheepish reply was, "Let them (the historical society) do it!"

* * *

A major initiative, one very close to Whalen's heart, sought to improve living conditions for families of low-to-moderate income. His aspirations were high enough and their realization full enough to support one of the legs on which the All-America City award was based.

Faced with little support from the federal government and with the state's programs stalled by scanty funding, Whalen aggressively explored alternate sources to help alleviate the crunch. Significant steps included the key decisions to merge the Albany Community Development Agency and the city's Department of Housing Development, aimed at increasing efficiency and coordination as well as encouraging innovative ideas. Critical to these efforts was the hiring in 1986 of Joseph Pennisi, who had been with the state's Division of Housing and Community Renewal, to be Housing Commissioner, and Steve Longo as executive director.

The Capital Affordable Housing Funding Corporation, which coordinates the involvement of banks in obtaining affordable housing funds, received major support from the city. Even more importantly, the Mayor incorporated the Capital City Housing Development Fund Company as a not-for-profit corporation acting as a low-income promoter in partnership with private developers. With Pennisi and Longo as the staff, this fund was able to build 30 new two-family houses each year at a $90,000 cost, to which the state contributed about $25,000. The homes sold at $60,000 to low-income families, who received a 15-year staggered tax abatement and the expectation that they could augment their ability to carry their costs by renting out the second dwelling. A Housing Trust Fund renovated 20 to 30 historic homes a year. In the South End, Arbor Hill, West Hill, and North Albany, neglected and disenfranchised neighborhoods started to change. A crucial bar had been raised for performance in providing homes for first-time homebuyers and others who, without such a helping hand, could barely dream of living in decent housing. Over one six-year period, for example, more than 1,400 such dwellings were opened up.

* * *

A revived appeal of city living—very much in line with Whalen's insistence that Albany had "come alive" with excitement—was evident in the mid-1980s. And it did pan out in the 1990 census, when fears of worsening in the population hemorrhage were revealed as merely alarmist.

Chart lines depicting prior history and the 1980s record provide graphic testimony as to the actuality of the Whalen premise. If one man could dam a flood, it appears that this is what happened in Albany within a decade.

Estimates looking ahead to the 1990 census pessimistically had placed the population of this Toqueville-on-Hudson at no more than 97,000 (compared with fractionally over 100,000 in 1980)[1] and perhaps as low as 94,000.

But contrary elements were at work. Among these can be counted the addition of housing units in the 1980s; abandonment of the traditional roller-coaster taxation practices (cynically labeled the "Welcome, stranger" policy); the reassurance implicit in the Albany Plan to combat drug abuse while providing employment for many young people at critical points; the rejuvenated, enjoyable climate for the performing arts; cooperative partnerships in encouraging business enterprise. And certainly not least a steadily growing confidence of fair play by a straight-shooting government.

In his late-1985 enumeration of key concerns as his first full term began, Whalen included a wistful objective to be reached before the coming census, then only five years distant. "Set a goal," he wrote, "for an increase in population by 1990."

Among the standards for judging leadership in elected officials is the ability to create programs reversing negative trends and perceptions. Whalen's timely responses to what he perceived as the factors in a decline in his city's livability were intended to positively impact Albany's status amid an era of transience.

A month later, he described[2] the declining population as "one of the most serious" among "clearly discernible trends that—if not dealt with early and carefully—could have a devastating affect on the city's future." He contended that central Albany, "losing a large part of its middle class to the suburbs," had sustained a depleted tax base: Family incomes in the remaining core were not only falling, they were down compared to households elsewhere in the region. Retailers' business downtown had plunged by 53% in a 20-year period.

In his 1986 inaugural address he declared that "those

dark days" of out-migration were past. He had already sensed a clue to potential improvement. As the remainder of the decade unfolded he could recognize further substantial indications that Albany now was really bucking the population trend. Buoyed by such a prospect, he worked diligently with all population-sensitive areas of his government to encourage collaboration in ensuring that every resident would be found and counted.

This effort was the beneficiary of an agreeable happenstance which he seized upon to help upgrade the head count. The regional director for the Census Bureau, Arthur Dukakis, had visited City Hall in the earliest months of Whalen's mayoralty. They found a variety of shared interests and as token of their congeniality Dukakis prescribed pointers for obtaining the best result in the oncoming census.

The outcome actually bore out Whalen's distant hope and justified all the special labors. The population's bottom line shunned those dismal prospects of 94,000-97,000 (which would have resulted in repercussions when state-aid formulas were applied). Contrary to all predictions, defying experience throughout northeastern industrial cities, and in the face of national trends, Albany's official population at the opening of the century's final decade was certified as 101,082, virtually identical with 1980.

This arguably was reflective of residents' (and potential residents') attitude toward Albany as a place to call home. And unofficial estimates in 1994 almanacs put the population at nearly 105,000 (as of 1993, Whalen's final year in office[3]).

The startling performance—reversal of the steady downward slide, and success in fighting losses experienced by old cities everywhere—almost surely would not have been accomplished in Albany except for a dynamic mayoralty. First, through a positive response to the large changes Whalen had initiated; second, through his energetic search for previously missed inhabitants; and, additionally, his constructive friendship with Dukakis. The record exemplifies the "pride" of which he spoke so often, the "spirit" with which he sought to endow his entire flock, a momentum of enthusiasm and activity.

It is as though the impossible was achieved because he willed it so; a tangible tribute to what he accomplished for his city. Not something to be determined by numbers alone; rather, validation by underlying circumstances that converted the barely plausible into a reality.

* * *

To make sure that Whalen was on top of the hourly demands of the Mayor's job, his office kept three identical appointment calendar books meticulously up to date.

He maintained one at his desk; his secretary, Jo-Ann Trim, had one always close at hand; and so did Pat Storm in the reception office. They needed to be current on where the Mayor should be, reminded of when he was expected elsewhere later—and, for the staff's information, where he was to be found when not busy in the mahogany-paneled corner office.

The obligations of a 60-hour to 70-hour weekly schedule were never-ending. Such a Mayor was inevitably tied to the requirements of the big picture, though his time and attention could be requisitioned by any one of tens of thousands of citizens and their seemingly endless desire to come together for meetings.

When there were late-morning meetings in the office, these frequently turned into impromptu lunches, with sandwiches brought in, ordinarily from City Hall's basement café. Whalen's order almost always called for turkey on rye with a little bacon and a bit of mayonnaise added, plus a container of coffee or iced tea, depending on the season.

* * *

Despite the demands on the Mayor's normal schedule, he insisted on making the time for a 30-question interview requested by a SUNYA graduate student as part of a proposed "scholarly study of the transition from Mayor Corning to you." The student hoped "to reach a better understanding of the informal processes of leadership in a city famous for its informal political processes."

This idea clearly intrigued Whalen, for even after the interview he elaborated on his responses in further detail. He wrote out more than 3,000 words intended to enrich the student's understanding of those "informal processes"—although the young man wasn't a constituent, and had addressed his request to *Mayor Whelan.*

* * *

A renewal of recreational and competitive rowing on the Hudson at Albany had its genesis in 1984, when Peter Kiernan and Lew Swyer paid a purposeful call on the Mayor. They had been approached by two young physicians who hoped to reintroduce the city's waterfront to rowing, a sport they'd mastered as college students. Would the city be interested officially in helping to make that feasible? They had chosen their intermediaries well, for both older men also had been skilled and ardent oarsmen and were especially well known to the Mayor.

At that point, Whalen was innocent of knowledge about rowing, though generally aware that in the late 1800s the Hudson's waters had offered classically challenging opportunities for privileged young swells. They were known to row, row their boats gracefully and speedily as far as Poughkeepsie in spirited races that often were paced by trainloads of spectators taking advantage of the water-level tracks. Sculls such as theirs are built in lengths varying from 27 to 62 feet, though scarcely a foot in width.

Everyone was correctly assuming that the idea needed the city's assistance as well as the advantage of an official blessing. In Whalen, they had found their man. Largely because of respectful regard for the two friends who were propositioning him, he readily gave them and the physicians several opportunities to talk over what steps were needed to turn their wish into reality.

An early outcome was a new boathouse built by the city along the river's shore. Swyer and Kiernan came up with additional sources of funding for purchase of shells—and the reintroduction of rowing on the Hudson was under way.

The second step was to recognize and encourage the sport's rebirth in a regatta. Whalen and several of his department heads involved themselves in promoting the idea. "With the city's blessing and material support," Whalen recapped the episode, "the regatta came into being and prospered with the guidance of Peter and Lew. I believe the idea inspirationally originated with Peter, who was an expert and enthusiastic oarsman." When the first challenge was held, the Mayor was pointedly on hand to observe with interest; he decided it all looked like fun—the active, demanding fun that always had captivated him and provoked a significant response. As the next season began, he was prepared to lower himself into a single recreational shell, one wide enough to make tipping over difficult. He rowed in it with mounting enthusiasm and commitment for a year. Predictably, he would go where there was action. John Krueger, another novice, provided company in a comparable shell. In another year, they graduated to racing shells. Later, Whalen became owner of both a double and a single shell.

Over a dozen intervening years, he planned to be on the river—in season—two mornings a week for some 40 minutes, from 6:45 to nearly 7:30, an ideal time because so little else would be going on. After a shower, he could arrive in his office by 8 o'clock.

In a collision on the river with another shell, Whalen sustained a severe injury one spring morning while still in office. He later resumed his routine, and gave up rowing only as he approached his mid-sixties.

The regattas grew into a major annual event for which he was extravagantly proud—matching his personal involvement—and was known to enthusiastically predict that the regatta would be a staple of the Albany recreational scene for many years. Within a short time of his leaving office, however, the city withdrew its support and the regatta was no more, perhaps a victim of latent class-conscious suspicions and antagonisms.

* * *

Encouraging "Albany citizens to be part of the renaissance of their city," in Whalen's words, brought about the formation early in 1985 of an Office of Volunteer Services. The first director, Dale Crary, set about the task for enlisting enthusiasts who could help staff a variety of services, some of them in City Hall departments and still more in unmapped areas that essentially were an outgrowth of the new-found activism. To avoid any impression that volunteers might replace city employees, they were assigned only tasks that did not involve payroll positions' work.

The inspiration for Volunteer Services was modeled on a program in Baltimore that had received national acknowledgement. On a visit there in the fall of 1984 to confer with Mayor William Donald Schaefer, Whalen was so impressed that he provided for funding for a similar agency in his second budget.

The volunteers—one of whom rather typically commented that the work was "a lot better than sitting in the house looking out the window"—might be doing clerical work in the water department, preparing documents for microfilming at the records center, assisting in researching historic buildings, or on the other hand engaging in more outgoing efforts: acting as a guide for tourists or as a receptionist in City Hall's rotunda, taking responsibility for flower beds in parks, visiting patients in nursing homes, even grooming the police department's horses.

A "Beautification Committee" headed by Mary Jo Mincy and Lee Lindstrom did acclaimed work for the Tricentennial year and, joined by Peter Rumora, continued with Academy Park restoration, flower boxes on public buildings and flowerpots on lamp posts. They splurged on decorations for holidays and for the annual "First Night." Parks Commissioner Dick Barrett cited his volunteers supervising the planting of tulips for the festival while others designed the summer gardens in Washington Park, drew up bid specifications, and supervised the contractor who did the major work. They were, the Commissioner said, "a rich treasure; without them there's no way we could care for 300 flower beds all over the city."

Once well under way, the volunteer program enlisted scores of people at any one time. Their committed efforts each year totaled 10,000 hours—the equivalent of some 1,400 full work days or nearly 300 weeks' worth annually. All this, said the Mayor enthusiastically, "enhanced the services of city government and broadened the scope of civic and cultural events held throughout the year." He used an engraved card, individually signed, as a thank-you for "volunteered time and talents enabling Albany to become a 'world-class city' and a lovely place in which to live."

"We have done much toward restoring a sense of heritage, of pride, and of the will to prevail," he wrote at the time of his reelection to a second full term.

* * *

Albany's "First Night" tradition had its first observance, fittingly, in the last hours of the Tricentennial year. But it had its origin earlier in 1986 in the Whalens' kitchen.

The idea had been voiced by Denie as she read the *Wall Street Journal* during breakfast. "You ought to try something like this," she suggested rather pointedly, handing over the newspaper folded to display the article which reported on the success of Boston's pioneering New Year's Eve celebration.

"I thought the concept was appealing," the Mayor said in a conversation about having adapted the observance for Albany. He cut out the article and took it to the office. ("Took it to work," actually was the nature of his old-time reference.)

After taking up the possibilities with two aides, he asked that they explore it further by buying Boston's advisory package of procedures for other cities' adaptation: "Let's see what's involved."

The first decision was a positive one: The venues provided by major downtown business centers and the areas many public buildings would offer adequate settings. The next question, one of sources of support, was quickly answered by banks and utilities, offering volunteered staffing and financing.

By the night of December 31, arrangements were completed for such entertainments as Irish step-dancing in the basement of St. Mary's Church, ballroom dancing at Norstar Plaza, gospel singing at Sweet Pilgrim Church, a rhythm band at the arts center, and Albany Pro Musica at St. Peter's Church. Nearly 8,000 people turned out for the first First Night, a number that progressively grew each year until Saratoga Springs began its own observance, which drained off a substantial number of First Nighters. In spite of this factor, the series continued a successful run into the new century, including events that witnessed the arrival of a millennium.

* * *

Although the selection of Albany as an All-America City was the unquestioned high point of a two-year deluge of honors, a quite different citation surely was even more appealing to the Mayor emotionally. It had a unique quality among all the citations that recognized not only the city's achievements in a variety of areas but also, either directly or implicitly, Whalen's personal dedication and labors.[4]

Among these, the award conferred in 1991 by the Kennedy Center Imagination Celebration, a national festival program, has to be ranked as the one that almost certainly would have been the most gratifying to him. It lacked the public attention and the obvious prestige of the All-America City award from the National Civic League, but sentimentally, on a personal level, being cited for contributions to the arts was deeply affecting. So much so that the citation itself is deserving of quotation here:

"Mayor Whalen has truly revitalized the City of Albany. His leadership has wielded enormous impact on the cultural climate of the state capital. Vital demonstrations of Mayor Whalen's support of the arts include city festivals designed for everyone, the Imagination Celebration, free public theatre in beautiful Washington Park—the wonderful musicals produced by Park Playhouse, Inc., and the absorbing performances by the Actors Shakespeare Company.

"Mayor Whalen has created a City Arts District. He provides rent-free facilities for various arts organizations and maintains an active city office which enriches life in Albany through the city's annual calendar of festivals, parades, and unique special events. The Mayor identifies outstanding performing companies, outside of Albany, such as L'Ensemble, Albany's Berkshire Ballet, and the Actors Shakespeare Company, and invites them to become resident companies in the capital city.

"He established a special committee to make recommendations for a long-range strategic plan for the arts in Albany and has now established an Arts Commission to implement these recommendations.

"Mayor Whalen is intent on making the arts a vital component of life in Albany. Beyond these unusual achievements, the Mayor not only supports the annual Imagination Celebration but participates in it personally each year. And this year, he had named the celebration the 'Arts Centerpiece' of Albany's 1991 'I Love New York Albany Festival.'

"For his unique role in the arts and arts-in-education, it is a great honor to present Mayor Whalen with the Kennedy Center/Alliance Award for Distinguished Leadership."

* * *

The All-America City designation was noteworthy for
a variety of reasons, including the credibility it bestowed on
Whalen's aims and effort over the years—and on the national
boost given to his stature in his home base where opponents
continued their unfriendly critiques. And surely it was balm
for his own esprit, because though the honor was in the city's
name, he knew that without Tom Whalen no such distinction
could possibly have come Albany's way. Sharing a podium at
the White House with President Bush to receive the award
must have brought him a share of the pride which he'd been
urging on Albany's citizens for so long.

NOTES

[1] The population had been 140,000 before 1950, about
130,000 in 1960, down another 12% to 116,000 in 1970, an additional 15,000 or 16,000 by 1980. The decline (made sharper by the
"South Mall" project of the 1960s) was nearly 30%, before being stabilized in the 1980s.

[2] In *City and State*, newspaper of public business and
finance, a publication of Crain Communications, Inc., January 1986.

[3] Unfortunately, the momentum was not sustained in the
post-Whalen years. The 2000 census for Albany showed a population of 95,658.

[4] A deluge of citations for Albany as "among the best cities"
in the country within certain categories were received in a single
year, 1991. The Zero Population Growth (ZPG) national organization termed Albany "the most livable city in the U.S." The Albany
real estate market was designated by *U.S. News & World Report* as
one of its "Top 25 Markets (where homeowners will do best)"; and
two closely related distinctions were cited by *Fortune* magazine,

which declared Albany to be "One of the 50 Best Cities for Business in America," while the *National Employment Review* called it "One of the 10 Hottest Places to Work." If these areas of recognition might be considered as transitory, two other citations undoubtedly were even more impermanent: "Fastest-growing financial center" and "Fifth-lowest office vacancy rate."

When the Party's Over . . .

". . . And there's a politician
That has read and thought. . . ."
—William Butler Yeats[1]

As the Nixon White House staff was cracking wide open in the spring of 1973, a presidential speech-writer resigned to become a columnist for the *New York Times*. In one of his first essays, he wrote obliquely about grand juries, and in passing quoted the acerbic G. K. Chesterton: "The horrible thing about all legal officials . . . is not that they are wicked (some of them are good), nor that they are stupid (several of them are quite intelligent); it is simply that *they have got used to it*."

In Albany, a young municipal court judge, upon reading the quoted paragraph, marked it, then clipped that column by William Safire and stored it away among his personal papers.

The concept of the well-meaning public servant who has stayed on too long had greatly impressed Tom Whalen. And it evidently jibed intimately with a doctrine of his own: As his six-year term in the minor judiciary approached an end in 1975, he declined reelection, and explained: "I always felt it was a one-term job."

* * *

Ten years after he tucked away the Chesterton gibe, Whalen was fated to succeed in office a mayor who hardly could be regarded as burdened by a Chestertonian sensitivity.

And just 10 years beyond *that*, he announced his personal decision to leave the mayoralty. In addition to the Chesterton comment, he had in later years come across a parallel and even more detailed advocacy of term limits. From it, he borrowed some of the language he used in his withdrawal announcement.

He expressed the hope that people from many walks of life would temporarily abandon their occupations or professions "and come and partake in the affairs of government," as he had. But, the Mayor added, "those called to public service should stay only as long as needed; after making their contribution they should return to their chosen vocations.

"And then others would come forward and do the same in an on-going process of participatory government."

He linked these motivating thoughts to a theory of the founding fathers who had originated the concept that "the farmer would lay down his plow, the teacher his books of learning, the doctor his stethoscope, and (like me) the lawyer his law books" for a relatively brief period of public service. (One of the Whalen commissioners, Michael Haydock of the Buildings Department, reached deep into history to cite a precedent in the context of temporary public service. Learning of the Mayor's decision, he wrote to him with praise for having chosen "the route of Cincinnatus.")[2]

The Mayor was describing this ideal transition on March 1, 1993, in the City Hall rotunda. A standing-room-only throng was on hand, awaiting disclosure of the future he would seek for himself and his city. In effect, it was the keystone in a review of a 10-year tenure.

In essence, his ideas—and his behavior—were wholly attuned to the term-limits principle as widely advocated (and less widely practiced) throughout the country. His career as Mayor, two whole terms and a sizable fraction (65%) of another, was a reasonable cutoff point. It's worth noting, however, that he did give active consideration to serving another term, and if he had decided to go for it, the principle would have taken it on the chin.

In departing so dramatically in spirit from his predecessor's historic career as a city's chief executive, Mayor Whalen underscored the many and significant ways in which he distanced himself from the expectations and performance of the Corning era.[3]

* * *

When *did* the Mayor decide that it was time to go—that slightly more than 10-1/2 years in office would be enough? That dramatic period, incidentally, was almost precisely one-quarter of Erastus Corning's tenure.

He frankly sought the opinions of a circle of friends who talked over with him his alternatives as the election year of 1993 approached. These gatherings tended to meld into the birth sessions of what came to be known, among a rather select circle, as the Albany Civic Forum.

The friends were split: Some advocated staying on. "You've got a good team. It's functioning well. Why drop it in midstream?"

"Don't be precipitous," Bill Hennessy, the party's former state chairman, urged.

Whalen heard counsel from others urging his retiring, but the factors for leaving were largely within his own mind. "If I don't leave now," he reasoned, "doors will close. I would be in my mid-60s. Some opportunities wouldn't be there. I want to leave office with a record of accomplishment—but good sense tells me that I've done that." Anita Loos put it more succinctly—"Leave them while you're looking good"—in *Gentlemen Prefer Blondes*, terming it "an old adage."

As the Mayor himself saw his situation, and as he described his ideas and feelings to these supporters, he recognized a "real tug-of-war" within himself.

"I would be comfortable to stay on," he said, adding, however, a qualifier: "*I think.*"

"Because I thoroughly enjoyed what I was doing," he explained later, "the decision was more difficult."

He weighed the negatives about remaining in office and found them unpersuasive: Difficult fiscal decisions would need to be made, as Dan Klepak had repeatedly—pointedly?—warned, but the economy was on the upswing after some tough years. The visible issues of governing the city appeared to be much like those he had experienced during the decade.

Klepak, a pessimist by nature, invariably provided a worst-case scenario. He was vivid now, true to his fashion, in arguing that the budgetary issues he presented merely pictured the reality of national doldrums the new Clinton administration was not likely to shake off. Whalen, for his part in these exchanges, was greatly inclined to discount much of Klepak's outlook. In shaping his ultimate judgment for or against a third term, he put aside the iffy fiscal circumstances. If he continued in office he and his administration would meet them head-on as just one more challenge.

"Even in the years when we were building the accumulated fund balance, this wasn't 'fat city,'" he rationalized, noting for the record that his administration had accomplished fiscal miracles in circumstances that were generally miserable for governments everywhere.

Family preferences weighed heavily for a return to private life and against the demands of public office. Ultimately, this very human emotional element appears to have been the main factor as he cast the deciding vote.

* * *

But where were the people who were going to "come forward" in what many Albanians might regard as an act of self-immolation?

Whalen's rather romantic view of how his progressive

stewardship of the city's affairs could be effectively extended was as unrealized in the event as unreal in prospect.

Repeatedly, he voiced the wistful hope that an unidentified citizen would emerge from the relative handful of clearly "acceptable" Albanians who would fit a profile that might be described in this way:

A male northern European, physically able and within an age range of 40 to 60, devoid of lurid scandal, untoward debt or other disagreeable handicaps such as an unduly strident anti-Organization record, but preferably bringing decent name-recognition or some heartwarming success story.

This formula, though never put into words, means that the pool of prospects necessarily was (and is) shallow, and not very wide.

Whoever the prospects might have been at the time, their thoughts clearly were elsewhere. Their motivation to "come forward" had been dulled by new economic realism. And ancient apprehensions hung over from days when volunteering was not healthy.

As a clincher, if other rationalizations weren't enough, the city had been regularly exposed to the example of the public thrashing a Mayor apparently could expect if his policies or personality offended an editor. This unquestionably would be a turn-off for any resident who otherwise might consider the position as a route to important public service rather than as an outlet for self-satisfying ambition.

"I should have been more serious about consolidating my political position," Whalen said in later years. "I really hadn't been much interested in the power that Judge Bergan could see for me. But I should have paid more attention. And been more active in looking for a successor."

His failure to have done those chores left him without a viable candidate he could support for the party's 1993 mayoralty nomination. Instead, two self-promoted alternatives— both of whom he regarded as unsuitable—were the available choices. His history with one of them—Harold L. Joyce, for the past two years the party's county chairman—was of dreary contentiousness marked by impatience on Whalen's part toward what he insistently saw as Joyce's Old Guard associations, attitudes, and abilities; and suspicions by Joyce about the Mayor's associations, attitudes, and loyalties. Harold's profile was of honest, stolid support for many of the old ways, with public-payroll jobs at the axis of the city's governance. He was thoroughly sold on the jobs-and-more-jobs credo. Whalen's distaste for such a policy weighed heavily in his failure to support Joyce although Jennings demonstrably bore much more ill-will to the Mayor than did Joyce. Whalen's strict adherence to what has been termed "mere principle" kept him officially neutral.

Joyce remained a hero among the party's Regulars who nettled Whalen because—as he saw it—they couldn't understand his aims and methods. Joyce had said—as Whalen drily remembered—that "I never would understand how to deal with the ward leaders; that I wasn't capable of doing that."

Joyce, in fact, seemed to be of at least two minds about what Whalen was doing for the city—and doing to their party. At one point in the Mayor's second term, he stood back for a perspective and delivered this assessment:

"When he first came in, a lot of people questioned who he was, where he was from, and where he was going.

"He has angered a few—but he has satisfied most."

These several words tersely—and fairly—sum up Whalen's imprint and impression though stopping short of weighing the value of his service. When put on the spot by reporters somewhat later Joyce was more diffident about finding positive words, as described previously in chapters "One Hundred Precious Days" and "Crossing the Delaware."

The record of the other alternative, Gerald D. Jennings, was so anti-Whalen that choosing Joyce would have seemed to be the Mayor's best option. But he appeared stuck in an idealism—in effect, "some patriot will step forward and take his turn"—which insisted that the ideal person would turn up, gratefully committed to carry on Whalen's policies and goals.

He deferred effective action until finally undertaking a late-hour search and then surrendering to inevitability.

Sorely stung by Jennings's attacks over the years, he was pardonably motivated to rebuff his candidacy. But, committed to a hands-off posture, he deliberately refrained from using the factual criticisms which he wrote out in several long-hand pages. If released, these might have won for Joyce a bitter primary with Jennings. For Joyce, it was "his to lose"—and he rather narrowly lost. Numerous reasons were offered, but an underlying cause likely was that enough Democrats, dubious about the Old Guard, turned to the only available alternative, his "maverick" opponent whose plausibility as a candidate had been validated—if not created—by his consistent press notices. Jennings's very public belittling of Whalen and its derisive personal quality had created an irreconcilable barrier.

So by virtue of Whalen's long-standing pessimism about successfully recruiting an attractive candidate, together with establishing lofty ideal qualities for such a person, he became unable to stop the one politician most responsible for making his mayoralty appear less successful than his record of accomplishment truly warranted.

* * *

Some four months before the end of his term, as he prepared a major speech,[4] the Mayor jotted a notation reminding himself that he "would love to weave" into his text three sentences written by Theodore Roosevelt.

Their brashly defiant language surely spoke volumes about Tom Whalen's view of his own career, just as TR's choice of phrase declared his thoughts about his presidency.

"It is not the critic who counts, not the one who points out how the strong man stumbled or how the doer of deeds might have done them better.

"The credit belongs to the man who is actually in the arena, whose face is matted with sweat and dust and blood, who strives valiantly; who errs and comes up short again and again, who knows the great enthusiasms, the great devotions, and spends himself in a worthy cause.

"Who, if he wins, knows the triumph of high achievement, and who, if he fails, at least fails while daring greatly so that his place shall never be with those cold and timid souls who know neither victory or defeat."

The goals, the challenges, the triumphs, and failings within the offices held by the Mayor of Albany late in the 20th century and the President of the United States eight decades earlier are on different planes. But nonetheless striking parallels are evident in the kind of person who dares to rise to his particular circumstance, draw his sword, and confront fate's dragon when others would sit or flee.

A vigorously upright approach—steadfastness in the face of peril, courage to prevail over looming defeat, satisfaction in the struggle—is to be found in many places. As a new century opened, a full 100 years after Roosevelt's voyage in history began, the nation responded to a crisis unparalleled in its challenge, demanding steadfastness and courage sufficient to test even TR's Rough Rider tradition. As an adage from the Spanish countryside cautions, "It is one thing to talk about the bulls—and quite another thing to get into the bullring."

For certain, Tom Whalen was actually in the arena, and he rightly took pride in his stance. He liked to quote a description once written about a former New York City mayor, John Purroy Mitchel: "He may make mistakes, but they are the kind of mistakes Teddy used to make—likable mistakes, and the mistakes of a strong fighter."

* * *

Having put into play an irresistible force—the calendar—Mayor Whalen was, in one camera's angle, only a spectator as the government he'd molded in his own image headed straight into the arms of another man.

Impressed subconsciously by the unthinking flurry of

"lame duck" talk, Whalen had expected his last few months in office to be undemanding and unproductive. Instead, he found his days much more fully occupied than he had anticipated.

"It is still a busy time," he wrote in October to Sol Wachtler, the state's former Chief Judge who had been a cordial Eagle Street neighbor of City Hall. "People want me to get things done on my watch. I expect we'll continue to be busy as we start to indoctrinate the new administration. I'm gratified with the knowledge that the city is in good shape, but also understanding that it has been a job that I have loved greatly. So it is with mixed feelings that I go. . . ."

"I certainly was not at loose ends from September through December," he later reported. "It was a fast finish—lots to do. Although I was not undertaking new initiatives, I was still making major decisions, right to the end, on matters that involved the city! And the government—I was still responsible for it." One decision was to refuse to agree on an out-of-court settlement of the Jesse Davis case. For nine years it had been limping through a series of legal maneuvers. For a proper resolution, in the absence of a settlement, the civil case against the city would have to go to trial.[5]

After the election, the Mayor pulled together his commissioners for a two-day retreat at the Rensselaerville Institute high in the Helderberg range. The purpose was to extract thoughts about the city's future, plus ideas that the incoming administration might profitably learn from. A formal document emerged, rather like a master plan, to be turned over to the Mayor-elect, though pessimism as to its future utility cynically dominated at least some of the contributors' expectations.

Not happily, he finally received an acceptance of his standing invitation for a meeting with his successor on elements of the transition. Two weeks before the end of his term, they spoke stiffly in the Mayor's office for 90 minutes. It was hard to put aside the strained relations stretching over ten years. "We have institutionalized many of the reforms," he had written to Judge Wachtler, "so that it would be very difficult [for any future administration] to bring City Hall back to 'the good old days.' They can tinker with it but I doubt that they can overhaul it."

And Albanians were still eager to hear from him. The day before conferring with Jennings, he talked to a sizable group of elderly members at a First Presbyterian Church luncheon. Albany's Rotarians—the most influential of the traditional service clubs—requested, and got, a retrospective view of his term.[6] Whalen could recap, with a figuratively triumphal "So there!":

"In 10 budgets, we held the line with an average of 1% a year—compared with the city school district's increases of 97% in that period." He could leave office with a surplus produced by having operated in the black in each of those years.

When a well-wisher inquired about his feelings on leaving office, his suggestive answer was, "I try not to dwell on it too much." At times, "The king is dead" seemed the prevailing sentiment and, disappointingly, Dan Klepak's presence conveyed this most pungently.

He was "bothered" by Klepak's belated revealing of an almost furtive decision to stay on as Budget Director rather than leaving with him as he thought they had agreed. He was experiencing difficulty in catching his aide's eye when they encountered one another.

When Klepak took on the budgeter's responsibilities, he went on record as expecting to stay for a couple of years. He'd already passed "normal" retirement age of 65.

But more than 12 years later, he was still at his desk, having lasted through the Whalen administration and into the third year of the successor's.

Only in the very last days of their work together did he find the words to explain to Whalen his decision. "Why are you avoiding me?" the Mayor had asked.

"I was ambivalent about staying in city employment," he informed Whalen, choosing to tell him in writing, a note delivered by the postman. "My daughter and friends had urged against it, but like the proverbial old war-horse I finally decided to stay for my last hurrah. . . . I feared you might be so convincing (in arguing that he also should leave) I would change my mind again."[7]

* * *

A few weeks before "the last of the ninth" he was toasted by 800 Whalenites at a party in—most fittingly—the one-time Union Station. Its conversion into a corporate banking center had begun in his first months and its completion, with his strong encouragement, had been hailed as a major step forward in the city's early prospects and ultimate gains. A video containing tribute from a coterie of admirers dominated the rather bittersweet evening. For his own part, the guest of honor signed off with a couplet from the exquisitely talented William Butler Yeats, who might well qualify as Whalen's favorite among all the poets:[8]

> "Think where man's glory begins and ends,
> And say my glory was I had such friends."

* * *

Still the showman and detail man, he rode the cherry picker crane again to place a suitably large wreath on Philip Schuyler's shoulder at City Hall. ("In front of the Capitol," said the *Times Union*, confusing Schuyler with Philip Sheridan astride Rienzi a bit farther up the hill.)

The final day mandated a round of farewells. Packing of some personal items—radio, pens, books, desk gadgets—had been accomplished. Gifts to the city which had added to the distinctiveness of his offices were segregated to remain as official property. Several last-minute notes were to be written. The Whalens' pastor had sent words of praise—"your energy, vision, and encouragement"—and offered good wishes; then, being a clergyman, he added, "and my prayers as well."

In his neat, round longhand, the departing Mayor

noted "I'm almost out the door," and spoke of the priest's "service to the city" and "to the people at St. Vincent's that you have nourished all these years."

Then it was time for one last family occasion in the darkening chamber which for them had stood for so long as a resource for latent pride but also as a barrier to the closeness that thousands of official hours might have meant to father, mother, sons, and daughter. (In an address accepting a "Citizen Laureate" award, he made a point of "a special tip of the hat to Denie and our five children for their encouragement in being a family full of love and support.")

Last sentimental farewells were spoken quietly to the loyal staff left behind to provide continuity in the days ahead for the incoming freshman.

Bill Kennedy had jested publicly that he'd be one Mayor who didn't go out of office feet first. Tom Whalen walked quickly through the offices, hit the light switch, and closed the door decisively, rattling its heavy hardware, and remembering to twist the knob for security's reassurance.

The little troupe marched poignantly through the revolving outer door and into the chill of the late evening. All that remained of the Whalen administration were the few hours' indulgence in Denie's special gift to Albany, her inspiration, "First Night."

He'd bade one final official favor: To be granted a few minutes executing a happy role which might be occasionally claimed by a town's No. 1 citizen but by few others: Accepting the conductor's baton and with zestful abandon leading the St. Cecilia's Orchestra for an appreciative gathering in St. Peter's Church a block down State Street's steep slope. Imaginative observers might also have discerned a passing similarity to the enthusiastic conducting of Professor Harold Hill in the pavilion of River City's village square.

Next came a stop at two hillside attractions—at St. Mary's Church and then at the Masonic Temple for African dances, then downtown to Kiernan Plaza—site of the big boost for his spirits and the city's early in 1984—for a L'Ensemble concert.

And there was time along the way for a ham sandwich with Champagne and for a bit more of First Night's manifold attractions, its music, dancing, and enough clowns to make the whole city laugh.

* * *

At dawn of his sixtieth birthday five mornings later, with new plain-citizen license plates replacing the "A" on his Olds, he headed north to the Wells retreat, where so much history had begun 3,877 days before.

NOTES

[1] From the poem "Politics," in *Poems of William Butler Yeats: A New Edition*, published by Simon & Schuster.   Copyrights 1940/1960 by Bertha Georgie Yeats.

[2] His allusion was to the Roman dictator Lucius Quintius Cincinnatus (5th century B.C.), of whom legend relates that he retired to his small farm immediately after leading a great military triumph: "A lofty ideal which we might all profit from," Haydock wrote. (President Harry S. Truman was said to have pondered the ancient example during his own dark days in the White House.)

[3] Later that year, in one of his final public statements, he referred to this as his "ultimate decision as Mayor—to step aside, to heed the wisdom and sound advice of Jefferson and Madison, Hamilton and Jay, to let others come forward to lead this great city and receive the invaluable psychic reward that can only come from public service." And, he advised, "Whoever is our next Mayor, he will do well to heed the wisdom of our founding fathers and stay only as long as required."

[4] The occasion was the presentation to him of the Nelson A. Rockefeller Award for distinguished service in public administration.

5 In 1984, Davis, a black man with apparent mental handi-caps, had been fatally shot during a violent outburst against two police officers who had been called to quell his tirades. He was unarmed although his behavior gave a contrary impression to the officers, they said. On his behalf, they and the city were sued. Whalen's preference at this critical though long-deferred stage was for a jury to decide if the officers had acted improperly. He rea-soned that although an out-of-court settlement would not constitute an admission of culpability, public opinion would remain unsettled and resentful of a deal. Against the legal advice he was receiving, Whalen prevailed in rejecting a settlement and forcing the case into the courtroom, where it ultimately would be resolved after he left office.

6 Vincent O'Leary, who had retired in 1990 as the president of the State University's Albany campus, tried to prepare the Mayor for the let-down he could expect when he left City Hall. They met frequently for lunch under portraits of Irish writers at the Ginger Man on Albany's Washington Avenue near the university's down-town campus, sometimes joined for reminiscences and repartee by the proprietor, Michael Byron, a Galway man. Improving student relationships with the natives was a regular topic, but as O'Leary remembered these shirtsleeved hours, "Many a fine afternoon Tom and I shared a back table, talking of politics, books, families, our-selves and each other." Such companionship inspired the Mayor to initiate the renaming of a block of Partridge Street as O'Leary Boulevard, honoring his friend.

Suggesting that the end of Whalen's mayoralty would not be unlike his own experience in stepping down to a professorship in Criminal Justice, O'Leary reported he'd found it not really "the end of the world." But he related his amazement in the speed of his descent from a teller of jokes producing appreciative laughter. His jokes now resulted in groans or pained deadpan expressions. And he repeated a retirement scenario described by Hugh Carey. When he took off his coat, the former Governor said, it simply fell to the floor—no eager hands were ready to take it.

7 Whalen deferred opening the note as was his not-infre-quent habit when he'd perceived that the contents would convey information he really didn't want to receive.

8 In one spring semester the Mayor would—in his own words—"sneak out of City Hall two afternoons a week and drive to

the Albany State campus to take a course taught by Mary Ann
Devane on the Irish literary renaissance." He earned a "B" for the
course—and "No one ever missed me at City Hall."